Celluloid Comrades

Celluloid Comrades

Representations of Male Homosexuality
in Contemporary Chinese Cinemas

Song Hwee Lim

University of Hawai'i Press
Honolulu

Library of Congress Cataloging-in-Publication Data
Lim, Song Hwee, 1965–
    Celluloid comrades : representations of male homosexuality
in contemporary Chinese cinemas / Song Hwee Lim.
        p. cm.
    Filmography: p.
    Includes bibliographical references and index.
    ISBN-13: 978-0-8248-2909-4 (alk. paper)
    ISBN-10: 0-8248-2909-3 (alk. paper)
    ISBN-13: 978-0-8248-3077-9 (pbk : alk. paper)
    ISBN-10: 0-8248-3077-6 (pbk : alk. paper)
    1. Homosexuality, Male, in motion pictures.
2. Motion pictures—China—History. I. Title.
    PN1995.9.H55L56 2006
    791.43'6526642—dc22
                        2006012837

Designed by University of Hawai'i Press production staff

Printed by Sheridan Books

For my mother

Contents

Acknowledgments

Most first-book acknowledgments begin with thanking one's PhD supervisors. I would like to go back a little further in acknowledging my intellectual and other debts. My first love was literature, and it was during my undergraduate days (1985–1989) at the National Taiwan University (Taida) that Ko Ching-ming and Wang Wen-hsing first demonstrated New Criticism–style close reading to me. I have vivid memories of my first lesson with Ko and getting no further than the first few lines of Wang's short story "Wanting" *(Qianque)* and of spending three hours every Saturday afternoon crawling through J. D. Salinger's *The Catcher in the Rye* in Wang's classes—not even completing the book by the end of the academic year. Ko also introduced me to Russian formalism. To both Ko and Wang I owe my rudimentary skills in textual analysis.

It was at Taida that my interest gravitated from literature to film. My undergraduate days coincided with the heyday of Taiwan New Cinema, and there were always free screenings of a Hou Hsiao-hsien or an Edward Yang film on campus to lure me away from classes. Outside campus, there were numerous MTVs (not the television channel but commercial enterprises offering small rooms where one could watch films on video or laser disc) and the fantastic Taipei International Film Festival, where I discovered, among others, Fassbinder, Pasolini, Jarman, Greenaway, Truffaut, and Rohmer. After graduation, I would return to Taipei many times for the film festival, where the Iranian director Kiarostami became a hit by word of mouth, Genet's *Un Chant d'amour* was the highlight of the special section on *tongzhi* cinema in 1992, and Fassbinder's *Berlin Alexanderplatz* left an indelible mark on me even though I slept through half of what I saw.

Back in Singapore to serve out my eight-year bond (1989–1997), which came with the sponsorship of my undergraduate education, I started a routine of watching films at the Alliance Française every Tuesday. There I met Tan Ing How, who taught me to see film visually and who has since sustained a conversation with me on film for more than a decade. On one occasion he phoned me from the Alliance Française, and I heard, in the background, his girlfriend (now wife) Dorothy and their visiting Japanese ex-classmate Tomoko from the Beijing Film Academy playing the tune *C'est le vent, Betty* from Beineix's film on the piano. I knew instantly that the boundary between life and cinema, for me, had become indistinguishable, and for the better, as Bertolucci's recent film, *The Dreamers,* attests.

By the early 1990s the focus of my reading had turned to cultural studies, and the annual arts conference at the Substation opened my eyes to an English-speaking intellectual circle in Singapore. To witness Chua Beng Huat, Kwok Kian Woon, the late Kuo Pao Kun, and Lee Weng Choy in action was truly inspiring. I am privileged to have got to know them since, and I continue to admire their commitment to intellectual work in Singapore. At Taida I could not envision continuing in postgraduate studies. My new interest in film, cultural studies, and gender and sexuality studies, however, was to pave the way along a different trajectory.

Embarking on a PhD upon completing the bond in 1997 had never been the plan. I can never thank Quah Sy Ren enough for being my guiding light when, in an early midlife crisis, I was at a complete loss about the future. I followed in his footsteps to Cambridge, where he was a constant companion and mentor for the next couple of years. True to Xu Zhimo's writing, Cambridge was simply heavenly. I was very fortunate to have had Susan Daruvala as my supervisor, for not only was she unfailing in her support and advice but also, more important, she challenged me to write clearly and to think honestly. The M.Phil. coursework I did with her in the first year was the best introduction one could get to the field of modern and contemporary Chinese literary studies.

Michel Hockx, who examined my M.Phil. dissertation on Tsai Ming-liang, has always been very encouraging towards my work, and the Southern England Modern Chinese Literature Seminar he organized with Susan Daruvala was the highlight of my postgraduate years. In November 1997 I was surprisingly reunited with an undergraduate classmate, Bernhard Fuehrer, who had been (and still is) teaching at the School of Oriental and African Studies. I thank him and his wife, Mei-chuan, for their hospitality during my many escapades to London, and I can only dream of emulating Bernhard's formidable example as a scholar. My first year at Cambridge was blessed by the company of my course mate, Lin Pei-yin, and my Trinity Hall kitchen mates, Stephen Edwards, Emma Hughes, and Douglas McCabe. My research trip to Taipei from January to May 1999 was enriched by the friendship of Foo Hong-cheng, Huang Ming-che, and Huang Hui-feng. Back in Cambridge, Violet Cheong, Julia Lovell, Hong

Jeesoon, Kang Jaeho, Yeo Wei Wei, and Yeo Ye kept me sane in my subsequent years of wrestling with the monster that is The Dissertation.

My postgraduate studies and research activities (1997–2001) would not have been possible without substantial grants from the following institutions and schemes: Overseas Student Bursary from the Cambridge Commonwealth Trust; study grants from the Lee Foundation, Singapore; Allen, Meek, and Read Awards from the Board of Graduate Studies, University of Cambridge; a research bursary and a travel grant from Trinity Hall; a travel grant from the British Association for Chinese Studies; and a PhD Dissertation Fellowship from the Chiang Ching-kuo Foundation for International Scholarly Exchange, Taiwan. For writing references for my various applications during those years, I am grateful to Kwok Kian Woon, Ko Ching-ming, Leslie Sharpe, Kuo Pao Kun, Susan Daruvala, David McMullen, Michel Hockx, and Bernhard Fuehrer.

My experience in academia has been marked, from the initial years, by the spirit of generosity displayed by many scholars, be it by pointing me to a source, sending me their writing, or sharing their ideas with me via e-mail or in person. I was overwhelmed with the number of responses and suggestions I received after posting a self-introduction note as a new member on the MCLC and H-ASIA lists. Nick Kaldis, in particular, was most candid and helpful in our e-mail correspondence. In fall 1998, despite his busy schedule, David Der-wei Wang spent an hour advising me on my project in his office at Columbia University. Wang pointed me to the work of Chong Kee Tan, who kindly gave me a copy of his PhD dissertation. My attending a talk by Rey Chow in London in 1999 led to her sending me her forthcoming article on *Happy Together*. For my PhD work I have benefited from exchanges with Leo Ou-fan Lee, Paul Julian Smith, Kwok Kian Woon, Peggy Chiao Hsiung-ping, Raymond Chu Wei-cheng, Sebastian Liao Hsien-hao, C. J. Wee Wan Ling, Audrey Yue, and Chris Berry. Thanks to Douglas McCabe for helping with the proofreading of my dissertation. My PhD examiners, Mark Morris and Li Ruru, gave me useful comments during the oral defense.

The road from dissertation to book has not been straightforward. I thank the reviewers for the University of Hawai‘i Press who provided many insightful suggestions, which I have tried to incorporate in my revision. The intervening years (2001–2005) have been spent at the University of Leeds, where I have enjoyed support from colleagues both at the World Cinemas group and the Department of East Asian Studies. A semester's sabbatical in 2003, coupled with a British Academy-Academia Sinica (Taiwan) Individual Research Visit Grant, gave me time and space to rethink the project. While in Nankang, Taipei, I again experienced Taiwanese hospitality, this time from colleagues at the Institute of Chinese Literature and Philosophy. Over these years I have benefited from exchanges with Teri Silvio, Fran Martin, Natalia Chan, Travis Kong, Lawrence Yim, Darren Aoki, Frances Weightman, and colleagues from the World Cinemas group, especially Lúcia Nagib, Stephanie Dennison, Diana Holmes, Lisa Shaw, Danielle Hipkins, and Paul Cooke. Danielle Hipkins also kindly took over the duties of general editor for *New Cinemas* in 2005, which allowed me to focus on the rewriting of the manuscript. Since 1997 many people have contributed to my project by supplying research materials or pointing me to various sources. I thank in particular Eva Tang, Tan Kay Ngee, Ng How Wee, Chan Cheow Thia, Mark Yong, Wong Koi Tet, Lin Pei-yin, Violet Cheong, Quah Sy Ren, Lai Chee Kien, Margaret Hillenbrand, Julian Ward, Elena Pollacchi, Pan Shao-yu, Kenneth Chan, Mark Williams, and Flemming Christiansen. Chen Zishan brought my work to the attention of Zhang Beichuan, who kindly gave me a copy of his book. Thanks also to Tsai Ming-liang for supplying me with video copies of his early work.

I could not have completed this book in the summer of 2005 without the following friends, who came to my last-minute rescue; to them I am immensely grateful: Jeroen de Kloet for making possible a most relaxing break in Amsterdam before the final leg of the writing began; Wong Koi Tet for his amazing ability to track down any source and for helping with the film stills and filmography; Chan Cheow Thia for commenting on parts of the manuscript and for lending a listening ear; Quah Sy Ren for always being there; Sam Geall for his assistance in copyediting, capturing the film stills, and compiling the glossary, filmography, and bibliography; Chris Wood for helping with the index; and Frances Weightman for proofreading and commenting on the entire manuscript and for being so supportive. I also thank the Universities' China Committee, London, for a grant toward the preparation of the manuscript; my copy editor, Bojana Ristich; my proofreader, Wendy Bolton; and my editors at the University of Hawai'i Press, Patricia Crosby and Keith Leber, for their professionalism and patience. Needless to say, all imperfections in the book remain mine.

An earlier version of chapter 1 was published as "Celluloid Comrades: Male Homosexuality in Chinese Cinemas of the 1990s" in *China Information* 16, 1 (2002): 68–88. An earlier version of chapter 2 appeared as "Contesting Celluloid Closets: The Politics of Representing Male Homosexuality in Chinese Cinemas" in *Tamkang Review* 33, 2 (2002): 55–75. An earlier reading of Wong Kar-wai's *Happy Together* is forthcoming in Chinese as "Piaobo liuli de tongzhi manyouzhe: Lun Wang Jiawei *Chunguang zhaxie* zhong de jiuqi / huigui yinying" (Gay *Flâneurs* in Diaspora: The Shadow of 1997 in Wong Kar-wai's *Happy Together*); in *Quanqiu hua yu "Zhongguo-xing": Dangdai wenhua de houzhimin jiedu* (Globalization and Chineseness: Postcolonial readings of contemporary culture), edited by Song Geng (Hong Kong: Hong Kong University Press). Various parts of the book have been presented in numerous conferences and seminars, and I thank participants from London, Cambridge, and Leeds to Turin, St. Louis, and Taipei for their feedback.

Finally, I want to express my gratitude above all to my mother, whose financial and spiritual support over the years, and in particular during my postgraduate studies, has been unfailing and unyielding. She dares to dream for me where I would not, and I dedicate this book to her.

S. H. L.
August 2005
Leeds, England

Note on Chinese Romanization, Translation, and Periodization

As a general rule I have used Hanyu pinyin for Chinese names and phrases throughout the book, except for habitual spellings such as Sun Yat-sen and Kuomintang, and where possible for names of those who come from outside mainland China. Names of film characters appear mainly as they do in the films' English subtitles. For the sake of clarity, names of characters whose first given names are the pinyin A (as in A Lan) are spelled as Ah (as in Ah Lan). Chinese names are listed surnames first, followed by given names, unless the persons concerned have authored in English and their names appear otherwise in their publications. Chinese characters for terms used in the volume are listed in the glossary. Translations of Chinese texts are mine unless otherwise stated. The historical eras mentioned in the book and their approximate dates are as follows:

Han, 206 BCE–220 CE
Ming, 1368–1644
Qing, 1644–1911
Republican China, 1912–1949

In effect the cinema is basically immodest.

Let us use this facility to enlarge gestures.

The camera can open a fly and search out its secrets.

—Jean Genet, "Notes on *Le Bagne*"

Introduction

In the last few decades, questions of gender and sexuality have become an increasingly important area of inquiry in many academic disciplines. Within the field of Chinese literature and culture, the focus of this inquiry has been on the female gender. More recently, scholars have begun to turn their attention to the male gender.[1] The study of same-sex sexuality, whether for the male or the female gender, can also be described as an emerging field.[2] At the same time, we have witnessed Chinese cinemas fast rising as one of the most vibrant areas of research within modern and contemporary Chinese literary and cultural studies, with a particular interest in the representation of gender and sexuality in film.[3] This book aims to contribute to this exciting development in scholarship by situating itself at the crossroads of Chinese studies, gender and sexuality studies, and film and cinema studies in its examination of the representation of male homosexuality in contemporary Chinese cinemas.

This study focuses on the contemporary period (that is, since the 1990s), as the proliferation of films from China, Taiwan, and Hong Kong featuring male homosexual themes and characters is a striking but fairly recent phenomenon. Indeed, an *Encyclopedia of Chinese Film* published in 1998 acknowledges that "as a theme, homosexuality did not receive serious attention until the 1990s" (Yingjin Zhang and Xiao 1998, 300). This book looks at the phenomenon from several aspects. First, it accounts for the engendering conditions for the representation of male homosexuality in Chinese cinemas, tracing them to the emergence of Chinese cinemas in the international arena since the 1980s. Second, it delineates how the issue of homosexuality is negotiated in contemporary Chinese societies and Chinese cinemas. Third, it examines the meaning, politics, and burden of cinematic representation and interrogates the related identity politics underpinning discussions of selected films. Fourth, it provides an in-depth analysis of key films and auteurs, reading them within contexts as varied as pre-modern, transgender practice in Chinese theater to postmodern, diasporic forms of sexualities. It argues that representations of male homosexuality in Chinese cinemas have been polyphonic and multifarious, posing a challenge to monolithic and essentialized constructions of both "Chineseness" and "homosexuality."

Theorizing Chineseness, Rethinking Chinese Cinema(s)

In our study of films from China, Taiwan, and Hong Kong, a construct known as "Chineseness" has been foregrounded in this book. However, the basis of this Chineseness, be it race/ethnicity, culture, language, or geopolitics, is often fraught with dispute.[4] In English-language scholarship in the last two decades, there have been two high-profile efforts at coming to terms with the concept of Chineseness and the meaning of being Chinese. The first is the Spring 1991 special issue of *Daedalus* (later edited as a book by Tu Wei-ming 1994b). The second is the fall 1998 special issue of *boundary 2* (also edited as a book by Rey Chow 2000b). While both books contain heterogeneous voices, the positions taken by the two editors are in such stark contrast that one could say the former (Tu) "seeks commonality among differences" *(yi zhong qiu tong)* whereas the latter (Chow) "seeks differences within commonality" *(tong zhong qiu yi).*

Tu's concept of "Cultural China" has since generated heated debate. For Tu, "Cultural China" can be classified into three symbolic universes. The first consists of societies populated predominantly by cultural and ethnic Chinese—namely China, Taiwan, Hong Kong, and Singapore. The second consists of Chinese communities throughout the world, usually referred to as "overseas Chinese" or, more recently, the Chinese diaspora. The third consists of individual men or women, regardless of their race or nationality, who have an intellectual interest and investment in understanding the Chinese world (Tu 1994a, 13–14). In this regard, this book shares Tu's construction of the first symbolic universe by studying films originating from societies with a predominantly Chinese population.[5] It is for this reason, as well as the convenience of not having to repeat the phrase "films from China, Taiwan, and Hong Kong," that I have chosen to use the term "Chinese" cinemas throughout this book.

However, I am equally if not more concerned with the project of challenging a monolithic and essentialized construction of Chineseness. Citing examples ranging from minority populations in China and the demands for the liberation of Tibet to the independence movement in Taiwan and the call for democracy in post-British Hong Kong, Rey Chow argues that various alternative forces have been gathering momentum in recent years, and "we have begun to see a gradual epistemic shift that seeks to modify the claim to a homogeneously unified, univocal China" (2000a, 6). Chow's comments, together with articles published elsewhere, can be seen as a response, if not a reaction, to the concept of "Cultural China" proposed by Tu.[6]

The question of Chineseness, I would argue, is inescapably political on many levels.[7] In geopolitical and territorial terms, there is no denying that, at least from the second half of the twentieth century, three different Chinese polities have existed: the People's Republic of China, the Republic of China (Taiwan), and the British Crown Colony of Hong Kong. As a result, the national and cultural identities that have grown out of this separation imply that people from Taiwan and Hong Kong—coupled with their extended period of colonial experience under the Japanese (Taiwan) and the British (Hong Kong)—can no longer be simply subsumed under the umbrella category of "Chinese."[8] While it is clear that "the problematic nature of 'Chinese' as a signifier should suffice to demythify 'Chineseness' as a pre-given, monolithic and immutable essence" (Yingjin Zhang 2004, 4), the tension between "seeking commonality among differences" and "seeking differences within commonality" cannot be easily resolved and is replicated in the definition of "Chinese cinema(s)."[9]

In his introduction to *New Chinese Cinemas,* Nick Browne recognizes this tension:

> The presumption that Chinese cinema is the monolithic cultural expression of a Chinese nation has been dramatically undercut by history. . . . The People's Republic, Taiwan, and Hong Kong and their cinemas are marked as socialist, capitalist, and colonialist, respectively. Yet to exaggerate these differences would be to overlook a common cultural tradition of social, ideological, and aesthetic forms that stands behind and informs Chinese cinema as a whole. This book locates the Chinese cinemas of the People's Republic, Taiwan, and Hong Kong between the elements of a common culture and the differences of form and significance wrought by history and political division. (1994, 1)

What is remarkable is the rhetorical manner in which Browne acknowledges the differences within the construction of Chineseness only to dismiss them immediately in favor of the commonality. In her review of *New Chinese Cinemas,* Yueh-yu Yeh criticizes the tendency to use the term "Chinese cinema(s)," whether in the plural or the singular, "to include Chinese-language films from Hong Kong, Taiwan, and mainland China without bothering to qualify the problematic nature of the term itself" (1998, 74). While the plural form at least acknowledges the diversity under the sign of "Chinese," it cannot be seen as the same as resolving the problem

(Chow 2000a, 18). Indeed, any attempt to distinguish cinemas from China, Taiwan, and Hong Kong as distinct "national" cinemas is nullified insofar as the three cinemas are subsumed under the umbrella term of "Chinese cinema(s)" (or, as we shall see below, "transnational Chinese cinemas"), a practice that has become an "apparent consensus" since the mid-1990s (Yingjin Zhang 2004, 4).[10]

The question of Chineseness in relation to cinema, therefore, demands a rethinking on the very notion of national cinema, which remains one of the dominant modes of scholarship and publication in film and cinema studies.[11] In his introduction to *Chinese National Cinema,* Yingjin Zhang begins by noting the irony of publishing another volume on national cinema at the start of the new millennium given the forces of globalization, post-coloniality, post-modernity, transnationality, and new technological development (2004, 1). In light of the redrawing of national boundaries across the world in the last decade or so (most notably in the former Soviet Union and the East European bloc), notions of the nation both as a people and as a state are undergoing contradictory waves of dismantling and regrouping, at once deconstructionist and essentializing. In terms of cinema, the challenges posed to the notion of the nation manifest themselves not only in terms of self-definition by peoples and states (not to mention different demands from diasporic communities), but also in terms of the mode of production, which is increasingly transnational. The theoretical concept of national cinema is not just "a messy affair" (a declaration by Tom O'Regan in relation to Australian cinema and echoed by Zhang vis-à-vis Chinese cinema; Yingjin Zhang 2004, 3); rather, it is in deep crisis and demands a paradigm shift.

In tandem with contestations to the use of the term "Chinese" in relation to cinema, two other conceptual frameworks compete to replace the Chinese national cinema(s) model—namely "transnational Chinese cinemas," proposed by Sheldon Hsiao-peng Lu (1997c), and "Chinese-language cinema" *(zhongwen dianying or huayu dianying),* promoted by Yuehyu Yeh (Yeh 1998; Lu and Yeh 2005a) and used in some Chinese-language publications.[12] While they rightly identify the shortcomings of the national cinema model, both frameworks nonetheless throw up new questions of their own.

In his introduction to *Transnational Chinese Cinemas,* Lu traces the historical development of cinema in China back to its origin and argues that "Chinese *national* cinema can only be understood in its properly *transnational* context" (1997a, 3; emphasis in original). Delineating the different levels in which transnationalism can be observed in the Chinese case, Lu seems to emphasize the "globalization of the mechanisms of film production, distribution, and consumption" (ibid.). While Lu's intention is clearly to decenter the sign of "China" and "Chinese" in relation to cinema, the subsumption of cinemas of China, Taiwan, and Hong Kong under the umbrella of *transnational* Chinese cinemas does not so much displace the nation as reinstate it within a larger framework. Not only is Lu's statement that "these three cinematic traditions have developed in separate directions and yet all attempt to signify a shared object: 'China'" (ibid., 12) open to debate, but also to focus on transnationalism chiefly as a mode of production and consumption does not address, much less challenge, the sign of "China" in either its symbolic or substantive senses.[13]

Yeh follows up her 1998 call for the use of the term "Chinese-language cinema" by arguing that it is "a more comprehensive term that covers all the local, national, regional, transnational, diasporic, and global cinemas relating to the Chinese language" (Lu and Yeh 2005a, 2). By Lu and Yeh's own admission, this model is also not without its problems, including "the linguistic hierarchy and social discrimination embedded in Chinese cinema and society" (ibid., 3), and I would argue that they have overlooked quite a few issues. First, by describing "a Mandarin-language film made and released in the People's Republic of China" as an example of when "Chinese-language cinema is synonymous with Chinese cinema" and "national boundary and language coincide" (ibid., 1), the issue of non-Han minorities and their languages, which cannot be classified as "Chinese," is not addressed.[14] Second, in their attempt to distinguish "Sinophone film" from some post-colonial cinemas by stating that "speakers of Chinese dialects around the world have been mostly ethnic Chinese rather than indigenous peoples who were forced or inculcated to speak the language of *external* colonizers" (ibid., 4–5; emphasis mine), they have neglected the processes of internal colonization that include, among others, the People's Republic's annexation of Tibet, the Sinification of aborigines in Taiwan, and the Kuomintang's (KMT) occupation of Taiwan and its associated language policy.[15] Third, as more and more directors from China, Taiwan, Hong Kong, and the Chinese diaspora begin to make films in non-Chinese languages—from Chen Kaige's English-language *Killing Me Softly* (2002) and Hou Hsiao-hsien's Japanese-English-language *Café Lumière* (*Kōhī jikō/Kaife shiguang,* 2003) to Fruit Chan's Korean-Cantonese-language *Public Toilet* (*Hwajangshil eodieyo?/Renmin gongce,* 2002) and the remarkable example of Ang Lee—such films attest to not just the transnational, but also the translingual and transcultural aspects of filmmaking that may or may not find a position within a configuration of Chinese cinema(s).[16] Finally, in their inconsistent switch between the terms "language" and "dialect" and by speaking of "'Chinese-dialect film' as a subgenre of Chinese-language film" (ibid., 7), they reinstate the very linguistic hierarchy they have identified elsewhere as prevalent in "both past history and contemporary cultural production" (ibid., 3).

In his use of "Chinese national cinema" to cover all films produced in China, Taiwan, and Hong Kong, Yingjin Zhang instructs the reader "to keep in mind all problematics or messiness . . . surrounding 'China' and 'Chineseness'" and suggests "we take the messiness of Chinese cinema *positively,* as a sign that producers, filmmakers, exhibitors, state regulators, critics and audiences in different Chinese geopolitical regions and over different periods of time have aspired to different constructions of the national" (2004, 5, 6; emphasis in original). Zhang's suggestion points to the question of agency in the negotiation of the meaning and construction of the national. Also focusing on the issue of agency, Berry argues for "recasting national cinema as a multiplicity of projects, authored by different individuals, groups, and institutions with various purposes, but bound together by the politics of national agency and collective subjectivity as constructed identities" (2000a, 161).

For me, the more important question is not whether Chinese (national) cinema(s) ought to be reconfigured as transnational Chinese cinemas or Chinese-language cinemas, laudable efforts though these are; rather, we should examine the function each configuration serves, the legitimizing discourse behind each mobilization, its efficacy in unsettling the sign of the national in all its guises, and the agents empowered and disenfranchised in the process. If the nation(al) is, like all classificatory or identity categories, a necessary evil, not only must the constructedness of any category be highlighted as Berry has done, as noted above, but also, as Chow proposes in relation to Chineseness, it must be "productively put under erasure—not in the sense of being written out of existence but in the sense of being unpacked" (2000a, 18), or, as Judith Butler suggests in relation to the sign of lesbian, "to have it permanently unclear what precisely that sign signifies" (1991, 14). Moreover, in a binding together of these national agencies, it is worth bearing in mind that Chineseness often "lies at the root of a violence which works by the most deeply ingrained feelings of 'bonding'" (Chow 1993, 25).

In a different way of taking the messiness of Chinese cinemas positively, I propose to pay equal if not more attention to agents that by their very nature necessarily trouble and resist subsumption under the sign of the nation. I refer to models such as Third Cinema (Pines and Willemen 1989), exilic cinema (Naficy 2001), women and feminist cinema (E. A. Kaplan 2000), and queer cinema (Aaron 2004), which transcend national boundaries to form alliances and identifications based on (equally constructed) categories other than the nation. In her introductory essay to a special section on "Chinese and Chinese Diaspora Cinema" in the film journal *Jump Cut*, Gina Marchetti argues the following: "The common experiences of the Chinese diaspora and the global links among various Chinese communities must not be dismissed. Particularly for those who traditionally may be at odds with a conservative Chinese patriarchy, such as many heterosexual women, lesbians, and gay men, the ability to cross borders and to participate in a wider, global sphere transcends ethnic and cultural ties" (1998, 72). While I am aware that we "should not assume that what is diasporic, fluid, border-crossing, or hybrid is intrinsically subversive of power structures" (Ong and Nonini 1997, 326), an interrogation into the relationship between the nation and these other identifications will throw light on both the institutions of power within the nation and their processes of negotiation with these agents. With regard to the thematic concern of this book, it would be interesting to explore, for instance, the invocation of the "nation" by queer subjects, exemplified by the activist group Queer Nation.[17] While I have outlined so far the problematic nature of the concept of Chinese cinemas in several of its configurations, I will revisit some of these issues by raising the possibility of a queer Chinese cinema in the conclusion.

Speaking of Homosexuality

By "male homosexuality" I refer to the expression of sexual desire between men in the films discussed, though this does not imply that the characters necessarily declare themselves as homosexuals or identify with an identity category known as "homosexuals" (in many cases they do not). As with the issue of Chineseness, I am concerned with a non-monolithic, non-essentialized understanding of homosexuality. Hence I do not enter into a discussion on the etiology of homosexuality because I do not believe it will enhance our understanding of the expression of homosexuality in the films.[18] However, I do have other thorny issues to address: first, what is homosexuality, and second, how is homosexuality understood and discussed in the Chinese context?

To answer the first question, as Kevin Kopelson notes, it is by now "a commonplace of Foucauldian criticism that homosexual identities, as opposed to homosexual acts, arose only after a number of relatively recent, and primarily sexological, discourses breathed life into them" (1994, 8). This understanding is based on a much-cited passage in volume 1 of Michel Foucault's *The History of Sexuality:*

As defined by the ancient civil or canonical codes, sodomy was a category of forbidden acts; their perpetrator was nothing more than the juridical subject of them. The nineteenth-century homosexual became a personage, a past, a case history, and a childhood, in addition to being a type of life, a life form, and a morphology, with an indiscreet anatomy and possibly a mysterious physiology. Nothing that went into his total composition was unaffected by his sexuality. . . . Homosexuality appeared as one of the forms of sexuality when it was transposed from the practice of sodomy onto a kind of interior androgyny, a hermaphrodism of the soul. The sodomite had been a temporary aberration; the homosexual was now a species. (1990, 43)

This passage has popularly been taken as evidence of a historical moment that separated the understanding of homosexuality as sexual act from homosexuality as sexual identity. While Foucault's argument relates to nineteenth-century Europe, the dichotomy between sexual act and sexual identity arising from this popular understanding arguably informs other historical accounts of homosexuality, usually with a time line dividing pre-modern and modern periods of understanding. In his account of the long tradition of same-sex relationships in China from antiquity to the late imperial period, Bret Hinsch highlights in particular the care to be taken when discussing same-sex sexuality in the Chinese context because classical Chinese language lacked a term comparable to "homosexuality" or "homosexual." Rather, "[Homosexuality] was usually discussed using poetic metaphors referring to earlier men or incidents famed for association with homosexuality. Chinese terminology therefore did not emphasize an innate sexual essence, but concentrated rather on actions, tendencies, and preferences. In other words, instead of saying what someone 'is,' Chinese authors would usually say whom he 'resembles' or what he 'does' or 'enjoys'" (1990, 7).[19] However, with the advent of Western sexological categories since the early twentieth century, Hinsch believes that the "fluid conceptions of sexuality of old, which assumed that an individual was capable of enjoying a range of sexual *acts,* have been replaced with the ironclad Western dichotomy of heterosexual/homosexual," and as a result, the "Chinese now speak of 'homosexuality' *(tongxinglian* or *tong-xing'ai),* a direct translation of the Western medical term that defines a small group of pathological individuals according to a concrete sexual *essence*" (ibid., 169; emphasis mine).

Hinsch's argument therefore echoes the popular understanding of Foucault that distinguishes between sexual act and identity by some temporal marker (nineteenth century in the case of Europe and twentieth century in the case of China), and the distinction is attributed to the advent of Western sexological discourses. To adopt this understanding amounts to positing that sexual identities did not exist before the respective time lines in these geographical locales and that after them it has become impossible to conduct sexual acts without impinging on the notion of sexual identities.

In a drastically different reading of the Foucault passage quoted above, David Halperin argues that Foucault's "schematic opposition between sodomy and homosexuality is first and foremost a discursive analysis, not a social history, let alone an exhaustive one. *It is not an empirical claim about the historical existence or nonexistence of sexually deviant individuals*" (1998, 99; emphasis in original). Rather, Foucault is "documenting the existence of both a discursive and a temporal gap between two dissimilar styles of defining, and disqualifying, male same-sex sexual expression," and in so doing, he "highlights the historical and political specificity of sexuality, both as a cultural concept and as a tactical device" (ibid.). Noting that "the term *identity* nowhere occurs" in Foucault's text, Halperin encourages an inquiry "into the construction of sexual identities before the emergence of sexual orientations," on the one hand, and urges the need "to supplement our notion of sexual identity with a more refined concept of, say, partial identity, emergent identity, transient identity, semi-identity, incomplete identity, proto-identity, or sub-identity," on the other (ibid., 109; emphasis in original).

Halperin's argument does not discount Foucault's claim about the impact of nineteenth-century sexology on the understanding of homosexuals as a species with a distinct sexuality. What Halperin objects to is the distinction between sexual act and sexual identity drawn with that time line and the construction of identity as unitary. Following Halperin, the distinction between sexual acts and sexual identities is not so much that the former is "what one does" and the latter is "what one is" (to borrow Hinsch's phrases); rather, the very concepts of act and identity must be seen as the *effects* of sexual discourses that not only distinguish one from the other, but also, by mobilizing this distinction, impose an arbitrary marker that separates the two concepts as mutually exclusive. For Halperin, his intent is "to indicate *the multiplicity of possible historical connections between sex and identity,* a multiplicity whose existence has been obscured by the necessary but narrowly focused, totalizing critique of sexual identity as a unitary concept. We need to find ways of asking how different historical cultures fashioned different sorts of links between sexual acts, on the one hand, and sexual tastes, styles, dispositions, characters, gender presentations, and forms of subjectivity, on the other" (1998, 109; emphasis in original).

I have brought in Halperin's refutation of the popular (mis)understanding of Foucault's account of the history of (homo)sexuality (which, as Halperin insists, is a discursive analysis, not a historical assertion; 1998, 111) because the distinction between sexual act and sexual identity arising from that (mis)reading is so prevalent that it invariably impinges on modern discourses of Chinese homosexuality, as shown by Hinsch's account. Indeed, it is precisely because I agree with the general observation by Hinsch that understanding of homosexuality in the Chinese-speaking world has shifted from one of fluid, possible multiple sexual acts to one of monolithic, essentialized sexual identity that it is all the more important to heed Halperin's call in order to dismantle the mythifying distinction between act and identity (and to propose different ways of conceptualizing their relationship), to emphasize the multiple manifestations of sexuality that either break down the unitary construction of identity or displace its centrality in the popular imagination, and to be attentive to the different ways in which these issues are negotiated in different cultures.

In regard to the second question—that is, how homosexuality is understood and discussed in the Chinese context—the centrality of identity in the Chinese understanding of homosexuality since the early twentieth century has been, as Hinsch argues, largely an effect of the advent of Western sexological discourses. I would highlight the role of language in the shaping of this understanding as these discourses are, of course, mediated through translation, or what Lydia H. Liu (1995) has termed "translingual practice."

In her study of the Chinese translation of Western sexological terms in Republican China (1912–1949), Tze-lan Deborah Sang notes that as *tongxing'ai* (literally "same-sex love"; read as *doseiai* in Japanese) was coined in Japan at the end of the Meiji (1868–1912) and the early Taisho (1912–1925) periods as Japanese intellectuals translated European sexology, there is "reason to believe that *tongxing'ai* was a direct adoption of the Japanese *doseiai,* based on which the Chinese then invented the variants *tongxing lian'ai* and *tongxinglian* [both also meaning same-sex love]" (1999, 278). While Sang concurs with Hinsch that the "range of Chinese discourses on homosexuality narrowed after the 1920s," she nevertheless argues that "the idea of there being an extraordinary homosexual nature confined to a small percentage of the population did not become the overruling paradigm for understanding homoerotic desire" (ibid., 297) because "*tongxing'ai* is primarily signified as a modality of love or an intersubjective rapport rather than as a category of personhood, that is, an identity" (ibid., 292–293).

While Sang argues (in the spirit of Halperin's call) for a conceptualization of homosexuality away from sexual act or identity, through the course of the twentieth century, however, *tongxing'ai* and *tongxinglian* have not only become the most common Chinese discursive terms for homosexuality, but also have gradually solidified into an identity category. The latter has perhaps been exacerbated in the past few decades with the arrival of post-Stonewall gay identities and discourses and the concomitant tropes of the closet and coming out. Moreover, there are differences in the development of these discursive terms in China, Taiwan, and Hong Kong. For example, while it is not uncommon for those familiar with Western gay parlance to directly use the English word "gay" in these societies, it has been transliterated as *gei* (meaning foundation) in Cantonese, the common language in Hong Kong, and is usually rendered as *gei-lo* (*lo* meaning male), which Wah-shan Chou reads as derogatory "since *lo* carries the connotation of a male who comes from the lower classes" and as sexist "because it totally ignores and rejects lesbians and bisexual women" (2000, 79). In Taiwan, there is a translation of the term "gay" as *gaizu* (*gai* functions as a transliteration of gay and means, among other things, lid or cover, while *zu* denotes clan or tribe), though as far as I am aware, it has never attained wide circulation.[20]

Up until the 1990s, *tongxinglian* and *tongxing'ai* remained the most commonly used Chinese discursive terms for homosexuality. This began to change with the appropriation of the term *tongzhi* (literally "same will"), the Chinese translation of the Soviet communist term "comrade," as a discursive term for same-sex sexuality.[21] The popular use of the original meaning of the term *tongzhi* can be traced to a quote by Sun Yat-sen (1866–1925), the founding father of Republican China, whose dying words were, "The revolution has yet to triumph; comrades still must work hard" *(Geming shang wei chenggong; tongzhi reng xu nuli)*. Following the establishment of the People's Republic of China in 1949, the term became the most common form of political address in the country. The term *tongzhi* was first publicly appropriated for same-sex sexuality by the organizers of Hong Kong's inaugural lesbian and gay film festival in 1989 and introduced to Taiwan in 1992 when the Taipei Golden Horse International Film Festival featured a section on lesbian and gay films.[22] It has since gained popular currency in Taiwan, Hong Kong, overseas Chinese communities, and on the World Wide Web, where it is widely used to refer to lesbian- and gay-related activities and publications, and it is used as well by the media and the general public. Even in China, where there is potential ambiguity and confusion in its use resulting from the conflation of its appropriated meaning with its political reference, the term is increasingly used to refer to same-sex sexuality.

The term *tongzhi* has replaced *tongxinglian* or *tongxing'ai* in most post-1990 publications in the Chinese language, especially in publications outside of mainland China.[23] The term's popularity can be attributed to "its positive cultural references, gender neutrality, desexualization of the stigma of homosexuality, politics beyond the homo-hetero duality, and use as an indigenous cultural identity for integrating the sexual into the social" (Chou 2000, 2). The term can even break down the dichotomy between homosexuality and heterosexuality, as evidenced in the oxymoronic term *zhitongzhi* (straight comrades), meaning heterosexuals who are supportive of gay rights. Since the mid-1990s, the term "queer" has also become popular in Taiwan, where it is translated as *ku'er* (literally "cool kid") or *guaitai* (meaning weirdo, or literally "strange fetus").[24]

Of the above Chinese discursive terms for homosexuality, I have chosen *tongzhi* as the derivation for the title of this book, *Celluloid Comrades,* not because I particularly identify with its connotation and/or politics but rather to acknowledge the temporal coevality (the 1990s) of its circulation with the emergence of representations of male homosexuality in cinemas from China, Taiwan, and Hong Kong. It is significant that the new discursive language for homosexuality in Chinese societies has been occasioned by the introduction of lesbian and gay films from all over the world and that its circulation started in cinematic circles in these societies. On the one hand, this attests to the order of the new global cultural economy, described by Arjun Appadurai (1990) as disjunctive, wherein global flows (such as the circulation of a discursive term for homosexuality) can take place because marginal elements and identities have global interconnections. On the other hand, it exemplifies how a new discursive language can use cinema as a vehicle to transcend national boundaries and, in the process, act as a catalyst for new identity categories and new forms of solidarity. While this coevality can be seen as a consequence of the term providing a timely discursive language for the films, it can also be argued that, on the contrary, these films have created a platform for the extensive use of the new discursive language, thus highlighting the enabling potential and constitutive aspect of cinema.

Because of the temporal specificity of the term *tongzhi,* however, and for reasons of consistency, I have avoided using *tongzhi* or any other Chinese discursive terms in my general discussion of homosexuality in the rest of this book. Similarly, I use the English terms "lesbian and gay" and "queer" predominantly in their temporal-political-activist (post-1970 and post-1990 respectively) and institutional-disciplinary-theoretical (lesbian and gay studies, queer theory) senses, with attendance to the double entendres of the term "queer." As a result, the terms "homosexual(s)" and "homosexuality," despite having their roots in clinical pathology and sexology, become the default general referents in the literal sense of same-sex. Less clumsy than "same-sex sexuality" and more flexible in their uses (as both noun and adjective), the terms "homosexual(s)" and "homosexuality," it seems to me, are also more capable of transcending the temporal and connotative markings of their discursive histories for general description in ways that "lesbian and gay" or "queer" are arguably not.

To sum up, both "Chinese" and "homosexual" are classificatory and identity categories that are prone to essentialized usage, and the coupling of the two terms can usher in new mechanisms, processes, and opportunities for inclusion and exclusion, legitimation and stigmatization, and empowerment and disenfranchisement. If a category known as "Chinese homosexual(ity)" is invariably invoked in the course or as a result of this inquiry, it is certainly not my intention to propose a Chinese expression of homosexuality or a homosexual expression of Chineseness. Rather, I wish to highlight the opposite—that is, whether it is "Chinese," "homosexual(ity)," or "Chinese homosexual(ity)," these are not essential qualities but expressions and constructs determined by social, economic, political, cultural, historical, ideological, and discursive forces. It is not *what* they are but *how* they have been constructed, spoken of, mobilized, by whom, for what purposes, to what audiences, and *why* that are the crucial questions.

Representing Homosexuality in Chinese Cinemas

As noted, this book is situated at the crossroads of at least three academic disciplines: Chinese studies, gender and sexuality studies, and film and cinema studies, thus foregrounding its invariably interdisciplinary nature. In terms of theoretical approach, it is also informed by critical theory, cultural studies, and post-colonial studies. It has to be emphasized, however, that the cinematic representations are my primary focus. I believe that rather than imposing themselves on texts, theories ought to illuminate textual elements alongside the latter's specific historical, cultural, social, and political contexts. Indeed, I would go as far as to argue that the complexity of textual elements often shores up the inadequacies of existing theories, thereby challenging us to reconfigure our theoretical undertakings.

Though I do not subscribe exclusively to any single school of thought, I find the position proposed by two British cultural materialists rather irresistible. For Jonathan Dollimore and Alan Sinfield, the approach of cultural materialism offers a combination of four elements: historical context, theoretical method, political commitment, and textual analysis. Primarily aiming at challenging traditional approaches to the study of literature, Dollimore and Sinfield elaborate on these four elements: "Historical context undermines the transcendent significance traditionally accorded to the literary text and allows us to recover its histories; theoretical method detaches the text from immanent criticism which seeks only to reproduce it in its own terms; socialist and feminist commitment confronts conservative categories in which most criticism has hitherto been conducted; textual analysis locates the critique of traditional approaches where it cannot be ignored" (1985, vii).

I believe the interplay and check between the four elements will create a tapestry that is not slanted to, or by, any single overriding imperative. Of the four elements, I should qualify what I mean by political commitment. Like Dollimore and Sinfield, I am committed to any efforts that confront conservatism and will undoubtedly align with minorities, subalterns, and marginalized groups of all variants in posing challenges to orthodox ideologies and cultural hegemonies of all forms. However, if I have a political commitment in relation to scholarship, it would be not to allow the arguments in this book to be dictated by the political dogmas of any imagined community. On the contrary, it is precisely because I am acutely aware of the necessarily essentializing nature of political activism and the communalizing tendency of identity categories that I strenuously argue against the rhetoric of a gay liberationist discourse and demands of political correctness prevalent in many readings of the films under discussion. Indeed, the central issues of representation—including the theoretical, textual-analytic, and political debates—are so deeply embedded in a contemporary climate of identity politics and multiculturalism that they warrant historical, theoretical, political, and textual analyses in themselves.

To begin with the historical, Kath Weston has written on what she calls the "Great Gay Migration" of the 1970s and early 1980s into major urban areas across the United States; it coincided with a gay movement that ushered in the so-called minority model of gay identity, the pitfalls of which she describes as follows:

> In the minority model homosexuality becomes an entity supposed to be discernible without respect to culture or context. To write unreflectively about "gay people" is to treat homosexuality as a presocial given. To say "I am a lesbian" or "I am gay" usually presumes a consistency of attraction to the same sex that makes an individual a different kind of person. When the minority model grants gay people ontological status as a finite, bounded group, it uni-

versalizes a Western classification in which sexual behaviors and desires are supposed thoroughly to infuse a self. (1995, 258)

Weston's historical account highlights not only the economic and geographical factors underlying what might seem like a natural formation of an identity, a community, a movement, and a politics, but also the theoretical implications of a minority model that assumes an essentialized, pre-social given. One result of this historical development is the valorization of the gay self/identity and the gay experience, to the degree that, to borrow Diana Fuss' exquisite construction, "who we are becomes what we know; ontology shades into epistemology" (1989, 113). In the process, knowledge becomes derivative of experience, and experience in turn bestows its own authority upon knowledge. In an essay that calls for a historicizing of experience, Joan W. Scott persuasively argues that

> we need to attend to the historical processes that, through discourse, position subjects and produce their experiences. It is not individuals who have experience, but subjects who are constituted through experience. Experience in this definition then becomes not the origin of our explanation, not the authoritative (because seen or felt) evidence that grounds what is known, but rather that which we seek to explain, that about which knowledge is produced. To think about experience in this way is to historicize it as well as to historicize the identities it produces. (1992, 25–26)

A theoretical approach to the question of homosexuality as a historical, discursive process will undoubtedly reshape the political debates surrounding its cinematic representations. This historical development has to be situated in the context of Anglo-American societies, as well as other societies informed by the politics of multiculturalism, for two reasons: linguistic and temporal. In terms of language, it might seem like an unusual denaturalizing gesture to bring to the reader's attention that this book is written in English and that I have been able to engage only with debates written in English and Chinese, the latter also entrenched in Anglo-American epistemologies and politics.[25] Contrary to the usual broad binary of East versus West, I would argue that within so-called Western societies, the epistemologies and politics surrounding "the gay issue" are organized very differently, especially in their legal, social, institutional, and cultural manifestations.[26] The politics underpinning many debates with which I engage throughout the book is therefore chiefly Anglo-American, and as Alice A. Kuzniar argues in her study on queer German cinema, there are many unquestioned preconceptions about "the progressive nature of gay and lesbian representation in cinema, the sexuality of the directors, and the prevalence of the coming-out narrative" in conventional constructions of film history that purport to survey lesbian and gay representations in a national cinema (2000, 16). Given this background, it seems superfluous, yet totally imperative, to reiterate that it is possible, if not necessary, to approach the question of homosexuality and its cinematic representations away from an Anglo-American-centric, identity-politics-based framework.

Temporally, then, because the films under discussion were mainly released in the 1990s, the debates surrounding their representations and the generation of scholars and critics involved in these debates are inevitably contemporaneous with the politics of multiculturalism that has dominated sociocultural discursive practices since the 1980s, to the extent that one could argue that few (debates or individuals) have not been impinged upon by this politics, and fewer would be self-reflexive enough to escape its stranglehold. There has been an obsession with identities in their innumerable configurations and permutations within the climate of multiculturalism, but one needs to be reminded more often that identity categories "tend to be instruments of regulatory regimes, whether as the normalizing categories of oppressive structures or as the rallying points for a liberatory contestation of that very oppression" (Butler 1991, 13–14).

Finally, the political climate of identity politics and multiculturalism cannot but have an effect on strategies of textual analysis. As Michael Warner admits, "what we may be less prepared to recognize is that the frame of identity politics itself belongs to Anglo-American traditions and has some distorting influences" (1993, xvii). While I cannot possibly claim to be totally free from such influences, I have throughout the book largely adopted a position that refuses to accept uncritically the terms of identity politics and gay liberationist discourses. Rather, by striving to liberate readings of films from the dictates of what has been called the "gaytto" (Jousse 1997, 20), I call for interrepresentation among different groups and identities, arguing that the representation of male homosexuality in Chinese cinemas invariably involves collaboration between gays and straights and that the latter's involvement in these filmic projects should not always be held with suspicion or dismissed as misplaced goodwill. In so doing, this book in fact ushers in "a new utopian imaginary" (Ong and Nonini 1997, 330) in its quest to illuminate our understanding of homosexuality in its irreducible multiplicity through cinematic representations that become sites of analysis drawing together textual elements with historical contexts, theoretical frameworks, and political debates.

Representation, therefore, is a central issue linking the chapters that study the celluloid comrades. To begin with the historical, chapter 1, "Screening Homosexuality," argues that the representation of male homosexuality in Chinese cinemas has been engendered by the marginal and interstitial spaces created by the disjunctive order of globalization. These spaces include the international film festival circuit, which has witnessed the emergence of Chinese cinemas since the 1980s and has served as a global public sphere upon which representations of male homosexuality in Chinese cinemas can come into being. Focusing on the theoretical and the political, chapter 2, "The Burden of Representation," locates *The Wedding Banquet* (*Xiyan,* 1993), by Ang Lee (Li An, b. 1954), within theorizations on the meaning of representation and debates on the politics of representation. Noting that the film has shouldered the heaviest burden of representation given its status as the first "gay film" in contemporary Chinese cinemas and its thematic concern with the position of homosexuality in a Chinese-Confucianist cosmology, it argues that the conjunction of Chineseness with homosexuality and the hegemony of a gay liberationist discourse have led to dominant readings of the film in the tropes of the closet and coming out in less than reflective ways. Chapter 3, "The Uses of Femininity," further problematizes the politics of representation by raising the question of the place of femininity—a debased cultural stereotype—within male homosexuality. Drawing from *Farewell My Concubine* (*Bawang bie ji,* 1993), by Chen Kaige (b. 1952), and *East Palace, West Palace* (*Donggong xigong,* 1996), by Zhang Yuan (b. 1963), I argue that the trope of femininity can provide a model for the reconfiguration of power relations in terms of both gender and sexuality, as well as in the sociopolitical realms through its dynamics of resistance-via-obedience.

Weaving the political with the textual, chapter 4, "Travelling Sexualities," explores diasporic forms of sexuality by highlighting the economic conditions for travel and the dialectic relationship between home and the diasporic space in *Happy Together* (*Chunguang zhaxie,* 1997), by Wong Kar-wai (Wang Jiawei, b. 1958). An allegorical reading of the film in the context of Hong Kong's 1997 return to the People's Republic of China also leads to an interrogation on notions of normativity in relation to homosexuality. The final two chapters adopt an auteurist approach by paying attention to two key directors. Chapter 5, "Confessing Desire," traces the poetics of Tsai Ming-liang's (Cai Mingliang, b. 1957) queer cinema, drawing representational tropes from his early theatrical, television, and documentary works to illuminate his films *Rebels of the Neon God* (*Qingshaonian Nezha,* 1992) and *The River* (*Heliu,* 1997). Deploying the Barthesian concept of *jouissance,* I argue that Tsai's focus on the poetics (of representation) rather than the psychology (of characters) renders his cinema queer insofar as it is impossible to pin down. By contrast, in chapter 6, "Fragments of Darkness," I propose to read Stanley Kwan (Guan Jinpeng, b. 1957) as a gay director through his "coming out film," *Hold You Tight* (*Yu kuaile yu duoluo,* 1998). Positing Kwan's documentary work against Rainer Werner Fassbinder's politics, this chapter identifies a moment when Kwan's filmmaking career and personal history collapse into each other to the extent that the issue of sexuality haunts the film like a darkness that threatens to engulf his cinematic representation of homosexuality. Finally, the conclusion investigates the plausibility of a queer Chinese cinema and its various implications.

Last but not least, some caveats. This book does not pretend to be a comprehensive survey of representations of male homosexuality in Chinese cinemas. I have not included in the discussion films prior to the 1990s, a prominent example being Yu Kan-ping's *The Outsiders* (*Niezi,* 1986), based on the eponymous novel by Pai Hsien-yung (Bai Xianyong). While it is not difficult to find in run-of-the-mill Hong Kong films homosexual caricatures that are usually set up as the butt of demeaning comedy, to study such representations critically demands a totally different approach from what this book aims to achieve. From the 1990s and beyond, there are other films featuring male homosexuality that, for reasons of quality or space, have to be left out of this study.[27] The cinematic representation of lesbianism is another project waiting to be undertaken. I also have to exclude many documentaries and short films. Nonetheless, it is hoped that the multifariousness, complexity, and richness of the representations I have chosen to study will challenge us to reflect upon many of our assumptions not only about how identities might be negotiated in relation to the matrices of ethnicity/race, class, gender, and sexuality, but also about identity itself and the pitfalls in contemporary multicultural politics. If I have always believed in deconstructing monolithic and essentialized notions of both Chineseness and homosexuality, that faith can only have been strengthened in the years of pondering over these films and writing this book.

Screening Homosexuality

Thinking of the cinema in terms of the public sphere means
reconstructing a horizon of reception . . . in terms of multiple and conflicting identities and constituencies. Indeed, the
cinema can, at certain junctures, function as a matrix for
challenging social positions of identity and otherness, as
a catalyst for new forms of community and solidarity.

—MIRIAM HANSEN, "Early Cinema, Late Cinema"

From the interracial couple in *The Wedding Banquet* and the diasporic
sojourners in *Happy Together* to the cross-dressing opera actor in *Farewell My Concubine* and the incestuous father and son in *The River,* the proliferating representation of male homosexuality in contemporary Chinese
cinemas was a striking phenomenon at the end of the twentieth century
that would not have gone unnoticed by any cinephile. There is a need to
account for this phenomenon as representations of a marginal sexuality
become increasingly prominent in the cultural and sociopolitical realms
in China, Taiwan, and Hong Kong. Moreover, as Chinese cinemas begin
to capture the attention of even mainstream American audiences with
films such as Ang Lee's *Crouching Tiger, Hidden Dragon* (*Wohu canglong,*
2000) and Zhang Yimou's *House of Flying Daggers* (*Shimian maifu,* 2004) and
with the wire-fu choreography of Yuen Wo-ping transforming Hollywood
products as varied as the *Matrix* trilogy and the *Kill Bill* series, scholarship
in Chinese cinemas must also move beyond the paradigm of national cinema and the reading of films primarily as national allegories in order to
properly address representations that cannot, and should not, be simply
subsumed under the sign of the nation.[1] Rather than seeing cinema merely
as providing textual materials for the understanding of a particular nation,
this chapter proposes to rethink, via the screening of homosexuality in
contemporary Chinese films, cinema as an enabling agent that is also capable of bringing about societal changes. It argues that the amalgamation of

the invariably global dimension of both cinema and homosexuality has engendered new visual representations of celluloid comrades hitherto unseen on Chinese screens.

Chinese Cinemas and Their International Fascination

The 1980s witnessed the simultaneous surge of new waves in the cinemas of China, Taiwan, and Hong Kong that caught the world's attention. In China, prominent figures from the Beijing Film Academy's first graduating class since the Cultural Revolution came to be known as the Fifth Generation *(diwudai)* directors, including Chen Kaige, Zhang Yimou (b. 1950), and Tian Zhuangzhuang (b. 1952). Buttressed by a nationwide "cultural reflection" and "historical reflection" in intellectual circles (Lu 1997a, 7), these directors abandoned the socialist revolutionary project of their predecessors to re-envision the nation. In Taiwan, a similar "obsession with histories," albeit of a different locale and in a different fashion, was evident in the Taiwan New Cinema (Taiwan Xindianying) of Hou Hsiao-hsien (Hou Xiaoxian, b. 1947), Edward Yang (Yang Dechang, b. 1947), and others; it resonated with a wider nativization movement on the island (Kuan-hsing Chen 1998, 557). Led by directors such as Ann Hui (Xu Anhua, b. 1947) and Allen Fong (Fang Yuping, b. 1947), Hong Kong cinema also experienced a new wave *(xinlangchao)*, devoted to exploring the bleak living conditions of the underclass, thereby offering an alternative to the (then) colony's signature genre films (Teo 1998, 550).[2]

The collective new voice of Chinese cinemas soon became an emerging power to contend with globally. Particularly since Zhang Yimou's *Red Sorghum (Hong gaoliang,* 1987) captured the Golden Bear at the Berlin Film Festival in 1988, films from China, Taiwan, and Hong Kong have become festival darlings, winning many major awards worldwide.[3] For most of these auteurist directors, however, the route to international film festivals is not a choice but a necessity. By the late 1980s the film industries in China and Taiwan were at the brink of collapse. Some mainland Chinese directors such as Zhang Yuan have been blacklisted by the state studios or banned from filmmaking altogether. Many Taiwanese directors cannot survive in the shrinking domestic market dominated by Hollywood block-busters and Hong Kong genre films. Though Hong Kong is the third largest film-producing region in the world (after the United States and India), its film industry is almost exclusively dictated by commerce, and the space for making art house cinema is arguably more limited than in China and Taiwan. International film festivals have increasingly become the only avenues for these directors to showcase their films. Exposure at these festivals can lead to the sale of screening rights, investment in future projects, and possibilities of transnational collaboration.

The convergence of Chinese cinemas and international film festivals —a chiefly Western institution—produces a cross-cultural exchange that invariably involves various kinds of politics and power play. According to Esther Yau, the "international fantasy" surrounding new Chinese cinemas since the 1980s can be traced to at least three image-making processes. They are "the rewriting of China's political and cultural complexities by young filmmakers; the diplomatic exhibition of artistic talent in support of an open-door policy by the government of the People's Republic of China; and the search for new varieties of art cinema by (mostly western) film critics" (1993, 95).[4] For me, what is significant in Yau's analysis is her suggestion that this fascination does not originate only from the West. As much as Western film critics and film festival scouts have been eager to discover new cinemas from the exotic East, the participation of Chinese cinemas in international film festivals may also mask hidden agendas of cultural diplomacy and attempts to gain cultural capital by obtaining a Western stamp of approval.

This observation is of particular importance because in any cultural exchange such as this that becomes embedded in the terms of Orientalism versus Occidentalism, First World versus Third World, often only half of the story is told. Nativist critics have been quick to point out the unequal power relations between Chinese cinemas and international film festivals and to accuse Chinese filmmakers of pandering to the West.[5] However, Yau's research shows that as early as the mid-1980s, studio heads, directors, and critics in China "began to speculate on the kinds of films that would impress foreigners," and some studio heads "allocated funds and personnel each year to the production of one or two films designed to enter foreign film festivals" (1993, 98). Similarly, since 1992, Taiwan's Government Information Bureau has developed an elaborate scheme for rewarding films that have participated in or won awards at international film festivals.[6] It would seem that the international fantasy is, in fact, mutual.

A representative argument in the nativist mode is offered by Yingjin Zhang, who posits that "oriental *ars erotica* as a mythified entity is fixed or fixated at the very center of Western fascination" with Chinese cinemas (1998, 116).[7] Zhang goes on to list the "essential" or "magic" ingredients in the formula for satisfying Western aesthetic taste: primitive landscape, repressed sexuality, gender performance, and a mythical or cyclical time frame in which the protagonist's fate is predestined (ibid., 118). However, these ingredients (except the last one) can also be found in Jane Campion's *The Piano,* which shared the Palme d'Or with Chen Kaige's *Farewell My Concubine* at the 1993 Cannes Film Festival. Does this imply that Australian cinema has also been serving "oriental *ars erotica*" to satisfy Western aesthetic taste? While some Chinese films might have borne the traits of this description, Zhang's argument is too totalizing to do justice to the varied and complex body of films from Chinese cinemas that have won international accolades since the 1980s.

More important, the theoretical framework and polemical argument of such critics present a discursive impasse that makes their own position untenable. Moreover, as Ben Xu argues, the nativist critics' turn to radicalism "happens at the same time that the Chinese official discourse is desperately in need of new theory to bolster its parochial national position in resistance to international criticism, especially that of the Western world" (1997, 156). By turning away from "domestic problems concerning the relations of culture and power and choosing international culture/power relations as the main area of critical attention," these critics, Xu claims, are articulating "complicitous silences" with the party-state, and their critical stance is hence marked "with a pathetic nativist tone" (ibid.).

The relationship between Chinese cinemas and international film festivals requires rethinking in terms that go beyond the limitations of Chinese-nativist post-colonial criticism. I propose to read Chinese cinemas as part of a new world cinema that is premised on a different cultural economy, with an audience that is invariably global. In the case of Chen Kaige's *Farewell My Concubine,* which for nativist critics is yet "another example of third world cultural dependency on the first world" (Xu 1997, 156), Shiaoying Shen analyzes the success of Chen's film in rather different terms: "Chen is, in fact, exposing an aspect of the marketing ecology of the international commercial film arena: there is actually not much difference between the East and the West today when investors and filmmakers attempt to forcefully access the global market: Hollywood has already successfully interpellated the global film-viewing subject—shaping the film-viewing habit of audiences around the world. To appeal to the gaze of that 'global subject,' the universally acknowledged formula is to pack spectacles of one form or another into a film product" (1995, 9).

I would like to extend Shen's notion of the global film-viewing subject beyond the so-called commercial arena to apply it to the so-called festival and art house circuit. If Hollywood has indeed interpellated the global commercial film-viewing subject, international film festivals and art house cinemas have arguably interpellated another kind of global film-viewing subject, whose devotion to a variety of alternative cinemas does not depend necessarily on the spectacular. International film festivals range from major ones that can make or break an auteurist film to specific ones that cater to audiences as varied as ethnic or sexual minorities and those with special interests such as anime or horror films. The relationship between Chinese cinemas and international film festivals, therefore, is as much about cross-cultural exchange as it is about market segmentation.

Linked not only to the sensory organ of the palate but also to that of the eyes, the notion of taste is key to understanding the dynamics of international film festivals and their audiences.[8] For Chinese cinemas to triumph at these festivals, they would have to appeal to panels of judges comprising Western film directors, critics, actors, and actresses—usually white, cosmopolitan, First World cultural elites—and to film festival scouts, journalists, and audiences of largely similar composition. Even if Chinese filmmakers do not intentionally cater to the taste of these global film-viewing subjects, the latter's attitude towards the cinematic encounter may have predetermined the mode of reception. As Martin Roberts observes, "For consumers in such [First World] cities, going to the movies and eating out have become more or less equivalent activities, with choosing a movie, like choosing a restaurant, a matter of selecting from a repertoire of available ethnic options. . . . The audiences for multicultural films may be as transnational as the films themselves, and watching them may be as much a way of reconnecting with one's own culture as of indulging a touristic curiosity about someone else's" (1998, 66). As Roberts reveals, the global film-viewing subject is not homogeneous. Any accusation of a *purely* touristic, voyeuristic, and exotic Orientalism on the part of the viewers therefore runs the risks of overlooking diasporic ethnic audiences seeking reconnection with their own cultures.[9] In a globalized world in which intermigration and frequent travel are increasingly commonplace, the multicultural, multilingual, and multiethnic (not to mention hybridized) nature of global film-viewing subjects makes assumptions about the reception of Chinese cinemas in "the West" rather hollow.

A paradigm shift is thus required to re-envision the relationship between Chinese cinemas and international film festivals away from the rhetoric of Orientalism versus Occidentalism. Using the entry of Iranian cinema into the international film festival circuit as an example, Bill Nichols situates this cultural exchange in the context of "global image consumption in the age of late capitalism." As he argues, "the discovery of new national cinemas and their filmmaker artists operates much more fully inside the model of a postindustrial economy and postmodern condition devoted to the circulation of signifiers or images as such" (1994b,

73). Indeed, the link between the circulation of cinematic images and nativist sentiments should be decoupled. Rather, it is more important to understand the relations of production and consumption, to assess the ever-changing taste of global-viewing subjects, and to evaluate how representations such as homosexuality in Chinese cinemas can capitalize on the political economy engendered by this cross-cultural exchange.

The New Global Cultural Economy and Public Sphere

Contemporary Chinese cinemas, therefore, should be situated in a new global cultural economy, which "has to be understood as a complex, overlapping, disjunctive order," wherein global flows occur in and through the growing disjunctures between what Arjun Appadurai calls "ethnoscapes, technoscapes, finanscapes, mediascapes and ideoscapes" (1990, 296, 301). The site of international film festivals is one such disjuncture, facilitating Chinese cinemas' participation in a global cultural economy. This exchange of global flows has not only raised the profile of Chinese cinemas in the world but, I would argue, has also introduced homosexuality as a legitimate discourse in Chinese cinemas in ways that may not have been previously possible.

One effect of the new global cultural economy is the undermining of the notion of nation-states and enabling cultural imaginaries to transcend national boundaries. As globalization leads to deterritorialization, even marginal groups and individuals can begin to imagine themselves on a global scale. The extensive use of the World Wide Web is the most obvious example of how global an "imagined community" (to borrow Benedict Anderson's ubiquitous term) can now be. While globalization often results in homogenization, particularly in cultural terms, it nevertheless also deterritorializes by breaking down traditional barriers, decentering orthodox power structures, and creating new alliances for marginal groups. Fredric Jameson argues as follows: "Although it may be an exaggeration to claim that we are all marginals now, all decentered in the current good senses of those words, certainly many freedoms have been won in the process whereby globalization has meant a decentering and a proliferation of differences" (1998, 66).

It is against this background that I situate the representation of homosexuality in contemporary Chinese cinemas. I suggest that precisely because of homosexuality's marginality and difference, the conjunction of homosexuality and Chinese cinemas lends itself comfortably to the growing disjunctive order of the new global cultural economy. This situation is analogous to Third Cinema, an emancipatory and militant cinematic form. According to Michael Chanan, "The survival of Third Cinema depends on its origins within the margins and interstices. Margins and interstices are different but closely related spaces. They are also global in their interconnections. . . . The global conditions of postmodern culture make it possible for margins and interstices across the globe to become aware of each other" (1997, 388).[10] Chanan's notion of "margins and interstices" echoes Appadurai's concept of "growing disjunctures." As the new global cultural economy becomes increasingly disjunctive, the representation of homosexuality in contemporary Chinese cinemas can proliferate in its margins and interstices, particularly at the site of international film festivals.

Some may question if international film festivals can be regarded as marginal and interstitial spaces. Undeniably, big festivals like Cannes have become a very "powerful motor propelling films from around the globe into the distribution and exhibition system," some to arrive at smaller, regional festivals, and some even to theaters in other countries (Sklar 1996, 20). However, the international film festival circuit is dwarfed in the face of the cinematic hegemony of Hollywood. As Nichols argues, Hollywood forms the backdrop against which Third Cinema, independent Western cinema, and all other cinemas differentiate themselves. The political economy of international film festivals lies in displacing, not bolstering, the center that is Hollywood (1994b, 74). Though it has been argued that "the differences between Hollywood and the festival circuits are more and more blurred" (Shen 1995, 9), the cultural significance of a "superpower" film festival like Cannes still derives from "its ability to construct a response to the Hollywood colossus" (Sklar 1996, 18).[11]

Another way of conceptualizing the marginal and interstitial spaces for different forms of cinemas is Jürgen Habermas' notion of the public sphere (1992). With globalization, the public sphere is no longer confined to the boundaries of nation-states but can exist globally and also virtually on the World Wide Web. Many scholars have borrowed Habermas' concept to construct the world of cinema as a public sphere.[12] To her comment in the epigraph at the beginning of this chapter, Miriam Hansen adds, "The category of the public retains a critical, utopian edge, predicated on the ideal of collective self-determination. This perspective mandates not only maintaining critical distinction with regard to commercially disseminated fare but also envisioning alternative media products and an alternative organization of the relations of representation and reception" (1993, 207–208).

Conceptualizing Chinese cinemas as a global public sphere with the potential to challenge orthodox ideologies has appealed to scholars writing on Chinese cinemas. Invoking the Habermasian concept of the public sphere, Ben Xu points out that "owing to the ideological control of the Party-State in China, public discussion often takes a roundabout route" via artistic forms such as film (1997, 161). Citing *Farewell My Concubine* as an example, Xu argues that "the focus on the moral and cultural dimensions of social transformation rather than on immediate institutional shake-up may be, in its intent and consequences, more effective in shaping a public space than a direct encounter with the state" (ibid., 161–162). Moreover, in a country where film directors have routinely been blacklisted and their films banned, the concept of transnational Chinese cinemas, with its emphasis on creating a public sphere that transcends national boundaries, may become "a viable strategy of survival and of resistance to a domestic hegemony" (Lu 1997a, 11). Using Zhang Yimou as an example, Sheldon Lu argues that "while intellectualist, elitist 'cultural reflection' was hushed in post-Tiananmen China, filmmakers are able to carry out their critical project with the support of transnational capital and the global market" (1997b, 132), which are premised on the engendering conditions of this global cinematic public sphere.

Having highlighted the deterritorialized and disjunctive cultural economy that ushers in a global cinematic public sphere, I believe it is possible to rethink the notion of cinema in terms of its enabling potential and constitutive effects. While cinematic representations are often regarded as a reflection of society or "reality," the margins and interstices generated by the global public sphere of Chinese cinemas may, in fact, bring some "realities" into existence. That is to say, rather than merely "reflecting the thinking of an era," cinema actually "makes possible such thinking," thus marking a "constitutive, not a reflective relation" with "reality" (Andrew 1986, 7). To illustrate this, the new mainland Chinese cinema has, "at least in its most important phase in the mid-1980s, succeeded in creating a hitherto nonexistent discursive space for the formation and transformation of individual identities and subjectivities" (Yingjin Zhang 2002, 6–7). Similarly, the Taiwan New Cinema of the 1980s opened the way for a varied and diverse film production that, in the 1990s, joined a proliferating global film culture in helping to "create a new, more open and democratic, Taiwanese public sphere" (Kellner 1998, 102). For example, Hou Hsiao-hsien's *A City of Sadness* (*Beiqing chengshi,* 1989) contributed in generating public discussion on the hitherto taboo issue of the February 28 incident.[13]

It may seem more difficult to make a similar case for Hong Kong cinema because its modus operandi is fundamentally different. Unlike its mainland Chinese and Taiwanese counterparts of the 1980s, the Hong Kong New Wave has never achieved a break with its cinematic tradition, which is rooted in melodramatic narrative and the star system (C. Li 1994, 160). Even the stylistically avant garde cinema of Wong Kar-wai cannot do without Hong Kong's glittering pop and movie stars in the leading roles. However, I would still argue that the "critical, utopian edge" inherent in the notion of the public sphere is not necessarily less pronounced in Hong Kong cinema as it is differently formulated, demanding a reading that looks beneath (or beyond) the surface to uncover its oppositional potential. In the case of Stanley Kwan's *Hold You Tight,* for example, it was the Golden Harvest Studio that approached the director to make a film starring the actress Chingmy Yau (Qiu Shuzhen), more popularly known for her soft porn flicks. As it turned out, the film features an openly gay character and another male character who has sex with women but secretly loves men. *Hold You Tight* is hence "a brilliant example of a film that straddles the industrial fence by turning what is intended as a vehicle for female sexuality in a heterosexual framework into a film about queer desire" (H. Leung 2001, 439).

While cinema can certainly function, as Hansen argues, "as a catalyst for new forms of community and solidarity," a project such as the representation of homosexuality in Chinese cinemas is dependent upon the engendering conditions of a global cultural economy that are far beyond the control and prediction of any individual film director or producer. In his evaluation of the Habermasian concept of the public sphere, Nicholas Garnham writes: "We have to raise the question of how much room for maneuver agents actually have within a symbolic system within which both the power to create symbols and access to the channels of their circulation is hierarchically structured and intimately integrated into a system of economic production and exchange, which is itself hierarchically structured" (1992, 372–373). Insofar as the global public sphere of international film festivals has hitherto engendered conditions favorable to the representation of male homosexuality in Chinese cinemas, the terms and relations of production and consumption are as ephemeral as they are hierarchized. The key to survival may lie in being sensitive to the ways the five "scapes" described by Appadurai interact with each other and in locating the disjunctures wherein the representation of homosexuality in Chinese cinemas can continue to proliferate in the margins and interstices. In what follows, by providing case studies of the production, distribution, exhibition, and reception of the films discussed in this book, I will delineate the negotiation of homosexuality in Chinese societies and Chinese cinemas. While this is not the place for a full-blown sociological account on the state of homosexuality in China, Taiwan, and Hong Kong—which, in any case, changes rapidly with time[14]—I will highlight aspects of these societies that impact on the roles of both agents and institutions in making the representation of homosexuality in Chinese cinemas possible or difficult.

Playing the Party Game in China

In China, though there is no specific law for the criminalization of homosexuality, homosexuals can be arrested and imprisoned under Article 106 of the Criminal Law Code, which is meant for the prosecution of hooliganism (Ruan 1991, 131). Reports have shown that the enforcement of this law is highly uneven and often left to the whim of policemen. Punishment can vary from a mild chiding or a small fine to a few days' detention with no record kept or a few years' imprisonment (Chou 1996a, 139–151; An 1995, 26–31; Li Yinhe 1998, 380–398; Ruan 1991, 126). Written accounts concur that so long as homosexual activities do not disrupt social order or involve sodomy with minors and are not coupled with other petty crimes, the punishment will tend to be light.

According to sociologist Li Yinhe, who co-authored the first full-length study on homosexuality in contemporary China with her novelist husband Wang Xiaobo, the greatest threat for homosexuals in China is not legal prosecution but "administrative and party disciplinary action" (Li 1998, 389).[15] Again, such punishment can be as varied as that carried out by the police, who, instead of prosecuting the homosexual criminals, often refer them to their work units *(danwei)* or threaten to do so, though the control of work units over the lives of civilians is diminishing in contemporary China. The tropes of mental breakdown and attempted suicide are particularly salient in the accounts of homosexuals who have faced such disciplinary action.

Outside of the new commercial gay venues that have emerged in big cities across China, homosexuals mainly interact in open public spaces, making them vulnerable to police raids and extortion. Because regulations prohibit local residents from staying in hotels, homosexuals seeking sexual liaisons often find themselves driven into the dark corners of public restrooms (Chou 1996a, 65–66). Police raids on homosexuals and sociological research coincided in a bizarre episode in the early 1990s. In 1991, several projects linked to AIDS education were set up in China, involving the famous gay activist Wan Yanhai, who was working at the China Health Education Institute and the Prohibitions Section of the Social Public Order Department of the Beijing Public Security Bureau—that is, the police. According to Wan's own account, at a work meeting for the research project in which the topic of how to make contact with the gay community was brought up, a police officer "suggested the police should take the gay men in, and then the researchers could do surveys and take blood samples for testing" (Wan 2001, 56–58).

This incident in fact became the trigger for Zhang Yuan's *East Palace, West Palace* (which refers to the two public toilets on either side of Tiananmen Square known for gay cruising) because the director, having read the story in a newspaper, wondered what would go through a straight policeman's mind during his arrest of a gay man and "what kind of relationship could be woven between these two men in terms of sex and power" (Reynaud 1997, 33). The film features a policeman responsible for conducting raids on homosexuals cruising in a park and his relationship with a gay man who finally succeeds in seducing the policeman into physical intimacy. Zhang's film therefore is a strange reconstruction of reality as fantasy and challenges orthodoxy by queering the very apparatus of surveillance and law enforcement.

While homosexuality is no longer regarded as an illness in the *Categories and Diagnostic Standards of Mental Illness in China* (third edition), published by the Chinese Society of Psychiatry in 2001 (Z. Cui 2002, 13), the main legitimate channels for public discussion of homosexuality are still predominantly in terms of health and medical discourse. For example, discussion sessions in which "psychiatrists, volunteers from the Women's Hotline, and a few individuals discussed homosexual issues" in the early 1990s were held "under the label of 'mental health research'" (He 2002, 10). That many homosexuals have indeed sought medical help and psychiatric cure (Ruan 1991, 129) attests to the extent to which ill-informed discourses have shaped even the homosexual subjects' understanding of themselves. This, for Harriet Evans, is a "violation of gay and lesbian rights in China through the denial of social and discursive spaces permitting the expression of homosexual identities" since such (mis)understanding "penetrates even the subject positions with which homosexuals themselves identify" (1997, 211).

With the unprecedented speed of the opening up of the Chinese economy at the turn of the twenty-first century, there have been clear signs of greater visibility of both "people who call themselves gay" and "semi-public spaces" such as "gay bars; weekly salon discussions, a national hotline; books, magazines, and videos from abroad" that cater to their needs (Rofel 1999, 451). At the same time, there are also continuing reports of official censorship of the Internet, the shutting down of Web sites providing AIDS information targeted to men who have sex with men and run by the scholar Zhang Beichuan (who has written a book on homosexuality), and the closing down of a lesbian and gay film festival to be held in Beijing University.[16] This attests to the disjunctive order, this time within a national space, which engenders contradictory flows that simultaneously permit and disallow expressions of homosexuality; it is also reflected in the negotiation of the making of the two mainland Chinese films discussed in chapter 3, *Farewell My Concubine* and *East Palace, West Palace*.

Given the official censure of homosexuality in China, transnational capital played an important role in the production of Chen Kaige's *Farewell My Concubine* and Zhang Yuan's *East Palace, West Palace*. Chen and Zhang are representatives of China's so-called Fifth and Sixth Generation directors respectively. Fifth Generation directors made their earliest films under the state studio system, which for a brief moment produced experimental films such as Zhang Junzhao's *One and Eight* (*Yige he bage,* 1984) and Chen's *Yellow Earth* (*Huang tudi,* 1984). By contrast, the Sixth Generation is mainly regarded as an underground movement existing outside the state studio system, "shooting films without acquiring official permits and shipping them overseas for exhibition" (Yingjin Zhang 2004, 289). However, by the 1990s, both generations of directors were operating in an economy in which the injection of transnational capital into Chinese filmmaking was increasingly the norm for those with an international cachet.

Farewell My Concubine was conceived when the Taiwanese producer Hsu Feng (Xu Feng) presented Chen Kaige with a copy of the eponymous novel by Hong Kong writer Lilian Lee (Li Bihua) at the 1988 Cannes Film Festival, where Chen's *King of the Children* (*Haiziwang,* 1987) was unceremoniously given the unofficial Golden Alarm Clock Award as "the most boring picture of the year" (Zha 1994, 402). Despite drawing early international critical attention with his debut film, *Yellow Earth,* Chen had heretofore not enjoyed the prestigious accolades won by his contemporary Zhang Yimou (Chen's cinematographer for *Yellow Earth*), who clinched a Golden Bear award at the 1988 Berlin Film Festival with his film debut, *Red Sorghum.* With its epic, historical narrative; its dazzling and flamboyant visual style; and the use of bona fide stars, *Farewell My Concubine* became, in 1993, the first film from Chinese cinemas to capture the Palme d'Or at the Cannes Film Festival.

Financed by Hsu's Taiwanese Tomson Group through its Hong Kong subsidiary and co-produced with the Beijing Film Studio (Rayns 1994b, 48, 57), the film's release in China was to follow a tortuous trajectory. According to a report (*China News,* February 28, 1994), *Farewell My Concubine* was initially banned for three reasons: homosexuality, depiction of the Cultural Revolution, and the "pessimistic" ending.[17] The ban was later lifted but not before three cuts had been made.[18] As to the turn of events, rumor had it that China's then president, Jiang Zemin, had disliked the film, prompting the minister for radio, film, and television to order the postponement of its scheduled release. However, the paramount Chinese leader, Deng Xiaoping, subsequently saw the film and apparently thought otherwise, saying it should be released as soon as possible "after modifications." After its release the film enjoyed box-office successes in Beijing and Shanghai (Rayns 1994b, 48).

Nonetheless, the Chinese Communist Party (CCP) machinery did not try to mask its objection even after the film's release in China. A 1994 article in *Qiushi* (meaning "seeking truth"), an official CCP journal, criticized the film for portraying "a kind of perverted [*biantai*] love." According to the article, "as we all know, together with drug addiction, prostitution, and gambling, homosexuality is regarded in Western countries as a social public nuisance." The author goes on to claim that in China, "homosexuality had long been swept clean after the [1949] liberation" (Ji 1994, 45–46). Wang Dan, one of the student leaders in the 1989 Tiananmen incident, published a rebuttal (*United Daily,* March 3, 1994), arguing that any artistic work criticized by the CCP would immediately gain popularity with the Chinese public. This was evidenced by the underground circulation of *Farewell My Concubine* on videotape following the attack on it in *Qiushi*. Calling this attack a "devious exposure of [Communist China's] cultural totalitarianism," Wang highlighted the disparity between official censure and public sentiments in contemporary China.

Criticisms of Chen's film have also come from outside China, albeit for different reasons. The film's portrayal of the homosexual character, Cheng Dieyi, has been attacked as "incarnating a homophobic fantasy of the hysterical faggot" (Berry 1993a, 21), and the erasure of Hong Kong (where in the novel Dieyi and his object choice, Duan Xiaolou, reunite after the political upheavals in China) from the film's narrative has also been criticized as mainland-centric (Lau 1995, 26; see also Leung Ping-kwan 1995, 361–362; Wang Hongzhi, Li, and Chen 1997, 224–226). Both accusations can be partly explained by Chen's dissatisfaction with the novel and his roping in of a scriptwriter from China to collaborate on the film adaptation. The resulting screenplay was to boost the female character, Juxian, "from a two-page walk-on [in the novel] to a full scale role [on screen] for Gong Li" (Rayns 1994a, 42). Chen admitted in an interview that the expansion of the female role was necessary to accommodate the mega-star Gong Li (*Yang* ± *Yin* 1996) who, as the most recognizable Chinese actress in both the East and the West, would have been crucial to the film's box-office success. While Chen defends Juxian's role as pivotal to the structure of the film (Chiao 1998, 106–107), it has been argued that this role prevented the film from dealing directly with the issue of homosexuality (Rayns 1994a, 42).

Released three years after *Farewell My Concubine* but generally hailed as mainland China's first gay film, Zhang Yuan's *East Palace, West Palace* received most of its financial backing from France and was produced by a French company (Reynaud 1997, 33).[19] Made outside the state studio system, Zhang's film was illegal by default and thus destined to be banned in China. When the film was invited to the out-of-competition section of the 1997 Cannes Film Festival, the Chinese authorities tried to block its participation. When this failed, China withdrew its official entry, Zhang Yimou's *Keep Cool* (*You hua haohao shuo*, 1996)—an ironic title in these circumstances. Then, also in retaliation, Zhang Yuan's passport was confiscated to prevent him from attending the festival. At the screening of the film, the organizers of the festival placed an empty chair on the stage to mark the director's symbolic presence (Rayns 1997; Reynaud 1997, 33; Berry 1998, 84).

Just as the punishment for engaging in homosexual activities in China varies from one enforcing authority to another owing to the disjunctive order of the state apparatus, what constitutes an official ban on filmmaking in China remains ambivalent. Apparently, there are interstices within the system that are wide enough for a banned filmmaker like Zhang Yuan to do his shoots in broad daylight. Zhang was blacklisted, together with a few other directors, in an official directive in 1994. However, policemen who subsequently saw Zhang shooting films would simply comment, "Oh, it's Zhang Yuan, isn't it? I see you are still making movies, then" (Berry 1996b, 40–41). In the case of *East Palace, West Palace,* the shoot was by no means low profile, as the film crew took over an entire park, but there was no intervention from any official figure. The explanation for this seemingly paradoxical situation lies, to quote Zhang, in the fact that "China is too big and one department cannot command another" (Rayns 1996, 28; see also Chiao 1998, 259). The trick, it would seem, is to beat the party at its own political games.

This probably explains why more underground films on homosexuality have since been made. Liu Bingjian, the director of *Men and Women* (*Nannan nünü,* 1999), was asked to write a "self-critical review" for making a film without official permission, though the "punishment" does not seem to have stemmed from the homosexual theme of the film itself. Consistent with underground filmmaking's practice in seeking foreign assistance, the film's negatives were shipped via French and Swiss diplomatic pouches to be developed abroad.[20] Into the twenty-first century, Li Yu's *Fish and Elephant* (*Jinnian xiatian,* 2001) has been hailed as China's first lesbian film, while *Men and Women*'s screenplay writer, Cui Zi'en, has also made a couple of gay films on digital video (*Enter the Clowns/Choujue dengchang*, 2001; *Feeding Boys, Ayaya/Aiyaya, qu buru*, 2003). Cui's film, *The Old Testament* (*Jiuyue*, 2002), was shown at the aforementioned lesbian and gay film festival held at Beijing University that was cancelled halfway through (Wang Qi 2004, 191), and *Enter the Clowns* was funded by the Jeonju International Film Festival in Korea. As Chris Berry notes, "Cui has had the advantage of the relative ease and cheapness of video production and the availability of an international gay and lesbian film and video festival circuit to counter-balance the sometimes restrictive political situation in China" (Berry 2004, 200). On top of these developments, Hong Kong director Stanley Kwan also managed to make *Lan Yu* (2001) with a predominantly mainland Chinese cast and crew in China without official permission.

Capitalizing on the Market in Taiwan

Taiwan is undoubtedly the most tolerant and liberal of all Chinese-speaking societies in terms of lesbian and gay representation, ranging from governmental policies and civil rights to cultural production and commercial enterprises. It is difficult to imagine the mayor of any other Chinese city who would follow the example of the Taipei mayor, Ma Ying-jeou (Ma Yingjiu), in appearing on the front cover of a glossy gay lifestyle magazine as Ma did on *G&L* in April 2000 to celebrate its fourth anniversary (Simon 2004, 83). It is equally hard to see another Chinese government (or even those in some countries in the so-called liberal West) that would propose a human rights bill that includes "a clause granting gays and lesbians the rights to form civil unions and adopt children," as the Taiwan Ministry of Justice did in June 2001 (ibid., 74). Not only can Taiwan boast of commercial enterprises aimed at the pink dollar such as gay bars, saunas, and bookshops, but also civil groups for homosexuals range from those devoted to political activism to those catering to students, teachers, Christians, and Buddhists. Together with the political energies unleashed by the lifting of martial law in 1987, gay activism has joined forces with other previously marginalized groups in demanding greater recognition and representation, culminating in a "transformation of the cultural configuration" (Wang Yage 1999, 30–31). There is certainly a market for homosexual-themed cultural products, including film, waiting to be tapped by enterprising businesses. In addition to being of interest to the commercial market, homosexuality is also a hot ticket for politicians eager to attract the pink or liberal vote. In progressive circles in Taiwan, it is considered politically incorrect to speak negatively about homosexuality. For all its inherent problems and hypocrisies, political correctness seems to have served homosexuality well, at least in the case of Taiwan.

One of the most salient representations of homosexuality in Taiwan has been in the field of cultural production, especially in literary writing. Since the publication of Pai Hsien-yung's groundbreaking *Crystal Boys* (*Niezi*, 1983), commonly regarded as Taiwan's first homosexual novel, homosexuality had, by the 1990s, become the most fashionable topic in literary writing. Three literary awards inaugurated in that decade, each with a top prize of one million New Taiwan dollars, were won by novels with a lesbian or gay theme.[21] In terms of literary and cultural spaces dedicated to the expression of homosexuality, Taiwan has at least two publishers, a handful of glossy magazines, two specialist bookshops, and the ubiquitous lesbian and gay section in fashionable chain bookshops. A booming industry of *tongzhi* and *ku'er* literature has also attracted academic attention, both within Taiwan and beyond, as has the translation of these works into English.[22] Moreover, literary and intellectual journals regularly feature articles and special issues devoted to the issue of homosexuality in its various expressions, ranging from literature, cinema, identity politics, and sexuality to queer theory, space, and architecture. Queer theory has become the latest fashion in academia, with a Center for the Study of Sexuality established in the National Central University, which also publishes a journal, *Working Papers in Gender/Sexuality Studies*. Lesbian- and gay-related activities such as film festivals, book exhibitions, talks, and conferences are organized regularly in Taipei and other major cities.

A momentous event in recent gay and lesbian history in Taiwan was the wedding between writer Hsu You-sheng (Xu Yousheng) and his Paraguayan-American lover Gray Harriman in November 1996.[23] Mirroring the characters in Ang Lee's *The Wedding Banquet* in their interracial coupling and middle-class, professional backgrounds, Hsu and Harriman received largely positive, front-page coverage of their wedding in almost all the major newspapers. A documentary based on the wedding, entitled *Not Simply a Wedding Banquet . . .* (*Buzhishi xiyan*, 1997) and directed by Mickey Chen Chun-chih (Chen Junzhi) and Mia Chen Ming-hsiu (Chen Mingxiu), has toured many lesbian and gay film festivals around the world. Though not legally binding, Hsu's wedding represents a certain "normalization" of homosexuality in Taiwan, where it has become nothing more than media hype, encountering little or no official or societal condemnation.[24]

As in China, there is no law for the criminalization of homosexuality in Taiwan, though this has not prevented the police force from conducting raids in public spaces known for gay cruising, as an incident on Changde Street in 1997 shows (Simon 2004, 80). While the gay bookshop Gin Gin (Jin Jin) generally enjoyed good relations in its neighborhood, its window was repeatedly smashed in 2001 (Martin 2003b, 15). However, there is no question that Taiwan looks most promising in terms of furthering civil rights for gays and lesbians within the Chinese-speaking world, as a broad alliance has been built across the realms of politics, academia, civil society, and artistic and literary communities to ensure that the tides would not be rolled back on Taiwan's progressive political agendas.

In contrast to China, where the cinematic representation of homosexuality is officially prohibited, the Taiwanese films discussed in this book—*The Wedding Banquet* in chapter 2 and *The River* in chapter 5—are productions of the KMT-backed Central Motion Picture Corporation (CMPC). While I am not suggesting that the KMT's cinematic machinery is actively promoting homosexuality, these films are in fact aimed at participation in international film festivals. Their production reflects the acute marketing acumen of the man at CMPC's helm in detecting trends in fashion and taste in the international film world. These films were made under the aegis of Hsu Li-kong (Xu Ligong), then CMPC's vice-chairman, who understands that taboo and marginality in the East often translate into desirability and marketability in the West.[25] Both films proved successful at winning top awards at the Berlin Film Festival, with *The Wedding Banquet* sharing the Golden Bear in 1993 and *The River* capturing the Silver Bear in 1997.

Behind-the-scenes accounts reveal, however, that before the 1990s, homosexuality was still taboo in Taiwanese cinema. When the first draft of the screenplay for *The Wedding Banquet* was completed in 1987, it found no backers because of its homosexual theme. Having won a 1990 competition for his screenplays for both *Pushing Hands (Tuishou)* and *The Wedding Banquet,* Ang Lee decided to film *Pushing Hands* first because it did not involve a controversial issue like homosexuality. After achieving critical success with *Pushing Hands,* Lee was still not convinced that the time was ripe for making *The Wedding Banquet.* Apparently, at the screening of *Pushing Hands* at the Berlin Film Festival in 1991, many gay people in the film industry warned Lee that gay subject matter was like a minefield that could blow one into pieces if not handled properly. It finally took Hsu's persuasion to convince Lee, who trusted Hsu's judgment, to make the film (A. Lee and Peng 1993, 39–41).

Once again, the international stage provided a vital platform for the representation of homosexuality in Chinese cinemas, and the producer of *The Wedding Banquet,* Hsu, cautiously planned the film's first screening.

Hsu chose to premiere the film in Berlin, before its domestic release, as he feared possible polarized reviews in Taiwan might adversely affect its international reception. The film's international accolades may have cushioned any negative reaction to its theme in Taiwan, where, by 1993, homosexuality was already less of a taboo. However, isolated incidents showed that there were still some pockets of discomfort about homosexuality. At the 1993 Golden Horse Awards, Taiwan's equivalent to the Academy Awards (Oscar), a panel judge threatened to hold her fellow judges responsible for the proliferation of homosexuality in Taiwan if they presented *The Wedding Banquet* with an award. Her reported comment (*China Times,* December 13, 1994) was circulated in cinematic circles as "a joke."

The situation was somewhat different for Tsai Ming-Liang's *The River* because, in its depiction of an act of homosexual incest between a father and his son, the film pushes the boundary much further than *The Wedding Banquet* did. The power of the taboo was exemplified by Tsai's difficulty in convincing the actor Miao Tian to play the role of the homosexual father. Described as the Chinese Jack Palance, Miao has had a long cinematic career starring in macho roles such as knights and swordsmen. Miao feared that playing an aged homosexual who has sex with his son, albeit unknowingly, would tarnish his reputation among the Taiwanese audience. An impasse ensued, with Tsai summoning respected figures from the film industry to try to persuade Miao, while Miao's family members in Taiwan and beyond objected vehemently to the proposal. Miao finally gave in when Tsai threatened to abandon the project should he refuse (Hu Youfeng 1997, 106–107). After the film's release, Tsai was severely criticized for the incest scene (Rivière and Tsai 1999, 98). However, as most of these criticisms came from within the film industry (Huang Wulan 1999, 239–245), they could be attributed to infighting within the industry rather than a veiled attack on homosexuality.[26]

Taiwan cinema has since produced more gay- and lesbian-themed films, including short films and documentaries. From his debut film, *Rebels of the Neon God,* to his recently released seventh film, *The Wayward Cloud* (*Tianbian yiduo yun,* 2005), Tsai Ming-liang's oeuvre, while not always directly representing homosexuality, can nonetheless be read as queer (see chapter 5) or as camp (Yeh and Davis 2005). Even Hsu Li-kong, Tsai's producer at CMPC, has made a film with a homosexual theme, *Fleeing by Night* (*Yeben,* 2000). Lesbianism is touched upon in *Murmur of Youth* (*Meili zai changge,* 1997), by Lin Cheng-sheng (Lin Zhengsheng), and in a sixty-minute film, *The Love of Three Oranges* (*San ju zhi lian,* 1998), by theater director and poet Hung Hung (Hong Hong).

The ambivalence of adolescent sexuality seems to be fast becoming a staple in the genre of youth films *(qingchun pian)* in Taiwan cinema. Yee Chih-yen (Yi Zhiyan), whose 1995 film, *Lonely Hearts Club (Jimo fangxin julebu)*, deals with homosexuality between young men, has won critical acclaim for his sensitive portrayal of teenage female same-sex attraction in *Blue Gate Crossing (Lanse damen, 2002). Formula 17 (Shiqisui de tiankong, 2004)*, by Chen Ying-jung (Chen Yingrong), and a short film, *Too Young (Yemaque, 1997)*, by Huang Ming-cheng (Huang Mingzheng), are two other examples. Meanwhile, documentary filmmaker Mickey Chen Chun-chih has been particularly noted for his direct portrayal of queer Taiwanese teenagers. After making *Not Simply a Wedding Banquet . . .* in 1997, which has not been screened publicly in Taiwan because the interviewees in it spoke on the condition of anonymity, Chen's next documentary, *Beauty for Boys (Meili shaonian, 1999)*, enjoyed a full house when released in Taipei.[27] Among the audience at its premiere were the principal and students of the high school Chen had attended, along with cultural celebrities who gave their support. Within a span of two years, not only did teenagers feel unafraid to appear in a gay documentary, but it is also now in fact considered quite "cool" to do so.

Hong Kong in the Shadow of 1997 and Beyond

As a British colony until 1997, Hong Kong experienced a key moment in relation to homosexuality with its decriminalization in 1991.[28] Prior to this, a homosexual act between men was a criminal offense under provisions proscribing "gross indecency" or "buggery," a law Hong Kong's colonial master discarded in 1967 on British soil. The decriminalization process in Hong Kong had been filled with controversy, encountering opposition from the Chinese and religious communities (McLelland 2000). It had inadvertently also heightened the public's awareness of the issue of homosexuality and might have helped to unite homosexuals in forming activist groups to fight for their rights (Chou and Chiu 1995, 175). Despite its cosmopolitan facade, it has been argued that the notion of a sexually permissive and progressively liberal Hong Kong is a myth and that decriminalization did not alter the stigma attached to homosexuality (Lilley 1998, 214–215).

Perhaps owing to Hong Kong's colonial legacy and a partially English-language education system, Western lesbian- and gay-related ideas and institutions are more readily imported. Hong Kong boasts the first lesbian and gay film festival in the Chinese-speaking world, and the organizers of the inaugural film festival, Mai Ke and Edward Lam (Lin Yihua), are prolific writers on gay-related issues. Homoeroticism and homosexuality have also found expression in avant garde theater performances.[29] Chou Wah-shan (Zhou Huashan), a British-educated sociologist, is responsible for most of the popular writing in Chinese on homosexuality (see Chou 1996a, 1996b, 1997). Homosexual groups began to flourish in Hong Kong in the 1990s and range from the political and cultural to the social and religious. Members of these groups tend to be young, middle class, consumeristic, Westernized, and male-dominated (Chou and Chiu 1995, 178–195).

With the looming of Hong Kong's return to the People's Republic of China (PRC) in 1997, there were genuine concerns with regard to the state of lesbian and gay rights in post-handover Hong Kong. While interracial coupling between Hong Kong and Western men was a prominent mode of gay relationship in colonial times, the handover has in fact led to the opening up of "gay tourism in Mainland China [as] a new way in which Hong Kong gay men can channel their sexual gratification" (Kong 2002, 43–44). The geopolitical reality of 1997 also impinges on the state of filmmaking in the final days of the colony. Fearing a possible tightening of the censorship system after 1997, many Hong Kong directors reportedly rushed to complete their films on homosexuality before the deadline (Peng 1997, 42). While it still remains to be seen if or when tighter censorship might be introduced, the poster advertising Wong Kar-wai's 1997 film, *Happy Together,* showing the gay couple in the film embracing and kissing on a rooftop, was banned in Hong Kong (Chiao 1997a, 18). However, fears of immediate change after 1997 were unfounded, as two films featuring homosexuality, Stanley Kwan's *Hold You Tight* and *Bishōnen . . . (Meishaonian zhi lian),* by Yonfan (Yang Fan), were released in 1998.

Unlike their mainland Chinese and Taiwanese counterparts, Hong Kong actors are usually mega-stars who double as pop stars, making the stakes higher if they are to play a homosexual character on film. For example, *Happy Together*'s explicit opening sex scene proved to be a problem for one of the lead actors, Tony Leung Chiu-wai (Liang Chaowei), who was apparently "devastated" after filming the sex scene and complained to the cinematographer Christopher Doyle, "Wong said that all I'd have to do was kiss Leslie [Cheung, the other lead actor, who was openly gay]. . . . Now look how far he's pushed me" (cited in Doyle 1998, 163). Some members of the crew of *Happy Together* also displayed their ignorance about homosexuality while filming in Argentina. On a night out on the town, the camera assistants went to a gay bar by mistake. They ended up drinking their beer through straws and refused to use the toilet. Christopher Doyle comments in his journal, "We've been filming two men simulating blow jobs and anal sex for weeks now, and 'my boys' still think you can get AIDS from a beer glass or a sweaty handshake" (ibid., 167–168).

Stanley Kwan, who came out to the Hong Kong audience via his 1996 documentary, *Yang ± Yin: Gender in Chinese Cinema (Nansheng nüxiang)*, has since moved from displacing his sexuality onto the women characters for which he is most famous in his earlier films to the direct representation of homosexuality in *Lan Yu* in 2001. Yonfan's trilogy deals in turn with transgenderism (*Bugis Street/Yaojie huanghou*, 1995), homosexuality (*Bishōnen . . .*), and lesbianism (*Peony Pavilion/Youyuan jingmeng*, 2001). Other films that portray homosexuality include *The Map of Sex and Love (Qingse ditu*, 2001), by Evans Chan (Chen Yaocheng); *When Beckham Met Owen* (2004), by Adam Wong; and a fifty-minute film, *First Love and Other Pains (Xinhui*, 1999), by Simon Chung (Zhong Desheng). Hong Kong cinema of the popular and generic forms has always been filled with homosexual characters of various guises (such as comic caricatures and drag swordsmen) and representations of masculinity, male bonding, and homoeroticism that open themselves to a queer reading.[30]

The making of *Lan Yu* deserves special attention here because it exemplifies, on the one hand, the marginal and interstitial spaces available for the cinematic representation of homosexuality even in unpromising circumstances, and, on the other hand, the transnational nature of Chinese cinemas at the turn of the twenty-first century. The film is based on a novel entitled *Beijing Story (Beijing gushi)*, which first appeared on the World Wide Web in 1996 under the authorial pseudonym of Beijing Tongzhi and was subsequently published in print in Taiwan in 2002. According to Kwan's account on the official Web site of the film, Kwan was approached in February 2000 by Zhang Yongning, who had read the novel and found it very moving. The film was made with "some ingenuity" ("I can't tell you how or where we shot it"), with the cast and crew mainly from mainland China. The lead actors who play the gay couple in the film are Hu Jun, whose previous gay role was as the policeman in Zhang Yuan's *East Palace, West Palace*, and Liu Ye, an up-and-coming actor hitherto best known for his role as a postman in *Postman in the Mountains (Nashan naren nagou*, 1999), directed by Huo Jianqi.

As the above account clearly shows, *Lan Yu* is a text that has travelled across nations, transmuted across media, and thrived in the disjunctive order of the new global cultural economy. The original form of the text belongs to the genre of *tongzhi* literature on the World Wide Web, whose anonymity allows, in particular, those from mainland China to participate in the writing of this officially censured subject.[31] Zhang Yongning, a Chinese national who lives and works in Britain, then decided to produce the film and single-handedly sourced international funding, secured the Hong Kong director, and coordinated the shoot in China. Initially, Kwan was apprehensive about shooting in China, but it turned out that Zhang, who had trained as an actor, was very familiar with the film industry there and knew exactly when to push the limits and when to be restrained (Zeng 2001, 50). While its box-office reception was less than enthusiastic in Hong Kong (Li Zhaoxing 2002, 62), the film won critical acclaim in Taiwan, where Stanley Kwan was awarded the best director and Liu Ye the best actor in the Golden Horse Awards in 2001. The combination of global capital, transnational cast and crew, and local knowledge managed to circumvent official censorship in China to produce a cinematic representation of male homosexuality that first existed in virtual reality and later found new incarnations in print and celluloid. With *Lan Yu*, screening homosexuality has entered a new mode.

The Burden of Representation

Ang Lee's *The Wedding Banquet*

If, after many years of struggle, you arrive at the threshold of
enunciation and are "given" the right-to-speak and a limited
space in which to tell your story, is it not the case that there
will be an overwhelming pressure to try and tell the whole
story all at once? If there is only one opportunity to make
your voice heard, is it not the case that there will be an intolerable imperative to try and say everything there is to be said,
all in one mouthful?

—KOBENA MERCER, "Black Art and the Burden
of Representation"

Ang Lee's *The Wedding Banquet* is generally regarded as the first gay
film in contemporary Chinese cinemas. It premiered in February
1993 at the Berlin Film Festival, where it clinched the Golden Bear award
(several months before Chen Kaige's *Farewell My Concubine* won the Palme
d'Or at Cannes in May 1993).[1] It was also the most profitable film in 1993,
when it achieved phenomenal box-office records both in Taiwan and
abroad.[2] As a high-profile film and the first to openly problematize the
relationship between homosexuality and the Chinese family, the film is
also a victim of its own success as it has attracted enormous critical and
popular attention, focusing particularly on identity politics relating to a
gay liberationist discourse.[3] It is my contention that among all the films
discussed in this book, *The Wedding Banquet* has had to bear the brunt of
the burden of representation, given its status as the first gay film in contemporary Chinese cinemas, its thematic exploration of the position of
homosexuality in a Chinese family, and the timing of its release, which
coincided with a heightened identity politics in an age of multiculturalism
both within Taiwan and beyond. However, as I shall argue below, there has
been a concomitant lack of (self-)reflection on the terms of criticism in

these debates, and the premises underpinning such liberationist discourses and identity politics should in themselves be brought into question.

The Wedding Banquet is the second installment of what has commonly been referred to as Lee's "Father Knows Best" trilogy. The first, *Pushing Hands,* deals with cross-cultural and intergenerational conflicts as a Chinese son marries a white woman in the United States, posing difficulties for the retired father, who has come to live with them from mainland China. The third, *Eat Drink Man Woman (Yinshi nannü,* 1994), explores the changing relationships between a father and his three daughters in Taipei, using the tropes of food and sex alluded to in the title. Sandwiched between the two and set in New York, *The Wedding Banquet* examines how a father negotiates the issue of his son's homosexuality vis-à-vis his own wish for patrilineal continuity, with the trope of cross-cultural communication reprised from *Pushing Hands,* as the son's gay lover is a white American.

In *The Wedding Banquet,* Gao Wai-Tung (Winston Chao/Zhao Wenxuan) is a Taiwanese property developer who has been living in New York for ten years and has a green card as well as a white partner, Simon (Mitchell Lichtenstein). In an attempt to end the constant pestering of Wai-Tung's parents (the late Lung Hsiung/Lang Xiong and Gua Ah-Leh/Gui Yalei) that he should get married and produce grandchildren for them, Simon suggests a paper marriage between Wai-Tung and his tenant, Wei-Wei (May Chin/Jin Sumei), an artist from mainland China staying illegally in the United States. Trouble begins when Wai-Tung's parents announce that they are coming to attend the wedding, leading to an elaborate wedding banquet. After the banquet, the guests indulge in ritual horseplay, forcing Wei-Wei and Wai-Tung into their hotel bed naked. In their drunken state, Wei-Wei throws herself on Wai-Tung and subsequently becomes pregnant, posing a threat to the relationship between the gay couple and resulting in Wai-Tung's coming out to his mother. At the end of the film, Wei-Wei decides to keep the baby, Wai-Tung's father tacitly acknowledges his son's homosexuality, the parents return to Taiwan, and the gay couple and Wei-Wei agree to bring up the baby together.

Representation as Mimetic, Performative, and Constitutive

The term "representation" has multiple meanings. For the purpose of this book, I will engage its two major aspects: representation as signifying practice (standing for) and as political or constitutional representation (standing for someone). As a signifying practice, the first aspect of representation (standing for) is predicated on the notion of mimesis, which assumes an epistemological if not an ontological relationship with a signified given. Existing before and readily summoned in the act of representation, this signified given/referent is also often regarded as "reality" itself. The emphasis on authenticity and accuracy in the mimetic notion of representation encourages the conflation of the signifier and the signified, resulting in the representation being overly identified with/as the represented. As Jack Goody explains: "Representations are always of something; hence they are re-presentations, not the thing itself, *der Ding an sich*. Yet they appear to present themselves as that thing (here understood as any entity whatever, including imaginary ones). So there is always the possibility that the signifier, words, actions, images, may get confused or overly identified with the signified, bringing about a situation in which that relationship needs to be made more distinct" (1997, 25).

Though Goody makes a distinction between "representations" and "re-presentations," his definition of representation as "a presenting again, a presenting of something not present" (1997, 31) still assumes the presence of that something by its absence. However, if representation is "*of* something or someone, *by* something or someone, *to* someone" (Mitchell 1995, 12; emphasis in original), the act of representation cannot be simply mimetic but is also performative and constitutive and thus raises the following questions. First, what is the relationship between the signifier and the signified, between the something or someone that is represented and its representation? Second, who performs the act of representation, how is it undertaken, and why? Third, who consumes the representation, and to what extent does the representation constitute "reality" for the consumer? The first question, related to an epistemological understanding of representation, will be my focus in this section, while the second and third questions, related to the production and consumption of representations, will be dealt with in the following sections.

Understood as "*of* something or someone," the mimetic notion of representation presupposes the pre-existence of that something or someone, which the act of representation strives to replicate in truth and accuracy. What this mimetic notion conceals, however, is the "performative qualities through which the act of representation brings about something that hitherto did not exist as a given object" (Iser 1987, 217). That is to say, rather than re-presenting something or someone already in existence, what every act of representation does is in fact to bring into existence that something or someone. Every representation is individual and unique. Even if based on the same subject or person, no two representations are identical, and each highlights an aspect of that subject or person that resides only in one particular form of representation.

Understanding representation as performative erases the arbitrary boundary between signifier and signified, because the former is now considered a performative of the latter, at once expressing and constituting it. The mimetic notion of representation functions by separating the two realms of the signifier and the signified, with "reality" as a referent of "representation" but not vice versa. Applied to film as a signifying practice, what appears on screen is often regarded as a representation of society, a fiction that bears the truth about a reality. However, it has been argued that "film and the culture and society in which it is produced are not two separate spheres"; rather, "the strategies of valorization and representation in film are not 'fiction' in relationship to a 'real' world that is in no way structured by the same sorts of strategies of valorization and representation that one finds in film" (Ryan 1988, 479).

Seeing film as drawing on and reproducing social discourses, as well as being a socially discursive force in itself, Michael Ryan rejects the "metaphysical doctrine of representation whereby the referent or object is posited as external to the system of signifiers" (1988, 480). For Ryan, describing the relationship between film discourse and social discourse as a "material circuit" implies that "there is no exteriority of the referent, no objective ground to the film signifier. Rather, the two are part of one system, or a multiplicity of interconnected systems that relay social ideas and feelings from the extracinematic culture to film and back into the culture, where they circulate further" (ibid.).

Ryan's argument can be illustrated with debates about positive and negative representations, as these are inextricably bound to the assumption of truth and accuracy in the mimetic notion of representation. When minority groups protest about negative representations on the premise that these are untrue or inaccurate, they fall precisely into the logic of mimetic representation, as if some representations, thus realities (whether positive or negative), are truer or more accurate than others. The question is not whether these representations can claim to find their referents in reality (hence are true or accurate); rather, both "representation" and "reality" should be understood as social discourses that, by their performativity, not only reify those images, but also codify them as positive or negative.

Representation, therefore, should not be seen as outside reality or merely signifying reality, but as a discursive force that is capable of constituting what some perceive as reality itself. Rather than protesting that negative representations are untrue, minority groups would do better to argue that the "projection of an inferior or demeaning image on another can actually distort and oppress, to the extent that the image is internalized" (Taylor 1994, 36). Representations can have actual constitutive effects when they are perceived and acted upon as real. For example, members of minority groups may internalize certain cinematic representations of their group, resulting in psychic effects impinging on their self-esteem and self-image, or they may be embraced or discriminated against by others on the basis of these representations, with consequences affecting their social status and social relations. The constitutive aspect of representation bears a particularly intimate relationship to the construction of identities, which deserves more delineation.

In his long essay on multiculturalism and "the politics of recognition," Charles Taylor argues that the "crucial feature of human life is its fundamentally *dialogic* character" and that we define our identity "always in dialogue with, sometimes in struggle against, the things our significant others want to see in us" (1994, 32–33; emphasis in original). The dialogic nature of identity construction suggests that insofar as one can make claims to autonomy, agency, selfhood, and subjectivity, the tropes with which one defines one's identity are often located outside oneself. In the process of identity construction, one is in constant dialogue with social discourses embodied by friends and strangers, historical figures and pop idols, characters from fiction and film, and all kinds of people and texts that one may chance upon. It is an enterprise situated as much in reality as in one's imagination, with representations providing many of the tropes for one's construction of identity.

Compared to many minority groups, homosexuals may have a greater stake in the issue of representation because the tropes for the construction of their sexual identities are not always available or immediately recognizable. While women, ethnic minorities, and people of different classes can look to identifiable role models for inspiration, lesbians and gays are often confronted with a world of invisibility and anonymity. Because homosexuals do not necessarily possess identifiable external features and because many still avoid proclaiming their sexuality publicly (this is certainly still very much the case in Chinese societies), the tropes with which homosexuals can grapple in their identity construction are to be found mainly in media representation, thus rendering a particular political urgency and importance to the struggle over the meaning of homosexual representation in a visual medium like film.

Homosexuals share with many minority groups the unequal power relation vis-à-vis a mainstream that maintains a greater control over many forms of cultural capital, including the capital to produce cinematic representations of minority groups. "Mainstream," as opposed to "minority," "alternative," or "marginal," should be understood as denoting not essentialized ideologies or forms but rather relations of power. Equally important to the struggle for representation, as Goody reminds us, are the resistance to and the absence of certain kinds of representation, the occasions of their absence, and the objections to their presence (1997, 2). The representation of homosexuality is compounded by the fact that it remains taboo in many societies, thus reducing the potential quantity of these representations, while the negative attitude behind some representations has constrained the quality and scope of the dialogic imagination for the identity construction of homosexuals. A jagged history of representation, marked by negation, resistance to, and/or absence of any group, invariably engenders a burden that befalls a new representation made in its name or by one of its group members.

Representing Selfhood and Otherness

The struggle of minority groups over representation has been predicated on the historical denial of their access to mechanisms of representation. The problematic of "standing for someone," however, will not be exorcised simply by self-representation by minority groups, as this in turn produces the burden of representation. This burden of representation can be appreciated on several levels. First, as minority groups contest a history of negative, stereotypical representation of their identities and cultures, it is precisely this history that becomes a burden against which their self-representation must be defined. Second, even though opportunities for self-representation have increased for minority groups, these cannot be seen as redressing the actual imbalances of power. As a result, there is often a heightened sense of anticipation and anxiety to utilize every new opportunity to its full potential, thus posing a psychological burden in representation. Third, minority groups are usually assumed to have the moral authority to speak the ultimate truth about themselves in their self-representation. While this moral authority conceals a myth of authenticity and essentialism that should be interrogated, it is also a weighty burden to be perceived as a "true" representative of one's community. I shall elaborate on these three aspects of the burden of representation below.

To begin with, the struggle against a history of (mis)representation is a burden shared by many minority groups, aptly captured in Salman Rushdie's description of post-colonial literatures, "The Empire Writes Back to the Center."[4] As the imagery of the phrase suggests, the act of writing back, as with the imperialist history of conquest and colonization, aims to reclaim lost territories, as well as establish one's own empire. This imagery conceals a narrative that is both linear and teleological, emphasizing progress and purpose, even hinting at a state whereby the battle will be won and the mission accomplished, thus privileging the end over the means, arrival over journey, and aim over process. This narrative may unwittingly lead minority groups to believe that historical (mis)representation is a burden that can be discarded once progress has been made in self-representation.

For minority groups, this narrative is invariably embedded in their struggle over representation because its emancipatory and utopian outlook points to a destination to be reached; thus the inherent notion of progress. However, their experiences have also shown that "progress" is not an irreversible, permanent state, as backlash and new forms of contestation can emerge at any time. In addition, so-called positive representations do not simply replace or nullify negative ones; rather, they stand alongside each other in competition for attention, authority, and legitimacy. To continue with the metaphors of battle and empire, territories can be gained and lost in the same day, just as empires can be established and dismantled overnight. The burden of historical (mis)representation is not a history of the buried past but rather a history that continues to exist in the present and extends forever into the future.

The second aspect of the burden of representation concerns the heightened sense of anticipation and anxiety of minority groups in their self-representation. This anxiety is fuelled by a desire to simultaneously rectify past (mis)representations and to construct politically expedient ones for the present—that is, to rewrite one's entire history almost in a stroke. Kobena Mercer has captured this anxiety succinctly in the passage quoted in the epigraph above.

To complicate matters, this burden of representation is not only experienced at the point of production, but also anticipated at the point of reception. For mainstream audiences previously unacquainted with representations of minority groups, these self-representations are often the only—hence the full—stories providing an insight into their subaltern Other. Moreover, audiences who are also members of the minority groups concerned will bring with them their own expectations and measure these self-representations against their own experiences, while simultaneously realizing that these may be taken as the definitive representations of their communities through which they will be perceived. This burden of representation, expressed as anxiety, anticipation, and expectation, can compound efforts of self-representation by minority groups.

The anxiety of representation is linked to the third aspect of the burden of representation, which is the moral authority presumed in self-representation. The assumption that one necessarily speaks the truth about a certain community because one bears its identity can become a burden of representation, as any self-representation then becomes the beacon of a truth for which one is responsible. However, the assumption of moral authority is a myth that reinvigorates essentialism precisely at the point where the contestation of negative stereotypes has been premised on the rejection of essentialism. This paradoxical situation attests to the observation that "theory deconstructs totalising myths and rejects essentialised articulations of identity whilst political activism and support for affirmative action nourishes them" (Shohat and Stam 1994, 342).

For Mercer, speaking in the role of a "representative" is a "highly ambiguous performative speech-act: the transition from 'I' to 'We' has an empowering communifying effect, but by the same token, its use can disempower others by denying them the specificity of their voices and viewpoints" (1990, 72). For example, such moral authority can be easily exploited to censor aspects of identities deemed as negative and unrepresentative within minority groups. Moreover, as identity is inevitably multifaceted, can one speak only from the position of a single aspect of one's identity thus representing one community at any one time, or is polyphonic enunciation possible? Filmmaker Richard Fung, a fourth-generation Trinidadian Chinese living in Canada, often finds himself in situations where he is either the gay representative among other Asians or people of color or, more frequently, the Asian (for which he claims to have very tenuous authenticity) among a shifting list of requisite minorities (1995, 123–124). For Fung, the burden of representation "cannot be transcended any more than the socially defined categories of race or gender can." He suggests that it is in "foregrounding the burden of representation and in making its dilemmas explicit" that the distance between one's socially mediated life as "minority" and the dominant privilege of speaking "as such" can begin to close (ibid., 129).

As Fung points out, the right to speak, even from the position of a minority, is already a privilege. If the burden of representation poses so many complications and dilemmas for minority groups involved in self-representation, these can only be magnified when those outside minority communities attempt to speak on their behalf. Taking representation in its political and constitutional sense of "standing for someone" raises the following questions: Who speaks for whom, for what purposes, in what terms, by what means, and to whom? What is the burden of representing otherness?

Since the last decade of the twentieth century, cinematic self-representation by directors from minority groups has become more common.

Spike Lee (*Do the Right Thing*, 1989; *Malcolm X*, 1992) is the most prominent example for African Americans, while Derek Jarman (*Caravaggio*, 1986; *Edward II*, 1991) and Gregg Araki (*The Living End*, 1992; *Totally F***ed Up*, 1993) are leading figures in the short-lived New Queer Cinema of the early 1990s. Straddling both the homosexual and the black communities, Isaac Julien's films (*Looking for Langston*, 1988; *Young Soul Rebels*, 1991) exemplify that identity is multifaceted. As argued above, since homosexuals are not necessarily identifiable by external attributes, one cannot assume that films featuring homosexuality are necessarily self-representations unless the directors are openly gay. Homosexuals are thus unique in that they have to come out in order to claim their minority status, but this may not be a viable option for filmmakers working in societies where homosexuality remains censured. Does it matter who makes what films? Is it possible to represent one's Other? Can straight men make gay films?

In an essay on the author and the homosexual, which takes as its frame of reference his 1990 book on films made by lesbians and gay men, Richard Dyer argues that "it does make a difference who makes a film, who the authors are" (1991, 185). For Dyer, what is significant is "the authors' material social position in relation to discourse, the access to discourses they have on account of who they are." In the case of lesbian and gay films, Dyer argues that filmmakers who are lesbians and gays could produce representations that could be considered lesbian/gay because they have an "access to, and an inwardness with, lesbian/gay sign systems that would have been like foreign languages to straight filmmakers" (ibid., 188).

Whether lesbian and gay discourses and sign systems are as exclusive or inaccessible to straight filmmakers as Dyer claims is open to question. In fact, one could argue to the contrary that lesbian and gay subcultural sign systems have had a huge influence on and have long been appropriated by popular culture (whether in advertising, fashion, show business, or the media in general) to the extent that they are an inextricable part of the mainstream consciousness. Dyer's argument not only constructs lesbian and gay discourses as exclusive, insular, and inaccessible, but it also risks perpetuating a separatist ghetto mentality and shutting the door of communication between lesbians/gays and the rest of the world. Deploying the metaphor of "foreign languages," Dyer seems to rule out the possibility of cross-cultural exchange in all its different guises. Can a foreigner not speak one's language better than oneself or a straight man behave gayer than a gay man?

In relation to the Chinese identity, Allen Chun writes of the "need to articulate the various contexts (of speech or practice) wherein facets of identity (such as ethnicity) are deemed to be *relevant*. That is to say, what kinds of contexts demand that one speak from a position of identity, and what contexts do not" (1996, 134–135; emphasis in original). In the case of Chinese cinemas, it may not be realistic to demand that only gay film-makers can represent homosexuality on film. Indeed, when the question "Why does a straight man make a film about gays?" is posed, one should interrogate the contexts in which directors have been asked to speak from a position of their sexual identity and how meaningful such a question is.[5]

As Gina Marchetti points out, *The Wedding Banquet* is a film that defies classification while fitting easily into "several categories, and therefore can be marketed to a variety of audiences as an Asian film, a Chinese film, a Taiwanese film, an Asian American film, a Chinese American film, a New York Chinatown film, a 'green-card' story, a popular comedy, a melo-drama, an 'art' film, a gay film, an 'ethnic' family film, or a 'multicultural' feature designed to raise the consciousness of viewers" (2000, 276). Among these various audiences, however, the harshest critique seems to have come from the gay community and those who subscribe to a gay libera-tionist discourse. I will illustrate this below specifically on the issue of coming out and the film's representation of gender, race, and class.

Coming Out and the Rhetoric of Gay Liberation

In terms of the cinematic representation of homosexuality, the logical corollary to the contestation of negative representation often means the creation of openly gay characters, since the rhetoric of gay liberation dic-tates that to remain in the closet is a sign of self-loathing, whereas to come out is an affirmative act of pride. Over the decades, the act of coming out has acquired such an unquestioning and sometimes unquestionable sta-tus that not to come out is seen as an unfathomable form of behavior. As Sally Munt argues:

> For lesbians and gays this temptation, to see our sexuality as the truth of our identity because it is perceived as the most oppressed part of us, belies an enduring fiction. To "come out" as lesbian and gay is to speak the truth of that oppression. . . . Michel Foucault saw the link between the confessional and the Christian religious ritual as endemic to Western practices of sexuality, and the confession is also structurally associated with testimony and witness, processes which evangelize experience as transcendentally meaningful. What is clear from this conjunction is the way feelings become performative: they material-ize and metamorphose into states of being and legitimation. (1997, 187)

To borrow a Cartesian formulation, the rhetoric of gay liberation beseeches the homosexual to declare, "I come out, therefore I am." As the waves of gay liberation and gay activism have arrived on Chinese shores, it has also become more commonplace to regard coming out as the rite of passage for homosexuals and the ultimate acknowledgement of one's sexuality by oneself and others. As with their Western counterparts, homosexuals in contemporary Chinese societies increasingly perceive their sexuality as an integral part of their identity, selfhood, and subjectivity. The search for positive homosexual representation in Chinese cinemas has also led film critics to champion the representation of the highly performative act of coming out for its presumed power of legitimation and its revolt against the oppression of homosexuality in Chinese societies.

In *The Wedding Banquet,* the homosexual protagonist, Wai-Tung, is arguably only halfway out of the closet because he has come out to his mother but not to his father. Even though the father realizes that his son is homosexual and tacitly acknowledges it, the film's "failure" to stage a coming out scene between the father and son remains problematic for some critics. Edward Lam, a Hong Kong film critic who is openly gay, questions, "Why would (male) homosexuals of the 90s still be willing to stay in the closet?" (1993, 70). Lam accuses the film of discouraging homosexuals from coming out by showing that even clean-cut, amiable gays find happiness only in the closet (ibid., 72).[6] This line of argument raises several questions: Who decides if homosexuals should come out? Does the act of coming out necessarily promote understanding and acceptance of homosexuality? If coming out is chiefly linked to Western epistemologies and practices (as argued by Munt via Foucault), should it be regarded as universal and imposed indiscriminately on other cultures?

To begin with, I suggest that there is no inherent moral high ground in coming out, the rhetoric of gay liberation notwithstanding. Demands on homosexuals to come out, whether in reel life or real life, often reflect the need of gay activists and critics for greater visibility, alliance, and support for their political cause. However, who would have to bear the consequences of coming out? Eve Kosofsky Sedgwick argues that when gay people come out to parents, it is "with the consciousness of a potential for serious injury that is likely to go in both directions." Particularly in a homophobic society, the gay person's coming out may in turn plunge the parents "into the closet of [their] conservative community" (1990, 80). Questions of ethics, responsibility, emotion, and family ties are so intricately intertwined that the rhetoric of oppression and liberation seems simplistic and naïve by comparison. It is highly possible that the complications and consequences of coming out may, for both the homosexual and the family, be so constricting as to make the closet a relatively liberating place to inhabit.

Indeed, coming out cannot necessarily be presumed to achieve the dual goals of liberating the homosexual from the suffocating closet and gaining the understanding of those to whom the homosexual comes out. As the coming-out scene in The Wedding Banquet shows, getting the message across is not always easy. After Wai-Tung comes out to his mother, she questions him: "Did Simon lead you astray?" "How can you be so confused?" "Didn't you have girlfriends in college?"[7] The ironic twist of the film is that the father, from whom all the other family members conspire to keep Wai-Tung's homosexual identity, seems to accept his son's sexuality more easily than his wife does. Rather than seeing this as a "flagrant implausibility" and "a wish-fulfilment fantasy" (Rayns 1994c, 208), I would argue that the film has made a forceful case for the danger in equating the act of coming out with an increased acceptance of homosexuality, exemplified by the contrast between the reactions of the father and the mother towards Wai-Tung's homosexuality.

It is during the fight between Wai-Tung and Simon because of Wei-Wei's pregnancy that the father realizes the truth about his son's sexuality. Assuming that the parents do not understand English, Wai-Tung and Simon fight in their presence; the father remains silent but repeatedly hushes the inquisitive mother up. As his later conversation with Simon reveals, the father actually understands and speaks a little English. He has maintained a "strategic" silence (Dariotis and Fung 1997, 201) in order to make a secret pact with Simon that nobody should know that he knows about Wai-Tung's homosexuality. For the father, the strategy works this way: "If I didn't let everyone lie to me, I'd never have gotten my grandchild!" While the father's overarching concern for the perpetuation of his family line has been read as "selfish" (ibid., 202), his acknowledgement of Wai-Tung's homosexuality is in fact quite remarkable. Initiating a walk with Simon, the father gives him a red envelope (hongbao) of cash as his birthday present. It is the same kind of red envelope that his wife had given earlier to Wei-Wei, their prospective daughter-in-law. Using Simon's birthday as a pretext, the father's gesture amounts to accepting Simon as his "child-in-law." When Simon asks the father if he knows, he simply answers, "I watch, I hear, I learn. Wai-Tung is my son—so you're my son also." The father's message is unequivocal: Simon has been accepted into the Gao family.

By contrast, despite Wai-Tung's having come out to her, the mother seems to find it difficult to fully accept Simon to the same degree. Her only attempt at knowing Simon better turns out to be asking questions about his family and wondering if his sisters, who live in San Francisco, are also homosexual. After learning about Wei-Wei's decision not to have an abortion, the mother still hopes against hope that maybe Wai-Tung's homosexuality is "just a phase" and that "when he sees his kid, he'll revert back to normal." In the final, parting scenes at the airport, Wai-Tung, Wei-Wei, and Simon gather behind the parents to look at the photo album from the wedding banquet. They all laugh heartily at the photograph in which the blindfolded Wei-Wei fails to recognize Wai-Tung as he kisses her on the cheek (figure 2.1). However, the mood changes when a photograph of Wai-Tung hugging Simon from behind appears (figure 2.2), and the mother abruptly closes the album, claiming it is time to go. After embracing Wai-Tung and Wei-Wei in turn at the departure gate, the mother freezes up when Simon gestures to give her a hug. It is the father who comes to the rescue and dissolves the awkward moment by taking Simon's hands and thanking him, rather than Wei-Wei, for taking care of Wai-Tung. The father's parting words to Wei-Wei are, "The Gao family will be grateful to you," demonstrating his clear distinction between the roles of Simon as Wai-Tung's partner and that of Wei-Wei as the carrier of Wai-Tung's child.

Finally, considering their roots in Western epistemologies and practices, should not the very notions of the closet and coming out be interrogated rather than deployed indiscriminately across cultures? As Martin F. Manalansan IV argues, while paying "lip service to cultural diversity," there is a "tendency in popular and scholarly literature to impose a modern, Eurocentric, and universal subjectivity" and to deploy "monolithic constructions of gayness and gay liberation" (1995, 429). For example, the "presumptions behind the labeling of silence and secrecy as 'closeted' and the tracing of the absence of explicitly gay-identified people in public arenas to 'homophobia' are not interrogated" (ibid.). This tendency, I would argue, is prevalent not only among critics based in the West, but also increasingly among those who subscribe to the rhetoric of gay liberation, wherever they may come from or are based. The imagery of coming out of the closet, though visually compelling, cannot be taken as a universal framework for defining the varied experiences of homosexuals throughout the world. In any case, the closet is not a single space, nor is coming out a single and simple act, as Sedgwick demonstrates: "The deadly elasticity of heterosexist presumption means that . . . people find new walls springing up around them even as they drowse: every encounter with a new classful of students, to say nothing of a new boss, social worker, loan officer, landlord, doctor, erects new closets whose fraught and characteristic laws of optics and physics exact from at least gay people new surveys, new calculations, new draughts and requisitions of secrecy or disclosure" (1990, 68).

In *The Wedding Banquet,* does the mother's failure to fully comprehend her son's sexuality, despite his coming out to her, shut the closet door back on Wai-Tung? Does the father's tacit acknowledgement of Wai-Tung's

FIGURE 2.1. All smiles as characters look at wedding photos in *The Wedding Banquet.* (Copyright Central Motion Picture Corporation/Good Machine, 1993)

FIGURE 2.2. Smiles disappear when intimate photo of Wai-Tung and Simon appears. (Copyright Central Motion Picture Corporation/Good Machine, 1993)

The Burden of Representation

homosexuality leave the closet door half open? It is clear from the above that the metaphor of the closet has its limitations, whatever the cultural context. More important, the political evaluation accompanying the issue of coming out must be brought into question. That is, an implicit acknowledgement of a family member's homosexuality may not always be morally less acceptable than an explicit one, and the atmosphere surrounding such tacit acknowledgement cannot be regarded as simply "homophobic." As the response of the mother illustrates, the act of coming out cannot be assumed to be the best, if not the only, "solution." Wei Ming Dariotis and Eileen Fung end their discussion of *The Wedding Banquet* with the following question:

> In a way, the wedding banquet signifies an ongoing containment of homosexuality; even at the end of the film, it is the photo album of the heterosexual tradition of marriage that brings all the characters closer together, literally and figuratively. . . . If the wedding banquet and the shadow of the father's mortality [the father suffers two strokes in the film] act as means to contain the "transgressions" of homosexuality, then can the father's revelation to Simon of his ongoing knowledge, and acceptance, of Simon and Wai-tung's true relationship disrupt this almost homophobic formulation within the film? (1997, 207)

Rather than insisting that the father openly acknowledge his son's homosexuality, I would argue (along with Manalansan) that it is precisely terms associated chiefly with Western gay liberationist and activist discourses, such as "transgression," "homophobia," and "coming out," that demand interrogation. Homosexuality does not necessarily have to be more "transgressive" than any other form of sexuality, and one should perhaps question what there is to be "transgressed."[8] As a form of liberationist discourse and identitarian politics, it is understandable that the rhetoric of gay activism and criticism is often couched in terms of transgression and resistance. However, as Nicholas Garnham argues in his response to Jürgen Habermas's notion of the public sphere, there is "a left cultural romanticism, increasingly prevalent in media and cultural studies, that sees all forms of grassroots cultural expression as 'resistance,' although resistance to what is not at all clear" (1992, 373).[9] The imperative to transgress a perceived orthodoxy or to resist a presumed domination, I would argue, can in itself produce its own form of hegemony that solidifies into a position that denies difference within its own community in the name of solidarity, as exemplified by some of the responses to *The Wedding Banquet* in relation to the issue of coming out. In terms of film analysis, this liberationist imperative often manifests itself in ideology overdetermining the critical project at the expense of close textual evidence, which is often more complex and nuanced than political expediency would allow.

Representing Race, Gender, and Class

Identitarian politics have tended to focus on only one given aspect of identity in relation to the minority group concerned. However, as identity is multifaceted, any discussion of (homo)sexuality would be incomplete without a concomitant engagement with matrices such as race, gender, and class. Indeed, it is precisely the cross-examination of these matrices and their intertwining relationship with sexuality that will debunk the myth that homosexuality is a monolithic construction premised solely on the index of sexuality.

Of all the films discussed in this book, the issue of race is most salient in *The Wedding Banquet,* as it features the only interracial couple: Wai-Tung is a Chinese from Taiwan, while Simon is a white American. The association of homosexuality with the West and the white race is a myth that continues to be perpetuated in Chinese societies.[10] While acknowledging that Wai-Tung "problematizes the myth that homosexuality is an exclusively 'white thing,'" Ling-yen Chua argues that the film still reinforces the association of homosexuality with whiteness, as "all the other homosexual characters in the film are white":

> By the same token, all the white characters in the film are also homosexual or at least pro-gay and involved in some form of gay activist work. There are no other Asian or non-white homosexuals. All of Wei Tung's Asian friends, as seen at the wedding [banquet], appear to be heterosexuals.[11] Therefore, despite the groundbreaking and sympathetic representation of Wei Tung as an Asian homosexual, *The Wedding Banquet* still seems to suggest that being gay is predominately a white thing. By depicting all Wei Tung's gay friends as white and his Asian friends as heterosexual, the film colludes with the popular stereotype that to be gay is to become "more white," or to be submerged into white culture. (1999, 105–106)[12]

Dariotis and Fung concur with Chua in their observation of the wedding banquet scene: "Significantly, all the Chinese people appear to be heterosexual while the white male couples upon which the camera quite often focuses appear to be gay" (1997, 206). What seems to have been overlooked in these observations is the setting of the film in New York, which makes it unavoidable if not more "accurate" to portray Wai-Tung's identity as an Asian gay man as a minority, if not an anomaly, among the predominantly white gay community. In fact, if "the film does little to support any notion of a history of [Wai-Tung's] gay life in Asia and [as an] Asian American" (Marchetti 2000, 286), the answer is simple: while in Asia, Wai-Tung did not have a gay life because he was still keeping up appearances of heterosexuality by dating girls, as he confesses to his mother in the coming out scene; as an Asian American, Wai-Tung does not participate in gay activism like Simon does, and the white homosexuals and gay-friendly characters at the wedding banquet are probably not Wai-Tung's friends but Simon's. Wai-Tung's situation is far from unique, and does his domestic partnership with Simon not count as some form of gay life, or must gay life equate the (stereotypical) gay scene?

If all of the white characters at the wedding banquet seem to be out and proud gays whereas the Asian guests *appear* to be heterosexuals, it is perhaps because the subcultural signification of gayness among Asian homosexuals, in the film at least, is less pronounced. Unlike Simon, who usually wears an earring and whose mannerisms are more effeminate, Wai-Tung, like his Asian guests, appears and easily passes as straight, which is precisely why he could stage a fake marriage without arousing suspicions about his sexuality on the part of either his parents or his guests. This interracial difference in the subcultural signification of gayness demonstrates that it is misguided to judge a person's sexuality by his or her appearance.

Rather than erasing homosexuality from the Asian representation (as these critics suggest), the film, I would argue, in fact gestures towards an even bolder statement—that Chinese culture is widely racist—by introducing the character of Little Sister Mao (Maomei, also known as Wu Ren-ren), a Taiwanese date flown into New York by Wai-Tung's parents and who, like Wai-Tung, is hiding the fact that she has a white boyfriend from her parents. By drawing a parallel between Wai-Tung and Little Sister Mao, the film implies that parents' acceptance of their children's choices of life partners hinges on more than (homo)sexuality and includes race, with the closet as "a function here of ethnicity as well as sexuality" (Chiang 2002, 278).

Moreover, beyond signifying gayness differently for the Asian and the white race, the film also attempts to reverse the Orientalist stereotyping of masculine white men and feminine Asian men.[13] In terms of gender, Simon is effeminate, temperamental, and a good housekeeper, whereas Wai-Tung works out at the gym and is invested with the masculine trait of an entrepreneurial spirit. The film's reversal of gender goes so far as to portray Wei-Wei, the biological woman who will bear Wai-Tung a child, as totally inept at cooking, in contrast to Simon, the stereotypical "woman" who excels in Chinese cuisine, winning even the approval of the hard-to-please Mr. Gao. The issue of class is also highlighted and reversed, as Wai-Tung's financial position is on par, if not stronger, than that of Simon, who works as a physiotherapist. Wai-Tung's masculinity and financial stability in combination thus reverse the double Orientalist hierarchization of gender and economic power. For David L. Eng, that the film "significantly revised this 'rice queen' dynamic, depicting a successful, savvy, and handsome Asian male *not* in a relationship of economic dependence with a homely white man twice his age marks a laudable departure from the pervasive stereotype of the white 'daddy' and the Asian 'houseboy' endemic to mainstream gay culture" (1997, 44; emphasis in original).[14]

Is there a place within contemporary Chinese cinemas for the representation of an interracial, bourgeois, gay couple in a stable relationship? In his book on Wong Kar-wai's *Happy Together*, Jeremy Tambling uses *The Wedding Banquet* as a contrast to argue that "*Happy Together* makes no attempt to 'Westernise' homosexuality by making it thoroughly bourgeois and linking it to a secure income and a stable relationship" (2003, 66). Noting that neither film is "made by 'gay-identified' directors," Tambling suggests that "every inscription of homosexuality is both a *representation* of it and a *production* of it, including a production of knowledge about it" (ibid., 66–67; emphasis in original). For him, the film's representation of Wai-Tung is "as bourgeois, capitalist, masculine and tender-hearted, just as he is all-American," and this image not only "subordinates Taiwan to Hollywood's neo-colonialism," but also "obscures other possibilities of representation" (ibid., 67).

Tambling's argument about the issue of representation echoes the opening section of this chapter, particularly the idea of representation as performative and constitutive, and thus as knowledge production. As I have tried to demonstrate in this chapter, what strikes me time and again is how often this knowledge production not only originates from a "left cultural romanticism," mentioned by Garnham, but also, by valorizing if not fetishizing "working-class" representation, as Tambling does with *Happy Together*, denies any representation and knowledge production of the bourgeois kind. Why do academics, who by definition enjoy a bourgeois income, insist on authorizing and authenticating filmmakers (especially those from the "Third World") only if they make working-class representations, speaking indeed the language of the powerless from a position of power?[15] Given the prowess of some East Asian economies, including that of Taiwan, must the idea of the bourgeois(ie) be associated exclusively with the West, or should one rather acknowledge that there is a Third World within the First World and vice versa? Given the disjunctive yet empowering flow of cultural products on a global scale (as argued in chapter 1), must one (bourgeois) representation necessarily obscure another (less bourgeois) representation, or must some forms of knowledge production be more equal than others?

Embodying the issues of gender and class even more sharply in *The Wedding Banquet* is the relationship between Wai-Tung, the capitalist landlord from Taiwan naturalized as an American citizen (and by extension the Gao family and Simon), and the struggling artist and illegal-immigrant-cum-tenant from China, Wei-Wei.[16] The early sequences of the film cast Wai-Tung in the unflattering light of an unscrupulous capitalist, visiting his barely inhabitable property to collect rent from the impoverished Wei-Wei and shouting the line "It's coming out of your salary" whenever an employee does not perform a duty to his satisfaction. Though he shows compassion towards Wei-Wei by accepting in lieu of rent one of her paintings (which he pretends to appreciate while invariably holding it up the wrong way), he frowns at her plea for the water pipe to be repaired.[17] To be fair, his frugality extends to himself, as his own office does not have air conditioning but only an electric fan to combat the summer heat. Back home, he confesses to Simon that money is tight but promises to take Simon on a holiday to Paris after the city council hearing on his next property development project. Thus the matrix of gender and class is also mapped onto geopolitical entities, with the male capitalist from Taiwan occupying the superior position in the hierarchy while the biological female from communist China and the feminized gay man from the United States both depend on Wai-Tung's goodwill to be either relieved of the burden of rent or taken on a holiday.

In her reading of Ang Lee's films in the context of globalization and minoritization, Shu-mei Shih delineates the unequal power relation between Taiwan and the United States that accounts for both Lee's cinematic representations and their reception. While I agree with the main thrust of her argument, I suggest that *The Wedding Banquet* stages not so much a replay of the familiar narrative of "a new kind of colonialism"— namely, "the US power to determine Taiwan's fate" (Shih 2000, 97)—but rather its reverse: a (re)territorialization of the United States by a Taiwanese property developer purchasing land in the United States. Unlike members of the Fifty-First Club (Wu Yi Julebu), a Taiwanese organization established in 1994 to promote "what they say was China historian John K. Fairbank's original suggestion to turn Taiwan into the 51st state of the

United States" (ibid., 95), in a reverse neocolonialism many Taiwanese have in fact, like Wai-Tung, bought (more than) a piece of American land and claim it as their own via economic migration. The film's representation of the issue of class and the flow of capital is not confined to a specific national boundary but is at once transnational and global.

More important, the transnational matrix of gender and class is also intertwined with the negotiation of sexuality. In his analysis of the film, Mark Chiang forcefully argues that the "consolidation of a transnational patriarchy of capital is fundamentally dependent upon the subordination of women and labor, and these are conflated in the film, so that woman becomes the very sign of labor" (2002, 281). This is established first when Simon proposes the idea of a paper marriage between Wai-Tung and Wei-Wei, convincing Wai-Tung on the grounds of gaining a tax break if he is part of a married couple. Such a move entails Wei-Wei's moving into their apartment and also learning all about Wai-Tung's intimate habits— her first laborious task. This is followed by the first encounter between the Gao parents and Wei-Wei, in which she volunteers to pull the heavy luggage while Mr. Gao approves of Wai-Tung's choice of Wei-Wei as a tenant by saying, "After all, my investment has not been in vain," and observes, "She'll have lots of babies," judging by the size of her pelvis. Mr. Gao's candid comments reveal, on the one hand, the patriarchal nature of the transnational capital through which Wai-Tung is but an agent charged with its investment, and forecast, on the other hand, that the woman (Wei-Wei) can benefit from the transaction of the paper marriage only by forsaking one form of labor (illegal manual work) for another (child-bearing).

Thus the film's final resolution of the seeming incompatibility between the father's desire for the perpetuation of his family line and Wai-Tung's homosexuality is premised upon the exchange of capital, concretized in the form of the red envelope first given to Wei-Wei by Mrs. Gao, then given to Simon by Mr. Gao. The two "daughters-in-law" are in a sense bribed into the deal, with Mrs. Gao securing the contract with Wei-Wei by using emotional tactics and an appeal to biological womanhood while Mr. Gao makes a pact with Simon to keep the father's knowledge of Wai-Tung's homosexuality from the rest of the family. For Chiang, the "baby that Wei Wei carries is the signifier for the vast Chinese labor force, and the money that is exchanged between Wai Tung's father and Simon is the symbol of their common interest as the owners of global capital" (2002, 283), and the "transformation of Wai Tung into a patriarch . . . can now be seen as fundamentally dependent not so much upon the reconciliation with his father as upon the solicitation of ideological consent from Wei Wei and her submission to his hegemonic dominance" (ibid., 282). However, this reading of Wei-Wei as a mere victim of what Leslie Sklair (1995) calls the "transnational capitalist class" denies her agency and ignores her desire for Wai-Tung, shown right from the start of the film. Her pregnancy, one could argue, is of her own doing, as "Wai-tung's saying 'no' and the positionality of Wei-wei could qualify [the wedding night scene] as a 'rape' scene" (Dariotis and Fung 1997, 204–205). The baby, while no doubt welcomed in the economy of the Gao family ideology, is also Wei-Wei's bargaining chip with Wai-Tung and a passport to a more comfortable life in America. It is a capital she decides to keep rather than abort, declaring her decision to Wai-Tung while chewing on a hamburger—the all-American food.

The Burden of the Chinese Patriarchal Family

As stated from the outset of this chapter, *The Wedding Banquet* sets out to problematize the relationship between homosexuality and the Chinese family, which is one of the modern challenges faced by a traditional patriarchy (alongside the challenges in the other two films in the "Father Knows Best" trilogy), seen as "resuscitated" by Cynthia Liu (1995). Many readings of the film have thus chosen to employ the same matrix for analysis. For Fran Martin, the film "stages a kind of postcolonial cultural clash between two regimes of sexuality: broadly, a 'Chinese-familial' regime, and a regime of 'American gay identity'" (2003c, 143), and Shu-mei Shih situates it at the crossroads of "nationalist patriarchy and gendered minoritisation" (2000, 90). Chris Berry contextualizes the film in the genre of the family melodrama that promotes "audience empathy and identification . . . with the Confucian family unit as it negotiates the interface with globally hegemonic American culture" (2003c, 183), and Sheng-mei Ma also locates the film genre as a "domestic tragicomedy," with family ethics "revolving around a patriarchal figure [which] is, after all, the foundation of Confucian cosmology" (1996, 193).

While the film certainly invites if not demands this line of analysis—(not) helped by Ang Lee's cameo appearance in the wedding banquet scene, in which he explains to the white guests bewildered by the ritualistic horseplay that "You're witnessing the results of 5,000 years of sexual repression"—my focus is again on the pitfalls embedded in this kind of analysis and the other roads not taken, so to speak. While there is undisputed textual and contextual evidence to support the examination of homosexuality in relation to the Chinese patriarchal family, I would argue that to pursue this overdetermined line of analysis does nothing to decouple the two but rather serves to perpetuate the myths that, on the one hand, the negotiation of homosexuality in a familial-patriarchal context is unique to Chineseness and, on the other hand, Western gay identities are happily family-free. This line of reading, therefore, risks essentializing the relationship among homosexuality, the patriarchal family, and a Chinese-Confucianist ideology when there is equally compelling evidence to suggest otherwise.[18]

In a popular British film, *Bend It like Beckham* (dir. Gurinder Chadha, 2002), football is used as a signifier for parental objection as Jess, a British-born Indian girl who has pictures of the English footballer David Beckham plastered all over her bedroom wall, devises ways to enroll secretly on a women's football team when all her mother wants is for her to learn Punjabi cooking and find a nice Indian boy to marry. Football also turns out to be the trope through which her best male friend, Tony, who plays football with her and is regarded by some as her potential suitor, comes out to her:

> TONY: I really like Beckham too.
> JESS: Of course you do. No one can cross a ball or bend it like Beckham.
> TONY: No, Jess. I *really* like Beckham.
> JESS: What, you mean . . . ?
> TONY: *(Nods his head.)*
> JESS: You're Indian!
> TONY: I haven't told anyone yet.
> JESS: God, what's your mom going to say?

As in *The Wedding Banquet,* ethnicity (this time Indianness) and the family are deployed in *Bend It like Beckham* as the main signifiers of homosexuality's incompatible counterparts. The film unequivocally underscores the patriarchal nature of the diasporic Indian family, with its huge extended family, close-knit community, objections to interraciality (Jess fancies her white Irish coach), emphasis on material possession and academic success, and the imperatives of marriage and procreation, all of which are at odds with a younger generation harboring different wishes and desires, be they football or (homo)sexuality. In his reading of Ang Lee's films, Jeroen de Kloet summarizes the Chinese-Confucianist family's characteristics as harmony, hierarchy, patriarchy, and piety (2005, 122). The parallels between *The Wedding Banquet* and *Bend It like Beckham* are obvious. Like Ang Lee's film, the latter is also unabashedly (self-) exoticizing in its colorful portrayal of the lavish engagement party and wedding ceremony and extravagant display of what has been called "food pornography." Though homosexuality is not the main theme of *Bend It like Beckham*, it nonetheless functions, along with football, as a metaphor for the intergenerational clash of values in a post-colonial, diasporic space in which fissures invariably surface as the tectonic plates of essential(ized) ethnic-based ideologies and Western lifestyle choices rub against each other.

While *Bend It like Beckham* does not portray whether Tony's homosexuality is reconciled within the Indian family, the 1985 Mexican film *Doña Herlinda and Her Son* (dir. Jaime Humberto Hermosillo) shows the elasticity of the family in accommodating both the son's wife and his male lover under the same roof. Like the father in *The Wedding Banquet*, the matriarch in *Doña Herlinda and Her Son* acknowledges her son's homosexuality without ever openly talking about it. Always proactive and resourceful, she keeps her son happy by inviting his male lover to move into their house ("Rodolfo has such a big bedroom," she says) while keeping up appearances for herself by arranging a marriage of convenience for her son with a woman who works for Amnesty International. The film could be seen in precisely the same terms as noted in some of the above-mentioned readings of *The Wedding Banquet*: the genre of family melodrama; the saving of face *(mianzi)*, which is commonly perceived as essentially Chinese; the formation of an unconventional neo-family; and the patriarch/matriarch's tacit acknowledgement of the son's homosexuality. Both *Bend It like Beckham* and *Doña Herlinda and Her Son* demonstrate that this matrix for negotiating homosexuality is not unique to Chinese cinemas or indeed Chinese societies.

As for the representation (and liberationist discourse) of seemingly family-free Western gay identities, illustrated in *The Wedding Banquet* by Simon, whose family members are living apart, have died, or else have lost contact with each other (thus are stereotypically Western and dysfunctional), this representation should be appreciated equally as a mythical construct, with evidence suggesting otherwise. A quick Internet search using the keywords "family" and "coming out" on the book section of Amazon.co.uk produces the titles of dozens of English-language self-help books advising Western lesbians and gays on how to come out to their families, as well as books for parents, siblings, and children of lesbians and gays. If coming out is a non-issue for Western lesbians and gays and their families, as some might have us believe, the market for these self-help books and organizations such as Parents, Families, and Friends of Lesbians and Gays (PFLAG) in the United States would not exist.[19] Indeed, homosexuals who have married members of the opposite sex, with or without the (tacit) knowledge of their spouses or families of their sexuality, are not uncommon in Western societies either.[20] Rather than essentializing the notion of the family in strictly ideological terms (Chinese-Confucianist versus Western-liberal-dysfunctional) and discounting its significance in Western societies, it may be more productive to see the family as a construct with multifarious economic, social, and cultural configurations impinging on the ways in which it may (or may not) negotiate the issue of homosexuality. The family, I would argue, is a burden of representation in relation to homosexuality that demands decoupling, not reinforcement.

In her reading of Ang Lee in terms of "the politics of flexibility," Shih asks, "What are the material consequences of flexibility?" (2000, 88). I would ask instead what are the *conditions* for flexibility—material or otherwise. If the overemphasis on the matrix of homosexuality and the Chinese-Confucianist patriarchy reflects critics' eagerness not just to champion minority rights, but also to oppose an orthodox ideology widely perceived as oppressive, the result is that very little room is allowed for flexibility within the construction of this patriarchy.[21] There is, however, a moment in *The Wedding Banquet* in which the patriarch reveals some flexibility in his own negotiation of his father's demands. Having arrived in New York and safe in the knowledge that his son is finally getting married, Mr. Gao decides to share a secret with Wai-Tung. Mr. Gao, a retired KMT army general, asks Wai-Tung if he knows why he joined the military in the first place and reveals that it was not, as the son had naïvely assumed, a response to General Chiang Kai-shek's call during the Sino-Japanese War. Mr. Gao explains: "No. I wanted to run away from home. So I joined the army. Your grandpa had arranged a marriage for me. I got mad and just took off. After the war, we fought the Communists. A relative escaped to Taiwan and brought me a letter from your grandpa. He told me that there was no longer a Gao family and that I should start my own family outside the mainland, to continue the family name. Son, imagine how I feel to be able to attend your wedding" (A. Lee 1994, 146–147).[22]

Overlooked by most critics, this speech provides a crucial clue to the father's eventual tacit acknowledgement and acceptance of his son's homosexuality.[23] Read as the father's coming out to his son with a long-kept secret—one that undermines his valorized image as a patriotic general, no less—the speech in fact unites the father and son as rebels who have both resisted a marriage imposed on them by their fathers. Having disclosed his own flexibility in dealing with his father, Mr. Gao would have to extend this flexibility to his dealings with his son, for their parallel experiences as rebels would have made it morally difficult for him to reject Wai-Tung's rebellion. I would suggest that the father's politics of flexibility also ushers in a category almost unmentioned and unmentionable in contemporary critical practice, that of the affective, which, it has been argued, is the governing tenet of parent-child relationships in the Confucian tradition (King 1994, 112). Within the diegesis of the film, affection *(qing)* would have been another reasonable mechanism of flexibility in the father's negotiation of the issue of his son's homosexuality. The ambiguous ending of the film, in which the father raises his arms while being frisked by the security officer, only accentuates the refusal of finality in the film's ideological construction.[24]

Towards Inter-Representation

As Mercer notes in the epigraph of this chapter, the burden of representation imposes "an intolerable imperative to try and say everything there is to be said, all in one mouthful" (1990, 62). This burden, I would argue, is multiplied when members from outside the groups concerned assume the task of representing those groups, raising the question of the ethics of representing otherness, as well as questions on their claims to authenticity and experience. Moreover, as the act of representation is inextricably linked to an identity politics in which a redress of injustice, discrimination, and imbalance of power is at stake, the concomitant expectation of what these representations can achieve is often of a utopian nature to the extent that they are doomed to disappoint.[25] In the case of *The Wedding Banquet,* this insurmountable burden of representation can be illustrated by comments such as, "Queerness and diaspora in Lee's film do not finally constitute any inherent challenge to local or global status quo" (Eng 1997, 46), while it remains undefined what the status quo is, what constitutes a challenge, and who is best placed to determine the effect of the challenge. Needless to say, it also remains unquestioned whether such a demand is fair or legitimate in the first place.

For Shih, Ang Lee's politics of flexibility can be explained by Lee's translatability, "a necessary mode for the minoritised to acquire access to and acceptance by the centre," and what she calls "decipherable localism," which is "the presentation of local national culture with the anticipation of ready decipherability by the non-local audience" (2000, 100). I would suggest that rather than translatability and "decipherable localism" being seen in negative terms, their potential should be reassessed and the strategies of their deployment reconsidered if reaching out for wider communication among different groups of people, marginal or otherwise, is indeed the common will of all concerned. I agree with Shih that "it is important to continue to ask on whose terms and on what terms that reaching is made possible" (ibid.), but I also wish to emphasize that opportunities for cross-group communication should not be foreclosed and the potential of goodwill from any party should not be dismissed simply as a fairy tale.

In her book on "the vicissitudes of cross-ethnic representational politics" (2002, viii), Rey Chow draws a parallel between John Berger's metaphor of the public zoo and "the politics of ethnicity in the context of capitalist liberalism" (ibid., 96). Using Fredric Jameson's (in)famous article, "Third-World Literature in the Era of Multinational Capital," as an example of "the unavoidable pitfalls of cross-ethnic representation" (ibid., 97), Chow argues that "however benevolent and complimentary the visitor might be, the image produced of the animal—in this case, the third-world cultural workers, the ethnics caught in the plight of postimperialist nationalisms—is bound to be out of focus because they are the products of a certain kind of gaze to which they are (pre)supposed to play *as,* to act *like,* to exist *in the manner of* something" (ibid., 100; emphasis in original). However, if pitfalls are indeed unavoidable, as are cross-group representations, what else is there to do besides the obvious task of critiquing those pitfalls? If minority groups still suffer from unequal access to the mechanisms of self-representation, is it not politically more expedient for them to re-envision their relationship with the mainstream (especially if the mainstream is benevolent and complimentary) as one that is based not on suspicion and antagonism but on good faith and collaboration?

In this new configuration, not only can mainstream culture participate in the representation of minorities, but also minorities can equally seek to represent mainstream culture. In addition, greater cooperation can be forged among minority groups so that they can speak up for one another. In this respect, *self*-representation can be reconfigured as *inter*-representation, and the significance of the latter is manifold. First, it will eliminate the victim mentality of minorities and their tendency towards self-ghettoization. Second, it means an openness to, not a rejection of, those segments of the mainstream society who speak for minorities that still may lack access to channels of self-representation. Third, it encourages cross-cultural and inter-group understanding not only among different minority groups, but also between minority groups and mainstream culture. This is particularly important because some minority groups have an antagonistic relationship not just with the mainstream, but also with other minority groups. To perceive each other as comrades rather than enemies promotes cooperation and understanding among minority groups, which will markedly increase their collective power in negotiating with the mainstream.

If the new configuration of inter-representation sounds utopian, it is precisely Ang Lee's filmmaking career that may illustrate its potential. For Lee and especially for his co-writer of the screenplay, Neil Peng (Feng Guangyuan), the making of *The Wedding Banquet* was almost a personal crusade inasmuch as the film was inspired by the real life experiences of a gay friend of Peng (A. Lee and Peng 1993, 13–14). The published Chinese screenplay includes articles on gay activism in the United States in the hope of promoting equal rights for homosexuals in Taiwan. Peng also initiated a petition protesting the exploitative portrayal of homosexuals on Taiwanese television (ibid., 247–283). During the filming of *The Wedding Banquet*, Ang Lee attended the Gay Pride March in New York City with the leading members of his cast (ibid., 244). According to a report (*United Daily*, January 24, 1995), several gay organizations in the United States presented Lee with awards for the film's contribution to the community. Moreover, Lee has shown that cross-cultural collaboration is more viable than some might have imagined. After his first three feature films in Chinese (the above-mentioned "Father Knows Best" trilogy), Lee has proceeded to make English-language films as diverse as a Regency period drama (*Sense and Sensibility*, 1995), a film set in the United States of the 1970s (*The Ice Storm*, 1997), an American Civil War drama (*Ride with the Devil*, 1999), and an adaptation of a classic American cartoon and television series (*Hulk*, 2003). At the time of this writing, Lee is also in post-production for his latest film, *Brokeback Mountain*, a film featuring gay cowboys in Wyoming that is bound to stir up controversy in America.[26]

While it may not be possible to totally obliterate the distinction between self and other, one should begin to realize how much of one's self is always already invested and implicated in the other and vice versa, and the boundary between self and other should continue to be blurred, if not broken down. Along with my call for inter-representation among social groups, I also propose that the notion of the multiple first person—the hybrid "I"—should be promoted to transcend the narrow essentialism still predominant in many forms of identity politics. As Allen Chun argues, "The polarization invoked both by subaltern studies and post-Orientalist studies, albeit from different directions, has galvanized 'identities' to such an extent that all writing invariably begins in the first person" (1996, 132–133). This invoked first person, however, is usually premised on one aspect of identity, be it sexuality, ethnicity/race, class, gender, or nationality; hence the separate forms of identity politics. For Ella Shohat and Robert Stam, the appreciation of the self as "a matrix for multiple discursive forms and identifications . . . is in no way to deny realities of race, class, gender, nation but only to complicate and dialecticize them" (1994, 344). While there will always be contexts that demand one to speak from a certain position of identity, the deployment of the hybrid "I" should highlight the multiplicity of identity, as well as debunk the myth of essentialism that bases the definition of the self on a single facet of identity.

In this globalized age, when the cultural economy of cinema can no longer be defined as national but has indisputably become transnational and international, when cultural flows and the public sphere for their discursive exchange are invariably fluid and interpenetrating, identities are also inescapably multiple, hybrid, and cross-cultural. Separatism and ghettoization, whether by nation, race, gender, class, or sexuality, should continue to be dismantled; in tandem with this, communication among groups should be promoted. To these ends, inter-representation must increasingly be seen not just as a possibility but a necessity. As an art form that can imagine as well as bring together societies and communities, the global sphere of cinema has the potential of fostering greater understanding among peoples and groups of diverse backgrounds. Seen as a socially discursive act in itself, film can, as Ryan points out, "help create a new social discourse by offering representations of new values, institutions, and modes of behaviour for collective identification and internalized modelling. Film discourse and social discourse intertwine as a struggle not only over how reality will be represented but over what that reality will be. Films play a role in the social construction of reality in that they influence collectively held representations or ideas of what society is and should be" (1988, 483).

In this sense, the representation of male homosexuality in contemporary Chinese cinemas should be of concern not only to homosexuals in Chinese societies, but also to all who believe in combating prejudices of all kinds. At the same time, these representations should not focus exclusively on sexuality, but should be cross-examined in relation to race, class, gender, and nation so that the concept and understanding of homosexuality are also complicated and hybridized. Most important, it is only by acknowledging that minority identities are not "any more 'multiple' than [those] of a straight white man, who is also raced, classed, gendered, and sexually oriented" (Fung 1995, 128) that the burden of representation may perhaps be lifted from the shoulders of those who have carried it for far too long and that the notion of representation may itself be reconceptualized, renegotiated, and reevaluated.

The Uses of Femininity

Chen Kaige's *Farewell My Concubine* and
Zhang Yuan's *East Palace, West Palace*

To obey, but to resist. There is the whole secret!
—EMILE CHARTIER ALAIN

"What is the place of femininity within male homosexuality?" Kaja
Silverman notes that "it seems politically impossible to ask [such
a question] at this moment in the history of representation" because "the
question itself appears to solicit a cultural stereotype which many homosexual men have struggled to put behind them" (1992, 339). In a book on
the representation of male homosexuality in Chinese cinemas in which
the films under discussion are drawn from the decade of Silverman's writing, femininity poses a problem both politically and discursively, albeit for
different reasons. Certainly Silverman's anxiety is also palpable in the context of this book, particularly with regard to Chen Kaige's *Farewell My
Concubine* (hereafter *Farewell*) and Zhang Yuan's *East Palace, West Palace*
(hereafter *Palace*). In the representation of male homosexuality, femininity is configured in both films through the trope of transgender practice
in Chinese opera, wherein female roles are played by male actors. However, my concern in this chapter is not so much the relationship of femininity to male homosexuality; rather, I am interested in the ways in which
femininity in male homosexuality has been used as a figure for a different
kind of relationship—that between the artist-intellectual and the state—
in the two films from mainland China.

The emphasis on the geopolitical region of mainland China is not
unintentional, and the relationship between the artist-intellectual and the
state is invariably allegorical because of the double taboo of politics and
homosexuality in China. Indeed, one might extend Silverman's question
by asking: What is the place of femininity within male homosexuality in
a country in which homosexuality as artistic/cinematic representation

and lived reality are both officially censored and censured? I have provided in chapter 1 an account of the difficulties faced by the directors in the making of these films. In this chapter, I shall ask to what extent the allegorical uses of femininity in male homosexuality offer different possibilities of reimagining the relationship between the artist-intellectual and the state.

Transgender Practice in Chinese Theater and Society

The prominence of the trope of Chinese opera in films with a homosexual theme is not unique to the two films from mainland China. Chinese opera also functions as a trope for homosexuality in the Taiwanese film *Fleeing by Night* and the Hong Kong film *Hu-Du-Men* (dir. Shu Kei, 1996). This has led Chris Berry to comment that it is "emerging as a privileged Chinese site or trope in the discursive construction of homosexuality" (1996a, 171). In her analysis of *Farewell*'s homosexual protagonist, Teri Silvio reverses Berry's construction to argue that "homosexuality is becoming a privileged trope for a Chinese allegorization of the opera" that demands an "overcoming [of] resistance—that is, by denaturalizing one's own subjectivity—[in order] that the opera star and the New Socialist Person can come into being" (2002, 187). I would suggest, however, that in employing the trope of femininity in Chinese theater's transgender practice to represent male homosexuality, *Farewell* and *Palace* not only allegorize the state's relationship with its homosexual subject, but also with its artists, intellectuals, and film directors, all of whom occupy a structurally feminized position in the unequal power relation. Femininity in the two mainland Chinese films does not serve to signal an essential quality of the homosexual subject (and this is where I believe charges of homophobia may be missing the point); rather, it functions as a figure for the marginalized subject—regardless of whether the marginalization arises from political or sexual dissidence—and his/her structural relationship to the state. Directors filming homosexuality in China have had to (and continue to have to) negotiate the state apparatus praxis of policies and policing and to devise strategies to circumvent the barriers imposed by them.

"To obey, but to resist. There is the whole secret!" This statement by Emile Chartier Alain (1868–1951) has been mobilized by Laurence Schneider (1980, 48) in his study of the Chinese poet Qu Yuan (338–278 BCE). Alain's formulation captures the paradoxical situation in which a feminized male subject invariably finds himself—that is, he has to obey orders yet finds ways to resist them. It is apt that my examination of the power politics embedded in femininity within male homosexuality should begin with Qu Yuan, for he is the archetypal embodiment of the feminized and (homo)sexualized relationship between a king and one of his officials. Transgender practice in Chinese culture and society enjoys a long history, dating back to antiquity. In particular, the relationship between a king and his official is often expressed in terms of male/female love. When the official loses favor with his king, they are frequently depicted as estranged lovers (Schneider 1980, 32; Kang 1996, 114). Qu Yuan's epic poem *Encountering Sorrow (Li sao)* is a prime example of linguistic transvestism as it employs the symbol of fragrant grasses *(xiangcao)* for the official seeking the favor of the king, the fair one *(meiren)*.[1] With the official occupying a similar positionality to that of the concubine—as evidenced in the Chinese expression "the way of the official and the concubine" *(chenqie zhi dao;* Kang 1996, 111)—the feminized, submissive position of the male official is predetermined in this transgender practice. In the case of Qu Yuan, there have also been debates about whether his relationship with his king bordered on homosexuality.[2]

In Chinese theater, particularly in Beijing (Peking) opera, transgender practice has long been an integral part of the performance, as well as of a courtesan culture in which prostitution by male actors who play female roles (known as *dan* actors) and their patronage by bureaucrats and upper-class men were commonplace.[3] Under both the Ming and Qing regimes' strict prohibition against the frequenting of houses of female prostitution by bureaucrats and upper-class men, *dan* actors were actively cultivated as substitute objects of desire (D. Wang 1997, 67). In certain historical periods the milieu of theatrical performances was primarily all-male, with women forbidden from performing under Qing law in 1772 (Vitiello 1992, 359) and from the audience until the early twentieth century (Mackerras 1975, 90–91).[4] The exclusion of women from these theatrical and social spaces undoubtedly contributed to the prominence and popularity of male-to-female transgender practice.

Siu Leung Li notes that "the climax of the sexually ambiguous figure of the male *dan* as a cultural obsession occurred in the golden age of Beijing opera, the 1920s to the 30s, culminating in the body of the ultimate icon Mei Lanfang (1894–1961)" (2003, 7). However, social pressures outside the theater mounted against the playing of female parts by male actors, resulting in the appearance of women on the Beijing opera stage in 1928 (Dolby 1976, 219). Despite efforts to eradicate homosexual practices in opera troupes and training schools (Mackerras 1975, 75), "the association of *dan* actors with a homoerotic subculture, while publicly denounced, was an integral element of theater culture and would not be easily expunged" (Goldstein 1999, 402). The assumption that the *dan* actor/prostitute necessarily takes the passive role sexually (Vitiello 1992, 361) inextricably ties femininity in transgendered homosexuality to submissiveness and powerlessness. The transvestite female role is therefore first and foremost a structurally submissive discursive position that can be occupied by any male so long as he adheres to the inherent power relation, thereby predetermining the terms of negotiation for his expression of homosexual desire. Indeed, I would argue that the expression of homosexual desire via transgender practice is not necessarily a result of identification with the feminine. Rather, the process may have been the reverse: it is because of its institutionalization and legitimatization in both Chinese theatrical tradition and sociocultural mores that this particular form of homosexual expression has been made possible in the first place. This reading thus brings into question the issue of agency in determining the modes of homosexual expression under specific historical circumstances.

It is particularly important to emphasize the issue of agency because unlike modern-day drag queens, who use their cross-dressing acts as deliberate attempts to subvert gender boundaries, the same cannot be assumed in the case of the transvestite female role in Chinese opera. Judith Butler argues that drag, in imitating gender, *"implicitly reveals the imitative structure of gender itself—as well as its contingency"* (1990, 137; emphasis in original). Such post-modern self-reflexivity is not present in cross-dressing in Chinese opera, as Siu Leung Li explicates:

> Butler's concern is the philosophical-deconstructive interrogation of performativity and citationality, subjectivity and agency. To her, any appeal to an interior, a priori identity is futile because it does not exist. But let me emphasize here that Tang Xianzu [a Ming playwright] and the transvestite actor [in Chinese opera] were essentialists in that they believed in the essence of a biological sex as given. In capturing the essence/psyche of the female sex, a male transvestite can be transformed into a "woman" that everyone takes as "real." (2003, 165)

The issue of agency therefore cannot be taken as a priori in the case of transgender practice in Chinese theater. Rather, the institutionalization of transgender practice may have unwittingly provided an outlet for the trafficking of homosexual desire. It is important to bear this distinction in mind to avoid anachronistic and retroactive readings, particularly in terms of gender and sexual politics. For example, the idea of transgression may not be embedded in transgender practice in Chinese opera as it is in contemporary gender performance. In her analysis of *Farewell*, Jenny Kwok Wah Lau argues that the transvestite role in Beijing opera "does not copy the woman but signifies her" and that femininity in this context is "a translation, not necessarily a transgression" (1995, 23).[5] In other words, though the gender boundary of male/female has been literally transgressed, the act itself may not have any transgressive or subversive value in terms of gender and sexual politics.

The two films discussed here offer an interesting contrast in relation to the issue of agency. In *Farewell*, the protagonist, Dieyi, is constricted in his expression of homosexuality by his structural position within the milieu of Chinese theater. By contrast, Ah Lan, the protagonist in *Palace*, is a self-identified gay man who employs transgender imagination as one of his many tropes for homosexual expression. The reason for their difference, as I shall illustrate below, is a question of agency. In my analysis of the films, I am concerned with the following questions in relation to femininity in homosexuality: What kind of discursive structure and space is built into the transvestite female role in Chinese opera? How do femininity and transvestism as defining features of this role determine the terms of negotiation in articulating homosexual desire? Does physical transvestism necessarily imply psychological transvestism, and if so, how does this impinge on the male actor's subjectivity? Finally, what is the significance of the continued deployment of a traditional transgender practice as a representational trope for homosexuality in Chinese filmmaking, and what implications does this deployment have for contemporary gender and sexual politics?

Farewell My Concubine: Feminization, Transvestism, Agency

In *Farewell*, Cheng Dieyi (the adult role played by the late Leslie Cheung Kwok-wing) is a *dan* actor in Beijing opera. As a child, Dieyi's (then known as Xiao Douzi) prostitute mother leaves him with an opera troupe, where he forms a special bond with a tough boy, Shitou, who becomes Duan Xiaolou (the adult role played by Zhang Fengyi).[6] They grow up to become stars of the troupe, assuming the leading roles in the classic play *Farewell My Concubine*, in which Dieyi plays the concubine Yu Ji to Xiaolou's King of Chu.[7] Over the years Dieyi develops a secret love for Xiaolou, but their relationship becomes strained after Xiaolou's marriage to Juxian (Gong Li), a prostitute, and Dieyi submits to courting by Yuan Shiqing (Ge You), a wealthy patron. Meanwhile, historical events unfold, taking the narrative through the Japanese invasion and the Nationalist takeover to the communist reign, culminating in the Cultural Revolution, when Dieyi and Xiaolou are forced to denounce each other and Juxian commits suicide. In their final performance of the classic play after the end of the Cultural Revolution, Dieyi slays himself with the sword carried by Xiaolou, turning drama into life.

As argued from the outset, in the context of transgender practice in Chinese theater, the expression of homosexual desire via transvestism may not be a result of identification with the feminine. In fact, the film begins by subjecting Dieyi to a series of feminizing rites of passage and shows his initial response to enforced feminization as one of rejection. First, Dieyi's mother chops off his extra finger so that he will be accepted by the opera troupe, a symbolic act of castration that serves to demonstrate the trauma of feminization and to foreground Dieyi's soon-to-be feminized position as a *dan* actor. Dieyi is then assigned the transvestite female role as a nun in a play, *Longing for the World (Sifan),* but he insists on reversing a gendered line.[8] Instead of "I am by nature a girl and not a boy," Dieyi repeatedly recites it as "I am by nature a boy and not a girl," suffering severe punishment by the troupe master as a result. On one occasion, Dieyi threatens to jeopardize the troupe's opportunity to perform for a powerful ex-Qing eunuch as he recites the line wrongly again. Eager to save Dieyi from punishment and to salvage the troupe's chances, Xiaolou inserts an opium pipe into Dieyi's mouth, twisting and turning it violently. This simulated oral sex results in blood flowing out of Dieyi's mouth, signifying his loss of virginity in this symbolic rape. Dieyi emerges from the experience a changed gender and recites the line as "I am by nature a girl and not a boy." Now feminized, Dieyi opens himself to sexual patronage according to the praxis of Beijing opera, and he is deflowered by the eunuch after performing for him. The physical rape immediately invokes in Dieyi a maternal instinct, as he adopts an abandoned baby in the street after leaving the eunuch's court, thus completing his initiating cycle of feminization.

Castration, loss of virginity, deflowering, maternity: femininity is used in the film, with all its none-too-subtle Freudian symbolism, to first and foremost mark a violence upon which transgender practice in Chinese theater must rest.[9] While violence is also inflicted on the other boys in the opera school, that which is enacted on Dieyi's body, both symbolically and literally, is different not only in degree, but also in kind. Precisely because the theatrical roles Dieyi has to play are transgendered, the film's deployment of Freudian symbolism suggests that physical transvestism cannot be convincingly achieved without a concomitant psychological transvestism, violently executed if necessary. Nevertheless, this has not always been the case, as shown by the preeminent *dan* actor Mei Lanfang, upon whom Dieyi's character is loosely based (Silvio 2002, 187), for Mei "made the body, rather than the psyche, the source of the self's coherence" as the Beijing opera actor "internalizes a gestural semantics into bodily, not psychic, memory, and then externalizes that memory into a performance text" (ibid., 194). In *Farewell,* however, "an interior psyche is constructed for Dieyi through a symbolic language that belongs to the *mise-en-scène,* rather than the actor," and for Silvio, "the excessiveness of this psychological symbolism" is "a register of how far the distance between stage and screen has grown in post-Mao China" (ibid.). That is, the film's psychologizing tendency necessitates that the violence inflicted on the body in the feminization process also leave its mark on the psyche, thus stitching up the gap between physical transvestism and psychological transvestism.

The psychological transvestism or gender inversion of Dieyi is most clearly illustrated in Dieyi's first (pseudo)sexual experience in the symbolic oral sex scene, as he consequently comes alive in his female role, reciting the line "I am by nature a girl and not a boy" with an unmistakably post-coital aura of *jouissance* and afterglow. Collapsing feminization and homosexualization into one, the phallic penetration of the pipe by a male into a male transforms the latter male into a female so that Dieyi occupies the discursive position of the feminine/feminized and henceforth negotiates his homosexuality as such. Contrary to suggestions that Dieyi might have developed homosexual desire for Xiaolou prior to this scene (Liao 1994, 202; Sang 1993, 60–62), I see their childhood relationship as one of mutual support, innocent friendship, and male bonding, which, despite being clearly homoerotic, is perhaps not quite consciously homosexual. Even the symbolic oral sex scene can be described as only pseudosexual at best, and to what extent it arouses a homosexual awakening in Dieyi is open to interpretation. I am more inclined to read, along with Wendy Larson, Dieyi's "difficult proclamation that he is a girl, and his subsequent behavior . . . as feminization rather than homosexualization" because the film "emphasizes the position Cheng Dieyi holds relative to the other characters and to the discourse of national cultural form, rather than any essentialized desire" and because his position "is one of weakness and inability to act, or symbolically that of the feminine within the social arena" (1997, 345n25).

I would therefore argue that Dieyi had to first and foremost identify with the trope of femininity embedded in the transgender practice in Beijing opera *before* he could discover the possibility of trafficking homosexual desire via the transvestite role. To suggest that Dieyi might have been homosexual since childhood seems to me to privilege Dieyi's a priori agency in determining his mode of sexual expression and runs the risks of overlooking the structural and material conditions for articulating sexual desire and constructing sexual identity within the cultural milieu of the

Chinese opera troupe. Indeed, Dieyi's homosexuality could not have been reified without the trope of femininity afforded to him in the transgender practice of Beijing opera. As we shall see below, because Dieyi's position is the structurally feminine/feminized, in his adult homosexual relations, this trope at once provides him with a mode of expression for his feelings towards Xiaolou (though these are constrained to his onstage perform-ance, which has no valence offstage due to Xiaolou's desire for Juxian) and renders him powerless to reject the courting of the wealthy patron, Yuan.

By focusing on the structurally feminized position occupied by Dieyi, I am highlighting rather than discounting the issue of agency, as well as its limitation or lack. The role of Juxian, the prostitute who later becomes Xiaolou's wife, is pivotal in underscoring Dieyi's incapability of finding an alternative mode for his sexual expression. It is significant that both Juxian and Dieyi are marginalized by society for their respective profes-sions as prostitute and *dan* actor (who is simultaneously regarded and treated as a prostitute, and for Dieyi, the son of a prostitute, it is a triple curse).[10] Though they are similarly circumscribed by society to an inferior, feminized position, Juxian is determined to take matters into her own hands where Dieyi is not prepared to. In particular, Juxian succeeds in buying herself out of prostitution and literally throws herself into a mar-riage with Xiaolou. Notwithstanding Dieyi's devotion to the art of his profession, his response to Xiaolou's abandonment of him for Juxian is to throw himself into decadent wantonness with Yuan. In his attempt to win Xiaolou back, Dieyi presents him with the sword Xiaolou first coveted at the eunuch's court in their childhood days—now possessed by Dieyi at the price of submitting sexually to Yuan. Xiaolou, in his state of drunken-ness on the night of his engagement ceremony, fails to recognize it, ren-dering Dieyi's prostitution futile. The scene recalls the phallic smoke pipe inserted by Xiaolou into Dieyi's mouth in the symbolic oral sex scene; Dieyi's claim to masculinity is tenuous as the phallic sword is doomed to be misrecognized when held in his hands.

The transgender performance of Dieyi, therefore, is highly restric-tive. His femininity is literally beaten into his body and psyche by the bru-tal regime of the Chinese opera troupe, and his successful identification with the feminine is achieved by a violent male force. For Dieyi, physical transvestism necessarily entails psychological transvestism, and the traf-ficking of homosexual desire via the transvestite role is not a deliberate choice but an institutionalized tradition. His adherence to the submissive, feminized position of the concubine predetermines his powerless negoti-ation of his homosexuality. How does one assess the film's representation of such a highly constricted form of homosexuality? It is perhaps appropriate at this juncture to address the question raised by Silverman and quoted at the start of the chapter—"What is the place of femininity within male homosexuality?"—and the difficulty of raising this question in light of the politics of representation.

Representing Femininity in Homosexuality

The difficulty of the question raised by Silverman is illustrated by the strong reaction against the inextricable link among (enforced) femininity, gender inversion, and homosexuality in *Farewell*. For many scholars and critics, the portrayal of Dieyi as a "hysterical faggot" is reminiscent of the traditional stereotype of the hysterical woman, implicating the director as both homophobic and misogynist (Berry 1993a, 21; Leung Ping-kwan 1995, 360; Liao 1994, 203–204). The suggestions that Dieyi's homosexuality is a result of gender inversion (Shu 1993, 19), victimization (Leung Ping-kwan 1995, 360), and the "othering" of the homosexual as the aesthete (Liao 1994, 204, 208) have also come under fire. Taiwanese scholar Chu Wei-cheng's (Zhu Weicheng) comment sums up the sentiments shared by the film's critics. While acknowledging that one cannot demand too much of any single film text, Chu argues that the film "overlaps too closely with the heterosexual imagination of homosexuality," making it impossible to challenge and question its portrayal within the film's narrative structure (1994, 145). A comment by E. Ann Kaplan, a feminist scholar, also exemplifies such criticism:

> Perhaps the film needs to be criticized from a gay/queer-studies perspective for perpetuating such negative gay stereotypes as the effete, seductive, and narcissistic opera patron [referring to Yuan], and for apparently utilizing an underlying traditional psychoanalytic understanding of queerness as a result of overidentification with the mother [referring to Dieyi]. On the other hand, Chinese cinema has only just begun to deal with gay sexualities, so Chen's introduction of these should be recognized as progress. (1997, 270–271)

The kind of critical project undertaken above can be classified as what Stuart Hall, in his study of black filmmaking in British cinema, calls the initial phase in the cultural politics of representation, which focuses on the contestation of negative stereotypes and the counterpositioning of positive representations (1996, 442). However, Hall also identifies a later phase, which marks "the end of the innocent notion of the essential black subject" and recognizes that "'black' is essentially a politically and culturally *constructed* category" (ibid., 443; emphasis in original). In both Kaplan's and Hall's accounts the history of representation (whether for homosexuals or blacks) is assumed to follow a teleological and developmental trajectory, with Kaplan's notion of "progress" and Hall's distinction of "phases." According to this logic, to take Kaplan's argument as an example, just as the development from no representation of homosexuality in Chinese cinema to Chen's negative representation can be seen as "progress," the mission will be accomplished when the negative representation one day leads to a positive representation of homosexuality. While this may have been the case in certain histories of representation, I suggest that this is not the only possible trajectory and that such a narrative betrays a myth that perhaps finds its roots in social Darwinism. More important, it seems to me there are two wider issues to be addressed, in addition to the point that (to echo Hall) in challenging negative stereotypes, the above-mentioned criticisms make assumptions about an essentialized and homogenized *group* when homosexuals are in fact heterogeneous *individuals*. These two issues concern the question of who speaks for whom and the agency of those for whom the speaking is supposedly done.

First, how does one determine the political efficacy of any representation—if it would do more harm than good and to whom? As Cornel West observes, contestation of negative stereotypes is often "rested upon *a homogenizing impulse* that obliterates differences within a community" (1990, 27; emphasis in original), and there is indeed "a thin line between refusing the constriction of the stereotype and denying difference" (Fung 1995, 127). Moreover, critics may not realize that in purporting to champion the interests of homosexuals, they may be utilizing the same language as those who censure homosexuality. In the case of *Farewell*, an article in the CCP journal *Qiushi* argues that many male actors who play female roles in Beijing opera are real men in real life, unlike Dieyi, who is affected, effeminate, and abnormal (Ji 1994, 46). Thus both discourses—those speaking for and against homosexuality—see femininity in homosexuality as somehow false. This recalls Michel Foucault's assertion that the production of discourses on homosexuality in the nineteenth century, which "made possible a strong advance of social controls into this area of 'perversity,'" also "made possible the formation of a 'reverse discourse'" that allowed homosexuality to begin "to speak in its own behalf, to demand that its legitimacy or 'naturality' be acknowledged, often in the same vocabulary, using the same categories by which it was medically disqualified" (1990, 101). However, in this instance, pro-gay critics of the film seem to be oblivious to the possibility of their discourse's being reversed for a truly homophobic purpose. It is worth bearing in mind Foucault's cautionary note that we must "make allowance for the complex and

The Uses of Femininity

unstable process whereby discourse can be both an instrument and an effect of power, but also a hindrance, a stumbling-block, a point of resistance and a starting point for an opposing strategy" (ibid.).

Second, these critics seem to have discounted the possibility that what they perceive as negative representations could be seen by others—particularly those on whose behalf they are presumably speaking—as positive. They also seem to designate only one possible reading position for the film's audience, that of passive reception and wholesale acceptance. Is it not possible that *some* homosexuals may not find these representations offensive but, on the contrary, celebrate Dieyi and Yuan as their role models? If audiences "are not univocally 'positioned' by films" but rather either accept or reject cinematic representations of the world and do so in accordance with the social codes they inhabit (Ryan 1988, 480), is it not possible that audiences are equally capable of discerning the social discourses mobilized by the director in his cinematic representation of male homosexuality and rejecting them as they see fit? While it is possible that the discourse inherent in these representations may be put to homophobic use, it is equally plausible that these images may be creatively appropriated by agents whose identifications are as individualized as they are multifarious. More important, suspicions about the former should not preclude the potential of the latter; otherwise, as K. Anthony Appiah argues, it is at this juncture that "someone who takes autonomy seriously will ask whether we have not replaced one kind of tyranny with another" (1994, 162–163).

While I do not wish to be an apologist for Chen or his film, I see the reactions against *Farewell* as symptomatic of the contemporary climate of identity politics and the multiculturalism underpinning them and a concomitant failure to realize its own restrictive politics, on the one hand, and to historicize and contextualize textual reading, on the other.[11] The focus of film reading should not be on whether a film's representations are seen as "positive" or "negative" by a contemporary audience; rather the reading should investigate the film's social context as a way of understanding the representations historically (Arroyo 1997, 72–73). In the contemporary climate that has led to Silverman's anxiety in raising the question of the place of femininity in male homosexuality, I want to highlight a different reading of *Farewell* that addresses this question historically.

While *Farewell* is set in the period between the early Republican era and the end of the Cultural Revolution, the relationship between Dieyi and his patrons "resembles that between the boy actors and their literati patrons in the late-eighteenth century more than the relations between actors and fans in the mid-twentieth century" (Silvio 2002, 186). Homosexuality in this historical and cultural context is usually associated with cross-class relations. The unequal power relation of patronage by upper-class men predetermines an actor's structurally feminized position, which in turn determines the latter's negotiation of his homosexuality. It is difficult to imagine someone like Dieyi being capable of developing an economically egalitarian form of homosexual relationship under the circumstances. One should also note that class is but one form of inequality in any (homo)sexual relationship and that power relations can be configured along many different axes, such as age, appearance, and physique, which are performing similar functions of privileging and discrimination in the contemporary gay milieu. Indeed, one could go as far as to lament the demise of cross-class relations while not discounting their socioeconomic inequality. In the Western context of the late twentieth century, it has been observed that the cross-class liaison between the effete gent and the "manly" lower-class boy "no longer seems the obvious choice for gay men" (Sinfield 1994b, 149, 151). The alternative, "that the most suitable kind of partner is someone whose outlook and interest are close to your own," which "matches closely the current heterosexual idea, especially in the middle classes, of companionate marriage," may, for Alan Sinfield, be "effecting a tyrannical confinement of the potential in gay relations" (ibid., 151).

More important, the relationship between femininity and homosexuality has not always been perceived as negative, or, as Jonathan Dollimore puts it, "the association between homosexuality and femininity is not necessarily insulting to either" (1991, 263). As Sinfield shows in his study of Oscar Wilde's century, effeminacy can become the dominant expression of homosexuality in a historical period because of the availability, or the lack thereof, of tropes for sexual imagination, and "we cannot assume that the available images of same-sex passion correspond to the desires, to the fantasies, of individuals" (1994a, 46). Nor does the trope of femininity need to be seen as necessarily constricting. For example, the transvestite stage of Beijing opera that Dieyi inhabits has been described as "an imaginative capaciousness," where "Dieyi can both represent and masquerade his genuine sensibility" (B. Zhang 1999, 104). Hence, while effeminacy or femininity in homosexuality may be eschewed as a negative trait in contemporary gay culture, in the case of Wilde and Dieyi, it could well have been a neutral expression in their days. Even though *Farewell*'s homosexual representation coincides with present-day prejudice against effeminacy, this does not disqualify its use of the trope of femininity when taken *on its own terms*. As Taiwanese scholar Sang Tze-lan (Sang Zilan) argues, those who see the representation of homosexuality in the film as negative in fact participate in a contemporary attitude that perceives femininity as shameful and as a social myth to be eradicated (1993, 58). Echoing my argument above for the potential for creative appropriation of seemingly negative representations, Sang suggests that in the film's return in historical time to search for and imagine a cultural milieu suppressed by the present Chinese official orthodoxy, it may even be creating and concretizing images of "homosexual pioneers" (ibid., 66).

Moreover, many discussions of the film presuppose an identity category that may not be applicable to Dieyi. I have repeatedly emphasized the feminized position that Dieyi occupies and cautioned the attribution of an agency for Dieyi's negotiation of his sexuality precisely because notions of identity category, particularly sexual ones, may not have been as commonplace in the time period of the diegesis' setting as they are today. Noting that the emergence of sexual identity categories are seen "to inhere in the psyche rather than the body," Silvio argues that "Dieyi is not gay" but rather that "his sexuality is a synecdoche for a whole way of being a Chinese person that had to be sacrificed in order for 'gay' to come into existence as a possible identity category" (2002, 194, 186). Even if we were to grant Dieyi a certain degree of agency in his sexual imagination, it is worth noting that sexual identity "depends not on a deep-set self-hood (though it may feel otherwise), but on one's particular situation within the framework of understanding that makes certain, diverse, possibilities available; which makes some ideas plausible and others not" (Sinfield 1994b, 11).

I hope I have shown that the taboo of femininity in homosexuality should not be taken as a given but should be seen as historically and culturally constructed. While *Farewell* clearly psychologizes homosexuality in its blatant use of Freudian symbolism, whether this has been borne out of a latent homophobia by the director is not my primary concern. Rather, I am more interested in tracing the historical development and reception of the trope of femininity in different cultural contexts and to argue for a reading strategy that is culturally sensitive and historically responsible. Most important, I want to highlight the possible means in which the trope of femininity may be employed and appropriated, not only for a film set in a context in which homosexuality may not have been conceived in terms of identity category, but also to echo Silverman's call that "we must be prepared to entertain the possibility that a gay man might deploy signifiers of femininity not only because to do so is to generate a counter-discourse, but because an identification with 'woman' constitutes the very basis of his identity, and/or the position from which he desires" (1992, 344).

The Virtue of Sacrifice and the Sacrifice of Virtue

To return to and by way of drawing to a close my discussion of the film, I would like to explore the uses of femininity in *Farewell* through the question of sacrifice. Like the ancient poet Qu Yuan, both the concubine and the wife in the film commit suicide when their king has let them down. Sacrifice in the form of suicide is constructed in these cases as virtuous, shoring up the moral bankruptcy of the king. Juxian's suicide after Xiaolou claims that he does not love her in a struggle session during the Cultural Revolution, for example, can be see as the virtue of love. The issue of virtue in Dieyi's suicide is more complex and demands a closer reading as it is intertwined with gender performance, performativity, and agency, as well as allegorized as the relationship between the artist-intellectual and the state.

The film ends with Dieyi and Xiaolou's final performance together after the end of the Cultural Revolution. The theater is now empty, and they are performing only to themselves for old time's sake. In this final scene, Dieyi is tricked by Xiaolou, who recites "I am by nature a boy...," which Dieyi completes with "...and not a girl," thus unwittingly repeating his childhood mistake of reversing the gender construction in the line. If "gender is an identity tenuously constituted in time, instituted in an exterior space through a *stylized repetition of acts*" (Butler 1990, 140; emphasis in original), the film shows that the reiterative force of Dieyi's performativity fails to concretize a stable (trans)gender identity in him despite decades of performing the transvestite female role. It therefore suggests an essentialist notion of gender identity as (over)determined by biological sex, as Dieyi somehow retains his "core" as irrepressibly male.[12] More to the point here, unlike Yu Ji, who kills herself so that the king can focus on the military battle in the classic opera, Dieyi's suicide is arguably self-serving and also a rare expression of agency, an agency that must premise upon its own denial and destruction—"I die, therefore I am." The virtue for which Dieyi has sacrificed himself, within the logic of the diegesis, is a paradoxical self-realization in both senses of the term: in order to fully occupy the position of the feminized (a femininity that must sacrifice its existence to fulfill the militaristic mission of the masculine), Dieyi must realize the futility of his gender performance and take his own life so as to bring his role as the concubine into realization.

It is noteworthy that the film's ending is different from the two original versions of the story written by Lilian Lee, one of which is a screenplay adapted by Lee for a Hong Kong television drama directed by Alex Law (Luo Qirui) in 1981 and the other being the original version of her novel, published in 1985. In Lee's versions, Dieyi and Xiaolou reunite in old age in a sauna in Hong Kong, where they relive their memories by singing lines from the play *Farewell My Concubine*. With the two male protagonists immersed naked in water (as seen in a clip from Law's television version in Stanley Kwan's documentary *Yang ± Yin*), this ending is homoerotic but absent in Chen's film.[13] In defending his change of the ending in an interview, Chen argues that "there is no other way of expressing the ending but death; this is the highest state [*jingjie*]," and to do otherwise, "for me, for Dieyi, he will scream, he will not be satisfied" (*Yang ± Yin* 1996). Note here that Chen unwittingly speaks of himself and Dieyi in the same breath, and his message for the film is clear: Dieyi must die. If Chen does indeed identify with Dieyi's sacrificial death and if, as argued above, Dieyi's suicide is the only means by which he can achieve self-realization, what is the virtue of the self that has been actualized in the act? Why is sacrificial death satisfying?

While critics have charged Chen for homophobia and mainland centrism, I suggest that Chen's motivation for changing the ending lies instead in the valorization of feminine sacrificial death as the highest virtue, an ideological construction that can be variously configured and that is also inseparable from my allegorical reading of the film's use of femininity as a figure for the relationship between the artist-intellectual and the state. Feminine sacrificial death has long been valorized in Chinese culture, as evidenced in the discourse on virtuous or chaste women *(lienü)* and the Qu Yuan lore.[14] According to Schneider, the Qu Yuan lore, "at least from the eighth century onward, was deeply enriched by efforts to understand and appreciate [Qu Yuan] as a nonconforming, uncompromising, obstinately individualistic person of integrity," and his suicide in particular "became a model for a political and moral style" (1980, 50). In Silvio's reading, Dieyi also represents "the Modernist purity of the artist who sacrifices all for his artistic vision" (2002, 187), as shown in Dieyi's willingness to perform for the Japanese and Nationalist generals as long as they appreciate Beijing opera. Along with the feminine virtues of chastity, integrity, and purity, the film simultaneously constructs Dieyi as the embodiment of an uncompromising artist with a moral high ground for his political dissidence and as an ineluctable self-allegorization for the director and his relationship with the state.

By valorizing the virtue of sacrificial death, the artist-intellectual places himself in a feminized position vis-à-vis the state. However, precisely because this feminized space is imbued, in both artistic and political terms, with the virtues of chastity, purity, and integrity, it occupies a discursive high ground that shores up the moral bankruptcy of the state. Read in this vein, *Farewell* invites a rethinking on femininity and transvestism, on how these tropes for homosexual representation can be used as a transforming force, not despite, but because of, their feminized position. The film therefore privileges art and aesthetics over politics and underscores vulgarity as another form, if not a more destructive form, of violence. The appreciation of Beijing opera by Yuan and the Japanese compares favorably with the vulgarity displayed by both the Nationalist and communist soldiers. Dieyi's sacrificial death can be seen at once as transcending politics and as an indictment of the different vulgar forms of politics that have left no room for artistic practice. When we bear in mind that art is traditionally associated with *yin* and politics with *yang* (Silbergeld 1999, 112), in the film the feminine is clearly privileged over the masculine.

Released in 1993 (several years after the June 1989 Tiananmen incident), the film can be read as a critique on the current political scene through its critique of the "unending, vice-like grip of revolutionary politics in earlier decades" (Silbergeld 1999, 96). In fact, the timing of Dieyi's suicide cannot be overemphasized. The opening and ending scenes that frame the film's narrative are set in 1977, when Xiaolou and Dieyi return to a theater to perform for themselves. In a conversation with an offstage voice, the tumultuous political events that led to the halt in Xiaolou and Dieyi's performing career are blamed on the Gang of Four. To the offstage voice's suggestion that "things are better now," Xiaolou and Dieyi's hesitant response and stutter indicate their reservations towards such optimism. For Jerome Silbergeld, while Dieyi's words ("Everything's fine now") tell us that "the horrors of this play-within-a-play are now past history," the stutter and the patent insincerity in Xiaolou's and Dieyi's responses imply that "the past is still present," that this post-Mao moment is really post-Tiananmen (ibid., 117). The Chinese censor's objection to the timing of Dieyi's suicide—"The Cultural Revolution is over. Why would he want to commit suicide?"—is revealing for its erasure of the past and enforced optimism for the future.

The feminized space of artistic practice for Dieyi (and filmmaking for Chen) is thus an indictment of the masculinist practice of politics. If filmmaking is regarded as "a form of prostitution" in China (Silbergeld 1999, 119) and if Chen's film has been accused by both nativist and Western critics as prostituting to the West, I would suggest instead that what Chen has achieved with *Farewell* is a subtle criticism of the Chinese state, on the one hand, and the positioning of himself as dissident filmmaker, on the other, through the trope of femininity. Schneider argues that from the Qu Yuan lore emerges the idea that the ill-fated official can use his literary talents as a political force, and an allegorization for Chen can be read in the following description if one replaces "literature" with "cinema."

> The linkage of politics and literature persists in the lore; however, literature is not depicted as an expression of power. Rather, it is seen as the product of frustrated political power. It becomes sublimated politics, a way of exercising power by another means. The poet-officials learn to deal similarly with the unyielding encroachments made by kings and by time upon their mortality: consistent with their ideas about the link between literature and politics, they sought the power of an immortality lodged in their literary creations. Through these, the officials thought themselves in control of all moral space. And the immortality which literature gave them guaranteed at least a share of the political space in which mortal kings were only temporary residents. (Schneider 1980, 44–45)

As the endurance and endearment of the Qu Yuan lore attests, feminine sacrifice, especially for a masculine cause situated at the apex of political power, remains a popular trope for the real or imagined relationship between the artist-intellectual and the state. Seventeenth- and eighteenth-century Chinese writers assessed Qu Yuan's suicide "as the result of his conscious search for a meaningful death. It was not that he took life lightly, but that he used his own death as an instrument to arouse his lord to the political truth" (*yi si wu jun;* Schneider 1980, 79). However, in the valorization of the virtue of sacrifice, what other virtues are inadvertently sacrificed?

While I do not wish to deny the violence of the political system against which Chinese artists and intellectuals have struggled (and continue to struggle), I want to highlight the assumptions that often go unchallenged in the type of (over)familiar construction of the relationship between the state and its artist-intellectuals delineated above. In this configuration, the artist-intellectual is imbued with the moral high ground and is seen as a beacon of truth; hence the intellectual's duty of "speaking truth to power" (Said 1994, chapter 5). However, the mythology of truth and the moral authority of the artist-intellectual are left unquestioned. In the Chinese context, the artist-intellectual's obligation even goes as far as to demand death in order "to arouse his lord to the political truth." However, what does one make of the economy of sacrificial death or suicide and the self-aggrandizing propensity to martyrdom of the artist-intellectual? While death is not to be feared, as the moral authority and artistic creation of the artist-intellectual may be endowed with the virtue of immortality, which will outlast the immoral political system, does not the quest for immortality and its underlying trope of hero(ine) worship belie a different desire for (absolute) power? If feminine sacrificial death is indeed the only viable option open to the artist-intellectual's struggle with the state, is this mode of thinking not premised upon a logic of violence that invariably entails the eradication of the self?

While Dieyi's adherence to the submissive discursive position of the concubine predetermines the powerless negotiation of his homosexuality, suicide as his final act of choice is but a confirmation of his loyalty to, and falls within the praxis of, his role as the concubine. Situating Dieyi's suicide in the discourse of the *lienü*, Lau notes that "in the original novel, written by a woman, there is no heroic death of any kind. For both characters [Dieyi and Xiaolou] life simply goes on in banality. It seems that the male fantasy, ideologized through thousands of years of popular Confucianism, still grips the imagination of a contemporary post-socialist artist" (1995, 24).[15] The valorization of the feminine, after all, may be a masculinist construction that overdetermines the imperative of sacrificial death by the feminized. However, the more interesting question for me is the choice between (if not opposition of) heroic death in the film and banal living in the original versions.[16] In contradistinction to the popular use of femininity as a trope for heroic sacrifice, I argue that the virtue being sacrificed in Chen's film is precisely the possibility of femininity as a trope for banality.

Within the logic of both the *lienü* tradition and the Qu Yuan lore, it is certainly more noble, but arguably also easier, to choose death than to lead a banal life. Locating the Qu Yuan lore in the early Republican period, Schneider argues that in periods of great national distress, suicide was a prominent mode of political protest, and the "melancholy figure" of Qu Yuan "helped to justify if not inspire the act of self-destruction" (1980, 93). Identifying this period as "an epoch with an insatiable appetite for heroes," Schneider notes that one of the two popular understandings of Qu Yuan during the first half of the twentieth century was of a radically individualist public hero as sacrificial victim, "as the superman whose genius bore sympathy for the masses, but nevertheless conflicted with and was ultimately crushed by them" (ibid., 87, 89).[17] While deploying the feminine trope of sacrifice, I would argue that the gesture of suicide, indeed the effect of suicide—becoming a hero and a superman—is masculinist, firmly situating itself in the public realm of nationhood, politics, and the collective good.

However, there existed in the same period another kind of writing, an *écriture féminine* (feminine writing), which focused on the banal, on details, and on the everyday. A prime example is Zhang Ailing (Eileen Chang), who in an essay posits a very different relationship to writing:

> I have noticed that those involved in literature often emphasize that which is active and exciting in human life and ignore that which is stable and calm. Actually the latter is the foundation of the former. It is as if they emphasize the struggles of life but ignore the harmony. Actually people struggle so they can obtain harmony.
>
> Emphasizing the active, exciting parts of human life gives something of a superhuman flavor. Superhumans are born only in certain eras, but the stable in human life has a flavor of eternity. Even though this calm stability is often incomplete and must be broken every now and then, it is still eternal. It exists in all eras. It is the spirit of humanity, and we can also say it is *the nature of women*. (1996, 436–437; emphasis mine)[18]

For Zhang, who claims in another essay that she does not know how to write stories about the proletariat (1984, 124), the emphasis on active struggle belies a masculinist superhuman instinct, which is set against a yearning for stability and harmony that she identifies as "the nature of women." The kind of writing proposed by Zhang, with its emphasis on "ordinary, weak people without the strength of heroes" but who are nonetheless "better than heroes in representing the totality of this era" (1996, 438), is a form of *écriture féminine* that has been marginalized in twentieth-century China, especially after 1949, as evidenced by the different reception of Zhang's works across the Taiwan Straits and her precarious position in PRC literary historiography.[19] The propensity to valorize the heroic and reject the banal, I would argue, underpins Chen's insistence on changing the story's ending so that Dieyi must die; it echoes a twentieth-century understanding of Qu Yuan in a "Nietzscheian sense of self," with sacrifice being "an expression of the perennial struggle between genius and vulgarity" (Schneider 1980, 106, 107).

In her study of femininity-as-detail, Rey Chow argues that the tension with the "historical" that Zhang Ailing's writings produce "offers us an alternative approach to history by resisting the lures of monumental structures of feeling" (1991, 120). Katherine Carlitz notes that the virtuous woman was "an icon of orthodoxy," invoked "by both men and women confronting invasion or dynastic fall, but at times of lesser stress or moment, she could be packaged for a variety of other ends," including "ethics as entertainment" (1991, 141, 118). For me, Chen Kaige's use of femininity-as-sacrifice in *Farewell* seems to be caught between a grand gesture towards history and orthodoxy as entertainment. Chen was baptized by the experience of the Cultural Revolution; his early film career developed in the milieu of the "cultural fever" *(wenhua re)* of the 1980s, which shared with the May Fourth period an "obsession with China" (Hsia 1971) and invariably a concomitant obsession with the role of the artist-intellectual and his/her relationship with the state. Such "monumental structures of feeling," however, were increasingly unpopular by the time of the film's making in 1993, when a general commercialization of culture swept across China to the extent that orthodoxy such as Mao's iconography was marketed as kitsch entertainment. The debate about the role of artist-intellectuals during the 1990s was whether they should "go commercial" *(xiahai)*. The use of Dieyi's femininity as sacrificial death, therefore, can be seen as a nostalgia for a lost era, when monumental structures of feeling were highly valued and the role of the artist-intellectual vis-à-vis the state, albeit feminized and submissive, at least had the paradoxical potential to become heroic and super(hu)man through suicide.

Citing Silverman's above-mentioned book in her reading of *Farewell*, Larson argues that the film "stages a symbolically feminized consciousness that is an attribute of a man who already 'knows' of lack and is completely possessed by his marginalization" and suggests that when "Chinese film is positioned within the transnational and transcultural market, any innocent notion of cultural representation immediately becomes simplistic and reductionist and reinforces the consumerist commodification of culture" (1997, 343). While Larson is more concerned with Chen's "archetypical feminine position" (ibid., 333) in the global film economy, my focus is Chen's feminized, if increasingly marginalized, position in his own country, with Dieyi as his alter ego embodying the Silvermanian "marginalized but superaware male consciousness" (ibid., 338). After making *King of the Children* in 1987, Chen had been living in the United States, and his 1991 film, *Life on a String (Bianzou bianchang)*, had been a failure both commercially and critically. The disavowal of homosexuality in *Farewell* mirrors the position of the self-exiled artist-intellectual's relationship to his nation, where he cannot find a place in the rapidly changing, crass commercialization of culture. In valorizing one form of femininity (sacrifice) while denying another (banality), the figure of homosexuality in which femininity resides becomes the unacknowledged Other, whose potential for heralding a new kind of male consciousness via femininity is not fully realized.

East Palace, West Palace: Confession, Voyeurism, Masochism

Following films on the disabled (*Mama/Mama*, 1991), rock musicians (*Beijing Bastards/Beijing zazhong*, 1993) and the alcoholic and unemployed (*Sons/Erzi*, 1996), *Palace* can be seen as a continuation of Zhang Yuan's exploration of socially disenfranchised groups in contemporary mainland Chinese society (Berry 1998, 84). Zhang was attracted to the issue of homosexuality after reading reports that the police force had helped to round up a group of homosexuals to facilitate sociological research on AIDS. This absurd situation made Zhang "want to meet gay people . . . and find out what (if anything) is different about them" (Rayns 1996, 28). The screenplay for *Palace* is co-written by Zhang Yuan and Wang Xiaobo, a novelist who co-authored the first sociological study on male homosexuality in contemporary China with his wife, Li Yinhe.[20]

The title of the film refers to two public toilets on either side of the Forbidden Palace on the north edge of Tiananmen Square in Beijing that are popular sites for gay cruising (Berry 1998, 42). The film takes place mainly in a police station and centers on the relationship between a homosexual writer, Ah Lan (Si Han), and the policeman who interrogates him, Xiaoshi (Hu Jun). Ah Lan's confessional narrative weaves reality with fantasy, the latter appearing in the form of a Chinese opera genre, *kunqu*. Identifying with the female convict at the mercy of the male prison guard in the *kunqu* sequences, Ah Lan plays out his masochistic fantasy in reality during his interrogation by Xiaoshi, eventually seducing Xiaoshi into physical intimacy. Ah Lan's engagement with authoritarian power through the tropes of femininity, transvestism, and masochism throws open the question of "the perverse link connecting the governed and the governing" (Reynaud 1997, 33) in general and the relationship between the Chinese authorities and China's artists and intellectuals in particular.

From the outset, it should be noted that in *Palace*, the tropes of femininity and transvestism function differently from those in *Farewell*. While a Chinese opera genre is deployed in the fantasy sequences to highlight the protagonist's identification with the feminine, Ah Lan does not assume the transvestite female role either in fantasy or in real life. In contrast to Dieyi's transgender practice in *Farewell*, the female convict in Ah Lan's fantasy sequences is in fact played by a woman (as is the male prison guard). Describing a transvestite who also frequents the park where he goes cruising, Ah Lan says, "He is different from us. He never has sex with us; neither do we have sex with him." Claiming that everyone has a theme in his/her life, Ah Lan concludes that the transvestite's theme is different from "ours." This distinction is not between masculinity and femininity, as Ah Lan is effeminate in his appearance and behavior, but between femininity (in homosexuality) and transvestism. This distinction is reinforced when Ah Lan initially resists Xiaoshi's demand that he put on women's clothes, protesting that "this is not what I want." For Ah Lan, transvestism resides only in his sexual imagination, without his assuming the transvestite role, and remains merely one of his many tropes for sexual expression. By representing an effeminate homosexual who rejects transvestism, the film decouples through the figure of Ah Lan the link between femininity in homosexuality and transvestism in the popular imagination of male homosexuality.

Ah Lan's identification with the feminine begins in his early childhood, when his fondest moment of the day was for the clock to strike so that his mother would stop her sewing work to breast-feed him. In adolescence, Ah Lan identifies with a female school classmate nicknamed "Public Bus" because it was believed that anyone could get on board to have sex with her. For Ah Lan, the attraction of "Public Bus" seems to be her premature puberty and presumed promiscuity, as her sexual activity and access to men are both desirable to him. In fact, "Public Bus" unwittingly plays an instrumental role in Ah Lan's first homosexual experience. During the interrogation, Ah Lan recalls how he and a male classmate became aroused after fantasizing about their female classmates, especially "Public Bus." With Ah Lan proclaiming that he is a woman and also a "Public Bus," the boys ended up in physical intimacy. Here femininity is used to circumvent the taboo of homosexuality, and it foreshadows Ah Lan's submission to Xiaoshi's enforced transvestism at the end of the film.

Unlike Dieyi, who is circumscribed by his circumstances in his homosexual expression, Ah Lan's manifold homosexual experiences and his active seeking out of the policeman attest to his agency vis-à-vis sexual identity and expression. Ah Lan's ability to construct a personal history in the confessional mode, flavored with scenes of sexual fantasy, reflects a subjectivity that has negotiated between the self, the sexual, and the criminal. This formulation appears repeatedly in his confession: "The convict on death row loves the executioner; the female thief loves the prison guard; we love you. Is there any other choice?" In these parallel pairings, the "convict/thief/we" are at once female/feminized, homosexual, dominated, and masochistic, whereas the "executioner/prison guard/you" are invariably male, law enforcing, and in power. As in *Farewell*, the discursive position for a transgendered homosexual desire is a feminized one; the difference is that in *Palace*, it manifests not only as transvestism, but also as masochism, where the potential for the subversion of power relations lies.

Following a Foucauldian reading, Jeremy Tambling argues that those addressed by a confessional discourse are "made to think of themselves as autonomous subjects, responsible for their acts" (1990, 2). In *Palace*, Ah Lan claims his subjectivity in an essentialized way as he confesses to Xiaoshi that "I am a homosexual" and "I am a woman" *(woshi nüde),* even though his sexual expression is polymorphous. Seducing Xiaoshi with his sexual imagination, Ah Lan says, "I can be a goddess, or I can be a slut; I can be a man, or I can be a woman; I can do anything; I can be anybody. You can do anything to me, especially you." Echoing the notion of gender performance, Ah Lan's sexual identity is fluid, shifting among values, genders, appearances, and corporeality. This fluidity allows Ah Lan to submit to Xiaoshi's demand that he put on women's clothes and is also instrumental in subverting the power relation between them.

Confession is an act that not only invariably involves two parties—the confessant and the confessor—but also highlights an unequal power relation, as it presupposes an "authority who requires the confession" (Foucault 1990, 61). Tracing the practice of confession from its origin in religious penance through the loss of its ritualistic and exclusive localization to its new position in a series of modern-day relationships, Michel Foucault recounts how the confessional mode now functions, privileging sex as a theme: "It is no longer a question simply of saying what was done— the sexual act—and how it was done; but of reconstructing, in and around the act, the thoughts that recapitulated it, the obsessions that accompanied it, the images, desires, modulations, and quality of the pleasure that animated it. For the first time no doubt, a society has taken upon itself to solicit and hear the imparting of individual pleasures" (ibid., 63).

Foucault's account reveals the complicit role of the confessor in soliciting information on forbidden sexual desire. As the confessor/policeman's duty in *Palace* is to solicit such information in the name of law and order, voyeurism becomes an inextricable part of his job, if not his subjectivity. However, the confessional practice is compounded in the film because it is Ah Lan who deliberately plays himself into the hands of the policeman. The power relation is thus reversed since the confession does not originate as a requirement by an authority, but rather it is the confessant who demands that his secret pleasures be solicited, imparted, and recorded by the confessor/policeman. Meanwhile, Xiaoshi is shown to have more than a passing interest in homosexuality beyond the call of his duty. In their first encounter Xiaoshi singles out Ah Lan from the group of homosexuals rounded up in a police raid in the park and asks him if he is only passing by, clearly intending to let him off, a favor that Ah Lan turns down. Taking Ah Lan alone to the police station, Xiaoshi is surprised when Ah Lan kisses him and runs off. Ah Lan later sends Xiaoshi a notebook with the words, "To my love—Ah Lan." Xiaoshi's voyeurism is highlighted when he then seeks out Ah Lan in the park and, discovering Ah Lan engaging in physical intimacy with another man, he observes for a moment before shining the torch on them. The phallic torch and penetrating light accentuate Xiaoshi's voyeuristic intrusion, and Ah Lan does not run away this time. Instead, in his subsequent confession Ah Lan turns Xiaoshi into an object of his masochistic imagination and eventually seduces him into sexual intimacy.

In his reading of the story "Venus in Furs," by Leopold von Sacher-Masoch (1836–1895), from whom the term "masochism" was derived (Stewart 1995, 162, 220), Gilles Deleuze highlights the contractual nature in masochistic practices. According to Deleuze, it is the masochist who is "in search of a torturer and who needs to educate, persuade and conclude an alliance with the torturer in order to realize the strangest of schemes" (Deleuze and von Sacher-Masoch 1991, 20). Ah Lan's masochistic sexual imagination, however, does not make Xiaoshi sadistic by inference. Questioning the very concept of an entity known as sadomasochism, Deleuze argues that "a genuine sadist could never tolerate a masochistic victim" and "neither would the masochist tolerate a truly sadistic torturer" (ibid., 13, 40–41). Rather, the policeman functions merely as an "element" in Ah Lan's sexual economy in Deleuzean terms, as Xiaoshi is "*in* the masochistic situation," playing "an integral part in it, a realization of the masochistic fantasy" (ibid., 41–42; emphasis in original). Indeed, Ah Lan's childhood fantasy was to be arrested by a policeman: when his mother threatened him with the police if he misbehaved, Ah Lan could not wait for one to turn up to arrest him. During the interrogation, Ah Lan clearly enjoys being handcuffed and slapped by Xiaoshi. Xiaoshi, on the other hand, is not totally unaware of his role in Ah Lan's sexual imagination. When Ah Lan resists Xiaoshi's attempt to unlock his handcuffs, Xiaoshi says, "Go buy yourself a pair [of handcuffs] if you fancy; this is public property." Far from being sadistic, Xiaoshi's treatment of Ah Lan shows that he is conscious of the complicit role he is playing in the interrogation/confession process. The film thus provides a variation to Deleuze's definition of masochism because while the relationship between Ah Lan and Xiaoshi is not explicitly contractual, the policeman unwittingly concludes Ah Lan's unilateral "alliance" by merely performing his duty.

In Deleuze's construction, the masochist needs to educate and persuade the torturer into a sexual alliance. In *Palace*, however, it is the torturer who displays a voyeuristic eagerness to learn from the masochist. Xiaoshi's complicity in Ah Lan's confessional process is underlined as he passes comments, seeks clarification, and selects materials to be put on record, betraying his curiosity about a sexuality that he is supposed to discipline and punish. When Ah Lan relates his experiences of picking up men for sex, Xiaoshi asks how he knows that they are "of a kind." When Ah Lan sings praises about a man's hands, Xiaoshi participates by asking if they are small and gentle. In fact, it is Xiaoshi who initiates physical contact with Ah Lan during the interrogation. When Ah Lan comments that he would like to have the hands of his sexual trick, Xiaoshi examines Ah Lan's hands with his handcuffs. When Ah Lan describes the pleasure he derives from being slapped, Xiaoshi slaps him gently and asks, "Is this the way?" In participating in role playing, Xiaoshi has unwittingly reenacted episodes in Ah Lan's masochistic sexual imagination by assuming the part of the torturer.

Because the confessor plays the passive role of listening, he is directed by the confessant's narrative rather than being in command of the situation. This is most clearly illustrated when Ah Lan, instead of answering Xiaoshi's questions, tells his own story. Weaving fantasy with reality, Ah Lan's confession can be seen, like autobiography, as a kind of "self-fashioning" that shifts between fact and fiction (Tambling 1990, 9).[21] While the crosscuts between the flashback and fantasy sequences are unambiguously executed, one can never be sure when fantasy overlaps with reality in Ah Lan's confession or if indeed it can not all have been made up, given Ah Lan's profession as a novelist.[22] If confession is a process for "telling the truth of sex which [is] geared to a form of knowledge-power" (Foucault 1990, 58) that privileges the confessor, what *Palace* shows is a reversal of the power relation in which the confessant dictates the process so that the truth about sex may never be known. After all, it is the confessant who holds the key to the secret knowledge of prohibited sex and thus the power to disclose it or do otherwise. The confessor may have the authority to demand a confession, but the film clearly demonstrates that it is the confessant who can twist the knowledge-power nexus to his advantage.

Criminality, Captivity, and the Genet Connection

In *Palace*, Ah Lan's criminality is predetermined because of his homosexuality. Since police raids are regularly carried out in the park, entering this public space with the intention of cruising for sex already constitutes the homosexual as a criminal susceptible to the enforcement of law and order by the policeman. Because of its overt coupling of homosexuality with criminality, *Palace* has invited comparisons with the work of the French playwright and novelist Jean Genet (1910–1986), especially his only film, *Un Chant d'amour* (1950). Indeed, it has been argued that "it is almost impossible *not* to think of Genet when seeing crime and homosexuality combined in films" (Giles 2002, 63; emphasis in original). The themes of Genet's work and life, as spelled out in his autobiographical novel, *The Thief's Journal*, are "betrayal, theft and homosexuality" (1967, 141). Like Ah Lan, who is constituted as a criminal because of his homosexuality, Genet's attitude towards crime is to embrace it.[23] Not only was he "*hot* for crime," Genet was also determined to aggravate his condition of being abandoned by his family "by a preference for boys, and this preference by theft, and theft by crime or a complacent attitude in regard to crime" (ibid., 8, 71; emphasis in original). The title of a section in Jean-Paul Sartre's study of Genet quotes from the criminal's words: "I decided to be what crime made of me" (Sartre 1988, 59). Ah Lan shares Genet's embracing of his homosexual-criminal identity, his defiant attitude towards crime, and the criminal's masochistic love for law-enforcing policemen.

Set in a prison, *Un Chant d'amour* portrays a voyeuristic prison guard who peeps into the inmates' cells and, through fantasy sequences, idealizes homosexual love among the inmates.[24] (The enclosed setting, claustrophobic ambience, and coupling of criminality with homosexuality are also found in Rainer Werner Fassbinder's film adaptation of Genet's novel *Querelle*.)[25] Richard Dyer argues that because Genet's name "evokes a flavour, a set of images, a world," one does not have to read his work to know what it means when something is described as Genetesque (1990, 47). While Zhang Yuan might not have heard of Genet (Rayns 1996, 5; Berry 1998, 84), *Palace* nonetheless exhibits a Genetesque sensibility, and *Un Chant d'amour* and *Palace* have in common a voyeuristic, law-enforcing policeman or prison guard who is fascinated by the homosexual-criminal. As Dyer argues, the voyeur is "unable to express his desire except through violence" in order to "get the 'little contact' his role denies him" (1990, 74, 84). In *Un Chant d'amour* the prison guard whips an inmate and puts a gun in his mouth because these are the only ways in which he can establish physical contact with the inmate. In *Palace*, Xiaoshi's violence towards Ah Lan is expressed in the form of enforced transvestism so that he can become physically intimate with the criminal at the end of the film.

Apt for the theme of criminality, the trope of captivity is deployed in *Palace* to underscore the subversion of the power relation between Xiaoshi and Ah Lan. When Ah Lan is brought to the police station, he is held

captive in a room, while Xiaoshi circles the corridor surrounding the building and watches Ah Lan through the windows, the circling movement
being in line with "the power-play and surveillance that is the film's general ambiance" (Berry 1998, 86). After his release, Ah Lan turns into the
voyeur by circling the corridor and looking at Xiaoshi. When Ah Lan puts
on women's clothes and makeup at Xiaoshi's demand, the film suggests a
link between Ah Lan's transvestism and feminine imagination by crosscutting it with a *kunqu* fantasy sequence in which the female convict is
held in a gigantic birdcage while the prison guard circles it, looking at her
passionately. When Xiaoshi returns to face a transvestite Ah Lan, he finds
himself turning into a captive in the labyrinth of Ah Lan's sexual imagination, as Ah Lan circles him repeatedly while delivering a hypnotic confession expressing his love, making physical contact throughout by lean-
ing on Xiaoshi's back, touching his shoulders, looking at him passionately,
caressing his face, and hugging his back. Having submitted to Xiaoshi's
demand for him to dress as a woman, Ah Lan asks Xiaoshi, "I love you.
Why don't you love me? I know what you're thinking. Actually, am I only
a woman?" Ah Lan's last question not only attests to his blurring of gender boundaries in his own sexual imagination and identity construction,
but also challenges these very notions held by Xiaoshi.

At the end of the film, Ah Lan fulfills his desire to be sexually intimate
with Xiaoshi. Arriving at a derelict building Ah Lan had previously used
for his sexual encounters, Xiaoshi fully plays, albeit unknowingly, the part
of Ah Lan's former sex partners as he slaps, strips, and insults him. When
Xiaoshi takes a hose and showers Ah Lan with water, the scene recalls the
practice of the "golden shower" in the gay sadomasochistic (S/M) subculture, in which one partner urinates on another. Held at waist level by
Xiaoshi, the hose droops in an explicitly phallic manner. Kneeling in front
of Xiaoshi, Ah Lan receives the water passionately with his hands and
face. Though their physical intimacy does not lead to copulation, the
highly symbolic S/M sex is sufficiently suggestive. What begins as the captivity of a homosexual-criminal who is to be released on the condition of
confession ends with the captivity of the sexually repressed policeman
whose release is conditional upon his participation in an S/M experience.
Through the overnight confession/interrogation, Ah Lan has not only
lured Xiaoshi into physical intimacy, but has also made Xiaoshi question
his own sexuality. In the "golden shower" scene, Xiaoshi looks stunned
when Ah Lan asks him, "You have questioned me on everything. Why
don't you question yourself?" As Xiaoshi leaves the building, Ah Lan's
expression is one of exasperated contentment. Rather than seeing Xiao-

shi's final departure as a confirmation of his repressed homosexual desire, the film suggests that it may be the beginning of his acknowledgement of his sexuality by ending with Ah Lan looking out to the sunrise.

The Uses of Allegory

Femininity is thus used in *Palace* to subvert the relationship between the homosexual-criminal and the policeman via the tropes of transvestism and masochism and, allegorically, the relationship between the artist-intellectual and the state. For Chris Berry, Zhang's films are concerned with "access to public discourse" in China, a problematic that is not only shared by the underground director "with gay men and the other Chinese social minorities he represents in his work," but is also "generalized across Chinese society today" (1998, 85). Arguing that some spaces of performance have a greater social visibility and hence a greater power to disseminate more widely than others, Berry suggests that Butler's insights into performativity's potential need to be grounded "both socially and historically if we are to understand how it does not simply smuggle the liberal free subject back into the picture but instead inscribes agency as regulated and deployed differentially" (ibid., 87). Berry reads *Palace* in an allegorically political vein by emphasizing not only the way in which Ah Lan's performativity "attempts to reconstruct and resignify his own identity differently," but also how that attempt "depends on the ability to seek out and obtain access to public space, public discourse and public record, however unpromising the particular circumstances might seem" (ibid., 87–88). Quoting examples of homosexual oppression in China provided by the director (ibid., 86), Berry highlights the oppressive nature of the Chinese regime and the unenviable position in which homosexuals in China find themselves.

Similarly concerned with the issue of access to public discourse by the gay subaltern, Shuqin Cui considers that the film's significance lies not so much in the gay image brought to the screen, but in "the construction of a gay discourse that the mainstream considers subversive" and "how a cinematic construction subverts hegemonic discourse and brings the gay subculture into cinematic representation and public discussion" (2005, 106). However, as Zhang's film is officially banned and denied public screening in China, any circulation or discussion of the film remains unofficial and underground, and the extent to which it "subverts hegemonic discourse" or brings gay subculture into "public discussion" is questionable. On the other hand, while I agree with Berry that the visibility of homosexuals in China continues to be constricted by the regime, the making of *Palace* and other underground films on homosexuality nevertheless attests to the existence, however interstitial and precarious, of both public and private spaces for the negotiation of homosexuality.

I suggest that the censorious situation in China forces us to rethink not only the definition of the public sphere, but also how the relationship between the so-called mainstream or hegemonic culture and the subaltern may be configured differently. Precisely because the subject cannot be assumed to be liberal or free and has to be recognized as regulated and deployed differentially, the *mode* of speech, rather than the actual content, becomes paramount. Tracing the historical use and abuse of allegory in Chinese discourse, Silbergeld notes that the "pervasive control of public speech and constraints on political thought that led to such literary subtlety and indirection, and to such 'abuse' of original texts, is not exclusively old or new. Rather, it unites the past with the present" (1999, 109). Arguing that there is a "continuing *need* for allegory" in China today (ibid., 110; emphasis in original), Silbergeld explicates how allegory works:

> As with deconstructive discourse, allegory stimulates "reading" but allows no *particular* reading, distributing authorship among the audience. As such, it remains the best rhetorical antidote to the intended ideological monopoly of totalitarian government. In this context, the weakness of allegory—the uncertainty of how to read it—becomes a strength. . . . Allegory, therefore, by any name, is a well-conditioned cultural response that no politically sensitive Chinese artist, visual or textual, modern or traditional in period, has needed to think too much about in order to use. (ibid., 111; emphasis in original)

When asked why he continues to make films despite an official ban, Zhang Yuan replies, "That's quite natural. I love my country and I love the Party, just like A[h] Lan in my film loves that policeman" (Berry 1998, 84). While Zhang's tone may have been sardonic, he implies, like Qu Yuan, that loyalty and dissent are not mutually exclusive values. More important, he highlights the feminized, submissive position from which he practices his filmmaking, and until and unless the political reality changes in China, he cannot but speak allegorically, as allegory takes its impetus from "the need to negotiate from a position of inferior authority" (Silbergeld 1999, 111). This structurally inferior position is defined in terms of power, but the artist-intellectual inspired by the lore of Qu Yuan assumes that he/she possesses the "legitimization of a challenge to authority on the grounds of a higher and more complete authority" (Schneider 1980, 5). This is arguably the premise that has sustained the uses of allegory throughout the centuries.

In *Palace,* Ah Lan's strategy of engaging the necessarily evil power of the state is not in the active, combative mode but in the passive, feminine, transgendered, and masochistic forms. As in the case of *Farewell,* this has proved problematic in terms of the politics of representation. Claiming that Ah Lan is far from being a positive image of a contemporary Beijing gay man, Berry suggests that if "the park is a heterotopic representation of the People's Republic itself then the film seems to imply that in a police state masochism is the only surefire road to fulfilment" (2000b, 192, 193). Similarly, seeing the film as freeing "the gay man from the closet but not, however, from the stereotype of a submissive figure," Shuqin Cui argues that positioning the gay character as passive "prevents the film from acknowledging a true gay identity" and concludes that "gay identities and homosexual issues in China remain at a rudimentary level in cinematic representation" (2005, 109, 110). I have expressed above in the chapter my reservations about discourses on positive and true gay representations and their teleological tendencies, and such responses serve as a reminder of Silverman's concern in raising the question about the place of femininity within male homosexuality. This, for me, reveals more about the context and politics in which these cinematic representations are situated than about the representations themselves, and I would suggest that the concomitant politics needs to be interrogated alongside the representations.

Finally, I would suggest that a more radical reading of *Palace* is in the positive light of its ending, in which the state, represented by the policeman, has the potential of acknowledging both the existence of the homosexual-criminal Other and its own repressed desire, for it is precisely this power relation that has been subverted in the film. The individual represented by the homosexual is always-already enlightened and fully conscious of his sexuality, modes of sexual imagination, and object of desire. It is the never-ever state, represented by the policeman, that awaits enlightenment, still in denial with regard to issues of sexuality and the meaning for its agents. If the police raid of homosexuals in the film is deployed to implicate a wider oppression in Chinese society in terms of individual freedom, the film's message is unequivocally clear: femininity expressed as transvestism and masochism can be a transforming and potentially subversive force. Moreover, both *Farewell* and *Palace* affirm that femininity is not biologically determined and exclusive to women; rather, femininity in homosexuality may indeed provide a model for the reconfiguration of power relations not just in terms of gender and sexuality, but also in the sociopolitical realms.

Travelling Sexualities

Wong Kar-wai's *Happy Together*

> How do different populations, classes and genders travel?
> What kinds of knowledges, stories, and theories do they
> produce?
>
> —JAMES CLIFFORD, "Notes on Travel and Theory"

Wong Kar-wai is undoubtedly the most hip director in contemporary Chinese cinemas and enjoys a cult following worldwide.[1] His debut film, *As Tears Go By* (*Wangjiao Kamen*, also known as *Rexue nan'er*, 1988), brought him critical attention in Hong Kong, but it was his subsequent films such as *Days of Being Wild* (*A Fei zhengzhuan*, 1990), *Ashes of Time* (*Dongxie Xidu* 1994), *Chungking Express* (*Chongqing senlin*, 1994), and *Fallen Angels* (*Duoluo tianshi*, 1995) that propelled him to international status. *In the Mood for Love* (*Huayang nianhua*, 2000) won Tony Leung Chiu-wai the best actor award at the Cannes Film Festival. Wong's latest film was the long-awaited *2046*, which was released in 2004. My focus in this chapter is his 1997 film, *Happy Together*, which won him the best director award at Cannes.

Shot in Argentina, geographically the antipodes of Hong Kong, *Happy Together* is a film simultaneously about home and being away from home. The film problematizes the intertwining relationship between sexuality, home, nation, and space. In this chapter, I propose to examine the trope of travel and how sexuality is negotiated vis-à-vis the diasporic identities of the protagonists. I want to raise the following questions: What does it mean to negotiate sexuality in a diasporic space as opposed to doing so at home? In what ways are the material conditions of travel and diaspora related to the figure of homosexuality in these representations? Or, to adapt James Clifford's questions in the epigraph above, how do different sexualities travel, and what kinds of representations do they produce? What is the relationship between the trope of travel, the locales of home and away, and sexuality?

Happy Together has been described as belonging to "the genre of the 'road movie' where the travel metaphor becomes a search for 'home' and 'identity' through the three male protagonists' (individual and collective) quests" (Yue 2000, 254). For Iain Chambers, to travel "implies movement between fixed positions, a site of departure, a point of arrival, the knowledge of an itinerary. It also intimates an eventual return, a potential homecoming" (1994, 5). Many discourses of travel and diaspora are embedded in a dialectic relationship with the notion of home as the origin of journeys to which one can eventually return from one's journeys. It is thus appropriate that I begin my discussion by situating *Happy Together* in the context of the home, which is Hong Kong and its return to the PRC on July 1, 1997.

Deviance and Defiance: Happy Together?

Inspired by Manuel Puig's novel *The Buenos Aires Affair, Happy Together* traces the troubled relationship between Ho Po-wing (the late Leslie Cheung Kwok-wing; henceforth Po-wing) and Lai Yiu-fai (Tony Leung; henceforth Fai).[2] The film is narrated mainly from Fai's point of view via voice-over, a trademark of Wong's films. In the opening sequence, the couple is in a hotel room, where Po-wing suggests to Fai that they start over. An explicit sex scene between the couple follows, accompanied by Fai's voice-over: "'Let's start over'—these are Ho Po-wing's favorite words. I admit these words are a killer for me. We've been together for a long time, and we'd broken up before in the process. But I don't know why each time I hear him utter these words to me, I'll be back with him again. Because of wanting to start over, I left Hong Kong with him. As we travelled, we ended up in Argentina."[3] The opening sex scene is almost a shock tactic towards the audience, as there are subsequently no more sex scenes between the couple, and none of the other sex scenes in *Happy Together* is quite as explicit. It recalls Jean-Jacques Beineix's 1986 film, *Betty Blue: 37°2 le matin,* which also features an opening sex scene (albeit heterosexual in this case) accompanied by the voice-over of the male protagonist, Zorg: "I have known Betty for a week. We made love every night. The forecast was for storms." The voice-over in both films provides an account of the history of the relationships between the protagonists.

The trope of travel is highlighted right from the start of *Happy Together:* inspired by a picture of the Iguazu Falls on a lampshade that Po-wing bought when the couple first arrived in Argentina, the couple embarks on a journey to the falls. Zorg's last sentence above also applies to the couple in *Happy Together* as, following the opening sex scene, the film shows their stormy relationship: they quarrel as they lose their way on the trip to the Iguazu Falls, and Po-wing suggests they break up and start over if they meet again. Back in Buenos Aires, Fai works as a door-man at a tango bar, whereas Po-wing survives by hustling. The couple is reunited after Po-wing has been severely beaten up by one of his sex tricks. Ministering to Po-wing's injury but keeping his passport, Fai regards Po-wing's recovery period as their happiest time together. During this period, Fai spots the man responsible for Po-wing's injury and hits him with a bottle, thus losing his job at the tango bar. He subsequently works in a kitchen at a Chinese restaurant with a young man from Taiwan, Chang (Chang Chen). Fai and Po-wing break up again after the latter has recov-ered. Chang quits his job to travel to Ushuaia before returning to Taiwan. Fai starts a new job at an abattoir. Saving enough money, Fai travels to the Iguazu Falls. Po-wing moves into the apartment previously occupied by Fai, where Fai has left Po-wing's passport. Fai returns to Hong Kong but stops over en route in Taipei in search of Chang.

In her analysis of *Happy Together*, Rey Chow consciously departs from the tendency, whenever a non-Western work is being analyzed, "to affix a kind of reflectionist value by way of geopolitical realism—so that a film made in Hong Kong around 1997, for instance, would invariably be approached as having something to do with the factographic 'reality' of Hong Kong's return to the People's Republic of China" (1999, 32). While I sympathize with Chow's desire to "counter the analytically reductionist readings, ubiquitous inside and outside the academy" (ibid.), I agree with Helen Hok-sze Leung, who, in her response to Chow's stance, argues that "to approach the film text as though it were hermetically sealed from the historic moment of its production also seems to me an untenable tactic" (2001, 446–447n27).[4] Drawing references from the film's diegesis, I will illustrate below why a reading of *Happy Together* cannot be totally divorced from the geopolitical context of 1997. One could in fact argue that 1997 serves as the main impetus for the production of the film.

For Ackbar Abbas, July 1, 1997, "is not just a terminal date that falls sometime in the future" but, for the time leading up to it, also serves as "an ever-present irritant, a provocation, and a catalyst for change" (1997, 22). Making a film about "deviant" sexuality immediately before Hong Kong's handover to a regime (in)famous for its high-handed treatment of homo-sexuals can be seen as an act of defiance. While authorial intention should not be taken simply at face value, it is nonetheless noteworthy that Wong reportedly said he was making *Happy Together* because Hong Kong needed a "real gay film" before 1997 (Liu Zeyuan 1997, 33).[5] Billed as "A Story about Reunion" in one version of the film's posters, the film's title, *Happy*

Together, works as an ironic suggestion—wishful thinking even?—that Hong Kong might be able to live happily together with its new mainland Chinese master. As Jeremy Tambling proposes, read as two interrogatives—Happy? Together?—the film's title also constitutes "an oxymoron," raising the question of whether happiness and togetherness are not mutually exclusive (2003, 77).

Indeed, the choice of location for the film cannot be unintentional. As Hong Kong's antipodes, Argentina provides a direct albeit unseen fast track between the two locales through the center of the earth, underlining the dialectic relationship between home and the diasporic space.[6] The opening credits are set against a glaringly bright red background, a color closely associated with communist China. Inserted in between the credits is a close-up of Po-wing's and Fai's Hong Kong passports (issued by the British authorities) being stamped by the Argentine customs officer. The disappearance of Hong Kong from the film's narrative, the impending change in its political status, and the tropes of travel and diaspora are simultaneously highlighted in this brief sequence. Hong Kong appears in the film only towards the end, when Fai wonders what Hong Kong might look like from Argentina, whereupon a montage of Hong Kong's cityscapes is shown upside down, literalizing the antipodal relationship between the two locales.

Happy Together poses a defiant challenge to China's claim to Hong Kong by introducing the factor of Taiwan, an antagonistic regime regarded as a renegade province by the PRC government. As Audrey Yue argues, "as either one or the other (of the other China), Taiwan can be considered as the third space that disrupts the reunification between Hong Kong and the Mainland" (2000, 260). Towards the end of the film, as noted, Fai transits at Taipei before returning to Hong Kong. The first scene in Taiwan—in a hotel room where Fai wakes up, specifically dated February 20, 1997—shows a televised news report of the death of Deng Xiaoping, China's then paramount leader who had expressed his wish to witness Hong Kong's return to China.[7] Taiwan's rebel status is reinforced as it is chosen as the site at which the denial of Deng's wish is announced. More important, the film does not end in Hong Kong but in Taipei, where the third protagonist, Chang, provides a possibility of the promise of "happy together" for Fai, suggesting that Taiwan might become Fai's preferred home over China-ruled Hong Kong. In "A Story about Reunion," *Happy Together* deliberately designates Fai's final destination not as Hong Kong but instead as Taiwan, where a militant independence movement rejects Taiwan's reunification with China.

Fai and His Friends: The Fassbinder Connection

Wong's above-mentioned comment on making a *real* gay film before 1997 must be understood in the context of Hong Kong cinema. Though many Hong Kong films have featured homosexual characters or touched upon the theme of homosexuality before Wong's *Happy Together,* most of these are slapstick comedies littered with gay stereotypes that do not deal with the issue of homosexuality in a serious manner. While what is a (real) gay film is open to definition and debate, *Happy Together* is arguably the first Hong Kong film that does not pathologize or caricature its homosexual protagonists but treats them as rounded characters worthy of engagement and empathy; nor does its representation aim to problematize homosexuality as a theme. As Tambling argues, *"Happy Together* contains no discussions of homosexuality whatsoever, nor any moments which imply that the film is trying to argue homosexuality as 'natural' or to place it in any context. It makes no attempt to work, therefore, as a 'gay' film. Like the characters who seem to have come from nowhere, insofar as they have lack [*sic*] histories, homosexuality is there but it is not spoken about" (2003, 21). Tambling's argument recalls Rainer Werner Fassbinder's comment on his 1974 film, *Fox and His Friends;* the comment can also be used to describe the position of Wong's *Happy Together* in the context of Hong Kong cinema: "It is certainly the first film in which the characters are homosexuals, without homosexuality being made into a problem. In films, plays or novels, if homosexuals appear, then homosexuality was the problem, or it was a comic turn. But here homosexuality is shown as completely normal, and the problem is something quite different; it's a love story, where one person exploits the love of the other person, and that's really the story I always tell" (Fassbinder 1975).

As it happens, while looking for an English (or foreign) title for the film, Wong and his crew started their brainstorming session with *Fox and His Friends* (Doyle 1997).[8] Another title suggested was *3 Amigos* (friends), the name of the bar where Fai and Chang hang out in *Happy Together.* For Tambling, the bar's name is significant for both the number and the notion of friends (2003, 55), though it must be qualified that Po-wing and Chang do not know each other in the film, thus making *3 Amigos* not as appropriate a foreign title as, for example, *Fai and His Friends.*

There is, moreover, another more significant Fassbinder connection in Wong's film: the abattoir where Fai works is reminiscent of a similar setting in Fassbinder's 1978 film, *In a Year with 13 Moons.* In the abattoir sequence in *Happy Together,* Fai pushes carcasses around (figure 4.1) and flushes the floor with a hose to wash away the blood. A shower scene in the communal bathroom of the abattoir accentuates the homoerotic flavor of Wong's film.[9] Fai's voice-over accompanying this sequence reveals that Po-wing has been in touch to ask for his passport, but Fai does not want to see him for fear that Po-wing might utter those deadly words ("Let's start over") to him. Not totally unlike the sequences in *Happy Together* and *Betty Blue,* the opening sequence of *In a Year with 13 Moons* features a sex scene, but it is more of a failed attempt at having sex: dressed as a man and having successfully cruised another man in the park, Elvira, the male-to-female transsexual protagonist, is beaten up halfway into the sexual act when the man discovers that Elvira has no penis. Like *Happy Together* and *Betty Blue,* Fassbinder's film has a voice-over recounting the protagonist's relationship with his/her lover, though this voice-over does not accompany the opening but the abattoir sequence. More important, the abattoir sequence in *In a Year with 13 Moons* also parades carcasses around (figure 4.2) and has scenes of blood being hosed away on the floor, and it is possibly where *Happy Together* drew its inspiration. The two films are clearly related on the visual, aural/narratorial, and thematic levels.

For Fassbinder, a love story is invariably about the exploitation of love, and the exploitation in *Fox and His Friends* "has to do with the social, and not the sexual, orientation of the characters" (Thomsen 1997, 183). In *Fox and His Friends,* the bourgeois son of a factory owner uses the money his proletarian male lover won in a lottery to salvage his father's ailing

FIGURE 4.1. Fai pushes carcasses around in *Happy Together.* (Copyright Block 2 Pictures/ Prémon H./Seowoo Film/Jet Tone Production, 1997)

business, only to dump his lover when the money dries up. If *Fox and His Friends* can be regarded as "a study of homosexuality and capitalism" (Shattuc 1995, 120), the social (or rather economic) condition of the protagonists is the aspect that has been neglected in most discussions of *Happy Together*.

Travelling Identities

Caren Kaplan argues that while the terms of displacement found in Euro-American critical practice rarely admit to material conditions that include modern imperialism, industrialization, and decolonialization (1996, 1), there is a tendency that the terms and tropes of travel and the metaphors and symbols used to represent displacement refer to "individualized, often elite, circumstances" (ibid., 4). For Kaplan, to question travel is to inquire into the ideological function of metaphors in discourses of displacement and to historicize the use of terms such as "sites, borders, maps, and diasporas as well as exile, nomadism, and migrancy" (ibid., 26).

Following Kaplan, I propose to examine the discursive terms vis-à-vis the diasporic identities of the protagonists in *Happy Together*. So far I have been using the term "travel" to describe the journeys the protagonists have taken from Hong Kong and Taiwan to Argentina and the terms "dias-

FIGURE 4.2. Display of carcasses in Fassbinder's *In a Year with 13 Moons*. (Copyright Tango-Film/Project Filmproduktion im Filmverlag der Autoren, 1978)

pora" and "diasporic" to denote the state or condition of their existence in the space away from home. Jana Evans Braziel and Anita Mannur concur that the term "diaspora" is often used as a catchall to speak of and for all movements, "however privileged, and for all dislocations, even symbolic ones," and hence argue that theorizations of diaspora "need not, and should not, be divorced from historical and cultural specificity" (2003, 3). It is my contention that the protagonists in *Happy Together* pose taxonomical, and thus epistemological, challenges to the trope of travel and that it is precisely the historical and cultural specificities that shore up the many discursive terms associated with diaspora that are far from clear-cut.

For example, Clifford has argued that diaspora is different from travel in that it is not temporary. It involves "dwelling, maintaining communities, having collective homes away from home (and in this it is different from exile, with its frequently individualistic focus)" (1997, 287). Clifford distinguishes travel from diaspora on the basis of temporality. However, as he has rightly asked in the context of "Fourth world [indigenous] peoples" claiming "'first-nation' sovereignty"—"How long does it take to become 'indigenous'?" (ibid., 288–289)—could we not also ask, "How long does it take for a traveller to become diasporic?" In *Happy Together,* the protagonists begin their journeys as travellers to Argentina but end up staying there for longer than intended as they have run out of money. Fai and Chang subsequently become what can be classified as (illegal) guest-workers, whereas Po-wing's economic dependence on his tricks and on Fai is even harder to define. These characters do not necessarily seek to integrate with their host country or with an existent overseas Chinese community, but as time passes, their status as travellers metamorphoses into a diasporic condition that may yet defy taxonomical classification. As Caren Kaplan notes, "The fact that the material conditions of displacement for many people blur these distinctions or that many modern subjects may participate in any number of these versions of displacement over a lifetime—never embodying any one version singly or simplistically— requires material histories of cultural production that would emphasize emergent subject positions and critical and cultural practices that are more responsive to transnational conditions" (1996, 110).

This is one of the reasons why Chow's alternative strategy of reading *Happy Together* in terms of Lacanian post-structuralism and Freudian psychoanalysis may not be any less problematic than a (possibly reductionist) geopolitical one, especially since, as Kaplan points out, dislocation is often expressed "in singular rather than collective terms, as purely psychological or aesthetic situations rather than as a result of historical circumstances" (C. Kaplan 1996, 4). While there is no suggestion that the characters in *Happy Together* are leaving Hong Kong because of the political changes about to happen in 1997 (Tambling 2003, 21), in light of the geopolitical reality it is certainly not far-fetched to see their sojourn as a participation in the collective exodus from Hong Kong, especially given that their deviant sexuality may not find favor with the new regime. This reading will add to, rather than reduce, the film's complexity, as Fai and Po-wing can be regarded at once as partly political refugees (though they have no recourse to seeking political asylum in such terms in their host country), partly sexual exiles, and partly tourists looking for a new locale to start their relationship over. As financial problems leave them stranded in Argentina, they assume new identities as illegal workers or even illegal immigrants (assuming their visas have expired), while simultaneously embodying their other diasporic identities delineated above.

In an examination of the material conditions that engender modes of travel, the issue of class inevitably surfaces on both the domestic and global levels. In his analysis of *Happy Together,* Tambling highlights the working-class background of the characters in contradistinction to the "thoroughly bourgeois" background in Ang Lee's *The Wedding Banquet* (2003, 66). While this is accurate on a micro level within the confines of Hong Kong and Taiwan, the fact that these working-class characters can afford to travel to Argentina (notwithstanding Fai's stealing of money from his boss)—and more important, that their travel is not borne out of an economic imperative to seek employment abroad—demands a reconfiguration of class status on a macro scale. That is, in a world where there are "first-world zones" in formerly "developing" countries and "third-world zones" in supposedly "first-world" nations (Braziel and Mannur 2003, 11), the working-class background of the protagonists at home should not obscure their comparatively privileged material conditions, which make their travel to Argentina—a country unquestionably lower on the global economic order than Hong Kong or Taiwan—possible in the first place, while it throws into question the usefulness of a world systems classification.

Therefore, diaspora and diasporic movement must be examined within the context of global capitalism (Braziel and Mannur 2003, 11). Tambling acknowledges that *Happy Together* responds to the power of globalization, as Taiwan has also been presented as "a place with an economic power Argentina lacks, for Taiwan has been exporting coach-loads of tourists to Buenos Aires" (2003, 63), where it is Fai's job as a doorman at Bar Sur to welcome them. While Chang distinguishes himself from these package tourists, his reasons for leaving Taiwan ("Because I'm unhappy") and for staying on in Argentina ("There's no point returning when you haven't thought things through") betray a luxury of travel that stems from a spiritual need for self-exploration rather than material poverty. To say the very least, despite their working-class background, none of the three protagonists seem to be the breadwinners on whom their families depend financially back home, and despite having to work illegally in manual labor (with the exception of Po-wing) in the diasporic space, they have been able to save enough money not only for a home-bound air ticket, but also for a visit to their chosen "holiday destinations" in Argentina before returning home. The confidence that Fai has in knowing where to locate Chang in the future, having visited the food stall run by Chang's parents in Taipei, is a confidence grounded, however unconsciously, in a sense of financial security that would engender the expression—even fruition perhaps—of his sexuality as "happy together."

As stated from the outset, many discourses of travel and diaspora problematize the relationship between home and away, with earlier models privileging "the geographical, political, cultural, and subjective spaces of the home-nation as the authentic space of belonging and civic participation, while devaluing and bastardizing the states of displacement or dislocation, rendering them inauthentic places of residence" (Braziel and Mannur 2003, 6). As *Happy Together* is one of the two films in this book (the other being *The Wedding Banquet*) whose diegeses are set outside of East Asia, its representation of diasporic sexualities travelling in Argentina cannot totally escape the problematic of home and away. As R. Radhakrishnan argues, "Diasporic subjectivity is thus necessarily double: acknowledging the imperatives of an earlier 'elsewhere' in an active and critical relationship with the cultural politics of one's present home, all within the figurality of a reciprocal displacement. 'Home' then becomes a mode of interpretive in-betweenness, as a form of accountability to more than one location" (1996, xiii–xiv).

In what follows, I will offer an analysis of *Happy Together* that focuses on the negotiation of travelling sexualities in the in-between space created as a site of tension between home and away. Delineating the relationship between Fai and Po-wing and that between Fai and Chang, I will show that the construction of sexualities vis-à-vis home and away is predicated on a set of opposing values and argue that the film's deployment of the spatial construction of sexuality reinstates the idealization of home.

Domesticity, Monogamy, and Private Sex

In terms of the relationship between home and sexuality, Fai is associated with home, a longing for home, and a difficult relationship with his sexuality vis-à-vis the figure of his father back home, whereas Po-wing seemingly has no home or no need for home and flaunts his sexuality wherever he is. (The third character, the sexually ambiguous Chang, is travelling around but with the intention of going home and is thus more aligned with Fai.) It has been noted that definitions of home shift across a number of registers: "home can mean where one usually lives, or it can mean where one's family lives, or it can mean one's native country" (Ahmed 2000, 86). The home away from home that Fai sets up in Argentina is where the drama of his relationship with Po-wing is usually played out, and this home can also be seen as Fai's symbolic longing for his home in Hong Kong.

The film sets up a corollary of contrasting values between Fai and Po-wing. Financially, Fai is more prudent and holds regular jobs, whereas Po-wing does not work and lives off his sexual partners. Emotionally, Fai tends to bottle things up and is prone to alcoholism and violence, whereas Po-wing wears his moods on his sleeves and often imposes them on Fai. Sexually, Fai is faithful and seeks monogamy while Po-wing is promiscuous. Socially, Fai is a domestic creature who returns home immediately after work, whereas Po-Wing is a *flâneur* who feels claustrophobic at home and loves cruising in the streets. Taken together, these opposing traits can be grouped spatially and ideologically into home-as-private-sphere versus city-as-public-sphere. They are also embedded in a discourse of sex and sexuality as private, personal, and intimate set against the notion of public sex as anonymous, promiscuous, and impersonal.

The private space for the realization of a monogamous, stable, intimate relationship in *Happy Together* is the home away from home established by Fai. It is during the period of Po-wing's recovery, when he is held captive in the confines of the home because of his injury, that, *from Fai's perspective*, they are happiest together.[10] *Happy Together* has a complex use of color scheme, alternating between full color and black and white, and the film uses both color scheme and music to denote the change in Fai's emotional state before and after this period.[11] The sequence at the start of the film, in which Fai and Po-wing first break up on their trip to the Iguazu Falls, is shot in black and white. This coloration is carried over to Buenos Aires, where, as a doorman at Bar Sur, Fai is shown to be impatient when taking photographs for a group of tourists (figure 4.3), chucking the camera in the tour guide's hands with the words, "Fuck it," as live tango music spills out from the bar. After he starts over with Po-wing following the latter's injury, the film switches into full-color mode. In a similar sequence, now shot in color, Fai is clearly in good spirits, smiling while patiently taking photographs for a tour group (figure 4.4). Set to the extra-diegetic tune of Astor Piazzolla's music *Prologue (Tango apasionado)*, it signals, as the music's title suggests, a new beginning for the couple.

Fai's idea of "happy together" is rooted in domesticity, as Po-wing's recovery period most resembles that of a monogamous marriage, with domestic details of cooking, eating, washing, sleeping, dancing, and endless bickering. As Po-wing's hands are bandaged, Fai plays the dual roles

FIGURE 4.3. Fai in a foul mood after breaking up with Po-wing (shot in black and white). (Copyright Block 2 Pictures/Prémon H./Seowoo Film/Jet Tone Production, 1997)

FIGURE 4.4. Fai in a cheerful mood after making up with Po-wing (shot in color). (Copyright Block 2 Pictures/Prémon H./Seowoo Film/Jet Tone Production, 1997)

of the responsible husband, who works and brings money home, and the dutiful wife, who feeds, cleans, and takes care of her partner. For Chow, this recovery period "may thus arguably be considered as the heart of the matter of Wong's (ambivalent) portrayal of happiness" (1999, 39). This portrayal of happiness is ambivalent, I would argue, because it belies a desire for control. As Po-wing gradually recovers, Fai's fear of losing control over him also becomes increasingly palpable. On one occasion, Fai returns to an empty home and suspects that Po-wing has gone out cruising. When Po-wing claims that he has merely gone to get cigarettes, the following scene shows Fai stocking up the room with cartons of cigarettes on the pretext of saving Po-wing the trouble of having to go out at night to get them. Seeing through Fai's act as a power play, Po-wing sweeps the cigarettes onto the floor, and the couple subsequently has more fights and soon breaks up again.

As the only direct reference to the film's title (besides the use of the eponymous song at the end of the film), Fai's definition of "happy together" deserves a closer analysis. The scene in which the definition comes is located at a time in the diegesis when Fai picks fights not only with Po-wing at home, but also with his colleagues at work during football games. While he earlier declined his colleagues' invitation to play mahjong and retreated to the kitchen to study a map to plan a trip to the Iguazu Falls, he now disregards financial prudence and joins in the gambling. Following the full-color shot of Fai playing mahjong, the film switches to black-and-white mode, depicting Fai in a reflective mood at home, accompanied by this voice-over: "One thing I never told Ho Po-wing: actually I didn't want him to recover so fast. The period when he was injured was the happiest time I had with him." Alongside an earlier tango dance scene between the couple in the kitchen, this black-and-white sequence is the most tender in the film, as Fai lovingly studies the face of the sleeping Po-wing and softly caresses his eyebrow.

This sequence, however, can also be read as the cruellest. The next scene reverts to full color: a bored Fai plays with a knife, while Po-wing looks on then turns off his bedside lamp to go to sleep, leaving Fai sitting in the corner of the room, flipping the knife despondently. In a single cut the home has turned from one imbued with love to one threatened with violence. More important, the black-and-white sequence defining Fai's notion of "happy together" is inserted into the full-color portion of the film. The black-and-white color scheme does not (only) serve the conventional function of signifying past events, but is also a register of Fai's emotional state. Sandwiched between the mahjong scene, highlighting Fai's loss of control over his financial prudence, and the knife-flipping scene, underscoring his impending loss of control over his violent tendency, the black-and-white sequence does not so much reflect Fai's reminiscence of the happiest time he has with Po-wing as it reveals his desire to return to the period in which he has the most control over him. While Fai's travelling sexuality yearns for a home away from home where a domestic, monogamous, and private relationship can reside, his desire for control remains the inextricable if not determining element in his definition of happiness.

Flânerie, Promiscuity, and Public Sex

In contrast to Fai's spatialization of sex in the private sphere of the home, the film portrays Po-wing as an active participant in a gay subculture that values "sexual adventurism, experimentation, and variety" in the public sphere of the city (Chauncey 1996, 253). Like the *flâneurs* who leisurely stroll in the streets and arcades of Paris in the writings of Charles Baudelaire and Walter Benjamin, the "prowling homosexual" has been described as "the perverted *flâneur*" (Betsky 1997, 10), with the public toilet being one of the main sites for cruising for sex. In George Chauncey's description, Po-wing probably finds "the very anonymity, unpredictability, and danger of encounters in public places to be sexually exciting" (1996, 253), whereas Fai is "as likely as the anti-vice societies to regard such encounters as shameful," for he expects "the same level of romanticism, monogamy, and commitment to be involved in gay relationships that bourgeois ideology expected of marriage" (ibid., 252). In Argentina, Po-wing's sexuality continues to travel from one partner to another, the diasporic space becoming his new sexual playground. Besides, unlike Fai, he has no hang-ups about home whatsoever.

The contrast between Fai and Po-wing's attitudes towards sex and sexuality is aptly illustrated by the tango dance, which in *Happy Together* serves as a metaphor for the seductiveness of sex, if not for sex itself.[12] Po-wing is, unsurprisingly, a master at the dance, whereas Fai is clumsy. During his period of recovery Po-wing teaches Fai how to dance the tango, and the couple's dancing scene in the communal kitchen is an embodiment of their being happy together. Crucially, while Fai has been rejecting Po-wing's sexual advances during this period, in this scene it is Fai who initiates a kiss, leading to more passionate kissing and groping between the two. The communal kitchen, usually bustling with tenants cooking and shouting, is emptied out to accommodate the intimacy between the couple, its semipublic status underlining Fai's rare open expression of his sexuality. When the couple breaks up on the trip to the Iguazu Falls, Fai realizes that Po-wing's "Let's start over" can have two meanings, which I understand as also meaning "Let's end it." Set to Piazzolla's music *Finale (Tango apasionado)*, the tango-dancing scene reminds us that as their relationship has to end before it can start over in Buenos Aires, their newly started relationship is also destined, as hinted by the music's title, to come to another end.

The two domains embodied by Fai and Po-Wing, however, are not mutually exclusive, as each can be the repressed desire of the other. In fact, Po-wing is "more desperately in need of the relationship than Fai is, although on the surface the opposite seems to be the case" (Stokes and Hoover 1999, 274–275). "Let's start over" is a suggestion uttered only by Po-wing, and it is Po-wing who keeps contacting Fai in an attempt to make up with him in Buenos Aires after their break up at the start of the film. As Chow observes, "ironically, it is the unfaithful one, the one who is always leaving, who most frequently desires to 'start over again' and rebuild the broken home" (1999, 37). After Fai's departure for the Iguazu Falls towards the end of the film, Po-wing moves into Fai's apartment and "begins to scrub and clean the apartment's floor in a manner that literally makes him resemble Fai" (ibid., 44).

Similarly, Fai is not unacquainted with the gay subculture of public sex or what Marc Siegel calls "ghetto knowledge": the skills at negotiating "the unspoken codes and unformalizable gestures of a sexual ghetto" (2001, 284). For Fai, the two seemingly separate realms of sexual expression collapse after the exit of both Po-wing and Chang from his life, leading him to succumb to the allure of public sex. Following Chang's departure, the film features a montage of Fai mingling with men in the city streets, with a shot of a man's bottom in denim jeans and another of drag queens waving from the rear of a car driving past, scored to the sexually suggestive lyrics of Frank Zappa's song *I Have Been in You*. This is followed by a sequence in which Fai visits a public toilet, where he deliberately bumps into another man to test if he is interested in sex, and a gay porn cinema, where a man performs oral sex on him. For Chow, there is a kind of "superhuman agency" at the "metanarrative level of the film as a whole" that serves the following function:

> In the case of the lovers, this superhuman agency lies precisely in its ability to yoke together—to render into one unity—entirely incompatible or incommensurate universes (such as promiscuity and fidelity, flânerie and domesticity), so that what begins as difference eventually turns into sameness. By the end of the film, precisely the kinds of details that used to distinguish the two men—having casual sex with strangers and performing tedious domestic chores—

have become instead the means of *visually conflating them*. Each man has, it seems, internalized the other to the point of changing places with each other. (1999, 44; emphasis in original)

While Chow's description is accurate on one level, the film's narratorial imperative emphasizes the couple's differences rather their similarities. Because Fai chooses to define his sexuality against that of Po-wing, he "expresses discomfort and confusion about this [public] sexual world" (Siegel 2001, 286). In an earlier scene, as Po-wing quizzes Fai on his relationship with Chang and teasingly asks if Fai has slept with the janitor at his lodging place, Fai retorts, "I'm not you." Fai's voice-over accompanying the public toilet scenes says, "Before I didn't like cruising in public toilets as I thought it dirty. Still I occasionally go for its convenience. I didn't expect to see Ho Po-wing there. Since then I've never been back. . . . I've always thought that I'm very different from Ho Po-wing. Turns out that in loneliness everyone is the same." For Fai, seeing Po-wing at the same cruising space seems to present a crisis for his own sexuality, which is irreconcilable with that of Po-wing. Likewise, compared to Fai's unwavering wish for a monogamous relationship located in the private realm of the home, Po-wing's repeated requests to start over highlight precisely his indecisive oscillation between togetherness and independence, as the lure of public sex in the city constantly draws this promiscuous *flâneur* away from the claustrophobic domestic space set up by Fai. In a film in which Fai mentions his wish to return to Hong Kong three times whereas Po-wing never expresses the same wish, their different attitudes towards going home embody their disparate travelling sexualities in Argentina.

Indeterminate Sexuality and the Anxiety of Heteronormativity

The introduction of a third character, Chang, in the second half of the film provides a contrast between the two kinds of (possible) relationships for Fai. As mentioned above, Chang is more aligned with Fai in relation to the issue of home. As in Fai's case, there is no question about Chang's intention to return home after his sojourn in Argentina. Just as Fai works the night shift at the abattoir to be back on Hong Kong time, Chang notes before leaving Argentina that it is evening in Taipei and wonders if the night market in Liaoning Street (where his parents operate a food stall) has started. Chang is thus united with Fai *in time* in two senses: their common consciousness of another time zone that is home and the possibility of a future relationship.

From the outset, Chang shows an unusual interest in Fai and in Fai's relationship with Po-wing. In his first appearance in the film, as Fai's colleague at the Chinese restaurant, Chang is washing dishes while listening to the hustle and bustle in the kitchen with his eyes closed. (In a later scene, he reveals that he had suffered from an eye problem as a child, and though it has since been cured, he cannot get rid of the habit of relying more on his ears than his eyes.) He hears Fai on the phone asking Po-wing what he wants for dinner and comments, "This guy loves talking on the phone. I could hear that his tone is happy. The other party must be someone he likes." While it is unclear how much Chang understands of Fai's conversation in Cantonese (the two usually conduct their conversation in a mix of Mandarin and Cantonese, with Chang showing adequate comprehension of Cantonese to respond), it makes Chang's interception of Fai's telephone conversation with Po-wing on one occasion suspect, as if Chang, looking stealthily after Fai returns to the phone, is trying to find out who or what the gender of Fai's mysterious partner is. This interception is, crucially, the trigger of one of the fiercest fights between Fai and Po-wing, leading Fai to throw Po-wing out of the apartment for the night. Thus Chang functions at once as a trigger to the beginning of another breakup between Fai and Po-wing and as a promise of a new relationship for Fai.

The film also designates Chang as an acute observer of Fai's emotional state, especially as it fluctuates vis-à-vis Fai's relationship with Po-wing. When Fai calls home to find that Po-wing is out, the film does not show much of Fai's unhappy expression but instead cuts to Chang's contemplative look, which serves as a thermometer both of Fai's emotional state and of Chang's affective investment in their affair. As Fai's relationship with Po-wing deteriorates and he starts playing mahjong with his colleagues, Chang looks on through the window of the kitchen, clearly concerned. Moreover, Chang shows little interest in women, as he rejects the advances of a female colleague in Fai's presence, claiming he prefers women with a deep and low voice, one that will make his heart beat quicker. When Chang proceeds to ask Fai what kind of woman's voice Fai prefers, his motive for asking the question is as ambiguous as Fai's answer, "It doesn't matter as long as you like it." While Chang might have been seeking confirmation with regard to Fai's sexuality, Fai's ambiguous answer could be equally suggestive to Chang.

The film shows the ambiguity of their relationship as reciprocal. After drinking in the 3 Amigos bar together, Fai gets drunk and has to be escorted home by Chang. As Chang undresses Fai and puts him to bed, there is a close-up of Fai's head facing the wall but with his eyes open, listening to Chang tidying up as if waiting for Chang to make a move on him. In the next sequence, in which they have a football game with colleagues, Chang is shown grabbing Fai from behind several times, the sequence ending with a pan to Fai looking at the distant Chang, as if contemplating the nature of their relationship. As they embrace before Chang leaves for his trip to Ushuaia, Fai's voice-over incorporates Chang's lover's discourse: "I cannot hear anything but my own heartbeat. I wonder if he hears it too." Chang has put the heartbeat back in Fai's life and offers Fai hope of a possible relationship.

For Fai, Chang and Po-wing could not have been more different. Where Po-wing is self-aggrandizing and self-centred, Chang is caring and sensitive. Po-wing enters and exits Fai's life according to his whims and fancies, with little regard for Fai's feelings. When Fai falls ill with a high fever during Po-wing's period of recovery, Po-wing nonetheless asks Fai to cook for him since his own hands are bandaged. By contrast, Chang is a good listener who provides Fai with stable companionship. Leaving for travel and sensing that Fai is unhappy, Chang offers to bring Fai's troubles in his cassette recorder to the lighthouse at Ushuaia, supposedly a place where one's unhappiness can be discarded. Rather than playing the role of caretaker to the unpredictable Po-wing, with Chang, for once, "Fai, too, can feel he is being taken care of" (Chow 1999, 41).

In a film driven by the desire to "start over" and to be "happy together," the motivation behind Chang's travel and the nature of his relationship with Fai become significant but prove elusive. Chang has said he is travelling because he is unhappy in Taiwan and there is no point in returning before he has thought things through. What is he unhappy about, and what does he have to think through? One suggestion is his sexuality, which remains ambiguous in the film. For Lisa Odham Stokes and Michael Hoover, Chang's problems "remain unspecified. Perhaps he's dealing with his sexual identity; perhaps not" (1999, 272). In a review of the film, Charlotte O'Sullivan sees Chang as being "on the brink of sexual awareness" (1998, 49). On the other hand, drawing upon Alan Sinfield's notion of "post-gay" understandings of relationships and Marjorie Garber's distinction between eroticism and sexuality, Helen Leung suggests that the film's ambivalence vis-à-vis the relationship between Chang and Fai "jettisons the idea that all relational bonds can be clearly demarcated as either *sexual* or platonic, and that people can be categorized as either straight or gay, according to their sexual preference" (2001, 438; emphasis in original). Tambling makes a similar observation that in *Happy Together* "no one makes any identity claim at all and the most interesting relationship is between two men who make no avowal of an identity to each other at all." For Tambling, whether Chang has any sexual interest in Fai "cannot be articulated for the reason that Chang seems to have escaped the necessity of defining himself in straight/gay terms at all" (2003, 74).

While the former group of readings focuses on Chang's emerging but undefined sexuality, the latter group celebrates this indeterminacy of sexual identities. This indeterminacy, I would argue, is not necessarily a "third way," offered by the film as a more fluid form of sexuality in contrast to the ones embodied by Fai and Po-wing. Rather, it serves as a promise of "happy together" for Fai as, in its representation of the different kinds of travelling sexualities, the film privileges one over the other. Towards the end of the film, as the digital clock turns from 23:59 to 00:00 in the apartment from which Fai has moved out, Po-wing is shown moving in, repairing the faulty revolving mechanism of the lamp with the picture of the Iguazu Falls that first inspired their trip and crying uncontrollably. The film then cuts to the Iguazu Falls, where Fai has finally arrived, with his voice-over lamenting Po-wing's absence. As the temporal marker signals a starting over, it is clear that Po-wing, stranded in Argentina, is drowned in sorrow, whereas Fai is due to return to Hong Kong and his unhappiness is, in an immediate following sequence, disposed of "at the end of the world" by Chang, who also arrives at his travel destination before returning to Taiwan. The impending return home by two out of the three protagonists thus appears to privilege the space of the home-nation, as in many discourses on travel and diaspora.

In the film, narrated chiefly from Fai's perspective through his voice-over, and with Chang also enjoying a voice-over but not Po-wing (Tambling 2003, 40), Fai's sexual economy and his potential relationship with Chang are indeed the driving forces. Three features unite Fai and Chang against Po-wing: similar work ethics, arrival at their respective travel destinations, and return home. In terms of work ethics, Fai and Chang are colleagues who work regular hours in a kitchen, whereas Po-wing lives off his sexual partners. As for travel destinations, Fai finally makes it to the Iguazu Falls but without Po-wing, while Chang arrives at the lighthouse at Ushuaia. With regard to home, both Fai and Chang manage to save enough money to return home, whereas Po-wing is left behind in Argentina. The film's designation of the three characters' final fate clearly favors domesticity over *flânerie,* monogamy over promiscuity, and private sexuality over public sexual activity. For Yue, the film's didactic treatment of the characters "exposes the straight-laced moral discourse of the narrative: excess of any nature is not tolerated." She further argues: "From the construction of the three male protagonists, it can be concluded that both Yiu-Fai and Chang are 'rewarded' in their quests through the neo-Confucian 'values' of decent hard work, thrift and normativity. The film's plot succeeds for both of them: they both reach their respective destinations. In the course of such a resolution, it appears that Wong [Kar-wai] has undermined the performative thrust of the film. The 'gay' theme appears to be contained by restraining Bao-Wing's [Po-wing] decadent excess" (2000, 255).

Yue's argument can be understood in the context of a dominant discourse in lesbian and gay studies and in queer theory that challenges heteronormativity. Lauren Berlant and Michael Warner situate the transformation in the cultural forms of intimacy in the history of the modern public sphere and the modern discourse of sexuality as a fundamental human capacity. They argue that both Habermas and Foucault "point to the way a hegemonic public has founded itself by a privatization of sex and the sexualization of private personhood." Both identify the conditions in which "sexuality seems like a property of subjectivity rather than a publicly or counterpublicly accessible culture" (1998, 559). By making sex private and personal, Berlant and Warner claim, heteronormative conventions of intimacy have blocked the building of non-normative or explicit public sexual cultures (ibid., 553). The stigmatization of public sex and promiscuity is therefore inseparable from the dichotomy of public/private and the demarcation of sex as personal and intimate.

Public sex as a means of challenging heteronormativity is a theme picked up by Marc Siegel in his analysis of the film, in which he focuses his attention on "the ghetto as the context within which the behaviors, spaces, and images in the film become meaningful." For Siegel, intimacy in *Happy Together* resides neither within coupledom nor in the private space of the apartment. Instead, the potential for intimacy exists outside the home, in the public sexual world (2001, 285). This leads him to conclude that *Happy Together* shares with Wong's other films "a concerted refusal to relegate intimacy to the private form of the couple or to the privatized space of the apartment" and that Wong's films "picture the limits of heteronormative constraints on intimacy" and "challenge the idea that intimacy can be confirmed within the form of the couple and within the realm of the private" (ibid., 286). I would argue, however, that to focus, as Siegel does, on the public sexual activities as "creative of potential new intimacies" (ibid., 285) betrays perhaps the critic's wish fulfilment, as it disregards the marginalization, not to mention stigmatization, of the sexual world embodied by Po-wing, who literally has no voice(over) in the film's narrative. Moreover, Fai's public sexual adventurism towards the end of the film is marked by a sense of abjection and contained by a patriarchal order located in the space of the home-nation.

Taking a different position and acknowledging the film's portrayal of happiness as ambiguous, Chow notes that this portrayal is "from the perspective of the faithful partner, the one who is repeatedly betrayed and stuck at home, and who is, moreover, forced to assume the maternal role of caretaker when the promiscuous partner comes stumbling back" (1999, 39). Unlike Yue's and Siegel's celebration of Po-wing's gay performativity and ghetto knowledge, Chow describes him as "an irresponsible scumbag" and a "jerk, who fucks around, and comes and goes as he pleases" (ibid., 36, 40). Instead, Chow defends Fai's act of confiscating Po-wing's passport as "of course by no means a reasonable or even practical move, yet its madness also embodies a kind of groping, a desperate attempt to be constructive in the midst of a destructive relationship" (ibid., 40). However, as the passport is the ultimate symbol of the freedom of mobility and travel, and given their diasporic identities, Fai's repeated refusal to return Po-wing's passport belies a deeper desire for domination and control. Rather than seeing the film as communicating "a compelling message about love in all its ambiguities" (ibid.), I would argue that Fai's desperate attempt to be constructive cannot mask a stifling possessiveness that in itself can be destructive in its desire for faithfulness.

If the two sexualities embodied by Fai and Po-wing are somehow represented as irreconcilable, we must question not only why the film privileges one over the other, but also why critics have chosen to either affirm or challenge the film's construction. As the Clifford quote asks at the start of the chapter, what kinds of knowledges and theories about travelling sexualities do these readings of the film produce, or indeed reproduce? This poses serious questions, which extend beyond the discussion of the film per se but which in fact form the unspoken premise upon which the above readings have been made possible. They concern the practice (and politics) of contemporary academic discourse in relation to lesbian, gay, and queer identity politics. As noted above, arguments such as Yue's, which challenge heteronormativity and celebrate gay performativity, have been the dominant discourse in the fields of lesbian and gay studies. In a book concerned with the representation of male homosexuality in contemporary Chinese cinemas, would it be possible to question the basis of this challenge to heteronormativity and ask at what price gay performativity is enacted?

In a different context but illuminating in an analogous manner, Fran Martin cautions us of "the trap of casting a particular culture and a particular history as the paradigmatic, illustrative example of the abstract quality that is currently privileged in academic discourse." She goes on to argue as follows:

Given that "cultural hybridity" appears to constitute for the current generation of scholars the object of collective desire that "cultural tradition" was for
a previous one, it would be all too easy merely to celebrate Taiwan's palpable
syncretic cultures as though their hybridity were itself proof against the continuing effects of unevenly held power. . . . One might ask: *Which people* in Taiwan, specifically, experience "in-between-ness" as productive or liberating? And
for whom does it constitute, on the contrary, an unlivable condition? (2003c,
35–36; emphasis in original)

Similarly, we might ask: Who benefits from a discourse that challenges
heteronormativity and that constructs gay performativity as homonor-
mativity? Who is excluded as a result? Following lesbian and gay studies'
self-definition against the heterosexual norm of coupledom symbolized
by domesticity, monogamy, and private sex, expressions such as *flânerie*,
promiscuity, and public sex become valorized to the extent that to suggest
the contrary would almost immediately invite accusations of homophobia and the aping of heteronormativity, while the assumption behind the
former's politics often goes unquestioned. Despite queer theory's emphasis on performativity, of which fluidity and (gender) border-crossing are
its hallmarks, the kind of discursive practice and identity politics arising
from this collective desire to define itself against heteronormativity has
paradoxically solidified into a paradigmatic—and arguably hegemonic—
discourse that precludes the possibilities of other forms of sexual intimacies, especially forms that bear similarities with those of the heterosexual
counterpart.[13] That is, as *flânerie*, promiscuity, and public sex are invariably
constructed as homonormative, domesticity, monogamy, and private sex
thus defy imagination as possibly equally homonormative, since the two
are supposedly mutually exclusive. Heteronormativity-as-homonormativity then becomes the Great Unthinkable, the ultimate taboo in hegemonic, liberationist discourses within lesbian, gay, and queer studies.

Returning to our discussion of *Happy Together*, we may wonder, for
example, why gay performativity has to be inextricably linked to "excess"
and opposed to the "neo-Confucian 'values' of decent hard work, thrift
and normativity." Is a hard-working, thrifty, (hetero)normal gay unthinkable—or unacceptable—and to whom? In a politics that valorizes the
transgressive, would it not be plausible to regard Fai's seemingly banal
pursuit of a domestic, monogamous, private relationship as radical rather
than a scandal? Conversely, what is so non-(hetero)normative about sexual promiscuity and excess?[14] If sexualities do indeed travel, it is literally
Po-wing's *flâneur*-like travel from one sexual partner to another and his

refusal to "settle down"—that is, to be "fixed"—that are privileged in Yue's reading, as she objects to "the fixity of the neo-Confucian fetish of the hardworking 'Asian' stereotype constructed through Yiu-Fai and Chang" that the film enables (2000, 256). In her writing on narratives of migration and estrangement, Sara Ahmed argues against Rosi Braidotti's valorization of the nomad as "a figuration for the kind of subject who has relinquished all idea, desire, or nostalgia for fixity" and of a nomadic consciousness as "an acute awareness of the nonfixity of boundaries" and "the intense desire to go on trespassing, transgressing." Instead, Ahmed asks, "We might consider how the very theoretical approach which privileges 'transgression' and 'subversion' and a lack of fixity does not necessarily define itself simply against the law, convention and boundaries, but may actually serve to reconstitute the law, conventions, and boundaries: we can ask, *how does the desire to go beyond fixity serve to fix? How does the law require transgression in order to exist?*" (2000, 84; emphasis mine)

Ahmed's challenging question acutely highlights the blind spot of theoretical approaches that appear to be progressive in their emphasis on transgression and subversion but are in fact also hostile and dogmatic towards those who may choose to be fixed and not to travel. I am not suggesting that the film's privileging of Fai's form of travelling sexuality—which, unlike Po-wing's, is driven by a fixation to establish a home as well as to return home—is necessarily beyond reproach. What I am arguing is that despite the conventional—and some might say conservative—form Fai's sexual economy takes, it cannot be dismissed outright as illegitimate or inauthentic. A truly inclusive and progressive politics cannot be built upon an immunity from any challenge to its own logic, and a radical theoretical approach such as queer theory might have to acknowledge that heteronormativity-as-homonormativity is equally performative in its discursive sense of being constitutive for certain agents.

Let's Start Over: Homecoming as Non-Arrival

If Fai's travelling sexuality is going to finally take him home, it is worth highlighting the only time when Hong Kong appears in the film. Sandwiched between the two abattoir sequences, the Hong Kong cityscape is shot upside down as Fai wonders what Hong Kong might look like from Argentina, having just discovered that the two locales are antipodal. It is clear at this point in the diegesis that Fai has decided to return to Hong Kong as he starts a new job at the abattoir to earn more money, and the night shift means he will be in sync with Hong Kong time. The upside-down shots of Hong Kong begin with a brief night scene, followed by a longer day scene, both shot from a vehicle travelling on busy roads, capturing overpasses crisscrossing and skyscrapers towering above (or rather below). The scenes are accompanied by low-volume radio broadcasts, which feature a call-in program, an announcement about typhoons, and a news item on a car theft. The disembodied voices on the radio and the upside-down shots of Hong Kong's cityscape, I would argue, do not evoke a sense of nostalgia and longing for home; rather, they serve to disorientate and defamiliarize Hong Kong and even, by their inversion, subvert (as it is, from below) Hong Kong to the point of no return. From Argentina, the images of Hong Kong conjured up by Fai are images of discomfort, underscored by the ominous messages in the disembodied voices.

The travelling shots of Hong Kong prefigure the closing scenes of the film, in which Fai rides on the Taipei mass rapid transport train. Just before the closing scenes, Chang had hoped to say goodbye to Fai before returning to Taiwan but could not find him in Buenos Aires. Fai, on the other hand, transits at Taipei on his return journey to Hong Kong and visits Liaoning Street in search of Chang. Removing Chang's photograph (taken at Ushuaia) from the parents' food stall, Fai feels assured that though he does not know when he will see Chang again, he now knows where he can find him. In contrast to the sombre Hong Kong scenes, the closing travelling Taipei night scenes are engulfed by bright neon lights on both sides of the train track, with the camera time speeded up to match the upbeat rendition of the Turtles' 1960s hit song *Happy Together*, by Danny Chung. With the line "I can see me loving nobody but you for all my life" played at high volume, the film signals a beginning rather than an end. As David Martinez comments on the use of music in Wong's films, "Music speaks just as evocatively as pictures, and in fact always has the *last* word. All Wong Kar-wai's films have one thing in common: they all end on a song which, from *Days of Being Wild* onwards, has always opened up the perspective of a fresh departure, a new story just beginning, for once giving the lie to the fateful title, 'The End'" (1997, 35; emphasis in original).[15]

With a faintly detectable smile on Fai's face, the cinematographer Christopher Doyle notes that this "looks like having the happiest ending of any WKW [Wong Kar-wai] film" (1998, 181). However, the referent in the title, *Happy Together*, is not what is shown in the film, for the relationship between Fai and Po-wing is anything but happy. Rather it points to what is not shown in the film: the relationship between Fai and Chang, extending beyond the scope of the film and remaining only a possibility. "Happy together" is therefore doubly absent in the film, as in Matthew

Arnold's lines in "Stanzas from the Grande Chartreuse": "Wandering between two worlds, one dead./The other powerless to be born" (1998, 81). Notwithstanding the upbeat music, could the ending not betray a deeper melancholia because the promise of "happy together" is deferred to the future, and the future—including Hong Kong's future—remains unknown?

I believe it is significant that Fai's homecoming results in his non-arrival at Hong Kong, and for this purpose, I would like to revisit a moment in Argentina when Fai decides on another form of homecoming, which is his attempt at reconciliation with his father. It has been noted that the absent father is a recurrent theme in Wong's films (Lalanne 1997, 22). In *Happy Together*, the absent father in the distant home of Hong Kong haunts Fai's existence in Argentina, creating an in-between space that interfaces Fai's negotiation of his sexuality. Before leaving Hong Kong, Fai has stolen some money from his boss, who is a good friend of his father. In Argentina, Fai has worked hard to save up in the hope of repaying the stolen money. However, it seems to me that Fai's feeling of guilt towards his father extends beyond this breach of trust, that Fai probably regards his homosexuality as a greater form of betrayal to his father and as something that, not unlike his theft, demands an apology. Following Fai's visit to the gay porn cinema, the film cuts to an exterior scene where Fai contemplates whether to call home in front of a public phone. His voice-over recounts his theft of the boss's money and expresses his wish to apologize to his father. When he finally picks up the phone to make the call, we hear him say, "Hello, Pa. It's Fai," but there seems to be no response at the other end. While in this scene Fai is wearing different clothes from the gay porn cinema scene, indicating that the two scenes are temporally distinct, the film suggests a (causal) relation between the two by editing them in immediate sequence. As if Fai is seeking the approval of his father for his public sexual activity, this phone call simultaneously reinscribes the patriarchal order in the film while cancelling out Fai's sexual adventurism.

If Po-wing's carefree loitering is "forever structured by a parasitical dependency on the other's seeming stability, conventionality, and homeliness—hence his pathological compulsion constantly to 'start over again'" (Chow 1999, 42)—Fai's own sexual loitering must be seen in relation to his father, whose trust Fai has betrayed. That is, what Po-wing is to Fai is precisely what Fai is to his father: the unfaithful one. For Fai, going home entails reconciliation with his father on the dual issues of money and sexuality.[16] Po-wing, on the other hand, has no such financial burden or sexual baggage. In fact, it is he who has squandered Fai's savings, resulting in their being stranded in Argentina. Fai's desire to establish a home in Argentina and to return to Hong Kong can be understood as (over)compensation for his infidelity to his father. His idealization of domesticity, monogamy, and private sex is governed by a patriarchal order located in Hong Kong. The opposing values embodied by Fai and Po-wing, delineated above, are not so much between Po-wing and Fai as between Po-wing and Fai's father.

Moreover, Fai's desire for reconciliation with his father borders on the incestuous. After the phone call, Fai sets out to write his father a Christmas card that turns into a long letter. In addition to saying he is sorry, Fai also "tells his father many things he [the father] has always wanted to know but has never dared ask," presumably a reference to Fai's homosexuality. Fai ends the letter by hoping that his father will treat him as a friend and that he will let Fai "start over again." By mobilizing the lover's discourse between Po-wing and himself to plead for a chance to start over with his father, Fai not only takes on Po-wing's persona of the unfaithful one, but also overlays his relationship with his father with an incestuous tone. As Fai posts the letter before the film cuts to the abattoir sequence, Zappa's song, *I Have Been in You,* appears for the second time and interfaces the two with its unabashedly explicit lines: "I have been in you, baby, you have been in me. And we have been so intimately entwined, and it sure was fine." When we recall that Zappa's song accompanies Fai's cruising scenes in its earlier appearance, does this betray, on a symbolic level, Fai's desire to penetrate or be penetrated by his father, or does it merely suggest the biological relationship between the father and son since it is the father's semen that has brought about the son's existence and is thus, in a sense, forever "in him"? Insofar as Fai's need for his father's acceptance of his homosexuality reinstates the patriarchal order in the film, it also suggests that his desire for home may after all not be directed at Po-wing but at his own father.

However, the film's ending in Taipei, which shores up Fai's homecoming as non-arrival, I would argue, serves to frustrate the patriarchal order governing Fai's negotiation of his sexuality. Towards the end of the film, having seen Chang's parents in Taipei, Fai suddenly understands why Chang can be so happy travelling around the world: at least he has a place to which to return. His voice-over then wonders what will happen when he meets his father and concludes, "We'll see." The final shot of the film shows the mass rapid transport train heading towards the blinding white light of a station at high speed and suddenly coming to a halt. The film suggests that having travelled half way around the world to Argentina, Fai might have chosen a different destination to call home, thus rejecting reconciliation with the patriarchal order. Read metaphorically in geopolitical terms, the film offers travelling denizens of Hong Kong a choice away from the reunion with China. However ironic the film's title might have been intended to be, the promise of "happy together" cannot be anchored in any particular location but is a journey on which travelling sexualities embark, then perhaps detour and never make their way home.

Confessing Desire
The Poetics of Tsai Ming-liang's Queer Cinema

Text of bliss [*jouissance*]: the text that imposes a state of loss,
the text that discomforts (perhaps to the point of a certain
boredom), unsettles the reader's historical, cultural, psychological assumptions, the consistency of his tastes, values,
memories, brings to a crisis his relation with language.
—ROLAND BARTHES, *The Pleasure of the Text*

As a filmmaker, Malaysian-born Tsai Ming-liang is best known for his representations of gender and sexuality, especially male homoeroti-cism and homosexuality, building an oeuvre that can arguably be called the first queer cinema in the Chinese-speaking world. However, he is notori-ous for resisting the label of "gay director." Unlike Stanley Kwan, who has come out openly as gay (see chapter 6), Tsai explicitly expresses his dislike at having his films labelled as "gay films" and feels that homosexuality has been turned into a kind of fashion and sensationalized in film circles (Chiao 1997b, 25). Paradoxically, perhaps more than that of Stanley Kwan, Tsai's oeuvre has generated a reception that is best described as queer—in both senses of the word. I argue in this chapter that despite Tsai's protes-tations of and self-distancing from such labels, he has constructed a poet-ics of desire in his works that not only invites but almost demands a read-ing that is invariably queer and has engendered a strange kind of queer cinema upon which a different kind of community may be imagined.

Based in Taiwan, where he has lived since his college days in the late 1970s, Tsai first made his mark on the Taiwan cultural scene as a theater director, playwright, and actor and subsequently established himself as a television drama director and a screenplay writer for film. He directed his debut film, *Rebels of the Neon God,* in 1992 and had, by 2005, made six more feature-length films and a short film, in addition to a couple of documen-taries and theater projects.[1] In this chapter, I propose to study Tsai's works as an oeuvre, as his interest in—indeed, obsession with—issues of gendered and sexual identities has been a consistent theme running through from his theatrical to cinematic works over two decades. I begin by situating Tsai in the context of Taiwan New Cinema, highlighting the confessional nature of his works, and tracing his "networks of obsessions" (Culler 1975, 146) from his theatrical works and documentary to his debut feature film. In the second half of the chapter I focus on his 1997 film, *The River*, in which the poetics of desire and the problematics of representation become the most acute in Tsai's *écriture* queer.

Confessing Identities: From Historical I to Private I

As an overseas Chinese working in Taiwan, Tsai has an ambiguous and at times also a difficult position in Taiwan cinema. Heralded as a representative of second-generation directors of Taiwan New Cinema (hereafter TNC), Tsai is without question the most prominent "Taiwanese" director on the international cinematic circuit after his predecessors Hou Hsiao-hsien and Edward Yang. Tsai's second feature film, *Vive l'amour (Aiqing wansui)*, shared the Golden Lion at the Venice Film Festival in 1994, and his third film, *The River*, won a Silver Bear at the Berlin film festival in 1997, thus propelling him to international status. However, his success has also been a mixed blessing, as Tsai was at the center of a controversy on film funding in 1998 in Taiwan, where his nationality was brought into question, leading Tsai to contemplate leaving Taiwan altogether (Wen T'ien-hsiang 2002, 201).[2]

Tsai's identity as an overseas Chinese is relevant here for his thematic departure from that of most TNC directors. On the one hand, though Tsai has been grouped with second-generation directors such as Yee Chih-yen and Chen Yu-hsun (Chen Yuxun) as initiating a cinema of the "new human species" (*xinrenlei*, loosely understood as Taiwan's Generation X) in the early 1990s (Wen T'ien-hsiang 2002, 88), his unrelenting examination of the isolated state of the individual finds more resonance with European high modernism than with Taiwan's native culture.[3] On the other hand, first-generation TNC directors, typically born immediately after World War II, have been strongly influenced by Taiwan's nativization movement since the 1960s. Their films are mainly concerned with history in a quest to come to terms with the island's troubled colonial past and tumultuous domestic conflicts, as well as with its long struggle for self-definition and self-determination as a people. This history is not one with which Tsai can easily identify—much less deal with—as a cinematic theme, though it must be qualified that Tsai's portrayal of contemporary urban Taipei has often been described as "terribly accurate" (ibid., 90).[4]

Making a rupture with the TNC tradition and marked by a shift from a "historical I" to a "private I," Tsai is nevertheless also obsessed with the issue of identity, albeit an identity that has little to do with the grand narratives of history and nation. While earlier TNC directors were preoccupied with such overtly political issues at a time leading to the lifting of martial law in Taiwan in the late 1980s, Tsai has been working under distinctly different sociopolitical conditions of the post-martial law period, when political battles are being fought on multifarious grounds, from aboriginal, women's, and gay rights to the Taiwanese independence movement. The multiculturalist premise from the 1990s means that such battles are now as much personal as they are communal, for it is precisely the previously suppressed—and often private—aspects of the personal that have now gained a political voice. Taiwanese novelist Chu T'ien-wen (Zhu Tianwen), a longtime collaborator (as screenplay writer) of Hou Hsiao-hsien, argues that history, once the motivating force behind TNC, has become baggage (1994, 165), and she hails Tsai's *Vive l'amour* as marking "a new milestone" (the title of her essay) for TNC. Chu mobilizes the Japanese concept of the *shishōsetsu*—often "*mis*translated as 'I-novel'" (Fowler 1988, ix; emphasis in original)—to discuss Tsai's film:

> It is not afraid of "small" subject matters. By small, I mean more appropriately like the "private" [*si*] in the "*shishōsetsu*" [*sixiaoshuo*]. There has never been this "private" in Taiwan cinema. . . . What is close to "private" is perhaps "confession." The tradition of confession comes from confessing to the priest, which traces back a long time. I therefore doubt if there has ever been such a thing called "private" in the Chinese world for a very, very long time. (Chu T'ien-wen 1994, 166)

Tsai acknowledges in an interview that "each time I make a film, it's in order to move a bit closer to the centre of that private self which I still haven't managed to master" (Rivière and Tsai 1999, 97). The Japanese *kanji* (Japanese writing using Chinese characters) for *shishōsetsu* reads literally as "private novel" in Chinese, which is why I have translated the first character into English not as "I" (the Japanese *watakushi* or *shi*) but as "private" (the Chinese *si*). In any case, Chu is not concerned with the Japanese literary form here but rather uses the interplay between the *kanji*/Chinese characters to make a point.[5] For Chu, the field of confession in Taiwan cinema has now been opened by Tsai (Chu T'ien-wen 1994, 167), and this also opens up a reading of Tsai's films at the crossroads of the Japanese literary form of the *shishōsetsu* and the Foucauldian explication on confession.

In *The Rhetoric of Confession: Shishōsetsu in Early Twentieth-Century*

Japanese Fiction, Edward Fowler notes that the *shishōsetsu* is "riddled with paradoxes": "Supposedly a fictional narrative, it often reads more like a private journal. It has a reputation of being true, to a fault, to 'real life'; yet it frequently strays from the author's experience it allegedly portrays so faithfully. Its personal orientation makes it a thoroughly modern form; yet it is the product of an indigenous intellectual tradition quite disparate from western individualism" (1988, xvi). Fowler distinguishes between the *shishōsetsu* and the confessional mode in the Western context, the latter of which "in the interest of atonement or self-analysis or even self-aggrandizement is the catalyst for some resolution or action that gives the work its shape and direction" (ibid., xx). In contrast, the Japanese writer compiled a record of his thoughts and actions "less out of a sense of his own self-importance than out of skepticism that experience other than his own could be recorded with complete confidence" (ibid., xxiv). While to "authorize a self was no easy task in a society unwilling to acknowledge the individual as a viable social unit" (ibid.), the *shishōsetsu* is nonetheless marked by "the diarist's or confessor's urge to transcribe lived experience, letting the course of the life itself determine the shape of subsequent transcriptions" (ibid., xxvii).[6]

By following Chu's cue in reading Tsai's films in the contexts of the *shishōsetsu* and the confessional mode (the relationship between the two is suggested in Fowler's book title), I am aware of the potentially problematic collapsing of both time and space in this operation. However, I believe this line of reading is worth pursuing—and the risks worth taking—because it encapsulates the intertwining relationship among the private sense of the self, the confessional mode, and sexuality, which is the preoccupation of Tsai's works. Moreover, not only is Fowler's explication of the formal features of the *shishōsetsu* apt for explaining the meandering qualities of Tsai's "narratives," but the sense of self portrayed in Tsai's works is also defined typically "by its separation and withdrawal from a society that normally demands strict allegiance from members, rather than by its confident confrontation with society" (ibid., xxiv).

The interplay between the Japanese and Chinese reading of the character *watakushi/si* creates a private sense of the self prone to the confessional mode, which helps to create "the private individual, measured by deep interiority and feelings, and by a personal history," thus encouraging "an essentialist view of the self" (Tambling 1990, 2). While confession has its roots as Eurocentric religious practice, it now has spread its effects far and wide, and one "confesses in public and in private, to one's parents, one's educators, one's doctor, to those one loves; one admits to oneself, in pleasure and in pain, things it would be impossible to tell to anyone else, the things people write books about" (Foucault 1990, 59). For Tsai, "making a film is a form of writing, writing about the things that concern me deeply," and "every time I make a film it's an attempt at dialogue with myself" (Rivière and Tsai 1999, 97). A quote by Theodor Adorno is particularly apt for Tsai, who has been living away from home for more than two decades: "For a man who no longer has a homeland, writing becomes a place to live" (1978, 87).[7] However, writing, like reading, is not an innocent activity (Culler 1975, 129). Before I examine Tsai's works from the theatrical to the cinematic, I would like to delineate Tsai's construction of a poetics of desire that engenders a kind of *écriture* queer that facilitates the representation of the unrepresentable.

A Poetics of Desire: *Écriture* Queer

More than those of any of the other directors discussed in this book, Tsai's works underline the precariousness of the representation of, and problematize the representability of, homosexual desire. In an essay entitled "Desire," rather than attempting to define what desire is, Judith Butler begins by questioning whether in trusting language to make something clear about desire one is not presupposing that "language itself has no vested interests in desire" (1995, 369). In a similar vein, Elizabeth Wright makes explicit the relationship between desire and language by explicating on the meaning of her book title, *Speaking Desires Can Be Dangerous: The Poetics of the Unconscious*: "Two meanings are . . . derivable from my title: meaning 1 (the gerund), *to speak our desires is dangerous* (since our words do not arrive at the desires we thought we had); meaning 2 (the gerundive), *the desires that are speaking are dangerous* (since they speak of what we do not want to know anything about). My title thus performs what it says, that desire works in the very structure of language" (1999, 2–3; emphasis in original). By drawing attention to the relationship between language and desire, both Butler and Wright question not just the limits of representation, but also the very possibility of representability. As Butler asks, "Does language give rise to desire and does it also set limits on the representability of desire?" (1995, 370). I would suggest that the question posed in the reverse is equally valid: Does desire give rise to language, and does it also set limits on the representability of language? I would also argue that the problematics of representation and representability concern not only the process of textual production, but also that of textual reception: the limits of representation and possibility of representability encountered by writers and filmmakers will also be faced by readers and viewers as limits and possibility of interpretation.

"My readers, says the narrator at the end of [Marcel Proust's] *A la recherche du temps perdu,* will become 'les propres lecteurs d'eux-mêmes': in my book they will read themselves and their own limits" (Culler 1975, 129). The problematic relationship between (homosexual) desire, (film) language, and (visual) representation is epitomized by Tsai's works and in particular in *The River.* In her reading of the film, Rey Chow argues that while Tsai's cinema is "rooted in a cosmopolitanism that is recognizably high-modernist in its thematic, narrative, and aesthetic designs," it also "poses questions, puzzles, and enigmas, confronting us repeatedly with the limits of our epistemological certainties, our comfort zones" (2004, 125). Tsai's corpus of work is, therefore, what in the epigraph quote Roland Barthes (1975, 14) has called a text of *jouissance.*[8]

Describing Tsai's films as "metaphorical" and "allegorical," Chow suggests that Tsai's cinema "should be approached in a way that goes beyond what is usually termed the 'interpretation of meaning'" (2004, 128).[9] Taking a cue from Chow but embarking on a different route, I propose to read Tsai's works in general and *The River* in particular in terms of a poetics of desire. If the "interpretation of meaning" belongs to the realm of hermeneutics, which "starts with texts and asks what they mean, seeking to discover new and better interpretations," Tsai's works can be more productively read in terms of poetics, which "starts with attested meanings or effects and asks how they are achieved" (Culler 1997, 61). Poetics, understood as "a totally intelligible structure of knowledge attainable about poetry, which is not poetry itself, or the experience of it" (Frye 1965, 14), can also lead to a mode of interpretation "where the work is read against the conventions of discourse and where one's interpretation is an account of the ways in which the work complies with or undermines our procedures for making sense of things" (Culler 1975, 130).[10] A poetics of desire thus bypasses the problematic relationship between desire and language/representation as it is not concerned with knowledge about desire but is an intelligible structure of knowledge attainable about desire. It asks what makes the unrepresentable representable.

Tsai's aforementioned filmmaking-as-writing can thus be seen as a form of *écriture* queer, with *écriture* understood, via Barthes, as a "mode of writing" that an author adopts, "a function he gives his language, a set of institutional conventions within which the activity of writing can take place" (Culler 1975, 134). What is queer about Tsai's works is not the literal representation of queer sexuality but rather its metaphorical unrepresentability, intelligible only because of the conventions that Tsai has constructed in his oeuvre, from the theatrical to the cinematic. Tsai's *écriture* queer, I would argue, is made possible (and more complex) because it

functions through poetic conventions such as metaphors and symbols—
"a personal and subconscious network of verbal obsessions" that Barthes
calls "style" (ibid.)—that open the texts to what Rey Chow calls "multiple
possible points of entry... leading to an irresolvable network of connota-
tions" (2004, 127). In what follows, I offer a reading of a selection of works
from Tsai's oeuvre that accounts for Tsai's *écriture* queer of a poetics of
desire. While my interest is in showing how Tsai's poetical conventions
work, I do not shy away totally from their hermeneutic interpretations
where they serve to illuminate the poetics of desire.

A Room with a Flying Closet

In his graduating year at the film and drama section of Chinese Culture
University's (Zhongguo Wenhua Daxue) Drama Department in 1982,
Tsai formed a theater company with some of his classmates; he wrote,
directed, and acted in his first play, *Instant Fried Bean Sauce Noodles* (*Sushi
zhajiangmian;* Wen T'ien-hsiang 2002, 30).[11] His second play, *A Door That
Can't Be Opened in the Dark* (*Hei'an li dabukai de yishan men,* 1983), with the
subtitle *Imprisonment (Qiu),* is a Genetesque play completely without dialogue in which an old male inmate rapes his younger male cellmate (ibid.,
32–33).[12] In 1984 Tsai premiered his third play, *The Wardrobe in the Room*
(*Fangjian li de yigui),* a one-actor play written, directed, and performed by
Tsai himself.[13] The unnamed protagonist is a playwright for television
drama, and the play takes place in his room, where he writes, receives a
long-distance phone call from a friend who has decided to get married,
and subsequently conducts a conversation with an invisible person he
believes is hiding in the wardrobe. *The Wardrobe in the Room* clearly contains autobiographical elements, with the protagonist acting as Tsai's alter
ego. Tsai was then working as a playwright for television drama; the protagonist mentions *Instant Fried Bean Sauce Noodles* as his first play for the
theater, and the long-distance phone call to the protagonist confirms Tsai's
diasporic identity.

In addition to the reference to a homosexual act in his second play,
The Wardrobe in the Room represents Tsai's earliest suggestion of homosexuality in his work, as shown by the telephone conversation between the
protagonist and his friend, during which, since it is a one-actor play, only
the protagonist's monologue is heard: "What time is it on your side? . . .[14]
I just sent you a parcel last week. Did you receive it? . . . Do you know
how much we now have in our bank account? . . . What? . . . You're getting
married? Are you crazy? . . . Didn't we say no marrying? Didn't we agree?
What am I doing here? . . . You know clearly that you're mine. . . . But I

won't give you my blessings" (Tsai Ming-liang 1993, 10–12). The bickering between the two, who have a joint bank account, suggests that they may be more than friends. Though the gender of the other party is unspecified, their argument over the issue of marriage because they have promised each other not to get married may also hint at a male homosexual relationship. After hanging up the phone following the above conversation, the protagonist cries and rips up letters (presumably sent by his friend). He then picks up the pieces, chucks them in a box and throws it into the wardrobe in the room. His reaction both during and after the phone conversation is that of a dumped lover, in this instance doubly betrayed because of a possibly homosexual, "no marrying" pact.

The wardrobe provides another clue to the queer subtext of the play, as the Chinese original of the term, *yigui*, is also the translation for "closet." It is difficult to ascertain if Tsai was aware of the metaphor of the closet vis-à-vis gay identity in early 1980s Taiwan, but the coincidence would have made it more uncanny had he not employed the term *yigui* intentionally.[15] In any case, Tsai's imaginative use of an invisible man residing in the wardrobe serves as an apt metaphor for a sexuality that still dares not speak its name.[16] In a statement written for the play's premiere, Tsai recounts his childhood experience when he would speak incessantly to a wall in a state of loneliness. Clearly referring to his young adult life in Taipei, Tsai goes on: "Later the days became a wandering; one walked the path of one's own choosing. Unfamiliar sceneries, polluted skies, fickle city. But a new name floated in the air, so I began to speak to the air again. You know that was the most stable moment in my entire life. . . . Now I face a wardrobe in the room, not knowing who to analogize it to. . . . Ah, if only he really is a wardrobe. . . . I hope the wardrobe really flies—in my play" (Tsai Ming-liang 1993, 51–52).

Loneliness and silence, both trademarks of Tsai's films, are already taking shape, if not yet perfectly formed, in his theatrical works: talking to the wall, talking to the air, a monologue by Tsai himself, a play with no dialogue whatsoever. *The Wardrobe in the Room* is also a confession by the protagonist, whether he is talking to his lover on the phone, to the invisible man in the wardrobe, or just to himself, in which he reveals his joy and pain, love and loss; in the process, his sexuality is invariably foregrounded. The "path of one's own choosing" exhibits a determination to be truthful to oneself (or one's sexuality perhaps?), and "a new name floated in the air" provides a momentary fulfilment of that wish. However, in a fickle city, the floating new name is also fleeting in its fulfilment, and Tsai's wish is for him—the friend/lover—to be a flying wardrobe/closet, at once signifying containment and freedom.

In the play, the protagonist speaks to the invisible man against the backdrop of a "Western song" with the line, "I know something about love" (English original), the record put on by the invisible man, who also asks the protagonist for a dance. Declining the invitation, the protagonist returns to his writing but feels bad when he discovers that the invisible man has retreated to the wardrobe: "Hey, are you really living comfortably in there? . . . I don't know about other people's wardrobes, but I chuck all the things I dislike in there. . . . What? You smell the sea. . . . Oh yes! I remember: it's that bag of shells! Yes! I went with him to the seaside last summer. . . . Me and him. . . . It was just the two of us then" (Tsai Ming-liang 1993, 37).

The wardrobe functions as a disposal unit in which items of dislike and memories of lost love are hidden away and rendered invisible. If the invisible man in the wardrobe represents a homosexual lover, this love is at best imaginary, and Tsai suggests that fulfilment—or rather displacement—is to be found somewhere else: in writing. When the protagonist completes his writing and "feels totally emptied out," he discovers that the invisible man has disappeared from the wardrobe. Writing is thus both salvation and sublimation, as the invisible man has now really become invisible, just as sexuality and desire are displaced—but perhaps not quite. At the end of the play, the protagonist returns to the room in an exuberant mood, as his play has just been successfully staged. He calls his overseas lover to share his joy, only to revert to tears of lamentation: "Why is it that nobody knows I care only about you? . . . Only you, only you will wait for me at the back door of the cinema, extending your hand to hold mine, waiting to go home with me . . . but . . . now . . . now where is your hand?" (Tsai Ming-liang 1993, 46–47). Having composed himself, the protagonist finally gives his blessings to his lover and hangs up the phone, while the wardrobe begins to fly behind his back, bringing the play to a close.

The Wardrobe in the Room can be read as Tsai's early confession of the self (though not necessarily of himself), a self marked by deep interiority and feelings and by a personal history, a solitary and lonely diasporic self whose only mode of speech is a confession-like monologue and an imaginary dialogue with an invisible man residing in a wardrobe.[17] The pathos of lost love and the longing for love point to a sexuality that must still be spoken in codes, made more difficult by its invisibility and by the heterosexist compulsion to marry. The flying closet remains wishful thinking, made possible on stage but not necessarily in life. The poetics of desire in the play, however, will not be lost on those who, like the protagonist, can also see the invisible. In the decade preceding the emergent gay movement in 1990s Taiwan, a queer, invisible community has been imagined in Tsai's play.

AIDS as a Metaphor (I): *My New Friends*

As Benedict Anderson suggests, "Communities are to be distinguished, not by their falsity/genuineness, but by the style in which they are imagined" (1991, 6). Fast forward to the 1990s, and Tsai's imagining of a queer community assumes the form of a documentary about AIDS, *My New Friends* (*Wo xin renshi de pengyou,* 1995). Featuring lengthy interviews with two gay men diagnosed with HIV, the film was commissioned as one of a five-part series entitled *Stories of the Red Ribbon (Hong sidai de gushi)* on the spread of HIV in Asia. Tsai defied the wishes of the producer by choosing to focus on gay men in Taiwan. As he recalls in an interview, "I remember at that time the production company kept asking me not to emphasise homosexuality. But I felt that prejudice against AIDS patients in Taiwan was often equated with homosexuality—as a double discrimination. Since this was the reality, why avoid it? In fact it should start precisely from here, so I insisted on filming it this way" (Wen T'ien-hsiang 2002, 223).[18]

Tsai chooses to go against the grain by challenging stereotypical representation through *not avoiding* stereotypical representation. The effectiveness of such a tactic, however, is not totally determined by the director but rather by the sociopolitical milieu in which the tactic is employed and received. I would argue that the issue here is not about representation—with its inherent assumption of falsity/genuineness—but about tactics, along the lines of Gayatri Spivak's idea of "strategic essentialism" (Landry and MacLean 1996, 204). I would also suggest that Tsai's queer tactic goes even further than strategic essentialism, as he turns AIDS from representation to metaphor, in the Aristotelian sense of "giving the thing a name that belongs to something else" (quoted in Sontag 1991, 91). If the discrimination against AIDS is embedded in the discrimination against homosexuality, instead of producing an educational documentary about AIDS, Tsai has, in a metaphoric operation, made one about homosexuality instead.

Envisioned as a transnational educational project on HIV and AIDS, the *Stories of the Red Ribbon* documentaries are the first non-official media representations made about these issues in Taiwan at a time when the government's health department was still "AIDS-phobic" (H. Hu 1998, 116). The equation of AIDS with homosexuality was certainly not restricted to Taiwan, and AIDS is at once individuating and communalizing, a personal illness that immediately identifies one as a member of a community.[19] As Susan Sontag writes, "Indeed, to get AIDS is precisely to be revealed, in the majority of cases so far, as a member of a certain 'risk group,' a community of pariahs. The illness flushes out an identity that might have remained hidden from neighbors, jobmates, family, friends. It also confirms an identity and, among the risk group in the United States most severely affected in the beginning, homosexual men, has been a creator of community as well as an experience that isolates the ill and exposes them to harassment and persecution" (1991, 110–111).

Tsai's documentary attempts to imagine such a community at a time when Taiwan's gay community is at best nascent and lacks the activism of a group such as the AIDS Coalition to Unleash Power (ACT UP) in the United States. For someone who has been at pains to dissociate himself from the gay label in his filmmaking career, Tsai's role in the documentary is all the more striking since he has to stand in for his interviewees as a talking head as the latter appear with their faces unseen. As Carlos Rojas argues, with Tsai's uncharacteristic "self-exposure" he literally "insert[s] himself into the film, effectively substituting his informants' anxieties about public exposure with his own" (2003, 86).

The documentary form is, of course, deeply confessional, with interviewees providing testimonies about the subject in question and the form itself (or the directors behind or, in this case, in front of the camera) demanding the testimonies. My interest in Tsai's documentary, however, is not so much what the interviewee/confessor has to say but rather the interviewer/confessant's role: after all, Tsai's face is the only one we get to see. As the interviewees asked for their faces not to be shown, Tsai's face "did the acting in their place" (Rivière and Tsai 1999, 93). Thus *My New Friends* can be seen as Tsai's queer performance through the confession of the interviewees and their sexuality. Using AIDS as a metaphor and acting on behalf of his interviewees, Tsai gives a performance that is also in itself a form of confession, his choice of words, response to the interviewees, and body language unveiling his own relationship to the imagined community of HIV carriers and homosexuals.

My New Friends consists of separate interviews with two gay men, Ah Bin and Hansen. It is clear from some of Tsai's questions that he has been mindful of the public education remit of the documentary series. He seems more guarded at the beginning of each segment but becomes visibly relaxed as the conversation flows. More telling is the physical proximity between Tsai and his interviewees, which closes ostensibly in the interview process. Compared to Stanley Kwan's perhaps unconsciously hostile interview of his mother in a documentary (see chapter 6), Tsai's physical performance creates an environment in which it is safe to be gay and HIV positive.

Writing on documentary, Bill Nichols notes that confession, "with its inadvertent revelation of truths (the past's structuring but invisible presence) by social actors who think they are giving testimony about the past rather than betraying how the past persists in them, in their very act of speaking, grants us the power to extract and manage (secret) knowledge —what the body knows but cannot openly say" (1994a, 5). Taking the cue from Nichols' last phrase, I want to highlight two moments in *My New Friends* in which Tsai's performance betrays the secret knowledge of what the body knows but cannot openly say. The first takes place towards the end of the first segment, featuring Ah Bin. The setup is initially rather formal, with interviewer and interviewee seated a few feet away and facing each other. However, as the interview progresses, Tsai stands up and paces around the room, finally assuming a kneeling position in front of Ah Bin. The second moment occurs in the interview with Hansen, when Tsai, still seated in a chair across from the bed where Hansen sits cross-legged, asks Hansen if he could rest his feet on the bed. Upon Hansen's invitation to do so, Tsai's feet are literally inches away from Hansen's before the two adjust their positions to create a comfortable space between themselves.

Despite being "the authority who requires the confession" (Foucault 1990, 61), Tsai undermines that authority by assuming an equal standing with his interviewees, physically taking up a position where his eyes are on the same level as theirs. However unconsciously, Tsai subverts the power relations by closing the physical distance between himself and the interviewees. By placing his legs inches away from Hansen, Tsai shows that he has no qualms about coming into physical contact (if necessary) with an infected body, thus unwittingly sending an educational message to the audience. More symbolically, by kneeling in front of Ah Bin, as if asking for forgiveness or the imparting of knowledge, Tsai suggests that rather than stigmatizing HIV-infected persons, they may in fact be in a position to offer valuable lessons about tolerance, courage, and love.

AIDS as a Metaphor (II): *Rebels of the Neon God*

Before *My New Friends,* Tsai had mobilized AIDS as a metaphor for homosexuality in his 1992 film, *Rebels of the Neon God* (hereafter *Rebels*). *Rebels* can be seen as the first installment of two different trilogies of Tsai's cinematic oeuvre, one organized by theme and the other by space or location. The first, Xiaokang's trilogy, consists of Tsai's first three films—*Rebels, Vive l'amour*, and *The River*—"linked by theme, structure and casting" (Rayns 1997, 15).[20] The second, the family trilogy, consists of his first, third, and fifth films—*Rebels, The River,* and *What Time Is It There?*—linked by the same domestic location used as Xiaokang's home and with the same actor and actress (Miao Tian and Lu Hsiao-lin/LuXiaolin; also known as Lu Yee-ching/Lu Yijing) playing his parents. As my concern in this book is the representation of homosexuality and as *Rebels* contains the only direct reference to AIDS in all of Tsai's films, I prefer to situate *Rebels* within the Xiaokang trilogy because it provides a more coherent reading on the use of AIDS as a metaphor in Tsai's queer cinema.[21]

Tsai's first three films are linked by the central character of Xiaokang (all played by Lee Kang-sheng/Li Kangsheng), with the queer theme developing from homosocialism through homoeroticism to homosexuality. In *Rebels,* Xiaokang is an adolescent (the *qingshaonian* in the Chinese title) rebelling against his parents and the college entrance examination system; while roaming the streets of Taipei, he finds himself attracted to a slightly older guy, Ah Ze (played by Chen Chao-jung/Chen Zhaorong). Xiaokang's incessant gaze on Ah Ze in *Rebels* is extended in *Vive l'amour,* in which Chen plays Ah Rong. The two run into each other in an empty apartment managed by a female property agent, Lin Meimei (played by Yang Kuei-mei/Yang Guimei). Both men gain illicit entry into the apartment by stealing the key from Meimei, and Xiaokang's attraction to Ah Rong leads him to plant a kiss on the sleeping Ah Rong towards the end of the film. In *The River,* Chen plays an anonymous young man who frequents gay saunas and has a sexual encounter with Xiaokang's father (Miao Tian), unbeknown to Xiaokang. Xiaokang, in turn, has sex unknowingly with his father in a sauna when the two travel to Taichung (Taizhong) to seek a cure for Xiaokang's neck pain. The representation of homosexuality in the trilogy develops from the implicit to the increasingly explicit.

In *Rebels,* gender identification and sexuality are intertwined with a challenge to the patriarchy via the trope of the rebellious Neon God (Nezha) in the title who, in Chinese mythology, cuts out his flesh and bone so as to sever all ties with his parents.[22] Xiaokang realizes that outside the safe environment of the home and the tuition school, there is a more titillating, if somewhat perilous, world out there. That freewheeling world is embodied by the buddies (Ah Ze and Ah Bin) and Ah Gui, a girl who initially has casual sex with Ah Ze's older brother before becoming Ah Ze's girlfriend. Generically, *Rebels* can be regarded as a buddy film with a twist: the protagonist, Xiaokang, is not one of the buddies but rather one who aspires to be like them. The adolescent Xiaokang is set in contrast to the slightly older buddies and thereby shown to be lacking in masculinity. Xiaokang's identification with Ah Ze, the more macho buddy, is complicated by an ambiguous attraction. Writing on the visual representation of men, Richard Dyer sums up the anxiety of adolescent male sexuality: "All anxiety about adolescent males has to do with the contradictory definitions of real manliness, on the one hand asserted and reproduced through compulsory heterosexuality but on the other hand most intensely expressed in the women-excluding buddy system, in a profound inculcation of woman-hating and in the celebration of tearaway, freewheeling, undomesticated adventuring" (1993, 88).

The three male characters in *Rebels* have much in common with the above description: while Xiaokang embodies the anxiety of compulsory heterosexuality, Ah Ze and Ah Bin are buddies who enjoy an undomesticated lifestyle. While the buddies are not altogether woman-excluding and certainly not woman-hating, there is no question that they place male bonding and comradeship above male-female relationships.[23] More important, Xiaokang, who has been excluded from the buddy system, is portrayed as a sad young man who, according to Dyer, is one of the four prominent gay types: "The sad young man is neither androgynously in-between the genders nor playing with the signs of gender. His relationship to masculinity is more difficult, and thus sad. He is a young man, hence not yet really a real man. He is soft; he has not yet achieved assertive masculine hardness. He is also physically less than a man" (Dyer 1993, 42).

Tsai's poetics of desire echoes a signifying system of homosexual representation that (cultural differences notwithstanding) readily identifies Xiaokang as queer. The opposition of the sad young man and the adventurous buddies is set up right in the opening sequence. Crosscutting between them, the film shows, on the one hand, Xiaokang trapped in his room preparing for the college entrance examination while the buddies, soaked in a heavy rain outside, retrieve loads of coins from public telephones with an electric drill. The buddies enjoy their freewheeling fun, whereas education becomes, for Xiaokang, a soft option so that he is safely shielded from the rain and shown to be "not yet really a real man."

There is, however, a rebellious streak in this sad young man: he is, after all, said to be the reincarnation of Nezha. During his half-hearted attempts at preparing for his examinations, Xiaokang breaks the windowpane and cuts his hand, drawing blood (figure 5.1). The blood is not just a symbol for his loss of innocence, as Xiaokang begins to rebel after this opening sequence; more important, it provides a link to the metaphor of

AIDS in which blood is the main channel of infection. This link is echoed towards the end of the film, when Xiaokang vandalizes Ah Ze's motorcycle and sprays the letters "AIDS" on it (figure 5.2).[24] Sandwiched in between the blood/AIDS metaphors is the main body of the film, in which Xiaokang trails Ah Ze in an attempt at gender identification that borders on male homoeroticism.

Steven Shaviro argues that identification is necessary to produce masculine identity, but this "idealized masculine self with which I identify is only an image, apparently belonging to somebody else, in any case remaining forever beyond my grasp" (1993, 185). For Kaja Silverman, identity is not "real" but has a powerful hold on belief. The ego, or *moi,* she explains, is "put in place through the subject's constantly repeated identification with images which have, at the level of the psyche, only a 'virtual' existence" (1992, 353). In *Rebels,* Xiaokang first spots Ah Ze riding a motorcycle with a girl (Ah Gui) holding him tightly from behind. Quietly looking from his father's taxi, he considers the couple an idealized image of the compulsory heterosexuality that embodies Xiaokang's gender and sexual anxieties. When Ah Ze shatters the taxi's side mirror in the rage of a traffic dispute with Xiaokang's father, he also shatters Xiaokang's hitherto sheltered, family-centered world to pieces. The broken mirror echoes the opening sequence, in which Xiaokang breaks his windowpane, and serves to reinforce the home/family's inability to domesticate Xiaokang as he

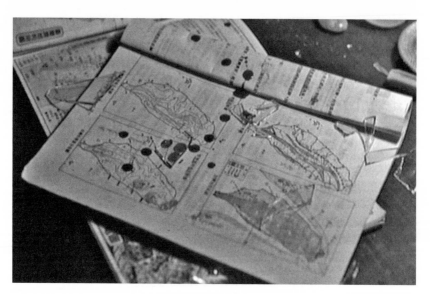

FIGURE 5.1. Blood drops on textbook with map of Taiwan in *Rebels of the Neon God.* (Copyright Central Motion Picture Corporation, 1992)

begins his odyssey in search of his gender and sexual identities. After a string of misdemeanors—withdrawing from the tuition school without his parents' consent and pocketing the huge refund, spending the night out trailing the buddies' criminal activities—Xiaokang ultimately vandalizes Ah Ze's motorcycle to a state beyond recognition.

The last act may seem like Xiaokang is seeking revenge on his father's behalf, but it belies his identification with Ah Ze, for the motorcycle is the ultimate phallic symbol in *Rebels:* Xiaokang rides a small 50cc scooter, whereas the buddies own full-blown motorcycles. It is significant that Xiaokang vandalizes Ah Ze's motorcycle at precisely the time, suggested by the crosscutting, when Ah Ze is having sex with Ah Gui, as it shores up his impotence: Xiaokang's only act of penetration is to insert glue into the keyhole of Ah Ze's motorcycle. This phallic symbol is what Xiaokang desires but does not own: indeed he is momentarily castrated when his scooter is towed away by traffic police because it is illegally parked. Gender identification collapses with a latent (homo)sexuality as Xiaokang displaces in the act of vandalism both his frustrations at failing to meet the compulsory heterosexual ideal and his homoerotic identification with Ah Ze.

This identification is brought out more clearly in a sequence the following morning, in which the film crosscuts between Ah Ze and a scantily dressed (only in underwear) Xiaokang doing the same things (washing

FIGURE 5.2. Ah Ze's motorcycle defaced by Xiaokang with the letters "AIDS" sprayed across. (Copyright Central Motion Picture Corporation, 1992)

their faces, drinking water) in their separate hotel rooms. The sad young man who never smiles is then thrown into a Nezha-like trance as he looks out from his window to find Ah Ze's distress at seeing his motorcycle vandalized, the Chinese characters "Nezha was here" *(Nezha zai ci)* sprayed on the floor. Xiaokang's final effort at identification with Ah Ze, however, is doomed to failure. Riding his scooter, Xiaokang approaches Ah Ze, who is pushing his defaced motorcycle, and asks if he needs help. Understandably in a bad mood, Ah Ze swears at him, and the camera suggestively pulls away, leaving Xiaokang stranded on the spot, diminishing in size.

Rebels problematizes Xiaokang's anxiety in gender identification and awakening sexual identity through Xiaokang's incessant gaze on Ah Ze. With the letters "AIDS" inscribed on the phallic symbol, repressed homosexuality in *Rebels* is imbued with abjection. Looking, as Shaviro explains in his reading of Fassbinder's film adaptation of Jean Genet's eponymous novel *Querelle,* can be dangerous: "If to be looked at is to manifest erotic power, then to be the one looking is to be exposed, to be made accessible to pain and loss. . . . This is the real 'danger' involved in 'finding oneself': a continuing potential for abjection subtends every act of self-identification and self-aggrandizement" (1993, 183).

In finding himself, Xiaokang rejects compulsory heterosexuality at the end of *Rebels.* In the final sequence of the film, Xiaokang steps into a phone-in dating club *(nan lai dian, nü lai dian)* where young men await anonymous calls from young women so as to establish some sort of liaison. The claustrophobic space is compartmentalized into beehive-like telephone booths, recalling the image of a closet. Xiaokang stares at the blinking red lights on the multi-line telephone set and decides to leave. The alarm-like red lights are echoed immediately in an exterior scene of the Taipei cityscape, signalling a crisis in Xiaokang's gender and sexual identities, and the film ends with the camera panning upwards to the blue sky at dawn. The impending break of day—typically signifying hope—points to a drawing out of Xiaokang's homosexuality, which is made explicit in Tsai's third film, *The River.*

Illness as Metaphor: *The River*

The River opens with Xiaokang's chance meeting with a female friend who works on a film set. Accompanying her to the film location, Xiaokang is persuaded by the director to act as a corpse floating in a polluted river. After showering in a hotel room, he has sex with his female friend. He subsequently develops a severe neck pain, and his parents escort him to seek cures of all kinds. Meanwhile, water begins to infiltrate the ceiling of his father's bedroom. The father tries to remedy the situation but to no avail. Both Xiaokang and his father are shown to visit gay saunas, while the mother has an extramarital relationship with a man who distributes pornographic videos. Travelling to Taichung in search of faith healing, Xiaokang and his father visit the same gay sauna separately and have sex with each other, unknowingly, in the dark. When the truth is revealed after the light is turned on, the father slaps Xiaokang, who dashes out. Later, both return separately to the hotel room where they have been staying. At the same time in Taipei, the mother discovers the source of the water infiltrating the father's room: a running tap in the empty apartment upstairs. She climbs up to the apartment and turns the tap off. The next morning, the father is informed by the medium at the temple that they should return to Taipei. He wakes Xiaokang up and goes out to buy breakfast. Xiaokang pushes open the door behind the curtain to find a balcony.

The synopsis above is not so much a summary as a listing of nearly all the action of what passes as a plot in Tsai's film. The film narrative is rendered mainly in silence; there is very little dialogue and no extra-diegetic music at all. Like a Chinese ink painting, in which the lacunae take up disproportionately more space than the painted portion, *The River* is devoid of dramatization of plot or psychologization of characters. It is impossible to explain the inner motivation of the characters or their actions without resorting to clichés about human alienation. The film insists instead on a reading that reorientates attention on metaphors and symbols: the poetical conventions of Tsai's works.

Echoing his earlier use of AIDS as a metaphor, homosexuality is signified as illness as a metaphor in *The River*. Xiaokang mysteriously develops a neck pain after immersing himself in the polluted river, while his father's bedroom begins to be infiltrated with water, as if inflicted by an illness brought home by Xiaokang. The two illnesses are set up as parallel; subsequently Xiaokang is subjected to all kinds of torturous treatment, while his father attempts to solve the problem of the leak by various means. Susan Sontag notes that in different historical periods and in relation to different illnesses, some diseases can be viewed as "forms of self-judgment, of self-betrayal" whereby "one's mind betrays one's body" or "one's body betrays one's feelings," while others are seen as "a form of self-expression" in which the disease "speaks through the body" and is "a language for dramatizing the mental" (1991, 41, 45). In the latter case, the illness "reveals desires of which the patient probably was unaware," and the "hidden passions are now considered a source of illness" (ibid., 46). Tsai's deployment of illness as metaphor can be seen in light of the relationship between the body and psychology explicated by Sontag. There is very little suggestion about the sexuality of the father and son in *The River* besides the episodes showing them paying random visits to gay saunas. Rather, the two illnesses afflicting them (neck pain, leaking ceiling) represent a sexuality that does not express itself psychologically but speaks through the body.

In *The River*, it is the ill corporeal that is privileged over, and often at the expense of, the psychological. The film devotes many sequences to the series of treatments that Xiaokang is put through since suffering the neck pain, including pain relief spray, faith healing at a temple, injections, two chiropractic sessions, massage, Chinese medicine, acupuncture, and hospitalization. The almost excessive representation of Xiaokang's physical ordeal is in stark contrast to the emotional detachment of the characters. It must be qualified that it is not as if the characters lack deep interiority—lack of emotional *expression* should not be equated with lack of emotion itself—but the film resolutely refuses to dramatize or psychologize it. In a paragraph that paraphrases Socrates' address to Phaedrus in Plato's *Phaedrus*, Gustave von Aschenbach, the protagonist of Thomas Mann's *Death in Venice* philosophizes, "But detachment, Phaedrus, and preoccupation with form lead to intoxication and desire, they may lead the noblest among us to frightful emotional excesses, which his own stern cult of the beautiful would make him the first to condemn. . . . Yes, they lead us thither, I say, us who are poets—who by our natures are prone not to excellence but to excess" (T. Mann 1971, 77). Mann's protagonist, who has written *The Abject* (ibid., 76) and is a "master of detachment," is "undone by 'the fantastic logic' of desire by which he is moved" (Butler 1995, 375). According to Butler, for Plato, "it is not that a desire emerges from a body, but that a body emerges *from* a desire" (ibid., 372; emphasis in original), and "the apparent 'detachment' of the Platonist is not a simple self-abnegation but a radical dissolution of the subject through desire, for the sake of desire" (ibid., 375). The excesses in Tsai's film are not emotional but corporeal. If emotional detachment dissolves the subject through desire, *The River* focuses instead on the body emerging from that desire and subjects it to an excessive regime of corporeal punishment. Human bodies, rather than human minds, are indeed "the primary site of drama" (Chow 2004, 126) in Tsai's queer cinema.

Food, Sex, Water, and a Pain in the Neck

The corporeal in *The River* is also the site of sexuality. The film makes an explicit link between the bodily need for food and for sex, recalling a famous saying in *Mencius* that "Appetite for food and sex is nature" (*shise, xingye;* Mencius 1970, 161) and the Chinese idiom "desire for food and sex" (*yinshi nannü*), literalized as *Eat, Drink, Man, Woman* in Ang Lee's 1994 film title. *The River* suggests that the two desires are inextricably linked by editing a sex scene immediately before or after a food scene or crosscutting between the two. These include the following sequences:

1. In the first sex scene of the film, Xiaokang's female friend brings food to the hotel where he has had a shower after acting as a corpse on the film set. The two subsequently have sex in the dark hotel room.
2. After sequence 1, the film cuts immediately to a scene in an equally dark gay sauna where a man makes a move on Xiaokang's father. After rejecting the man and having a shower, the father returns home to eat.
3. The father drinks in a McDonald's restaurant while being cruised by a young man from outside. They continue cruising in the corridor outside. Cut to Xiaokang eating at home. Cut to the young man looking at himself in a mirror at the sauna. Cut to Xiaokang dressing up in front of a mirror in his room. Cut to the young man initiating sex with Xiaokang's father.
4. The father and son have food in the hotel in Taichung where they stay while seeking faith healing for Xiaokang's neck pain. Cut to Taipei, where the mother visits her extramarital lover and feeds him food even though he is half asleep on the sofa. She continues eating and drinking beer. Aroused by the sound of pornographic videotapes being reproduced en masse in the sitting room, she spreads herself on top of her lover and makes moves on him, but he does not respond. Cut to Xiaokang visiting a sauna in Taichung, where the sex scene between the father and son will take place.
5. In the sauna in Taichung, Xiaokang unknowingly enters the dark room where his father is. Unable to see each other in the dark, the father hugs Xiaokang from behind and masturbates him. After Xiaokang has come and they have wiped themselves clean with tissue, Xiaokang turns around to perform oral sex on his father. Cut to the mother eating alone at home and discovering that the father's room is flooded. Cut to the sauna, where the father turns on the light to discover that he has just had sex with Xiaokang. He slaps Xiaokang, who dashes out. Cut to the mother knocking on the door of the upstairs neighbor to no avail. Soaked in the rain, she climbs up the railings to the empty apartment above and turns off the running tap that has been the cause of the flood in the father's room. Cut to the father returning to the hotel room in Taichung, where Xiaokang is already in bed but not asleep.

Tsai's poetics of desire, therefore, not only sets up eating food and having sex as parallel bodily activities and needs, but these are also interwoven with the metaphors of water and illness (particularly in sequence 5). Both Xiaokang and his father's bedroom are ill, sharing a common cause, which is water.[25] Xiaokang's pain in the neck also serves as a metaphor for homosexual representation. As has been suggested, Xiaokang's neck is a displaced penis: in the Chinese language, the *bo* in *bozi* (neck) and the *bo* in *boqi* (erection) have the same pronunciation and share a same radical (Wu Jintao 1998, 103). In one sequence, Xiaokang's mother gives him an electronic massager to ease his neck pain.[26] The massager looks and works like a vibrator, and the reaction of the three family members to its penetrating sound in their separate rooms is contrasted with crosscuts. Watching a pornographic videotape presumably supplied by her extramarital lover, the mother tucks a pillow tightly between her legs. The father, already troubled by the leaking ceiling, throws a towel over his face while Xiaokang soothes himself with the massager. With the massager acting as a symbolic penis rubbing against the displaced penis, this sequence grants a metaphoric expression to Xiaokang's sexual desire, whereas those of his parents (whether heterosexual or homosexual) are invariably silenced in the realm of the family.

The film's structure sets up the two water-inflicted illnesses as parallel with crosscutting, eventually bringing them together to suggest that a cure for both can be found. As detailed in sequence 5 above, the suggestion that a cure for both—with all its metaphoric implications—may lie in having them "come" together is, to say the least, provocative. For Chow, the sex scene between the father and son is "so challenging that it preempts one's relation to the entire film" (2004, 123). In line with my intertextual reading of Tsai's oeuvre, it is necessary to bring in another of Tsai's obsessive metaphors—Nezha—to fully appreciate the poetics of desire in this scene.[27]

Love Thy Father: Oedipus' Wrecks

Writing on the Nezha myth, popularized in the Ming novel *Investitures of the Gods (Fengshen yanyi)*, anthropologist P. Steven Sangren notes his surprise "at finding so rebellious a figure—particularly one whose murderous hostility toward his father so defines his persona—worshipped and beloved in a culture that otherwise so relentlessly and consistently emphasizes filial piety" (2000, 196).[28] While the Nezha myth clearly has Oedipal undertones, I agree with scholars who caution against the reading of the Nezha story (Sangren 2000, 189–196) or the sex scene between the father and son in *The River* (Chow 2004, 138) entirely in terms of Freudian psychoanalysis. However, the same-sex sex between the father and son in *The River* problematizes the typical cross-sex Oedipal representation in terms of gender (for example, the mother-son incest in Pier Paolo Pasolini's 1967 film *Oedipus Rex* and the father-daughter incest in Volker Schlöndorff's 1991 film *Voyager*).[29] Moreover, the focus of the Nezha myth is on the challenge to the patriarchy, not on intergenerational incest.[30] What *The River* does have in common with the Oedipal story is that the "incest" happens when the parties involved are unaware of their blood relations,[31] and it is thus first and foremost about the problematic of chance and coincidence.[32] Like Oedipus, Xiaokang the Nezha causes wreckage in the family by unwittingly having sex with his father.

While the Oedipal trope is embedded in the problematic of chance and coincidence, the sex scene between the father and son in *The River* opens itself to even more radical reading. In sequences 2 and 3 described above, the father is shown to prefer younger men to older ones. His aggressive reaction after discovering that he has had sex with Xiaokang is at once complex and ambiguous. In addition to the obvious fact that the part of his life that he has hitherto safely compartmentalized is now broken down and unveiled before his son, would it be possible that he has harbored, however fleetingly, a secret desire for Xiaokang? Is his slap simply a manifestation of anger at having been found out by his son and/or having found out about his son's sexuality, or could it also be directed at himself for having unwittingly fulfilled a taboo desire? By rethinking the "incest" scene as not just coincidental but possibly consensual (if given the opportunity), this reading pushes the limits of both representation and interpretation even further than the Oedipal logic.

Whatever the case might have been, despite the father's being the party inflicting physical violence on Xiaokang, I would argue that the symbolic patriarchal order embedded in the Nezha trope is undermined by the *mise en scène* in this post-sex scene.[33] After the light is turned on, the camera frames the father in a low-angle shot in the background. While low-angle shots are conventionally employed to enhance a character's power or significance by enlarging his/her presence, here the father actually appears smaller as he is framed in the background, compared to Xiaokang's back, which arises from the bottom left of the screen in the foreground. The low-angle shot highlights the father's impotency as, given the circumstances, if there has to be a hierarchy in the father-son relationship, it is clearly the father who, bearing the double burden of being both husband and father, is in a weaker position in claiming homosexuality compared to his son. What the shot underscores is not a powerful patriarch but a feeble father desperate to undo—with a slap—the sex he has had with his son. Xiaokang may have to bear the pain of the slap, but it is the father who has been placed in a more vulnerable position in simultaneously discovering his son's homosexuality and disclosing his own.

For Sangren, patrilineal institutions themselves can be viewed in part as "attempts to institute fantasies of much the same sort as those that manifest in mythic narratives. Patriliny itself is, in other words, an institutionalization of a desire—a desire for radical autonomy, a form of 'will to power,' in which, via the conceit of worshipping transcendent father figures, one produces oneself as a patriarchal producer" (2000, 192). In the myth, Nezha cuts off his flesh and bones and returns them to his parents as a symbolic gesture of severing his relationship with them, while in *The River* it is semen that Xiaokang has returned to his father in the latter's own hands. If the Nezha myth is read as giving "form and sanction to otherwise illegitimate sentiments and values" that are "autonomy and freedom from overbearing patriarchal authority" (ibid., 195), this desire has not reproduced itself as a patriarchal producer in *The River*. Rather, what is radical about the film is precisely the production of semen—capable of literally producing offspring to uphold the symbolic patriarchal order—in a non-reproductive context that simultaneously undermines the patriarchy. It is even more remarkable that semen is presumably produced by both father and son in this scene, and as they wipe with tissue before disposing of it, the final liquid form to appear in the film empties out its reproductive function in a perverse act of *écriture* queer. Instead of severing the father-son relationship by the return of the son's bodily parts, the co-production of semen by both father and son inaugurates a new kind of father-son intimacy, at once reversing "the oedipal logic of punitive inevitability" (Chow 2004, 138) and reimagining an almost utopian form of community.

The End: To Be Continued

Chow concludes her analysis of *The River* by drawing attention to the film's closing and Xiaokang's opening of the door: "This closing—or opening, rather, which is placed visibly at the center of the scene—is as enigmatic in its indeterminacy as it is refreshing in its sidestepping of the classical-tragic/psychoanalytic-traumatic conclusion. It marks the discursivity of Tsai's film with one more thought-provoking surprise, endowing his allegorical social figures with an unpredictable, rather than fatalistically determined, sense of the life still to come"(2004, 138–139).

The endings of Tsai's films are typically marked by a refusal of closure, each pointing to a continuation in some unknown place and some unknown time in the future, "the life still to come." At the end of *Rebels*,

Xiaokang's rejection of compulsory heterosexuality as he leaves the phone-in dating club is represented by Taipei's cityscapes, with red flashing lights lining both sides of the road signalling his identity crisis. The final shot pans upwards to the sky at the break of dawn, suggesting another day in waiting. At the end of *Vive l'amour*, Xiaokang, who had been hiding under the bed while Meimei and Ah Rong had sex the previous night, wakes up in the morning to find Ah Rong asleep alone in bed. Lying next to him, he plucks up the courage to plant a light kiss on Ah Rong's lips. Meimei walks in a desolate park, sits on a bench—and in the famous final scene that lasts about six minutes—starts sobbing uncontrollably, stops to smoke, then starts sobbing again. After the "incest" scene in *The River*, the father and son return separately to the hotel room where they have been staying. They sleep with their backs to each other, tears welling up in their eyes. The following morning, the father wakes Xiaokang up and goes out to get breakfast. Xiaokang pushes open the door by the side of the bed to find a balcony. In a long take with the balcony framed through the door in the background, Xiaokang steps out and disappears momentarily from the door frame before returning to it. With Xiaokang still rubbing his neck and looking towards the sky, the film ends.

In her reading of Tsai's films, Fran Martin notes that the final shots of *Vive l'amour, The River,* and *The Hole* "gesture ambiguously at a space of possibility beyond yet also within the contemporary urban life-spaces of the films themselves." Calling these spaces *"situated* utopias," Martin sees them as "new spaces of possibility opening up within the constrained conditions of everyday life in the dystopian cities of Taiwanese (post)modernity" (2003c, 179–180; emphasis in original). Martin captures the paradoxically utopian tone of the endings of Tsai's films in their unmistakably dystopian settings, and her reading can be complicated by noting the use of sound in these endings. For a director who uses extra-diegetic music very sparingly, the diegetic sound captured in Tsai's films invariably carries a disproportionate weight.[34] In *Rebels*, the prolonged ringing of the telephones accompanying Xiaokang's departure from the phone-in dating club signals a state of emergency in his gender and sexual identification, counterbalanced only by the more melodic extra-diegetic music of the following exterior scene. In *Vive l'amour*, a police car with its siren raging greets Meimei as she makes her way to her car, which will take her to the park. While the siren signifies the perilous promise of love for Meimei, underscored by her lengthy sobbing in the final shot, this dystopian outlook is offset by Xiaokang's planting of a kiss on Ah Rong—the tiniest of utopian gestures. In *The River*, when Xiaokang pushes open the door, the traffic sounds pouring in are accompanied by those of birds chirping. Xiaokang's stepping out to the balcony recalls the image of the closet/wardrobe and the dark room whose door cannot be opened in Tsai's theatrical works. With light let into the dark room and the sounds of birds chirping, notwithstanding Xiaokang's possible contemplation of suicide when he disappears from the door frame, the ending of the film can only be read, however perversely, as hopeful—and utopian.[35]

On a line by Gertrude Stein, "A dog that you have never had has sighed," Culler comments on "the power of words to create thought or of the peculiar dislocatory force of that linguistic agent which has no existence in nature: the negative" (1975, 151–152). I have argued above that one way of reading Tsai's poetics of desire is to focus on the lacunae rather than the representation itself. The lacuna finds resonance in Culler's notion of the negative, rendered more suggestive in the context of film. To read negatively is thus to read the reverse, a way of reading that, like the text of *jouissance,* introduces a new relationship with representation to the reader. Recalling that the text of *jouissance* unsettles the reader's historical, cultural, and psychological assumptions, Tsai's *écriture* queer inscribes instances such as the "incest" scene, which "we do not yet have the tools to resolve" (Chow 2004, 135). Illustrating with the line by Stein, Fredric Jameson writes, "Every work is clear, provided we locate the angle from which the blur becomes so natural as to pass unnoticed—provided, in other words, we determine and repeat that conceptual operation, often of a very specialized and limited type, in which the style itself originates" (1971, 9).

Tsai's cinema demands a conceptual operation in which a special queer angle engenders the blur as natural or clear. The queer in Tsai's perverse *écriture* queer is not so much an essentialist sexual identity as it is a specialized way of looking. This is where I believe Tsai's greatest contribution to queer cinema lies: rather than simply providing representations of homosexuality, he problematizes the act of representation itself and with it the act of interpretation, thereby challenging us simultaneously to face our own limits (to recall Proust's narrator) and to expand our horizons to incorporate a new, queer way of reading.[36] Employing a poetics of desire that is deeply confessional, I want to finally suggest that Tsai's queer cinema reorientates our attention to that critical anomaly called love.

A Lover's Discourse: The Tender Narrator's Answer

It is revealing that both Chow (2004, 131) and Martin (2003c, 178) read Tsai's films as "redemptive." The "incest" scene, in which the father embraces his son from behind, with just enough light to illuminate the upper bodies of the two, thus giving it an almost religious aura, has been compared to Michelangelo's *Pièta* (Jones 1998, 167). Chow notes the "strong sense of pathos" but the lack of "any idealized romance" in this scene and stresses the "reciprocal tenderness" shown between the father and son in sex (2004, 132).[37] Comparing Xiaokang and Meimei in *Vive l'amour*, Taiwanese critic Tsai Kang-yung (Cai Kangyong) writes, "At the end of *Vive l'amour*, the man who once attempted suicide by cutting his wrist does not cry; the woman who always keeps herself on the trot cries. The man who could only despairingly love in secret does not cry; the woman who was pursued and fulfilled her sexual desire cries. . . . This is perhaps because the man knows for sure that he has loved, and the woman knows for sure that she has not" (1994, 163).

Developing his idea that "the story is cruel but the narrator is tender," Tsai the critic thinks that Tsai the filmmaker has provided a tender answer to a cruel question, and that answer is "perhaps love" (Tsai Kang-yung 1994, 162–163). Echoing Barthes' statement that "the lover's discourse is today *of an extreme solitude*" (Barthes 1990, 1; emphasis in original), Kevin Kopelson questions, "Why is 'love' less fashionable than 'sex' or 'desire'?" He goes on to argue, "Critical theorists tend to see love as an outmoded and incoherent epistemological anomaly that has no place among the discourses that construct sexuality as an epistemological field. . . . But even if conceptions of love are now passé and fragmentary, they are not necessarily inconsequential. They are active, if residual, cultural elements that have played and continue to play a crucial and underexamined role in the construction of sexuality" (1994, 1–2).

If Tsai's queer cinema has proved to be notoriously difficult to interpret, it is perhaps because, as Kopelson argues, we fail to ask the question, "What's love got to do with it?" (Tina Turner's song title) or that we suggest "nothing" as its answer (Kopelson 1994, 1). Tsai's poetics of desire is unequivocally bleak, yet the love he provides as hope cannot be dismissed as utopian either. Fassbinder, "politically radical and highly critical of bourgeois society, but also thoroughly non-utopian" (Shaviro 1993, 161), has made films with titles such as *I Only Want You to Love Me* (1976) and *Love Is Colder than Death* (1969). Hailed in the Western media as Taiwan's Fassbinder, Tsai recalls bursting out in tears in 1982, when he read about Fassbinder's death in the morning paper (Wen T'ien-hsiang 2002, 24, 209). In an interview published in the screenplay for *The River*, Tsai recounts his experience of watching a Fassbinder film: "Yesterday I watched Fassbinder's *Fear Eats the Soul* again and still enjoyed it.[38] Because its content is about encouraging people to love courageously. This in fact serves as a reminder to the people watching it. Actually everyone is not living very happily but we must still have hope" (Chen Baoxu 1997, 64).

As Tsai suggests, via Fassbinder, it is not the lack of love but the fear of love and of loving that eats the soul, cripples the human, and accounts for the absence of affection. This is non-utopian in the sense that love is no panacea, evidenced by Tsai's ironically titled *Vive l'amour.* Love may not last forever—or indeed very long—but it does offer hope. Soft and tender, it is like the kiss that barely touches the other's lips, the ray of light let into a dark room, the faint sound of birds chirping. If the lover's discourse is of an extreme solitude, it is perhaps in the extreme solitude of cinematic spectatorship and in the darkness of sight and sound that one may find again in Tsai's queer cinema the courage to love.

Fragments of Darkness
Stanley Kwan as Gay Director

> Thus sex gradually became an object of great suspicion
> ... the fragment of darkness that we each carry within us:
> a general signification, a universal secret, an omnipresent
> cause, a fear that never ends.
>
> —MICHEL FOUCAULT, *The History of Sexuality*

Stanley Kwan is the first prominent filmmaker in the Chinese-speaking world to have come out openly as gay. Though he was on record stating that "I became gay very early in life" in an English-language film journal as early as 1993 (Kwan 1993, 13), it was with his performance in his 1996 documentary, *Yang ± Yin: Gender in Chinese Cinema (Nansheng nüxiang),* that his sexuality became newsworthy, particularly for audiences in Hong Kong and Taiwan. I call it a performance not only in the sense that the act of coming out is performative as well as a performance; more to the point here, Kwan's 1996 coming out was, unlike his earlier unequivocal statement, much more ambivalent in attitude, indirect in manner, and complex in meaning. This documentary is central to understanding Kwan's filmmaking career both pre- and post-coming out; it also foregrounds the significance of Kwan as the first openly gay director in Chinese cinemas.[1]

In this chapter, I propose to study Kwan's 1998 film, *Hold You Tight,* against the background of his coming out. As his first post-coming-out feature film, *Hold You Tight* encapsulates Kwan's ambivalence towards the issue of homosexuality in a manner that mirrors his ambivalence towards his own coming out. Unlike his later, more openly gay *Lan Yu* (2001), *Hold You Tight* captures a moment when Kwan's personal history and filmmaking career collapse into each other and serves to illuminate issues of gay identity politics in a Chinese context. This reading is thus deliberately autobiographical, for it is precisely in the negotiation of one's sexuality that the personal not only becomes the political, but also embodies the political in all its contradiction and struggle.[2]

Absent Father, Abject Filmmaker

Kwan opens *Yang ± Yin: Gender in Chinese Cinema* with a short chapter entitled "Absence of Father (I)." In the voice-over, set against scenes of naked men in a bathhouse from his 1991 film, *Actress* (*Ruan Lingyu*, also known as *Center Stage*), Kwan describes a love for his father that borders on the incestuous:

> When my father took me to a bathhouse, it was the first time I'd seen so many male bodies. These shots from my film *Actress* evoke that memory. My father died when I was fourteen. My memories of him are mostly memories of longing for his love because I always felt that he preferred his daughters to his sons. We were so poor when I was young that I had to sleep with him, head to toe on a sofa, and I recall touching him while pretending to be asleep. I also vividly recall the smell of his body. This picture is one of the few that I have of him. He didn't like to be photographed.[3]

This opening chapter sets the tone for the documentary, in which Kwan attempts to account for his sexuality by combing through family history, personal biography, and Chinese cinematic culture. Kwan's narration of the absent father is striking for his tone of abjection (defined as the "condition or estate of one cast down; abasement, humiliation, degradation" [*OED*]): he always felt his father preferred his daughters to his sons. Kwan acknowledged in an interview that making the documentary was a means for him to satisfy his longing for his father (Li Xiaoxian 1997, 56).[4] The abject filmmaker thus idealizes the image and his memory of his absent father, and as Steven Shaviro argues in his discussion of Fassbinder's film *Querelle*, abjection is "always already presupposed, as the unacknowledged ground of idealization" (1993, 185).

After the brief opening chapter, *Yang ± Yin* moves on to Kwan's filmmaking career, which, until then, was best known for films centered on women, including *Red Rose, White Rose* (*Hong meigui, bai meigui*, 1994); *Actress; Rouge* (*Yanzhi kou*, 1988); and *Love unto Waste* (*Dixia qing*, 1986). Kwan asks in the voice-over, "Why do I make so many films about women? Does it mean that I'm rather feminine myself?" He goes on to provide his own answer: following his father's death, he suddenly became the official head of the family as the eldest son, and the lives of all the women in the family became secondary to his. His sisters had to quit school to work to finance his education, his mother labored tirelessly to support the family, and Kwan confesses to feeling more like a protected child than a surrogate father. This story of a family struggling to cope after a father's death seems familiar enough, yet it is precisely this unremarkable familiarity that underlines the patrilineal tradition and patriarchal nature of the Chinese family, which continue to exercise a strong hold on its members even in modern times. Despite his being at the tender age of fourteen, there was no question that Kwan was the symbolic head of the family, that his education was more important than that of his sisters, and (though unmentioned in the above episode) that he would be expected to get married and to produce male offspring to carry on the family name.

The last issue was crucially intertwined with his sexuality in the closing chapter of the documentary, entitled "Absence of Father (II)." Considering Kwan's preoccupation with the theme of the absent father and his obsessive longing for his father's love, one wonders if, given the opportunity, he would have preferred to come out to his father—and, if so, how. However, Kwan's father did not like to be photographed; had he still been alive, it would be unlikely that he would have agreed to appear in his son's documentary, especially if Kwan had insisted upon declaring his almost incestuous love for his father. In any case, in the absence of his father, Kwan's mother became the lone parent—and surrogate father—to whom Kwan could come out. The closing chapter begins with, and is largely taken up by, a study of Yam Kin-fai (Ren Jianhui) and Baak Suet-sin (Bai Xuexian), two female stars of Cantonese cinema of the 1950s and 1960s who performed as a couple on screen (with Yam in the cross-dressing role) and lived as such off screen.[5] Kwan's mother had been a huge fan of the couple and exhibits a candid humor when talking about their charm ("I might have chased after Yam if I weren't burdened by children"). The remarkable film careers and private lives of Yam and Baak—they were accepted as a couple both in reel life and real life, no questions asked—act as a trope for Kwan's negotiation of his sexuality.

From the outset of this chapter in the documentary, Kwan introduces the Chinese concept of *taijiao* (literally "fetus education"), which proposes that the fetus can be influenced by outside stimuli, as a means of foregrounding his sexuality. Kwan "wondered if my own character was somehow shaped by all those Yam Kin-fai films my mother watched" when she was pregnant with him. The word "character" functions as a euphemism for Kwan to talk about a love that still dares not speak its name, as he asks his mother if she ever wondered why her son did not make more masculine films about men but instead was known for his women's films. In a reply punctuated by pauses and hesitations that indicates either her discomfort with or inability to articulate about the subject, Kwan's mother reiterates that "each person has his own *wish* [*yuanyi*]" and "each person has his own *will* [*zhixiang*]" (emphasis mine), the two italicized terms serving a similar euphemistic function as Kwan's choice of the word "character." Nevertheless, it is clear what Kwan is alluding to in his reference to his women's films, and it is also clear that his mother respects his choice, whatever that might have been.

However, if Kwan's mother inadvertently turned her son gay by overindulging in Yam Kin-fai films when she was pregnant with him, she now has to deal with the issue of her son's disinclination to impregnate a woman. In a sequence that recalls Fassbinder's interrogation of his mother in an episode in the *portmanteau* film *Germany in Autumn* (1978), Kwan questions his mother's attitude towards his sexuality vis-à-vis the issue of the perpetuation of the family name:

KWAN: So, do you now accept my relationship with William
  [presumably Kwan's partner's name]?
MOTHER: It doesn't matter. . . .
KWAN: *(Interrupts.)* How do you see it?
MOTHER: Well, if it's a daughter, she's been married off *(laughs);*
  if it's a son, he's got a wife. That's it. How else otherwise?
  If I didn't accept it, I wouldn't be living here [presumably
  with Kwan and William].

Cut to the next scene:

MOTHER: My concept nowadays is not about perpetuating the
  family line and that there must be male sons. It doesn't
  matter to me. . . .
KWAN: But I'm the eldest son. Don't you hold on to any
  traditional ideas?
MOTHER: No, no traditional ideas at all. *(Pause and silence for
  about five seconds.)* It's very common; it doesn't matter in
  today's society. I'm not anxious that I must have grandchildren, and male ones at that. Well, if something
  happens to you . . . once you close your eyes, you won't
  know anything else. Isn't that right? *(Laughs.)* It's very
  simple, it's really very simple.

This sequence is noteworthy for Kwan's insistence on having his mother talk about his sexuality and to do so in terms related to the perpetuation of the family line by her eldest son, who assumed the official role of the head of the family at the age of fourteen, some twenty-five years previously.[6] Kwan's mother, who did not have much formal education and who was clearly supportive of her son by the fact that she appeared in the documentary, was put in a situation where she had to deal with a very personal and complex issue—in front of a camera.[7] Her eloquent articulation after the five-second pause is revealing in that she suddenly found a language familiar to her, the language of death: "If something happens to you . . . once you close your eyes, you won't know anything else."[8] That she tried to reassure herself by repeating "It's very simple" yet simultaneously took out a handkerchief suggests that despite her best intentions, her son's homosexuality is still a fact hard to swallow and that she would probably find real peace of mind only in death.

Equally suggestive is Kwan's cinematic treatment of this sequence, which also ends the documentary. In the final moment after his mother utters the phrase "It's very simple," her act of retrieving a handkerchief from the pocket of her trousers and moving it towards her face is rendered in slow motion and with extra-diegetic music—both hitherto absent—followed immediately by the closing credits. With the documentary ending precisely at the moment the mother's handkerchief approaches her face, the audience does not get to see the mother wiping her tears, though it is clear that her voice has begun to crack and that tears are welling in her eyes. The audience is left with a reflective mood generated by the blackness of the screen and the evocative, if somewhat melancholy, music. The ending thus creates a rather emotive impact as it hangs precariously on the edge of violence, an emotional violence ending in tears. In the absence of the father, it is the mother who has had to bear the full force of a son's attempt to come to terms with his sexuality. Because the son's attitude towards his father is one of abjection/idealization and since "idealization is itself the source of the aggressivity it refuses to recognize" and every idealization is "a violent imposition of power" (Shaviro 1993, 161–162), it is to the issues of violence and power that we must now turn.

Violence and Terror: The Coming Out Story

What, then, is the ethics of coming out? If, as Eve Sedgwick argues, when gay people come out to parents, it is "with the consciousness of a potential for serious injury that is likely to go in both directions" and that in a homophobic society, the gay person's coming out may in turn plunge the parents "into the closet of [their] conservative community" (1990, 80), what is often missing in the celebratory rhetoric of gay liberation ("Out and proud") is the recognition that coming out can be an act imbued with violence and terror precisely because of the repressive force of the closet. In this context, if the private pain of suffering in the closet can be released only by coming out to one's parents, what does it mean for Kwan to engage his mother in his performance of coming out in a documentary meant for public consumption, especially in Hong Kong, arguably a rather homophobic society where he and his mother both live? If there is indeed injury inflicted in both directions in this instance, does Kwan's repressive pain of having been in the closet override his mother's pain of having to talk about it in front of a camera?

This is where I believe a comparison with Fassbinder's cinema in general, and his interrogation scene with his mother in *Germany in Autumn* in particular, is apt. Like Kwan, Fassbinder was known for his women's films and had a difficult relationship with his sexuality.[9] For Thomas Elsaesser, the central experience in Fassbinder's cinema—"one might go so far as to call it the trauma that motivates his productivity"—is "emotional exploitation" (1980, 25), a point Fassbinder himself freely admitted in interviews.[10] Elsaesser elaborates:

> [Fassbinder's] films are fictionalised, dramatised, occasionally didactic versions of what it means to live within power structures and dependencies that are all but completely internalised, and as such apparently removed from any possibility of change or development. . . .
>
> Whether the roots of this trauma necessarily have to be sought in Fassbinder's private life is immaterial. As far as the films are concerned, they attempt to prove, with varying degrees of conviction, that the personal predicament has a wider symptomatic significance. (ibid., 25–26)

Emotional exploitation is also a familiar theme in Kwan's cinema: an introduction to his films is entitled "Stanley Kwan: Narratives of Feminine Anguish" (Tam and Dissanayake 1998). Prior to his coming out in the documentary, Kwan focused on making films about women in which he projected his sexuality onto the female characters (Li Xiaoxian 1997, 58).[11] Talking about his films about women in an interview, Kwan acknowledged that he had been "too indulgent in the female characters." Citing Ruhua (Fleur) in *Rouge* as an example, Kwan said, "How much Ruhua is hurt, that's how hurt I am; how hurt I am, that's how hurt I want Ruhua to be" (ibid., 59). As with the case of Fassbinder, one could ponder what it means for Kwan to have lived within and internalized a power structure governing his sexuality—the repressive force of the closet—and to what extent this personal predicament has a wider symptomatic significance. His 1993 article proclaiming his sexuality ended with this statement: "However, I still don't know whether it is right to tell my mom what I am" (Kwan 1993, 13). When he decided to do so in 1996, the violence and terror embedded in the repressive force of the closet were unleashed.

I am not suggesting that Kwan intended to hurt his mother by making her confront his sexuality in the documentary. In fact, Kwan confessed in an interview that "I am very concerned about my mother's feelings. For example, after the programme [referring to the documentary] aired, I became very sensitive: my ears would prick up every time a relative phoned. The only thing I want to apologize to my mother for is that she has to face certain things that I don't have to" (Li Xiaoxian 1997, 57). Nevertheless, the sequence in the closing chapter quoted above does have the effect of emotional exploitation and recalls a similar sequence in Fassbinder's contribution to the *portmanteau* film *Germany in Autumn*.[12] Set against the background of West Germany in the autumn of 1977, when the president of the Employers' Federation was kidnapped and murdered by terrorists, Fassbinder's segment of the film includes a fierce argument between Fassbinder and his lover and with his mother. His lover "wants all the terrorists to be shot," whereas his mother "wants to annul democracy, she wants one terrorist executed for every hostage killed, . . . and above all she wants an authoritarian ruler, who—as she says with an apologetic smile—'is very good and very kind and decent,'" despite the fact that she grew up in the Nazi period herself (Thomsen 1997, 251, 253). Like Fassbinder, Kwan insists on framing his mother in a situation with which she may not be equipped to deal, either psychologically or intellectually.[13] In the interview sequence, Kwan is seated to the left of the screen in the foreground, with his mother occupying the center-right of the screen in the background. As he asks the first questions, Kwan holds a cigarette in his right hand, the symbolically phallic object pointing in the direction of his mother like a shotgun, smoke rising at its tip. In another scene, with Kwan's mother speaking in close-up, the smoke lightly clouds her face as if engulfing her. Kwan's temperament may not have allowed him to exercise the type of emotional terrorism characteristic of Fassbinder, but the undercurrents of violence and terror, both implicit and symbolic, are nonetheless present in this sequence. To pursue the Fassbinder trope further, this also reminds one of the Oscar Wilde line sung melancholically by Jeanne Moreau in Fassbinder's film adaptation of Jean Genet's novel *Querelle*: "Each man kills the thing he loves."

The Personal and the Political

Describing Fassbinder's response to those closest to him in *Germany in Autumn* as one of "psychological terror," Christian Braad Thomsen argues that unlike the other directors who contributed to the film but kept their personal selves out of the political events that triggered it, "Fassbinder shows that political and private frustrations are most intimately related, that terrorism begins in the private sphere and that the private in turn is destroyed by political developments" (1997, 252).

What political frustrations might have been intertwined with private ones for Kwan? Between the release of *Yang ± Yin* in 1996 and *Hold You Tight* in 1998, Kwan made a relatively unknown documentary, *Still Love You After All These* (*Nian ni ru xi;* hereafter *Still*) in 1997, the year of Hong Kong's return to Chinese rule. As the timing of its making indicates, *Still* serves as a transition for my reading of Kwan's 1998 film, particularly since both make explicit the link between the personal and the political. While making *Still*, Kwan was invited to contribute to a *portmanteau* theater production entitled *Journey to the East (Zhongguo lücheng 97)*, in which directors from China, Taiwan, and Hong Kong would individually produce a twenty-minute play. Kwan reflects upon this period in *Still:* "Suddenly many friends around me are enthusiastically doing many things. Actually everyone is hoping to finish the work before July 1. Nobody knows what it will be like after that. Even I have asked the question, but of course nobody can answer you."

Indeed, it has become virtually impossible to discuss contemporary Hong Kong culture without invoking Hong Kong's 1997 return to China or, to put it differently, Hong Kong's disappearance into the geopolitical boundary of the PRC. Ackbar Abbas argues that an unprecedented interest in Hong Kong culture was precipitated by the imminence of its disappearance (1997, 7). It would seem from Kwan's reflection in *Still* above that there was a general mood to "seize the day" before Hong Kong's disappearance. Kwan's representation of the intertwining relation between personal and political frustrations in *Still* and *Hold You Tight* can be appreciated against this background and through the concept of decadence.

According to Matei Calinescu, the Latin noun *decadentia* (and its derivatives in European languages, such as "decadence" in English) was not used before the Middle Ages. The myth of decadence, however, was known to nearly all ancient peoples with mythical-religious traditions, marked by the motifs of "the destructiveness of time and the fatality of decline" (1987, 151). Calinescu suggests that the modern idea of decadence is linked to the view of time and history brought about by the Judeo-Christian tradition, whose eschatological character makes the progression of time linear and irreversible. As the "approach of the Day of Doom is announced by the unmistakable sign of profound decay," decadence "thus becomes the anguishing prelude to the end of the world. The deeper the decadence, the closer the Last Judgment" (ibid., 152–153). The Christian view of decadence is also characterized by "an acute and feverish sense of urgency," which brings about "restlessness and a need for self-examination, for agonizing commitments and momentous renunciations" (ibid., 154).

Just as the signing of the Sino-British Joint Declaration in 1984 and the Tiananmen incident in 1989 have been a double trauma for many Hong Kong people (Abbas 1997, 6–7), July 1, 1997, can be seen as the equivalent of the biblical, apocalyptic Day of Doom for Hong Kong. Especially in the aftermath of the Tiananmen incident, which exacerbated the exodus of Hong Kong emigrants, many people in Hong Kong began to wonder if life would remain the same after 1997. As the linear and irreversible borrowed time under British rule was ticking away, the fatality of decline in terms of civic and democratic rights under Chinese rule seemed certain. It was indeed a time, in Calinescu's words, "for self-examination, for agonizing commitments and momentous renunciations"—the hallmarks of decadence. I would argue, however, that the two films by Kwan reverse Calinescu's description to demonstrate, almost in defiance, that the closer the Last Judgment, the deeper the decadence.

Both *Still* and *Hold You Tight* use Tsing Ma Bridge (Qingma Daqiao), a suspension bridge linking Hong Kong and its new offshore Chek Lap Kok Airport, as a metaphor for Hong Kong's uncertain post-1997 future, held in suspense. The opening sequence of *Still* features shots of the bridge accompanied by the following voice-over by Kwan:

> Last year I asked a friend: if he wanted the person he loved the most to give him a present, what would it be? At that time we happened to be on the bus from the New Territories to Kowloon. Pointing across the sea at the Tsing Ma Bridge, still under construction and full of scaffolding, he said: I want him to give me this, and for no one else to be allowed to walk on it. In our leisure, the two of us will take a stroll on it and look at the sunset. I interrupted: Do you want him to give you the new airport as well?[14]

Political frustration is here rendered as a personal joke: the image of two (gay) men strolling leisurely on a bridge pregnant with political symbolism but claimed for their exclusive use and the idea that both the bridge and the airport can serve as personal gifts are at once defiant and decadent. As a concept, decadence is inseparable from degeneration, decline, and decay (Calinescu 1987, 151–153), and in its popular usage, it is defined as signifying a decline from established artistic and moral standards, which is equivalent to degeneracy (Bullock and Trombley 1999, 201). However, it is a different kind of morality that Kwan is proposing here. The Chinese translations of "decadence" include the more commonly used *tuifei* as well as *duoluo,* and the Chinese title of Kwan's *Hold You Tight, Yu kuaile yu duoluo,* literally means "the happier the more decadent."[15] If we bear in mind the political shadow of 1997, the coupling of decadence with happiness may have been ironic wishful thinking, but the stance is decidedly defiant: the closer the Last Judgment, the deeper the decadence. For Kwan, decadence is not a form of degeneration but rather something to be celebrated. To reverse his Chinese film title: the more decadent, the happier.

What would make one happy in the face of political frustration? In *Hold You Tight,* Hong Kong's change in political status is marked metaphorically by the relocation of its international airport: the film opens with a scene at the old Kai-Tak Airport and ends with two of the male protagonists (Tong and Wai) driving on the Tsing Ma Bridge, which leads to the new Chek Lap Kok Airport, opened in June 1998. Early in the film, the Chinese leader Deng Xiaoping's death (in February 1997) is announced on the televised news, marking the film's diegetic time as spanning from pre-handover to post-colonial. Deng had expressed his wish to see Hong Kong returned to its "motherland," and the announcement of his death in the film seems to highlight—for once—his political frustration instead of that of the Hong Kong people. However, in the film's closing scene, Tong asks Wai if he remembers what he was doing on September 16, 1984. It was the day British prime minister Margaret Thatcher tripped on the steps on her way to negotiations with Chinese leaders on the Sino-British Joint Declaration (Luo 2002, 65). The relocation of the airport is an exchange of an old space for a new one. In the case of Hong Kong's relocation into the geopolitical boundary of the PRC, the old space has also become part of the new, thus disappearing into the new. With Thatcher unwittingly exhibiting Britain's weakness in the face of Deng-ruled China, Hong Kong's future is kept in perilous suspense as the protagonists make the metaphorical cross from the old to the new regime via the bridge.

For those who chose to stay in Hong Kong after 1997, there remained the question of how to deal with the might of the PRC. In a most explicit statement linking his sexuality to the political situation in Hong Kong, Kwan quotes in *Still* a classic line from a Cantonese opera, *Princess Chang Ping (Dinühua),* which had been performed by Yam Kin-fai and Baak Suet-sin—"I deny! I deny! . . . Yet in the end there's simply no denial" *(buren buren huan xu ren)*—and comments: "This line has always been an apt description of my process of growing up, especially in relation to my sexuality. Time has gone by, and this line seems to relate to the identity [or identification] of the Hong Kong people at this moment. I have not imagined that I would have to encounter the identity crisis entangled in this line twice in half my lifetime." For Kwan, the line "I deny! I deny! . . . Yet in the end there's simply no denial" sums up his dual identity crisis as a homosexual and as a prospective citizen of Hong Kong as a Special Administrative Region of the PRC.[16] The recognition (and acceptance) of his identities is borne not so much out of a positive affirmation but the futility of repeated denial, with an overdose of abjection. Tracing the development of the concept of decadence to the Italian *decadentismo,* Calinescu suggests that Italian critics agree on the fundamental link between *decadentismo* and a consciousness of crisis. Quoting Leone de Castris's *Decadentismo e realismo* (1959), Calinescu writes, "decadentism contains even the possibility of a new realism, a realism of inner life, of consciousness, interested primarily in the self that experiences the crisis and less in the naturalistic representation of the milieu" (1987, 220). In my following analysis of *Hold You Tight,* it is the consciousness of crisis by the self on which I will focus. The line "I deny! I deny! . . . Yet in the end there's simply no denial" echoes throughout the film as a background of the political crisis, as well as a backdrop to, and undercurrent of, the realism of the experience of crisis, which invariably impinges on the characters' abjection and their homosexual relations.

A(nother) City of Sadness: Duality, Geopolitics, Sexuality

The following reading situates *Hold You Tight* at the crossroads of two indices. First, as a film made at the turn of Hong Kong's handover to the PRC and with its use of Hong Kong and Taipei as somewhat parallel or mirrored locales, the film portrays dislocated characters who straddle the two cities and problematizes issues of duality and geopolitics. Second, as Kwan's first feature film since he came out publicly and as his first film to deal directly with male homosexuality, the film's representation of homosexuality is by no means unambiguous and seems to be dominated by the trope of displacement. I will show that the two indices are inextricably linked and that the displacement of sexual desires by the dislocated characters cannot be read outside the context of duality and geopolitics in which the film is set. As Helen Hok-sze Leung argues, the film "is indeed not about gay identity but about the ambivalence and fluidity of desire and its capacity to weave disparate people together during a time of crisis" (2001, 440).[17]

Hold You Tight, set initially in Hong Kong, explores the entangled relationships involving three men and two women. The male object of desire is a computer programmer, Wai (Sunny Chan Kam-hung/Chen Jinhong), who is newly married to Moon (Chingmy Yau/Qiu Shuzhen), an ambitious career woman who dies on a business trip to Taipei. Two men are attracted to Wai: Tong (Eric Tsang/Zeng Zhiwei), a middle-aged property agent, and Jie (or Xiaozhe, played by Ko Yu-lun/Ke Yulun), a young Taiwanese man who works as a lifeguard at the swimming pool in the apartment estate where Wai and Moon live.[18] Jie initiates a sexual relationship with Moon while harboring a secret desire for Wai. After Moon's death, Tong develops a platonic friendship with Wai, whereas Jie returns to Taipei, where he meets Rosa (also played by Yau), a Hong Kong businesswoman who owns a boutique there. It is through Rosa that Jie finally picks up the courage to express his love for Wai, making Wai reflect on his relationship with Tong.

The film's narrative structure is more complicated than the above synopsis would suggest. As in Krzysztof Kieślowski's 1991 film, *The Double Life of Véronique,* the two women in *Hold You Tight,* Moon and Rosa, are played by the same actress and linked by the key role they assume in Jie's relationship with Wai. Both women, oblivious to each other's presence, appear in the opening scene at the airport, where Moon is soon to die on her business trip to Taipei.[19] The first half of the film mainly comprises a flashback to Moon's marital life with Wai and extramarital affair with Jie. The opening airport scene is then reprised to mark the end of the flashback and the beginning of linear time after Moon's death. The second half traces Tong's friendship with Wai in Hong Kong and Jie's relationship with Rosa in Taipei. Hence the notion of duality is deeply embedded in the film's structure in terms of its employment of dual roles for the same actress, its spatial straddle of Hong Kong and Taipei, and its narrative temporality, switching between the past and the present, with Moon's death as the dividing marker.

While using the two airports in the opening and closing scenes as an enveloping signification of Hong Kong's return to China, the film also ushers in Taiwan as a parallel or mirroring element in duality, as the camera lingers suggestively on a film poster that takes center stage in Tong's living room (figure 6.1). The film on the poster, *A City of Sadness,* by Taiwanese director Hou Hsiao-hsien, was billed as a film about Taiwan's Tiananmen when competing at the 1989 Venice Film Festival, where it won the Golden Lion award. Hou's film was made in the immediate post-martial law period in Taiwan, when some taboo issues were brought into public discourse for the first time. It deals with Taiwan's bloody encounter on February 28, 1947, with a Chinese regime (this time Nationalist rather than communist) that had made sovereignty claims on the island at the end of Japanese colonial rule. *Hold You Tight* therefore suggests unequivocally a parallel between Hong Kong and Taiwan in terms of their shared destiny of "returning to the motherland" *(huigui zuguo)* after many decades of colonization, each case foreshadowed or overdetermined by a brutal massacre. In the time period in which Kwan's film is set and produced, the Hong Kong in the post-Tiananmen climate leading to the 1997 handover can indeed be aptly described as a(nother) city of sadness.

As Hong Kong's parallel, Taiwan is at once disruptive and mirroring—disruptive because as an antagonistic regime opposed to communist China, Taiwan often functions as the "third space" in China's political equation in relation to Hong Kong (Yue 2000, 260) and serves as a reminder that the CCP does not always get its way in claiming territorial and political sovereignty, and mirroring because Taiwan seems to be projected as Hong Kong's alter ego in Kwan's film, continuing Hong Kong's existence after its 1997 disappearance. The film opens at the old Hong Kong airport, and the destination of the two female characters is Taipei. For Andrew Grossman, this "flash-forward image" points to "a post-1997 progression from formerly democratic HK to still-democratic Taiwan" (2000c, 175). In diegetic terms, the opening scene also marks the death of

FIGURE 6.1. Hong Kong as "a city of sadness" in *Hold You Tight*. (Copyright Golden Harvest / Kwan's Creation Workshop, 1998)

the Hong Kong woman (Moon) while ushering in her Taiwanese counterpart (Rosa), who can be seen as the former's reincarnation.[20]

In addition, the tropes of dislocation and displacement are underlined in relation to geopolitics and sexuality. The choice of locations for the opening and closing scenes is not without its symbolic significance. As a site of international transport and communication, the airport is also the exit point for dislocated emigrants and the starting point of diaspora. The huge exodus of Hong Kong emigrants after Tiananmen and pre-1997 is captured in the film via another mode of transport—the Mass Transit Railway (MTR). One early scene shows a quarrel between an anonymous gay couple on the MTR train, as one of them plans to move to Vancouver, thus incurring the wrath of his lover. Geopolitics and sexuality are intertwined here as the political crisis threatens to break this couple up even as Hong Kong is due to reunite with China. Using this physical mode of transportation, the film also hints at the unfolding emotional and sexual entanglement and displacement among its characters, as it is on this MTR train that Tong first notices his future object of desire, Wai, standing despondently on the platform.[21] The circulation of the gay gaze is heightened as, at the same time, Jie is fixing his eyes on Wai while standing farther back on the platform.

In addition to alluding to the geopolitical, a city of sadness also signifies the sexual. The film poster is a gift from Tong's ex-boyfriend, Eric, who now lives in London. Though it is unclear if their separation is the result of the political uncertainties of 1997, the film suggests a correlation by placing Tong as the witness to the gay couple's quarrel on the MTR train. For Tong, sadness is tied to mourning for love lost as well as lives lost vis-à-vis homosexuality. In an early scene, Tong is informed by a friend that Eric's boyfriend in London has died (presumably of AIDS), but he is unsure about Eric's state of health. As Tong subsequently washes the dishes in the kitchen, the camera pans to the poster in the living room, highlighting the year in which the gift was presented—1989, another suggestion of the parallel between the Tiananmen incident and Taiwan's February 28 incident.[22] The duality of Hong Kong and Taiwan is further underlined as Tong hums a line from a song while doing his dishes—not a Cantonese song, as one might expect, but a Taiwanese Mandarin ballad entitled *You're My Only One (Nishi wode weiyi)*—"Though you're my first, though you're my last, though you're my only one."[23] Unlike the two female characters and Jie, Tong does not physically commute between Hong Kong and Taipei. His collection of books on Taiwanese cinema and his love for Taiwanese pop music, however, connect him to Taiwan on the level of cultural identification.[24] (Wai is the only character who bears no relation to Taiwan.) For Kwan, whose films have long enjoyed critical acclaim and popular reception in Taiwan, the cultural references in *Hold You Tight* to Taiwan are perhaps his oblique way of paying homage to Taiwanese cinema.[25]

In what follows, I will analyze the displacement of desire, which lies at the heart of the film's representation of homosexuality. With regard to same-sex relations, three possibilities are delineated through the three male characters. Tong is an openly gay man who secretly desires Wai; Jie loves Wai but displaces this desire onto sexual relations with women; and Wai is not repelled by the two men's attraction to him. Because the object-choice, Wai, is a married and hence presumably heterosexual man, Tong's and Jie's desire for him is displaced, if not misplaced. Tong's desire for Wai is displaced through denial, whereas Jie uses Moon as a substitute for Wai. While the banality of both heterosexual marriage and heterosexual man are portrayed in a manner that demystifies the fable of marital life as a happy ending, the film's expressions of homosexual desire are invariably displaced and remain largely unfulfilled. I will focus my analysis on the three men and their respective relationships with homosexuality and argue that homosexual desire is displaced as a heterosexual ideal since the object of desire in the film is a heterosexual man.

Abjection and Denial: Displacing Misanthropy as Philanthropy

The character who most embodies the sense of abjection and denial is the openly gay man, Tong. A middle-aged man who is past his prime in terms of physical attributes in the ruthlessly youth- and beauty-oriented gay world, Tong's outlook on life is decidedly misanthropic. However, precisely because he seems to have ruled out possibilities of future love relationships in his life, Tong is able to displace misanthropy as philanthropy by exhibiting a generosity of spirit towards others, particularly men, often underpinned by a covert but harmless sexual interest. When a male colleague asks to borrow his car and jokingly assures him that he is eyeing only Tong's car but not him, Tong's reply, "I'm not the slightest bit worried," is overlaid with sexual innuendo but falls on deaf ears. Though Tong is no longer in touch with Eric, when he hears that Eric's boyfriend has died and that Eric might be evicted from their flat in London, Tong offers help through a mutual friend, emphasizing that money is not a problem. These incidents suggest that Tong channels his misanthropic resolution and displaced sexual interests through his philanthropic kindness.

If philanthropy is Tong's mask for concealing his misanthropy, his relationship with Wai poses the question of where philanthropy ends and

misanthropy begins. Tong is clearly attracted to Wai, as he actively culti-
vates a friendship with Wai during their chance encounters. However, if
Tong freely showers his philanthropic kindness on Wai, his misanthropy
also prevents him from expressing his true feelings for Wai. Learning that
Moon (Wai's wife) has recently died, Tong maneuvers to fill the void in
Wai's life, listening to his sorrows and lending him a shoulder to cry on.
For all his efforts to get close to Wai, including inviting him home for a
sumptuous dinner, Tong stops short at expressing his love for Wai.[26] In his
conversations with Wai, philanthropy slips into misanthropy, as Tong
laments that he is "out of fashion" and is lucky to have bars that will
"adopt" bachelors like him. Describing himself as an illegal immigrant
who often has to hide his identity, Tong is in fact open with Wai about his
sexuality but hides his love nonetheless.[27]

When Jie enters the equation, Tong's repressed desire for Wai is
brought to the fore. Jie has been stalking Wai for some time and begins
work as a bartender at the gay bar that Tong and Wai frequent. On one
occasion, the drunken Wai has to be driven home by Tong and Jie. Since
Jie insists that he alone will help Wai from the car to his apartment, Tong
must have become suspicious and jealous as Jie keeps Tong waiting for a
considerably long time.[28] When Jie finally returns to the car and initiates
a conversation, Tong coldly rebuffs him, "I have no interest in your story."
Jie's intrusion into Tong's relationship with Wai, his deliberate exclusion of
Tong from physical contact with the drunken Wai, and his youthfulness
must have triggered Tong's misanthropic sentiments. In this instance,
Tong's philanthropic kindness has no room for Jie since his object of
desire, Wai, is at stake.

Tong's inability to confess his love for Wai is compounded by his sense
of abjection, here expressed as self-pity, self-loathing, and self-denial. At
the end of the film, it is Wai who has to confront Tong about Tong's desire
for him. Wai has been pondering why he has turned to Tong for help in
times of crisis. Tong replies, "Well, it can't be because I am handsome,
right?" This rhetorical question betrays Tong's low self-esteem, which is
central to his misanthropic outlook, as he thinks he does not deserve Wai.
When Wai asks Tong if he fancies him, Tong pauses for a moment, and
instead of admitting it, he chooses to reassure Wai: "I have not fancied anyone for a long time and have no plans to do so. Don't worry." Advising Wai
to look to the future, Tong says, "Sooner or later, you will meet someone
again. You will be very good to him and he will be very good to you.[29]
When the time comes, you will forget all the unhappiness you have now.
... The most important thing is to give yourself a chance."

Despite his frequent philosophizing in his conversations, which can often be read as double entendres about his sexuality, Tong does not practice what he preaches. When his colleague wonders if anyone would be interested in an apartment because of its unconventional layout, Tong suggests that different people have different tastes. When Wai remarks that he has never been in a line for such a long time in his life (referring to the two days he and Moon lined up for the apartment), Tong suggests that it is good to try new things as life is short. However, when Wai asks Tong in return whether he also gives himself a chance or merely stares at the poster at home, Tong has no answer. This conversation is set on a beach, with the sound of waves surging quietly in the background. As they leave and drive on Tsing Ma Bridge, the soundtrack of a song entitled *Dark Surges (Anyong,* or Undercurrents) underlines Tong's economy of love. As Tong is consumed by his abjection and misanthropy, his love for Wai will remain as dark surges raging in the heart but never expressed. Because of his fear of rejection, Tong instead rejects in advance the possibility of love. For Tong, a description borrowed from a Fassbinder film title seems apt: Fear eats the soul.

Body Double: Displacing Homosexuality as Heterosexuality

The character that most exemplifies the notion of duality is Jie, and I shall focus on his relationship with the two female characters. To begin with, the film employs many layers of double coding in Jie's characterization. Born in Taiwan, where his mother passed away when he was young, Jie now lives in Hong Kong, where he has no relatives and is not in contact with his father, who is supposedly living in Shenzhen. In terms of national and cultural identity, Jie is dislocated in both Taipei and Hong Kong, as he tells Rosa he has no home. Linguistically, he switches between Taiwan-accented Mandarin and Cantonese in his conversation. Sexually, he seems to be indeterminate as he obviously desires Wai but instead has a sexual relationship with Moon.

The most important aspect of Jie's duality concerns the two female characters, Moon and Rosa, who individually provide a pivotal link to Jie's relationship with Wai via the trope of the scent of perfume.[30] Following a sequence of scenes at a swimming pool in which Jie gazes incessantly at Wai, Jie is shown masturbating in the shower—clearly with Wai as his object of fantasy.[31] In Jie's initial non-sexual relationship with Moon, he confesses that he goes crazy every night thinking about what Moon and Wai are doing (presumably having sex). He then presents Moon with a bottle of cologne that is meant for men, claiming that this is the only way he can find out how his favorite scent smells on the person he fancies. It is obvious that Jie intends Moon as his substitute—indeed, his body dou-ble—in his sexual imagination of Wai.[32] By presenting Moon with the cologne, Jie seems to hope that its smell on Wai will rub off on Moon, thus providing him with a delayed aftertaste of Wai.

However, before that can happen, Jie initiates sex with Moon the very same evening in the elevator to her apartment. The film subsequently digresses into an extended sequence of happy moments and physical inti-macy between the two, with clichéd scenes of the couple taking a boat cruise, walking in a park holding hands, chasing each other by the sea, and having sex on the beach. This sequence is accompanied by a song by the late Taiwanese singer Teresa Teng (Deng Lijun) and recalls popular Taiwanese films of the romantic genre in the 1970s, in which Teng's songs were almost ubiquitous on the soundtrack.[33] Abruptly disrupting Jie's latent expression of homosexuality, the film inserts a narrative segment stylistically rooted in a different period and incongruous with the rest of the film.

Rather than seeing this sequence as nostalgia for a lost era in the face of present reality (Wang Zhicheng 1999, 42), I would argue that the dual slippages in narrative and style gain an ambivalent complexity when appreciated as Jie's displacement of his homosexuality as heterosexuality. In Freudian psychology, displacement takes place when the object dis-placed is "divorced from its context and consequently transformed into something extraneous" (Freud 1991, 415). In this instance, "a socially acceptable object stands for the forbidden desire" (Gray 1992, 236), with the object to which the displaced desire is transferred associated with the original forbidden object of desire (Hawthorn 1997, 27).[34] Since Jie's homo-sexual desire for Wai is, for him at least, forbidden, it is displaced as a heterosexual relationship and transferred onto a socially acceptable object, Moon, who is associated with Wai.[35] The happy moments shared by Jie and Moon can thus be seen as Jie's displaced desire to share these moments with Wai. This reading is reinforced by the editing of the film, as the romantic sequence is preceded by a scene in which Moon tries the cologne on herself. By spraying the scent meant for men on her female body, Moon symbolically undergoes a transgender transformation and becomes Wai's body double. As Grossman argues, this "masculinization" allows Moon to become "a gay version of her husband Wai" (2000c, 175). Just as Jie presents the cologne to Moon in the hope of smelling its scent on Wai *through* Moon, in this romantic sequence, Jie is, on an unconscious level, also trying to make love with Wai *through* Moon, who acts as Wai's body double.[36]

On the occasion when Wai gets drunk and has to be taken home, Jie finally gets to find out how the cologne smells on Wai. As the drunken Wai sleeps in his bedroom, Jie gets a glimpse of the life that Moon and Wai shared. Jie has found out about Moon's death only that evening, and he now has direct access to Wai. Discovering the cologne he had given to Moon, Jie stares momentarily at the sleeping Wai before spraying it on him (figure 6.2). Jie's act of spraying cologne all over Wai's nearly naked body—stripped to his underpants presumably by Jie—is the most homoerotic scene in the film, with the senses of smell and touch, which the sight and sound of moving images cannot transmit, accentuated. If we recall Jie's earlier act of masturbation with Wai as the object of his sexual fantasy, it is tempting to read Jie's spraying of the cologne as his symbolically ejaculating all over Wai. Now that Jie finally knows how the cologne smells on Wai, its scent acts as an erotic agent that gives expression to Jie's repressed homosexual desire.

As Moon exits from the story, Rosa enters Jie's life to provide a continual link to his relationship with Wai. After Moon's death, Jie returns to Taipei, where he wanders into Rosa's boutique. The scent of the cologne serves as a parallel between the two women, as Rosa immediately recognizes that Jie is wearing it.[37] The role that Rosa plays, however, is initially different from Moon's. While Moon is unaware of her status as Wai's body double in Jie's sexual economy, Rosa encourages Jie to confront his desire for Wai. As Luo Feng notes, Rosa's appearance does not trigger in Jie a remembrance of Moon; rather, it helps him affirm his homosexual desire

FIGURE 6.2. Jie spraying cologne on the sleeping Wai. (Copyright Golden Harvest/Kwan's Creation Workshop, 1998)

for Wai and confront his own sexuality (2002, 64). On one occasion, Rosa and Jie visit a gay disco. The following conversation illustrates Jie's repression of his homosexuality:

JIE: The men here are all quite good looking.
ROSA: Do you like them?
JIE: What? . . . Me? . . . Why would I like them?
ROSA: It's all right if you do. . . . I have girlfriends whom I like also. . . . Aren't you quite fond of Wai?
JIE: No. . . . You haven't heard me clearly.
ROSA: I have indeed heard you very clearly.

Though a confession is not shown diegetically, it is apparent from this conversation that Jie has told Rosa about his encounters with Wai in Hong Kong. Rosa has detected Jie's repressed desire for Wai, and the visit to the gay disco could be her way of helping Jie confront his homosexuality.[38] When they leave the disco, Jie throws up by the side of the road and expresses his wish to "tell him once." Seeing that Jie cannot even utter the name of his object of desire, Rosa takes out her mobile phone and urges Jie to call Wai. The film reinforces Jie's repression by not showing what he has to say to Wai; in fact, Jie does not confess his love to Wai personally as Wai is not at home. Rather, Jie's telephone message is recounted by Wai to Tong; in it Jie reveals he was the one who sprayed the cologne on Wai.

Ultimately, the film does not resolve Jie's repression of his homosexual desire. The film instead suggests that Jie and Rosa have sex later that night, thus completing the double coding of the two women as Jie's objects of displacement for Wai. Now that Rosa has provided the crucial connection to Wai as Moon once did, the women's roles as body doubles in Jie's sexual economy are reprised. Like the cologne he secretly sprays on Wai, Jie's relationship with his homosexual desire seems to evaporate quickly, even as it leaves a lingering presence.

That Obscure Object of Desire: Banality as Attraction

The two male characters discussed above are both attracted to a heterosexual man, Wai. Tong displaces his misanthropy as philanthropy, thereby denying his homosexual desire for Wai. Jie, on the other hand, displaces his homosexuality as heterosexuality, thus repressing his love for Wai. However, Wai's attraction as an object of desire remains obscure, as he is portrayed as a totally banal person in the film. A computer programmer, Wai displays a single-minded obsession with his own world, disregarding even the person who is closest to him. When they move into their new apartment, Wai keeps himself busy by arranging his records and fixing his computer in his study, leaving Moon to coordinate the movers unloading their furniture. When the exhausted Moon asks him to clear the rubbish at the end of the day, Wai excuses himself on the grounds that he has just taken a shower. Jie describes Wai as a robot for his focused, task-oriented purposefulness when he goes swimming. Wai's marriage to Moon is portrayed as equally banal, and the couple seems to lead separate lives in their new home.[39] One scene shows Moon talking on the phone in the sitting room while Wai works on his computer in the study, leaving Moon to retire to bed on her own. Wai is also devoid of emotional expression, causing Moon to break down on one occasion, pleading for his affection. The only expression of affection between the couple takes place the night before Moon is scheduled to fly to Taipei, as Wai prepares a bowl of noodles for her and they later have sex.

What, then, makes this banal heterosexual man so attractive to Tong and Jie? I suggest the answer is twofold. On the one hand, both heterosexual men and heterosexual marriage, despite their banality, exude a strange attraction for homosexual men precisely because they are unattainable. Tong dismisses the possibility of finding love within a gay milieu as he tosses away a telephone number given to him by another man at the gay sauna.[40] Jie displays no interest in a group of ostensibly gay young men who make passes at him at the swimming pool. Both Tong and Jie seem to prefer a masochistic fixation on Wai, punishing themselves with a secret desire that may never be reciprocated. This masochistic tendency points to the other side of their desire for heterosexual men: homosexual men's abjection. Tong's denial, Jie's repression, and their displacement of homosexual desire betray a deep self-loathing, albeit in different fashions, in relation to their sexuality. Their pursuit of a heterosexual man is a reflection of their masochistic self-loathing because this object of desire is unattainable and because they believe, however subconsciously, that they do not deserve Wai.

The film therefore structures its economy of desire in a hierarchical way: the heterosexual man is desired by both men and women, while the homosexual men remain unfulfilled desiring subjects. Moreover, heterosexual women are mobilized only as channels through which a sexually indeterminate man can gain access to his object of desire. This has led one critic to describe the film's sexual hierarchization as "women third, gay men second, straight men first" (Lam 1998, 81). In this sense, the film risks being perceived as both heterosexist and misogynist.[41] However, as I have argued in relation to the romantic sequence of heterosexual love featuring Jie and Moon, the obscure attraction of the banal heterosexual man as object of desire must be seen not just as the privileging of heterosexuality, but also as the displacement of a homosexual ideal. That is, by having both the homosexual men and a heterosexual woman attracted to the heterosexual man—and we must bear in mind the condition of the film's production as a vehicle for the actress Chingmy Yau—the film can be seen as an attempt to normalize or equate homosexual desire with heterosexuality by showing that they share the same object of desire while managing to traffic a substantial amount of homosexual desire into the diegesis.

The ending of the film, however, hints at a change of heart for the banal heterosexual man and the possibility of a relationship between Wai and Tong. This is suggested, on the one hand, by Wai's emotional reaction to Jie's telephone message—a sharp contrast to his emotionless self in the past—to the extent that Wai begins to reflect on his own relationship with Tong and even asks Tong if he fancies him. At the very least, Wai seems to have become sensitized to his own feelings, and he also assures Tong that he is not worried if Tong fancies him. On the other hand, the possibility of a relationship between Tong and Wai is suggested by a song and the film's editing at the end. The use of pop songs to lend intertextual meaning is a familiar ploy in Hong Kong cinema. *Hold You Tight* closes with the aforementioned song, *Dark Surges,* providing a vital clue to the film's English title:

> Fearful that tragedy will replay / In my life and my fate / The more beautiful a thing is the more I shouldn't touch it / History repeats itself / In such a chaotic city / There is no reason that love can be without dark surges / Actually what is the point of my loving you again / Who knows that my holding you tight this time will not be in vain?

While wondering if "holding you tight" will be in vain, the song (which appears twice and in two different versions) hints at a possible relationship between Tong and Wai. Towards the end of the film, Tong invites Wai to his place for a sumptuous dinner and subsequently drives him home. On his return journey, Tong hums along to the song, which is playing on his car's stereo system. This is the original version, sung by the Chinese pop star Faye Wong (Wang Fei), and the arrangement is light and upbeat, reflecting Tong's jolly mood, evidenced by his smile. Earlier in the film, Wai hummed the same tune while listening to it through headphones; thus the connection between the two men is made more explicit.[42] While driving home, Tong receives a call for help from Wai, who is devastated after listening to Jie's telephone message, and this leads to the closing sequence by the beach.

The editing in these closing scenes recalls the film's dual narrative structure, but this time it draws a parallel between Tong and Wai's relationship and that of Jie and Rosa. Crosscutting between scenes of Tong and Wai's conversation by the beach and Rosa and Jie in a bedroom, the film sets up the two couples as parallel. When Tong asks Wai what else Jie has said in the message, the film cuts to Rosa, who, like a sexual predator, looks at the bed in which the near naked Jie is asleep (and it recalls a similar scene with Jie and Wai). Echoing the song title, the film shows sea waves surging onto the shore, followed by Wai asking Tong if he fancies him. Tong pauses for a moment, and the film cuts to a scene in which Rosa, now lying next to Jie, touches him and kisses his nipple, before Tong replies in denial. The sequence ends with Tong and Wai smiling after their conversation, and the film cuts to Rosa looking out of the window, presumably after having had sex with Jie. The view from the bedroom is the break of dawn, as is the closing scene with Tong and Wai driving on the Tsing Ma Bridge. Hackneyed as it may be as a metaphor, the arrival of a new day for both couples suggests a new beginning in their respective relationships. If Rosa and Jie have had sex early that morning, given the crosscutting and dual narrative structure of the film, it seems to suggest that a sexual relationship may also develop between Tong and Wai.

This reading is reinforced in the last scene in three other ways: the use of another version of *Dark Surges,* the conversation between Tong and Wai, and the metaphor of the bridge. First, the song accompanying the closing scene of the film is a cover version by Anthony Wong (Huang Yaoming), originally from the pop duo Tat Ming Pair (Daming Yipai), perhaps best described as the Pet Shop Boys of Canto pop (Cantonese pop music). Specially commissioned for the film, Wong's rendition is slower and full of pathos, and because he is widely associated with a queer sensitivity, his version of *Dark Surges* lends a gay subtext to the film that will not be lost on a knowing audience.[43] Second, the conversation between Tong and Wai begins with the aforementioned date of September 16, 1984, when the negotiations on the Sino-British Joint Declaration took place, leading to a new chapter in Hong Kong's history. The date's function here can also suggest that a new chapter will open in the relationship between the two men. Finally, Tsing Ma Bridge leads to the new Hong Kong airport and, coupled with the break of dawn, signals a new beginning for the two men, concurring with David Martinez' description of Wong Kar-wai's use of a song at the end of his films: "[it gives] the lie to the fateful title 'The End'" (1997, 35).

Decadence: Fragments of Darkness

In a film that expresses an ambivalence towards the prospect of being held tight either personally or politically, does Kwan's representation of homosexuality live up to the promise of the dictum in the Chinese title, "the happier the more decadent"? It would seem from my analysis above that none of the characters is truly happy in his/her decadent sexuality, and though the film's ending points to the possibility of a relationship between Tong and Wai, the tone of the entire film remains one of darkness, echoed by the repeated use of the song *Dark Surges*. As noted in my argument above on the intertwining of the personal and the political, in experiencing the consciousness of the political crisis, the characters in the film seem unable to rise above the concomitant personal crisis. This ambivalence reminds one of Kwan's confessional line in *Still*: "I deny! I deny!...Yet in the end there's simply no denial."

In her reading of the film, Helen Leung concludes that "like the fragrance that wafts through the air heedless of boundaries, eroticism permeates these characters' lives, crossing the boundaries conventionally drawn between friendship, sexuality, love, jealousy, and guilt. It fosters new modalities of intimacy that flourish in a world where strangers need to, and do, take care of each other" (2001, 443). I agree with Leung that new modalities of intimacy occur in the film, but I would question their significance to the characters at the end of the day. Jie's repression of homosexual desire will not be resolved by his relationship with Rosa, and will Tong really be happy if his relationship with Wai remains platonic? Yes, strangers do take care of each other in times of crisis, but the real test for these new modalities of intimacy is whether they will last and, more important, if they mean anything beyond taking care. These new modalities, when push comes to shove, may just be new masks for the old face of denial.

Even if one chooses to read the film's ending as a happy one, Calinescu's explication on the notion of decadence (via Nietzsche) is instructive because decadence is deceptive:

> For Nietzsche, the strategy of decadence is typically that of the liar who deceives by *imitating* truth and by making his lies even more credible than truth itself. Thus, in its hatred of life, decadence masquerades as admiration of a higher life, and, because of its mastery in the art of seduction, it is able to make weakness look like force, exhaustion like fulfillment, cowardice like courage. Decadence is dangerous because it always disguises itself as its opposite. (1987, 180; emphasis in original)

It is with this understanding of decadence as deception that we can see why some critics have chosen to read the film in a more positive light. Luo Feng argues that the character Tong can be seen as Kwan's ideal human type because of his positive attributes, which include being considerate to others and understanding human relations (2002, 63–64), while Huang Shuxian sees Tong's character as the most perfect in the film (2000, 253). For Helen Leung, unlike the cruising scene in Wong Kar-wai's *Happy Together*, the sauna scene in *Hold You Tight* is shot without pathos because "Tong does not cruise out of pain. For him, cruising is simply a fact of life, one of the many ways he reaches for connection in an alienating city" (2001, 441).[44] Contrary to the above readings, I suggest that Tong is the darkest character in the film. Despite his attempts to be upbeat about life, Tong can be described as a living dead whose abject misanthropy betrays itself as a form of decadence, "a loss of the will to live, which prompts an attitude of revengefulness against life and which manifests itself through *ressentiment*" (Calinescu 1987, 181).

The general dark tone of *Hold You Tight* can also be illustrated by its trope of birth and death. A subplot of the film concerns Moon's interest in having a baby, first shown in a conversation with the pregnant owner of the video rental shop. On the night before her travel to Taipei, Moon and Wai have sex, and Moon pulls off the condom on Wai before his penetration and wears a contented post-coital expression, as if anticipating pregnancy. Rather than allowing space for hope brought about by a possible birth, the film frustrates her wish by having her die on the following day, her journey to the airport accompanied by Faye Wong's light-hearted rendition of *Dark Surges*. The ghost of death also dominates the film in other places: the poster of *A City of Sadness* features some characters carrying a dead man's photograph and his memorial tablet, a scenario to be echoed by Wai carrying Moon's ashes back in an urn from Taiwan; in addition, Tong's ex-boyfriend's boyfriend dies in London. Leung sees the trope of loss and lack in the film as signalling "the new possibilities that emerge from mourning and desiring" (H. Leung 2001, 442), and the second half of the film, following Moon's death, does open with the birth of the video shop owner's baby. However, while it is Moon's death that brings the three men together for the first time at the gay bar, the title of the Mandarin song in the background is *Can't Get a Share of Your Love (Fenbudao nide ai)*, suggesting that Jie and Tong will not get a share of Wai's love despite Moon's death. It is hardly surprising then when the video rental shop, whose name is Brightness (Qinglang), becomes the only shop to suffer from an electricity blackout and is shrouded in darkness, the neon light sign announcing the shop's name is rendered futile.

Writing on Kwan's earlier films, Abbas describes *Love unto Waste* as "a kind of Felliniesque study of decadence" and argues that in *Rouge*, "decadence reveals a complexity that challenges any easy moralizing" (1997, 27, 43). However, decadence for Kwan can also be appreciated as an aesthetic style. According to Calinescu, a "style of decadence is simply a style favorable to the unrestricted manifestation of aesthetic individualism, a style that has done away with traditional authoritarian requirements such as unity, hierarchy, objectivity, etc." (1987, 171). Calinescu also cites the French critic Désiré Nisard's argument that a decadent style of art places "such emphasis on detail that the normal relationship of a work's parts to its whole is destroyed, the work disintegrating into a multitude of overwrought fragments" (ibid., 158). Commenting on the narrative structure of *Hold You Tight,* Leung writes, "The narrative structure of *Hold You Tight* also offers a way of apprehending Hong Kong in transition. . . . This idiosyncratic structure reproduces the experience of living in uncertainty, when the illusion of life as being an orderly tableau that unfolds linearly must be replaced by the more accurate depiction of life as being incoherent fragments of delayed knowledge, startling discoveries, irreparable losses, and random delights" (H. Leung 2001, 442).

If *Hold You Tight* is a collection of fragments held tenuously together by its narrative structure, I suggest these are also fragments of darkness that echo Foucault's hypothesis of how bourgeois society in the nineteenth century produced discourses about sex, as referred to in the epigraph of this chapter (1990, 69). As I have above situated the film against the background of Kwan's coming out, what Kwan is dealing with here, however obliquely, is the subject of his sexuality, which, at the end of twentieth-century Hong Kong, remains an object of great suspicion. For the film's characters such as Tong and Jie, homosexuality seems like a fear that never ends. Kwan acknowledges in an interview that Tong is a projection of middle-aged gay men like himself (Shan 1998, 70). As Kwan's first foray into films featuring a homosexual theme after his coming out, *Hold You Tight* reveals a shadow of darkness whose persistence is as enduring as the repeated line of "I deny! I deny! . . . Yet in the end there's simply no denial." Seen in the context of Kwan's filmmaking career, it is not until *Lan Yu* in 2001 that his treatment of homosexuality gains an air of freedom and confidence that is missing in *Hold You Tight.*

Kwan has reiterated that "although I'm gay, I'm not particularly eager to deal with 'gay issues' in the films I make."[45] His refusal to be pigeonholed as a gay director signposts the problematics of gay identity politics in a Chinese context while paradoxically underlining his significance as the first prominent gay director in the Chinese-speaking world. The complexity and ambivalence of *Hold You Tight* do, as Helen Leung argues, deflect expectations that his films should reflect "authentic" gay experiences (2001, 439). However, the burden of representing homosexuality in a cultural milieu where the production, politics, and premise of such representation continue to be contested may haunt Kwan for some time yet.

Conclusion

In examining the representation of male homosexuality in contemporary Chinese cinemas, I have investigated the enabling conditions of these representations in the global cultural economy at the turn of the twenty-first century, the burden and politics of representation in relation to the reception of the films, the various tropes of representation, and the works of some key directors. I have emphasized from the beginning of this book that it is not about constructing a Chinese expression of homosexuality or a homosexual expression of Chineseness. Similarly, in his study on gender and sexuality in Spanish and Spanish American literature, Paul Julian Smith argues that adopting a thematic approach is inappropriate where sexuality is concerned. For Smith, this approach would lead, in his study, "either to a scrapbook of Hispanic erotica or to the vindication of some reassuringly stable 'Latin' temperament." He is thus less concerned with "the specificity of Spanish or Latin American 'experience' of sex, as with the enabling conditions of sexual difference itself" (1992, 2–3).

Smith's argument highlights the difficulty of writing on sexuality thematically without simultaneously reifying an essentialized identity, sexual or ethnic, or indeed a combination of the two. If an identity or classificatory category is ineluctably invoked in this study, the focus is not on what it is but rather on how one mobilizes it as a discursive tool while underlining its constructedness and using it to pry open other configurations of power. It remains for me in this conclusion to interrogate one final question: can the body of films discussed in this book be described as Chinese gay films, or can one begin to speak of a *tongzhi* or queer Chinese cinema?

To begin with, there are conceptual as well as linguistic issues to address. While it is widely regarded in Anglo-American discursive practice that the term "gay" marks the immediate post-Stonewall homosexual identity and that the emergence of a queer identity is linked to AIDS activism in the 1990s, the distinction between the two is not always clear; nor does the latter term supersede the former in popular use.[1] In relation to cinematic practice, the impetus behind the labelling of films as gay was rooted in the gay liberation movement of the 1970s, which believed that "an appropriate response to invisibility and a history of negative images was the construction and circulation of positive ones" (Arroyo 1997, 71). The New Queer Cinema movement of the early 1990s, then, can be seen as a reaction to the straightjacket dictates of gay film by its deliberate construction of challenging representations that range from HIV-positive, homicidal queers on the road in Gregg Araki's *The Living End* to the Genet-inspired love between prison inmates in Todd Hayne's *Poison* (1991).[2] However, most film festivals devoted to representations of homosexuality still bill themselves as lesbian and gay, while community support groups continue to add new sexual formulations to their abbreviations, culminating in the increasingly common LGBTQ (lesbian, gay, bisexual, transgender, queer).

In the Chinese language, while the term *tongzhi* is generally seen as a local appropriation of a political form of address (notwithstanding its Soviet roots) for a sexual identity, it is also usually taken to equate with the English "lesbian and gay." More confusingly, while the term "queer" has been transliterated as *ku'er*, it is also used in tandem with *tongzhi* and *guaitai*.[3] Therefore, when one reads any writing in the English language about Chinese "gay" films or "queer" Chinese cinema, it is difficult to ascertain which classificatory term in the translated language the author might have in mind, unless she/he makes explicit the translingual markers in her/his use. In any case, the distinction may well-nigh be impossible. While my book title, *Celluloid Comrades*, takes its derivation from the term *tongzhi*, I have also mobilized the term "queer" to describe Tsai Ming-liang's cinematic poetics and the term "gay" to refer to Stanley Kwan, though I generally avoid designating any film I discuss as gay, queer, or *tongzhi*.

What I am attempting to highlight here is not so much that these classificatory and identity categories overlap in the English language as well as in the Chinese language or that the discursive terms in the two linguistic realms do not map onto each other neatly. Rather, the untidiness of the linguistic and translinguistic practice should suffice to alert us that each discursive mobilization is contingent, contemplated, and at times contested, be it labelling by others or a self-identificatory strategy. As always, the crucial questions to ask are not what is a gay film or whether a body of films can be classified as queer cinema. Instead, we should examine the legitimizing discourse underlying each appeal to a certain classificatory category, the agents initiating the mobilization and their intentions (if at all possible to ascertain), the mechanisms of empowerment and disempowerment, and those who stand to gain and lose from such an enterprise. More than merely discursive terms, classificatory categories such as gay film or queer cinema are discursive practices that are imbricated with the nexus of knowledge/power themselves.

With the appearance of these hitherto unseen representations of male homosexuality in Chinese cinemas, scholars, critics, and journalists alike have invariably written about them as gay films and/or queer cinema. On the receiving end, directors of these films have been plagued by the use of such labels. Just as discourses have histories, so the application of these classificatory categories to films from Chinese cinemas cannot ignore their historical baggage. In Anglo-American discourse, the category of gay film has been described as a "Holy Grail," assumed to be somewhere out there, waiting to be made once the shackles of negative stereotyping have been thrown off (Medhurst 1984, 61). As a result, every film that incorporates representations of homosexuality is, "in the majority of writing and discussion by gay people, implicitly measured against the mythical Gay Film, and, of course, is found wanting" (ibid.).[4] It is thus unsurprising that the directors studied in this book have generally been ambivalent about the labelling of their films as gay, particularly in the contexts of Chinese cinemas and Chinese societies, where homosexuality is not universally accepted.

One of the most common strategies employed by directors to dissociate their films from the labels is to make claims to a universal humanity or a larger concern; such a claim may serve to circumvent censorship or to dispel a taboo in order to appeal to a wider audience. For example, while acknowledging that *Farewell My Concubine* is "a story about a man who loves another man," Chen Kaige emphasizes that the film is ultimately about "human nature" (Zhang Jingbei 1994, 73). Similarly, Tsai Ming-liang claims that *The River* is not about homosexuality but about "man and his suffering" (Ma Yingli 1997, 42). Wong Kar-wai does not like *Happy Together* to be seen as a gay film because the story, in his view, "could happen between any two people. It just happens that in this story, it happened between two men" (Havis 1997, 16). Though Zhang Yuan is not averse to the suggestion that *East Palace, West Palace* is China's first "gay film" (Rayns 1996, 29), he has also reiterated in an interview (*Minsheng Bao*, May 2, 1997) that the film is about the exploration of the relationship between sex and power.

Sometimes, filmmakers also declare their position with regard to the relationship between their films and the state of gay activism in the societies in which they live. Some go out of their way to champion gay rights, an example being Neil Peng, who co-wrote the screenplay of *The Wedding*

Banquet. Though Peng states that it is not a gay film, he nonetheless hopes the film will generate discussions that might help promote equal rights for gays in Taiwan (Lee and Peng 1993, 16). Some are at pains to draw the line between themselves and gay activism, in spite (or because?) of having come out as gay. In an interview given shortly after his coming out, Stanley Kwan stated that his coming out would not make any difference to his filmmaking; he would not necessarily label himself as a gay director or make gay films, nor would he use his filmmaking to promote the gay movement (Li Xiaoxian 1997, 57). Some others have commented on the category of gay film itself. On the designation of a special section on lesbian and gay films in Taiwan's international film festival, Tsai Ming-liang expressed his displeasure in seeing homosexuality being turned into some kind of fashion and sensationalization (Chiao 1997b, 25).

While there may be many different reasons why directors might choose to either distance themselves from or affiliate themselves with labels such as "gay film" or "queer/*tongzhi* cinema," it is also understandable that the convenience of these labels appeals to scholars and critics in their writing. Since the 1990s, the English term "queer" has increasingly been used to describe gay films from Asia, often highlighting the cultural specificities of the region. In a short piece introducing queer films from Asia, Chris Berry focuses on how these films challenge "the presumed universality of the post-Stonewall Anglo-American models of gay identity, which now appear as more historically and culturally specific" (1997, 14). In his preface to an edited volume on queer Asian cinema, Andrew Grossman underlines the role of the English language through which "queer politics and theory have been most encoded and disseminated worldwide" (2000a, xvi). In her book on queer representation in Taiwanese fiction, film, and public culture, Fran Martin sees the translingual mutation of queer as *tongzhi, ku'er,* and *guaitai* as examples of "glocalization in the domain of sexual knowledge: critical, selective appropriations and reworkings of terms and concepts that originated elsewhere" (2003c, 23). All three situate their mobilization of the English term "queer" for Asian cinema at the interface of global and local negotiation.

As the term "queer" is currently more fashionable than the term "lesbian and gay" in academic and intellectual circles in Anglophone societies and with the advent of queer theory and politics in the Chinese-speaking world, I believe each mobilization of the term "queer" in relation to Chinese cinemas must foreground its translingual and political aspects.[5] While the term "queer" is probably the most encompassing, non-essentialist, and deconstructionist category available in the English language, its use in both English and Chinese should not obscure its exclusionary effects, particularly in relation to class and age. As I have argued elsewhere, in order to fully appreciate the "coolness" of the transliteration of queer as *ku'er* (literally "cool kid"), one has to be familiar with queer theory's epistemological roots in post-structuralism and queer politics' roots in AIDS activism. Such knowledge invariably implies an elitist educational background and a cosmopolitan outlook; it also arguably ushers in a generational bias given that queer theory and politics, which emerged in the 1990s, generally inform a younger generation of scholars and critics.[6] Moreover, by positing not against the heterosexual but the normal (Warner 1993, xxvi), queer politics has also excised itself from homosexual expressions that appear seemingly (hetero)normal while failing to question the very definition of normality in a queer context.

There is no question that "queer" remains the most flexible term in use, as it can also denote a way of reading texts, both literary and cinematic (as in "queer reading," or *waidu* in Chinese).[7] However, the term has also been mobilized, in both the English- and Chinese-speaking contexts, as an identity category. In this regard, I would caution the assumption that the category of queer is necessarily more progressive, because teleological, than lesbian and gay or homosexual, so that queer becomes the terminator of same-sex discourse and identity. Rather, the term "queer," not unlike the terms "homosexuality" and "Chineseness," can equally be mobilized in essentialized ways to exclude and stigmatize those whom it otherwise claims to embrace and celebrate.[8] Whether known as homosexuality, lesbian and gay, or queer, the expression of same-sex sexuality in any cultural context may be too broad for a single discursive term to encompass. Similarly, in reference to its cinematic representation, "queer cinema," "lesbian and gay films," and "homosexual films" are not concentric circles with the former occupying the outermost space; rather, they overlap and shore up each other's deficiencies and efficacies.

In one of the earliest English-language surveys of the representation of homosexuality in (mainly Hollywood) cinema, Vito Russo argues that the more interesting films are those that take difference for granted and that "do not view the existence of gay people as necessarily controversial" (1987, 325, 326). B. Ruby Rich, credited for coining the term "New Queer Cinema," has also pointed to the earlier example of Fassbinder in creating representations that "explored a libidinal politics without ever leaving gender, race or class politics behind" (1993, 86). Having endured many terrible screenings at lesbian and gay film festivals, where films are typically made by, of, and for queer subjects, one is sometimes tempted to join Russo in his call for "no more films *about* homosexuality" (1987, 326; emphasis mine). This book has shown that representations of male homosexuality in contemporary Chinese cinemas, regardless of the sexualities of the directors, can enrich our understanding of same-sex sexuality in a Chinese-speaking context while problematizing homosexuality's relationship with race/ethnicity, class, gender, and nation. Heeding the call of the "national father" *(guofu)*, Sun Yat-sen, these celluloid comrades must continue to work hard, not necessarily to bring about a revolution but to destabilize and demythify constructions of homosexuality and Chineseness and indeed of "queer Chinese cinema."

Notes

Introduction

1. See Zhong 2000 and Louie 2002.

2. See Chou 2000, Sang 2003, and Martin 2003c.

3. Many new publications were appearing as this manuscript was being completed, and I have been able to incorporate only some of them in my discussions in this book. They include Berry and Lu 2005, Lu and Yeh 2005a, Pang and Wong 2005, and Yeh and Davis 2005.

4. While "race" as a classificatory term has been largely called into question—and put in quotation marks—in scholarship it is not always possible completely to distinguish its use from "ethnicity." See, for example, Fenton 2003, Guibernau and Rex 1997, and Bulmer and Solomos 1999.

5. I regard Singapore as fundamentally different from China, Taiwan, and Hong Kong, as it does not make claims—nor is it being claimed—to be part of China as a polity, notwithstanding dissenting voices within China, Taiwan, and Hong Kong on the demarcation of this polity. I exclude Singapore from the discussion in this book also because while there has been a surge in filmmaking at the turn of the twenty-first century, there has yet to be a film made on my thematic concern of homosexuality (Roystan Tan's 2003 film, *15,* borders on homoeroticism). Though Singapore filmmaking has been included in a recent study under the rubric of "Chinese-language film" (Lu and Yeh 2005a), I suggest the case of Singapore opens up a different can of worms on the issue of Chineseness. See Lim forthcoming-d.

6. See Ang 2001 and Chun 1996.

7. On whether Chineseness or being Chinese is political, compare the concluding remarks in the essays by Tu Wei-ming and Ien Ang. Tu writes, "The meaning of being Chinese is basically not a political question; it is a human concern pregnant with ethical-religious implications" (Tu 1994a, 34). For Ang, "if I am inescapably Chinese by *descent,* I am only sometimes Chinese by *consent.* When and how is a matter of politics" (2001, 36; emphasis in original). Tu's act of designating the question of Chineseness to the ethical-religious realm is, of course, in itself political. As Aihwa Ong and Donald M. Nonini point out, "The essentialization of Chineseness as Confucian has become a convenient meta-inscription of, and prescription for, pan-Asianness among the elites of the so-called new dragon nation-states of the Asia Pacific. Asian politicians of many nationalities have come to find strategic resonance with the diasporic Chinese imageries of Asian modernity, especially in framing disputatious issues vis-à-vis the West, such as trade barriers and human rights" (1997, 328).

8. See Brown 2004.

9. While I have heard a scholar state matter of factly at a conference that understanding identities as constructs is a "no-brainer," one must not underestimate the continual hold of essentialism on many brains, including those that appear at academic conferences. When I presented a paper on "Queering Chineseness" at Harvard in October 2004, an audience member from Mainland China suggested that I had overlooked the "sacred" aspect of Chineseness, which he summarized as "the harmony of heaven and human" *(tianren heyi)* for the Chinese in China and "falling leaves return to their roots" *(luoye guigen)* for the overseas Chinese.

10. Notable exceptions that list Chinese, Taiwanese, and Hong Kong cinemas as separate entries without mobilizing the umbrella term of "Chinese cinemas" include Hill and Gibson 1998, in which they appear under the rubric of world cinema, and Nowell-Smith 1997, in which they are classified in the section "Cinemas of the World."

11. It cannot be overemphasized, however, that the problematic definition of national cinema is not unique to the Chinese case. Spanish cinema's relation to Basque cinema and Catalan-language cinema or the relationship between Quebec cinema and Canadian cinema, to name but two other cases, invites a comparative approach in the rethinking of national cinema. Some scholars have begun to reconfigure "national cinema" as "cinema and the nation." See Berry and Farquhar 2001 and Hjort and MacKenzie 2000.

12. See Li Tianduo 1996; Ye, Zhuo, and Wu 1999; and Tay 1995.

13. As Lu also acknowledges, "the greatest irony of contemporary Chinese cinemas seems to be that some films achieve a transnational status precisely because they are seen as possessing an authentically 'national,' 'Chinese,' 'Oriental' flavor by Western audiences" (1997a, 12).

14. It must be qualified that this also applies to non-Han minorities in Taiwan and Hong Kong. On the discourse of race/ethnicity in China, see Dikötter 1997, Berry 1992, and Mullaney 2004. For a study on minority film, see Yingjin Zhang 1997.

15. On Taiwan as a problematic case for post-colonial theory, see Liao 2000 and Teng 2004.

16. Citing the "intentionally *hybridized* linguistic practice" in Hong Kong films since the 1980s, Yingjin Zhang notes that "'Chinese-language cinema' may also be a *narrower* term because it is misleading to assume that what binds Chinese cinema together are its common linguistic features" (2004, 5; emphasis in original). Berry also states that "because foreign languages are used in many diasporic films, even the currently fashionable concept of 'Chinese-language film' *(huayu dianying)* is not broad enough" (2003b, 2).

17. See Berlant and Freeman 1992.

18. For a debate on the etiology of homosexuality in terms of biological determinism or social constructionism, see Stein 1992.

19. In their survey of Sinological studies on sexualities in pre-modern China (including Hinsch's book), Liu Jen-Peng (Liu Renpeng) and Ding Naifei (1998) note that scholars have been prone to conclude that homosexuality was "accepted" based

on the numerous historical records on the subject. They argue that the existence of such records says nothing about the societal attitude toward homosexuality and may in fact mask a "politics of reticence," whereby differences are subsumed under the rhetoric of "tolerance."

20. The term *gaizu* probably makes its first appearance in the science fiction of Taiwanese writer Chang Hsi-kuo (Zhang Xiguo), though it does not signify same-sex sexuality. The use of *zu* to denote a subcultural group probably comes from the Japanese *zoku* (same Chinese / *kanji* character), which since as early as 1971 has been used in a same-sex context in Japan with the publication of the gay magazine *Rose Tribe* (*Barazoku / Qiangweizu*; Aoki 2004, 14).

21. I suspect the Chinese translation of comrade as *tongzhi* (same Chinese / *kanji* characters but pronounced *doshi* in Japanese) may have also been borrowed from the Japanese; the term has been used in homosexual argot in Japan since at least the end of World War II. On *doshi,* see McLelland (2005, 81, 98n25).

22. Chou Wah-shan dates Hong Kong's inaugural lesbian and gay film festival as 1989 and attributes the appropriation of the term to the two organizers, Mai Ke and Edward Lam (Lin Yihua) (1997, 360). Xiao Wenhui, however, dates the inauguration as 1991 and credits only Lam for the term's appropriation (1994, 55). The official Web site of the Hong Kong Lesbian and Gay Film and Video Festival (http://www.hklgff.com; accessed August 29, 2005) lists the inaugural year as 1989. Mai Ke (2003, 244–247) claims credit for himself for appropriating the term but attributes its popularization to Lam.

23. This is reflected in the titles of books published on homosexuality in China. See, for example, Fang 1995, Li Yinhe 1998, Li Yinhe and Wang 1992, and Zhang Bei-chuan 1994. Even a Taiwanese publication on homosexuality in China (An 1995) uses the term *tongxinglian* in the book title. In Hong Kong, Chou Wah-shan has consistently used *tongzhi* in the titles of his books, including one on China (1996a). This arguably does not reflect the term's usage among its subjects of inquiry who, according to An, use a host of terms other than *tongzhi* (1995, 80–82).

24. On the translation of "queer" as *ku'er,* see Lim forthcoming-b.

25. It must be qualified here that the term "Anglo-American" is a shorthand for the English-speaking world, which includes not only, among others, Australia and Canada, but also scholars and critics (regardless of their ethnicity) who are based all across the globe but write in the English language. It also applies to those who write in Chinese but have been educated in Anglo-American universities or shaped by multicultural politics in Anglo-American societies.

26. See, for example, the French case in Martel 1999, the Dutch case in Duyvendak 1996, and the German case in Kuzniar 2000. See also Michel Foucault's rejection of the politics of coming out in Macey 1995.

27. These include Chou Teng's (Zhou Teng) *Golden Paddy Field* (*Huangjin daotian,* 1992); Yee Chih-yen's (Yi Zhiyan) *Lonely Hearts Club* (*Jimo fangxin julebu,* 1995); Yonfan's (Yang Fan) *Bugis Street* (*Yaojie huanghou,* 1995) and *Bishōnen . . .* (*Meishaonian zhi lian,* 1998); Shu Kei's (Shu Qi) *A Queer Story* (*Jilao sishi,* 1996); and Liu Bingjian's *Men and Women* (*Nannan nünü,* 1999).

Chapter 1: Screening Homosexuality

1. "Wire-fu" is a new term invented to describe the use of wire in achieving the high-flying choreography in some kung fu fighting scenes.

2. It should be noted that the Hong Kong new wave is generally regarded as having begun in 1979 (C. Li 1994, 160).

3. To list just some of the top awards, *The Wedding Banquet* and Xie Fei's *Women from the Lake of Scented Souls (Xianghunnü)* shared the Golden Bear at Berlin in 1993; *Farewell My Concubine* shared the Palme d'Or at Cannes in 1993 with Jane Campion's *The Piano;* and Hou Hsiao-hsien's *A City of Sadness (Beiqing chengshi)* took the Golden Lion at Venice in 1989. As for the American Academy Awards, *Crouching Tiger, Hidden Dragon* was nominated in ten categories and won in four in 2001.

4. Though Yau deals only with mainland Chinese cinema in her essay, her last point is also applicable to Taiwan and Hong Kong cinemas of the 1980s and beyond.

5. See, for example, Dai 1991, Yin 1996, Zhang Yiwu 1995, and Yingjin Zhang 1996.

6. For a full list of the schemes available, see *Zhonghuaminguo bashiyi nian dianying nianjian* (1992).

7. It must be qualified that the nativist mode finds a counterpart in the skeptical Western mode, exemplified by Geremie Barmé's similar argument about the West's fascination with Chinese cinemas. Barmé is highly skeptical of directors such as Zhang Yuan who negotiate the economy of filmmaking between a repressive China and a West hungry for local dissent. Describing Zhang's films as "bankable dissent," Barmé formulates a detailed "formula for success" for such directors, culminating in the assertion that all Zhang needed to secure success for his films was an official ban (1999, 188–198). For Barmé, "bankable dissent" materials include "nonofficial or semi-illicit works, be they in the fields of art, literature, music, or film, that, owing to the repressive state control, could accrue a certain market value—and street cred—regardless of (even, in some cases, despite) their artistic merits" (ibid., 188). As with Yingjin Zhang's account, there is doubtless some accuracy in Barmé's description, but his formulation leaves no room for agency or the valuation of merits for artists, writers, musicians, and filmmakers who find themselves ineluctably caught in this cross-cultural economy since whatever they produce can be couched, in the eyes of these critics, only in terms of either cashing in or selling out.

8. While the taste buds are situated in the palate, taste is also linked to the visual. When one is commended for having good taste—say in fashion or interior decoration—it means having an "eye" for color, texture, composition, etc. Martin Roberts gives an account on how the eyes and the palate might be related: "It is no coincidence that exotic food is often the central subject of exotic films themselves. . . . One can watch Ang Lee's *The Wedding Banquet* or *Eat Drink Man Woman* and eat out at a Chinese restaurant afterward. In such cases, the difference between eating and watching, consuming exotic food and exotic film, becomes virtually imperceptible, the consumption of the exotic is literalized within the film itself" (1998, 79n15). In this regard, it is interesting to note that the published English collection of these two screenplays

is accompanied by full-color recipes of six Chinese dishes spread over eight pages (see A. Lee 1994).

9. Similarly, Arjun Appadurai speaks of the creation of "new markets for film companies, art impresarios and travel agencies, who thrive on the need of the deterritorialized population for contact with its homeland" in the age of globalization (1990, 302).

10. Though I draw an analogy between Chinese cinemas and Third Cinema, the philosophy behind the two is fundamentally different, as Third Cinema regards liberation as the goal and cinema only as a tool. The emphasis of the analogy is on their similarly marginal position, not the nature of their cinemas. On Third Cinema, see Pines and Willemen 1989.

11. The blurring of the difference between Hollywood and the film festival circuit can be described, in Robert Sklar's terms, as "blockbuster Hollywood" versus "boutique Hollywood" (1996, 19). This impression was reinforced in the early 1990s, when a string of American independent films ("boutique Hollywood") won the Palme d'Or at Cannes, including Steven Soderbergh's *sex, lies and videotape* (1989), David Lynch's *Wild at Heart* (1990), Joel Coen's *Barton Fink* (1991), and Quentin Tarantino's *Pulp Fiction* (1994). It must also be qualified that though it might not have been responsible for producing these independent films, Hollywood has generally become a byword for American films.

12. See Kluge 1981/1982, Dissanayake 1996, and Hansen 1983.

13. The February 28 incident refers to the day in 1947 when the Taiwanese clashed with the Mainlanders following pent-up frustration with the rule of Taiwan under the KMT regime after the Japanese surrender at the end of World War II. According to Alan M. Wachman, the "violence continued for two weeks," and this "was followed by several months of terror imposed by the KMT, which had troop reinforcements sent from the mainland to Taiwan." While the "precise number of executions, if it was ever known by the authorities, has not been released," Taiwan's government offered a formal apology in 1993—a few years after the release of Hou's film—acknowledging "the KMT's role in the affair" (1994, 99).

14. See Chou 2000 for such an account.

15. I am citing from the 1998 single-authored version, in which Li Yinhe expanded upon her 1992 co-authored book.

16. On recent official censorship and censure, see the report on "Restrictions on AIDS Activists in China" on the Human Rights Watch Web site (http://hrw.org/reports/2005/china0605/5.htm; accessed August 10, 2005) and news reports collated in the Global Gayz.com Web site (http://www.globalgayz.com/china-news03-05.html; accessed August 10, 2005).

17. Apparently, a negative depiction of the Cultural Revolution remains a taboo in China. According to a report in *China News* on February 28, 1994, the ending, in which the homosexual character commits suicide, was objectionable because of its timing in 1977 since, for the authorities, "the Cultural Revolution was over; why would he want to commit suicide?"

18. Of the three cuts made, only one concerns homosexual expression, while the

other two have to do with the Cultural Revolution (Rayns 1994b, 48). It should be noted that demands for cuts could also be made for commercial reasons. After Miramax acquired the film's rights for all English-speaking territories, it negotiated fourteen minutes of cuts with the director, and the original English title, *Farewell to My Concubine*, was abridged (Rayns 1994a, 41). The downfall of a supporting character, Xiaosi, for example, has been "edited out of American-released versions but [is] available in Japanese distribution" (Silbergeld 1999, 324n35).

19. In a report (*Minsheng Bao*, May 2, 1997) Zhang Yuan revealed that the film was financed by a scheme under the French Foreign Office and Ministry of Culture, which provided 900,000 francs. It also received 200,000 RMB for its screenplay from the Rotterdam International Film Festival (Chiao 1998, 259).

20. For an interview with the producer of the film, see Shelley Kraicer, "Deng Ye Talks with Virtual China," http://virtualchina.com/leisure/film/060200-dengyetalks .html. I first accessed this page in 2001, and the link did not work when I accessed it again in 2005.

21. They are Ling Yan's *The Silent Thrush (Shisheng huamei)*, winner of the *Independence Daily* novel prize in 1991; Chu T'ien-wen's (Zhu Tianwen) *Notes of a Desolate Man (Huangren shouji)*, winner of the 1994 *China Times* novel prize; and Tu Hsiu-lan's (Du Xiulan) *Rebel Woman (Ninü)*, winner of the Crown popular fiction prize in 1996. For an English translation of *Notes of a Desolate Man*, see Chu T'ien-wen 1999. For an English translation of *Crystal Boys*, see Pai 1995.

22. For an early list of homosexual literature and related research, see the appendix in Chang 1996. Fran Martin (2003a and 2003c) has extensively researched and translated queer literature from Taiwan.

23. For an analysis of the wedding, see Wang Yage 1999, chapter 5.

24. The only condemnation came from a Christian group that staged a protest outside the venue of the wedding. On protest by Christians at the gay and lesbian festival sponsored by the Taipei City Bureau of Civil Affairs in September 2000, see Simon 2004, 84.

25. An analogous example is the 1993 Cuban film *Strawberry and Chocolate (Fresa y chocolate*, directed by Tomás Gutiérrez Alea and Juan Carlos Tabio), which made US$2 million in sixteen weeks of release in the United States. As Paul Julian Smith observes: "Once more a homosexual theme proved no disadvantage to the niche marketing of small, foreign language films in the US" (1996, 147). On Hsu's marketing strategies at international film festivals, see Tang Qiandai and Xu 1995.

26. Infighting within the film industry partly stemmed from the film subsidy system run by Taiwan's Government Information Office (GIO). Tsai had been successful in securing subsidies from the GIO for all his films. Because he is a Malaysian who attended university in Taiwan before remaining there to work in theater, television, and film, his nationality was even used as a pretext in these attacks (Huang Wulan 1999, 241–242). I therefore see these attacks as mainly professional jealousy but with the issues of homosexuality and Tsai's nationality providing a convenient pretext.

27. For a review of *Beauty for Boys*, see Wang Ping and Parry 2000.

28. For a study on the decriminalization of homosexuality in Hong Kong, see Ho 1997.

29. For an account of queer theater in Hong Kong, see Lilley (1998, chapter 6).

30. For a queer reading of masculinity in seemingly straight-acting films, see Kong 2005.

31. On the rise of *tongzhi* literature on the World Wide Web, see Cristini 2005. The identity of Beijing Tongzhi, the author of the original novel, remains a mystery, though there is speculation that the author is actually a woman by the name of Linghui who now lives in the United States (Chen Yongcheng 2001, 52). As Giovanni Vitiello points out, the very nature of the medium of the Internet "guarantees, even encourages, all sorts of drags. No one can tell you for sure whether behind a 'gay novel' there isn't a heterosexual Shanghai housewife" (cited in Cristini 2005, 9). In the postscript of the printed novel, published in 2002, the author writes of her/his experience of living in the United States since 1994, though she/he states that she/he started writing and posting the story on the Internet in 1998 (Beijing Tongzhi 2002, 258–261), contradicting the information on the film's official Web site, which claims that the "first of three instalments appeared in 1996. Each instalment was given a different title; the final, unifying title for the ten-chapter work was *Beijing gushi (Beijing Story)*." See *Lan Yu's* official Web site at http://lanyu.gstage.com/english/qa.html (accessed March 11, 2002). When I accessed the site again in 2005, it required registration to enter the site, which was not the case before.

Chapter 2: The Burden of Representation

1. For an account of the film's participation in the Berlin Film Festival, see Zhang Jingbei (2002, 106–117).

2. Made with a modest budget of US$750,000, *The Wedding Banquet* was the most profitable film in 1993, with a global box-office intake of US$32 million (Zhang Jingbei 2002, 117).

3. Chris Berry notes that most existing critical discussion of the film "focuses on issues of identity politics" and that this is not surprising because the film "can claim to be the first mainstream Taiwanese and possibly even the first Chinese-language film to portray homosexuality seriously and sympathetically" (2003c, 183).

4. Rushdie's description has been borrowed for the title of a reader in post-colonial literatures. See Ashcroft, Griffiths, and Tiffin 1989.

5. The quoted question was posed to the Chinese director Zhang Yuan in an interview in *Sight and Sound* (Rayns 1996, 28). In his interview with Ang Lee, Chris Berry also wondered why "this married man with children would be so eager to make a gay film" (1993b, 54). I suggest that these questions reveal more about the interviewers and their position vis-à-vis identity politics than about the interviewees.

6. For another similar response by a gay viewer posted on the World Wide Web, see Marchetti (2000, 281).

7. As Sedgwick has also argued, "In the process of gay self-disclosure, . . . questions of authority and evidence ["How do you know you're really gay?"] can be the first to arise" (1990, 79).

8. For challenges to the notion of transgression, see Wilson 1993 and Foucault 1998.

9. Similarly, Rey Chow has argued that "if there is a metanarrative that continues to thrive in these times of metanarrative bashing, it is that of 'resistance'" and that "'resistance' has become the rhetorical support of identitarian politics, the conceptualization that underwrites discourses of class, racial, and sexual identity" (1998, 113). Lydia H. Liu also writes in relation to post-colonial theory: "I am struck by the irony that, in the very act of criticizing Western domination, one often ends up reifying the power of the dominator to a degree that the agency of non-Western cultures is reduced to a single possibility: resistance" (1995, xv–xvi).

10. Chris Berry (1996a, 158–159) cites two examples to illustrate the perpetuation of the association of homosexuality with the West by those representing orthodox ideologies in Chinese societies. One example involves Singaporean foreign minister Wong Kan Seng, who, at the 1993 United Nations World Human Rights Conference in Vienna, declared that "homosexual rights are a Western issue, and are not relevant to this conference." The other is a reported claim by a film critic from the PRC at the 1993 Berlin Film Festival that *The Wedding Banquet* was a lie because there was no homosexuality in Chinese culture. He argued that if there was any truth at all to the film, it was that it represented the corruption of Chinese manhood by Western decadence. For an illustration of the association of homosexuality with whiteness in Asian and Asian American communities, see Chiang (2002, 276–277).

11. Chua's transliteration of the protagonist's name is slightly different from that which appears in the film's subtitles and in the published script.

12. Marchetti's observation is strikingly similar: "All of the gay characters in the film are Caucasian men—with the crucial exception of Wai-tung. All of the Asian characters in the film are presented as heterosexual—again with the exception of Wai-tung. In other words, the film posits a not-so-subtle division in which a figure such as Wai-tung, who is both Chinese and gay, becomes an anomaly. Gay Asian Americans, gay Chinese, and all gays of color have a single representative in the figure of Wai-tung. Or, to put it another way, gay Asians disappear into the character of Wai-tung" (2000, 285–286).

13. For a classic example of such Orientalist stereotyping, see David Henry Hwang's play, *M. Butterfly*, which is inspired by Puccini's opera *Madame Butterfly*. Hwang's play was adapted into an eponymous film directed by David Cronenberg in 1993. For a discussion of Hwang's play, see Garber (1993, chapter 10). For a reading of Cronenberg's film, see Suner 1998. In *The Wedding Banquet*, Little Sister Mao bursts into an aria from Puccini's *Madame Butterfly*, though I find it difficult to judge if the deployment of this aria is coincidental or intentional and if it were the latter, whether it is meant to be a critique on Orientalism or an ironic statement. For a reading of this scene, see Marchetti (2000, 290).

14. In his essay on interracial gay relationships, Wei-cheng Raymond Chu argues that "*not* to represent such relationships as racially complicated *at all* can be judged only as uninformed romance or as escapist fantasy" (1997, 230; emphasis in original), and Chu wonders how Wai-Tung and Simon in *The Wedding Banquet* "are able to

reverse the role configuration of the stereotypical Caucasian-Oriental relationship" (ibid., 231). I would first suggest that while the film does not problematize interracial relationships in terms of the legacy of colonialism (the frame of reference in Chu's essay, which focuses mainly on relationships between blacks and whites), the entire premise of Ang Lee's film can be said to be precisely located in the realm of race—the wish of a *Chinese* patriarch for his son to perpetuate his family line complicates Wai-Tung's interracial relationship, leading the white Simon to consider leaving Wai-Tung, having put up with the Gaos for about a month. Second, the reversal of Orientalist construction in their relationship is achieved partly because of Wai-Tung's strong financial position, class being a category conspicuously absent in Chu's analysis. Moreover, I find Chu's colonial framework overdetermined, as it leaves no room outside of the master/slave deadlock not just for interracial but also for *intra*-racial relationships, as he claims that "even ethnic gay men's unlikely desire for one another, when it does happen, may be sutured by the raciality that spills over from *white* desire for these racial others" (ibid., 232; emphasis in original).

15. Moreover, as Rey Chow sharply observes (via Arif Dirlik), the "Orientalist has a special sibling" called the (Western) Maoists, whose white guilt (which Chow qualifies not as an essential category but a discursive position) engenders a discursive productivity: "Typically, the Maoist is a cultural critic who lives in a capitalist society but who is fed up with capitalism—a cultural critic, in other words, who wants a social order opposed to the one that is supporting her own undertaking. The Maoist is thus a supreme example of the way desire works: What she wants is always located in the other, resulting in an identification with and valorization of that which she is not/does not have. Since what is valorized is often the other's deprivation—"having" poverty or "having" nothing—the Maoist's strategy becomes in the main a *rhetorical* renunciation of the material power that enables her rhetoric" (Chow 1993, 10–11; emphasis in origin). Chow poses a challenge to those who assume this pose of "self-subalternization" (ibid., 13): "What academic intellectuals must confront is thus *not* their 'victimization' by society at large (or their victimization-in-solidarity-with-the-oppressed), but the power, wealth, and privilege that ironically accumulate from their 'oppositional' viewpoint, and the widening gap between the professed contents of their words and the upward mobility they gain from such words" (ibid., 17; emphasis in original).

16. The film intentionally sets up the relationship between Wai-Tung and Wei-Wei to be read as a geopolitical allegory, using wordplay in their first encounter, with Wai-Tung calling himself the "landowner" *(dizhu* rather than *fangdong)* and Wei-Wei claiming that the floor on which she is living has been "liberated" *(jiefang)*. For a political allegorical reading, see Marchetti (2000, 276–280).

17. The film repeatedly contrasts Wai-Tung's (representing Taiwan) lack of appreciation of culture (he frowns when Little Sister Mao bursts into an aria from Puccini) with Wei-Wei's (representing China) embodiment of culture (she comments eloquently on Mr. Gao's calligraphy).

18. Moreover, as Dariotis and Fung point out, the binary terms of East versus West set up in *The Wedding Banquet* (and, I will add, reinforced in these readings),

"eliminate a good deal in their division of the world; Africa and South America, for example, simply disappear" (1997, 201).

19. See, for example, Bono with Fitzpatrick 1998, Borhek 1993, Wythe et al. 2000, Herdt and Koff 2000, Sutcliffe 1996, Savin-Williams 2000, and Gottlieb 2004. For more on PFLAG, see http://www.pflag.org (accessed August 29, 2005).

20. See, for example, Ross 1983. In West Yorkshire, England, where I am based, a sexual health organization, Yorkshire MESMAC, runs a support group for gay men who are married to women (see http://www.mesmac.co.uk/groups/marriedmen.htm; accessed August 29, 2005), and there are similar groups throughout the United Kingdom and the United States.

21. In her study on the roots-searching school of literature *(xungen pai)*, Xueping Zhong notes that "to most PRC Chinese and to many contemporary Chinese intellectuals, traditional Chinese culture tends typically to mean mainly one thing: the negative remnants of Confucianism" (2000, 153). While "many contemporary Chinese oppositional critics . . . insist on identifying the CCP with the oppressive and conservative aspects of Confucianism" (ibid., 154), I would suggest that for oppositional critics in Chinese societies outside the PRC and Western critics, these "oppressive and conservative aspects of Confucianism" are more commonly identified with the patriarchal family.

22. The screenplay published in Chinese (A. Lee and Peng 1993) is the original draft, which is considerably different from the film. Here I quote from the published English screenplay on which the film is based.

23. Only two out of the many scholarly essays I have come across seem to have commented on this speech. Marchetti merely notes that "in the 1940s, then, Mr. Gao found himself in a situation similar to his own son's" (2000, 278), while Berry acknowledges that "the ethical parallels are clear" before qualifying that "it is also clear that Mr Gao's own experiences include the negotiation of parallel tensions" (2003c, 186).

24. The open-ended final shot, of course, invites all kinds of interpretation. For Dariotis and Fung, it is "a gesture of surrender, of one generation's sacrifice for another" (1997, 202). For Berry, the film's ambivalence "is itself an ideological move appropriate to the sustenance of globalised liberal capitalism, for it enables that system by finding a way to maintain simultaneously two otherwise incompatible value systems that it brings into proximity. In this way, it produces a new melodramatic hybrid appropriate to the negotiation of the 'moral occult' of globalism" (2003c, 189).

25. As Ernst Bloch remarks in a conversation with Adorno, "each and every criticism of imperfection, incompleteness, intolerance and impatience already without a doubt presupposes the conception of, and longing for, a possible perfection" (1988, 16).

26. For a report on the film, see Harris 2004.

Chapter 3: The Uses of Femininity

1. Wendy Larson's (1997) reading of *Farewell* also notes the transgendered expression of ruler-subject relations and the source to Qu Yuan, citing W. Li 1993. It should be noted that the poet "actually depicts himself in the first part of the poem as a

woman and later as a man. In the female role, he competes with jealous, slandering courtesans for the king-lover's attention. As a man, throughout most of the poem, he actively, though vainly, quests after his beloved" (Schneider 1980, 32).

2. See Sun 1944 and Wen Yiduo 1948.

3. Beijing opera is but one among the more than three hundred traditional operatic forms existing in China today, though it has dominated the Chinese stage for more than a hundred years and is still regarded as the leading form among all regional operas (S. L. Li 2003, 19). For a general study on cross-dressing in Chinese opera (both male-to-female and female-to-male), see S. L. Li 2003. On boy actors and homosexuality, see C. C. Wu 2004, chapter 5.

4. According to Colin Mackerras, while there were no major public acting companies with women throughout the Qing dynasty, actresses always existed and there were even exclusively female troupes in the late Qing (1975, 69–70).

5. Though she does not quote it as a source, Lau's formulation of "translation, not transgression" seems to have been borrowed from Roland Barthes, whom Ben Xu cites in his analysis of the same film (1997, 166). For the original source, see Barthes (1983, 53). In her study on female-to-male transgender practice in Taiwanese opera (koa-a-hi or gezaixi), Silvio notes that "in Taiwanese (and Chinese) performance studies, cross-gender acting in local operas is largely seen as a historically contingent tradition dating back to the fourteenth century and therefore no more transgressive than any other nonrealist aspect of Chinese opera performance" (1999, 587).

6. For the sake of convenience, I shall refer to the characters' adult names throughout.

7. For the source of the story on which the play is based and the different incarnations of the play over time, see S. L. Li (2003, chapter 3, especially pp. 72–73).

8. Sifan is a kunqu play revived by Mei Lanfang (Silvio 2002, 189). (Kunqu is a specific style of singing and music that prevailed from the mid-sixteenth century to the nineteenth century and remains the most revered form in China [S. L. Li 2003, 10]). Different parts of the play have been welded together to facilitate Dieyi's performance in the film. For the original play, see Yu (1982, 383–392). I am indebted to Wang Hongzhi, Li, and Chen (1997, 238n29) for pointing this out and for the reference to the source of the play.

9. See Silvio 2002 for an excellent reading of how both the opera academy and Cultural Revolution struggle sessions demonstrate the ways in which identities are violently unmade and remade.

10. Throughout the Qing dynasty, opera actors were classed as members of a "mean profession" (jianye), along with prostitutes and slaves, which prohibited them from sitting for the official examinations, the traditional path to upward social mobility (Goldstein 1999, 382; Mackerras 1975, 79). Since the Republican era, "actors (like fallen women) have always been the lowest of the low, the ninth and last of the professional grades, or what Maoists like to call 'the stinking ninth'" (Silbergeld 1999, 111).

11. One example is a reading by Taiwanese scholar Liao Ping-hui (Liao Binghui), which charges the film for not giving homosexuals the status they deserve and for not

facing up to sexual politics and the new social reality (1994, 196, 208). I do not believe it is the film's prerogative to promote gay rights or to deal with a sociopolitical condition temporally beyond its context. There is indeed a danger of this kind of criticism slipping into political correctness (PC). As Ella Shohat and Robert Stam write: "While the laudatory goal behind PC is to stimulate respect and mutual answerability in a reciprocity that takes past oppressions into account, in practice it often degenerates into the sadomasochistic self-flagellations of guilty liberals and a competition for oppressed status among the subaltern—victimhood and 'one-downs-personship' as cultural capital in a fluctuating identity stock market" (1994, 341).

12. This is confirmed by Chen Kaige's assertion in an interview that Dieyi "is ultimately a man; no matter what kinds of clothes he uses to camouflage himself, he is still a man. This story is about a man who loves another man" (*Yang ± Yin* 1996).

13. In Kwan's documentary, the year of the television version is credited as 1982, whereas other sources have identified the year as 1981 (see http://rthk27.rthk.org .hk/php/tvarchivecatalog/episode.php?progid=182&tvcat=3; accessed May 3, 2005).

14. Beginning with Han dynasty author Liu Xiang's (80–9 BCE) *Biographies of Notable Women (Lienü zhuan)*, there has been a long discursive tradition on virtuous women in China, particularly in the Ming and Qing dynasties, with the husband-wife relationship corresponding to the ruler-minister relationship (Carlitz 1991, 118, 121). For more on *lienü*, see Carlitz 1991 and S. Mann (1997, chapter 2).

15. It should be noted, though, that women were also active in the writing (if not the actual production) of their didactic tradition, as "elite Ming women subscribed funds for the publication of *Lienü zhuan* editions, and they are known to have edited such editions during the Qing" (Carlitz 1991, 123).

16. Interestingly, it is the feminized/women (Dieyi and Juxian) who perform the act of heroism in the film and the biological men (Dieyi and Xiaolou) who led a banal life in the novel.

17. The other notion was "heavily populist and emphasized the democratic pathos of merging with the people and heroically sacrificing one's life on behalf of the collectivity" (Schneider 1980, 89).

18. I quote from Wendy Larson's translation.

19. On *écriture féminine*, see Moi (1985, chapter 6). On Zhang's position in PRC official literary historiography, see N. Huang 2003.

20. The screenplay is slightly different from the film and is published in Wang Xiaobo 1998, in which *East Palace, West Palace* also appears in the form of an eponymous play that has been staged in Beijing and Brussels (Wang 1998, 371; Rayns 1996, 29) and as a short story entitled *"Sishui rouqing"* (Love tender as water).

21. It must be qualified here that Tambling uses the phrase "self-fashioning" to describe autobiography but not confession, as the former has "full knowledge of its fictional status," though he also acknowledges that self-fashioning seems inherent in Augustine's writings (which Tambling designates as a confessional discourse) and "its fictionalising of the self" (1990, 9). I agree with Tambling that "the intertwining of the two forms seems important" (ibid.), and it is for this reason that I am using the phrase to describe Ah Lan's narrative, which fuses confession with autobiography.

22. One example is Ah Lan's claim that he is married to his female schoolmate, "Public Bus," and, as a result, is despised in the homosexual community. There is no way of verifying this claim in the film. When Xiaoshi asks Ah Lan if he is really married and to whom, Ah Lan evades the question and talks instead about his first homosexual encounter. It is possible that Ah Lan is using "Public Bus" and his "marriage status" to arouse Xiaoshi's interest in his narrative, only to subvert the power relation by telling his own story.

23. In 1942, homosexuality was made illegal in France for the first time since 1791 and remained so until 1982 (Dyer 1990, 62).

24. For a close reading of *Un Chant d'amour* and a description of films inspired by or related to Genet, see Dyer (1990, chapter 2) and Giles 2002.

25. For an analysis of the film *Querelle* (1982), see Dyer (1990, 90–96) and Shaviro (1993, chapter 5).

Chapter 4: Travelling Sexualities

1. On Wong's cult status, see Bordwell (2000, 271) and the link to Web sites devoted to Wong and his films listed on *Senses of Cinema* at www.sensesofcinema.com (accessed August 29, 2005).

2. *The Buenos Aires Affair* was the working title of *Happy Together*. In the "making of" documentary *Buenos Aires Zero Degree* (*Sheshi lingdu, chunguang zaixian*, 1999), the clipboard on the set of *Happy Together* has the words "B.A. Affair" on it; it can also be seen in the photo-journal published by the cinematographer Christopher Doyle (1997). For an account of the film's context of Buenos Aires, see Tambling (2003, chapter 3).

3. I have rendered the voice-over in a more literal manner than the film's English subtitles. This also applies to my translation of the voice-over and dialogue below.

4. It must be noted, however, that Leung was referring to a different statement by Chow, in which Chow claims that she is not "too enthusiastic" about reading *Happy Together* in the context of Hong Kong's return to China in 1997 "because it would require one to reduce all narrative and imagistic significations more or less to a 'national allegory' type of reading and thus, by implication, to confirm the film work within an ethnic ghetto" (Chow 1999, 48n17; H. Leung 2001, 446–447n27). For a different analysis of the film in relation to Fredric Jameson's idea of Third World text as "national allegory," see Tambling (2003, chapter 2).

5. Further evidence of the significance of 1997 to Wong is his latest film, *2046*; it signposts exactly the fiftieth year dating from 1997 and alludes to the late Chinese leader Deng Xiaoping's promise that Hong Kong would remain unchanged for fifty years after the handover. The figure 2046 also appears as the hotel room number in *In the Mood for Love*.

6. As Wong reveals in an interview, "One of the reasons I chose Argentina was that it is on the other side of the world, and I thought by going there, I would be able to stay away from 1997. But then, as you must understand, once you consciously try to stay away from something or to forget something, you will never succeed. That something is bound to be hanging in the air, haunting you" (Ngai and Wong 1997, 112).

7. Drawing the link between the political and the metaphorical in the film, Tambling writes, "Deng was, famously, waiting for the moment when he could tread on Hong Kong soil, when it would not be the property of the colonizer, and would not visit Hong Kong before June 30, 1997. It was his version of reaching the Iguazu Falls" (2003, 80–81).

8. Christopher Doyle's photo-journal (1997), from which the above reference is taken, has no page numbers. An abridged version published in 1998 does not include the above-cited entry.

9. As Marc Siegel concurs, "Regardless of Wong Kar-wai's intentions with this scene, the intimate images of an abattoir in a film dealing with homosexuality will, at least in a Western gay context, evoke a relationship to Fassbinder's images" (2001, 285).

10. The trope of home-as-imprisonment points to another Puig reference, the novel *Kiss of the Spider Woman* and its film adaptation, directed by Hector Babenco (1985), noted by Tambling for the nursing of one inmate by another (2003, 70).

11. While all the sources I have encountered refer to black and white scenes, strictly speaking, these scenes are often tinged with a colored filter.

12. On the film's use of tango as music and as dance, see Stokes and Hoover (1999, 273–274) and Tambling (2003, 43–46).

13. In any case, what constitutes normality and its desirability is an ongoing debate within the so-called gay community. See, for example, Warner 1999, Sullivan 1995, Simpson 1996, and Bawer 1996.

14. I am deeply indebted to an anonymous reviewer of the book manuscript for challenging me to rethink the issue of heteronormativity. As the reviewer argues, in traditional China, "promiscuity was the prerogative of males, especially privileged ones, for whom polygamy and the sponsoring of prostitutes were normative practices." In this light, it would indeed be ironical for lesbian, gay, and queer theorists to acknowledge that their valorization of contemporary sexual promiscuity/performativity unwittingly colludes with traditionally sexist and economically asymmetrical forms of "normative" promiscuity.

15. On another take on the role of music in Wong's films, see Yeh 1999.

16. For Tambling, Fai's destiny has to do with "reconciliation with his father, which implies a movement back towards the centre" (2003, 70).

Chapter 5: Confessing Desire

1. For a list of Tsai's multimedia works, see Wen T'ien-hsiang (2002, 238–251).

2. The controversy was triggered by Tsai's withdrawal of his fourth film, *The Hole* (*Dong*, 1998), from participation in Taiwan's 1998 Golden Horse Awards, as he expressed his disappointment at the choice of some judges on the panel. This resulted in some judges withdrawing from the panel while others called for Tsai to return all governmental funding of his previous films since he did not have Republic of China citizenship. See Huang Wulan (1999, 239–246) and Rivière and Tsai (1999, 117–118).

3. Comparisons have been drawn between Tsai's works and those by Antonioni (Lee Ou-fan 1998, 170), Fassbinder (Wen T'ien-hsiang 2002, 24), and Beckett, Pinter,

Ionesco, and Kafka (Chow 2004, 126). Tsai acknowledges his influences in an interview: "I would say that my films are closer to European films of the '60s and '70s because I liked watching European films when I was a college student. I watched a lot of Visconti, Truffaut, Fassbinder, Fellini, and Antonioni. Those were the highlights of film history; they have had a direct influence on my films" (Kraicer 2000, 584–585).

4. Tsai reveals in an interview: "There is very little about history in my films because my films are very personal. Since I am an overseas Chinese from Malaysia, I have no interest in Taiwan history nor any understanding of Taiwan history" (Kraicer 2000, 584).

5. A well-read novelist whose mother is an eminent translator of Japanese literature into Chinese, Chu is unlikely to conflate the two terms but is perhaps more interested in their associative potential.

6. For more on the *shishōsetsu*, see Suzuki 1996 and Hijiya-Kirschnereit 1996.

7. For an elaboration on Tsai's diasporic condition expressed as the sentiments of *rensheng ruji* (human life is a transient abode), see Chow (2004, 136–138).

8. As pointed out in the note accompanying the translated text, the original French term *"jouissance"* is perhaps better rendered as "coming" rather than "bliss" (Howard 1975, v–vi), while Jonathan Culler has translated it as "ecstasy" (1983, 98).

9. Chow offers a reading of the film in terms of "a production of discursivity" that operates "in the manner of an archaeological excavation," from which "the *remnants of social relations,* which are presented by Tsai as *images with little or no interiority*—in the form of bodies, gestures, movements, and looks"—are excavated (2004, 129; emphasis in original). For another reading that focuses on the film's rewriting of "the meaning of the patriarchal *jia* [home / family] itself in the light of the internality of homosexual knowledges to its constitution" as "perverse utopianism," see Martin (2003c, chapter 6).

10. As Culler explains, "From the point of view of poetics, what requires explanation is not the text itself so much as the possibility of reading and interpreting the text, the possibility of literary effects and literary communication" (1975, 127). I would only add that a reading of Tsai's works from the point of view of poetics shores up the impossibilities as much as the possibilities in Culler's statement.

11. In the play, François Truffaut's film *Les 400 Coups* (1959) is projected onto a mosquito net on the stage (Wen T'ien-hsiang 2002, 31), prefiguring Tsai's celebrated cinematic affinity with Truffaut. In Tsai's fifth film, *What Time Is It There? (Ni nabian jidian,* 2001), Tsai's alter ego, Xiaokang (Lee Kang-sheng / Li Kangsheng), watches a videotape of *Les 400 Coups* in Taipei while Truffaut's alter ego, Jean-Pierre Léaud (the lead actor in *Les 400 Coups*), appears in a cameo role in Paris.

12. The play recalls Jean Genet's silent film, *Un Chant d'amour* (1950), in which a voyeuristic prison guard spies on the male inmates in various acts of sexual arousal.

13. The play was restaged by Taiwan's Min-hsin (Minxin) Theater Company in 1992.

14. As evidence of Tsai's consistent thematic concern over a long period of time, the original Chinese phrase here is *"Ni nabian jidian (le),"* which is to become the Chinese title of Tsai's 2001 film, *What Time Is It There?*

15. Wen T'ien-hsiang (Wen Tianxiang) thinks that the phrase "coming out of the closet" did not exist in Taiwan in 1984 (2002, 37). However, given that Tsai had wanted to use the film *The Boys in the Band* (dir. William Friedkin, 1970) as a model for his second play, *A Door That Can't Be Opened in the Dark* (ibid., 32), his familiarity with Western gay culture may not have precluded knowledge of the phrase, which was already popular in the West by the early 1980s.

16. In line with the general queer reading of the text, the gender of the invisible person, referred to as the gender-free "that person" *(naren)*, is here assumed to be male.

17. As evidence of the autobiographical nature of the play, Tsai reveals in an interview that a member of the audience came up to him after the play's performance and said, "Actually you're producing this play just for one person," a statement Tsai did not deny (Wen T'ien-hsiang 2002, 213).

18. For another account by Tsai in a different interview, see Rivière and Tsai (1999, 92–93).

19. For the case of the United States, see Crimp 1988.

20. While acknowledging that his first three films can be seen as "Xiaokang's films," Tsai dislikes calling them a trilogy, as he thinks it is clichéd (Chen Baoxu 1997, 53, 56). It should be noted that Tony Rayns' observation was made in 1997, when he was reviewing Tsai's third film, so he could not have foreseen that his criteria for calling Tsai's first three films a trilogy continued to apply in Tsai's later films.

21. Tsai's fourth film, *The Hole,* features a mysterious virus that infects Taiwan at the turn of the millennium; it can be seen as "a symbol for, among other things, HIV" (Rojas 2003, 66).

22. It should be noted that "Nezha" is more commonly pronounced as "Nuozha" in Taiwan.

23. For example, Ah Ze misses a date with Ah Gui and joins Ah Bin instead to steal computer motherboards from a games arcade. When Ah Bin is later beaten up as a result and longs to hug a woman, Ah Ze, who by then has had sex with Ah Gui but whose relationship with her is on the point of breaking up because he has left her alone in a hotel after sex, "sacrifices" Ah Gui and asks her to hug Ah Bin.

24. It is noteworthy that Tsai had originally wanted to end the film with this sequence, but the producer added another part to it as the ending, claiming that the film would otherwise be too short as a feature and thus would have qualified for governmental subsidy (Rivière and Tsai 1999, 92).

25. Water assumes various forms in the film, from the shower in the hotel and the sauna, the pouring rain, and the urine and flushing water in the toilet bowl to the sweat perspired and sperm ejaculated during sex. It has been argued that the Chinese character for water, *shui,* is a broader category than the English word "water," and it can refer to "river," "flood," "to flood," and "water" itself (Allan 1997, 32). Although the river in the film's title disappears after the opening scenes, critics have pointed out that it has "molecularized" (Huang Jianhong 1998, 52) or "metamorphosed" (Wu Jintao 1998, 102) into different forms of water throughout the film. Tsai has said that water is often a symbol for sexual desire in his work (Chiao 1997b, 23). In *Rebels,*

water is bound to Xiaokang's object of desire, Ah Ze, whose apartment is flooded. In *Vive l'amour,* the characters are frequently shown drinking water, quenching the unquenchable thirst for sex. The metaphors of water and illness are also employed in *The Hole.*

26. This sequence also combines food and sex as Xiaokang's mother feeds him durian, a tropical fruit (recalling Tsai's origins from Malaysia) that, when pried open, can be seen as a symbol for the female genitalia.

27. Another intertextual reading to note is the sex scene between the father and son in *The River* and that between the male inmates in Tsai's play *A Door That Can't Be Opened in the Dark.* Both feature intergenerational sex, both are rendered in silence, and the use of light (or rather darkness) is key to both scenes (Wen T'ien-hsiang 2002, 34).

28. See, in particular, chapters 12–14 of *Investitures of the Gods.*

29. Pasolini's film draws its inspiration from Sophocles' classic, whereas Schlöndorff's film is based on Max Frisch's novel *Homo Faber.*

30. As Sangren points out, even though Nezha is forced to recognize Li Jing as his father in the story as told in *Investitures of the Gods,* "one should not be misled by Nezha's eventual submission; it is his rebelliousness that impresses itself most clearly upon Chinese consciousness" (2000, 204).

31. Posing the question, "can incest actually happen between father and son," Chow argues that the categories of both incest and the Chinese term *luanlun* are inadequate to describe what happened between the father and son in *The River,* which she proposes to read as "an enigma" (2004, 125, 135). I have thus chosen to refer to this scene as "incest" (in quotes).

32. While the problematic of chance and coincidence is more often employed in melodrama, as Jane Shattuc argues, it can also "become central to the art cinema plot" such as in films by Fassbinder (1995, 121). I would, however, qualify that the distinction between art film and melodrama, especially in the case of Fassbinder, is not always useful. Similarly, while Tsai is generally regarded as an art cinema director, the Oedipal chance and coincidence in *The River* can in fact be seen as a typical melodramatic device. On melodrama, see Dissanayake 1993 and Gledhill 1987.

33. Most scholars concur that the symbolic patriarchal order has been undermined, rather than reinstated, in this scene. Fran Martin, for example, argues that the "painfully ironic and unjust situation in which the father punishes the son for the same behaviour in which he himself also engages and which they have just enacted together, surely evacuates the moral authority of the father, who is now revealed as hypocritical and unjust" (2003c, 175). Invoking Chang Hsiao-hung's (Zhang Xiaohong) argument, Rey Chow also sees the father as "dephallicized" (Chang's term) so that "his penis is just a penis" in the "clandestine sexual economy" of the bathhouse (2004, 135–136).

34. *Rebels* uses a piece of extra-diegetic music—a variation on a four-bar melody —that won the composer, Huang Shu-chun (Huang Shujun), an award at the 1992 Golden Horse Awards. There is no extra-diegetic music in *Vive l'amour* and *The River,* though Tsai has shown his preference for old Mandarin ballads from the 1930s to the

1960s; these feature in *The Hole, Goodbye Dragon Inn* (Busan, 2003), and *The Wayward Cloud* (*Tianbian yiduo yun*, 2005).

35. In a scene in the hotel room in Taichung preceding the "incest" scene, Xiaokang is shown trying to suffocate himself with a pillow before discovering the door behind the curtain. In an earlier scene at the hospital in Taipei, where his parents pass him by in the corridor without recognizing him, Xiaokang bursts out crying in a rare expression of emotion and says he does not want to live anymore.

36. As Culler writes, "How better to facilitate a reading of oneself than by trying to make explicit one's sense of the comprehensible and the incomprehensible, the significant and the insignificant, the ordered and the inchoate. By offering sequences and combinations which escape our accustomed grasp, by subjecting language to a dislocation which fragments the ordinary signs of our world, literature challenges the limits we set to the self as a device or order and allows us, painfully or joyfully, to accede to an expansion of self" (1975, 129–130).

37. While Chow's observation of reciprocal tenderness in this scene is accurate, it must be noted that in another sex scene between the father and the anonymous young man (played by Chen Chao-jung), there is no such tenderness, as the father repeatedly tries to make the young man perform fellatio on him by pressing his head down, leading the young man to resist and leave as a result.

38. While the title of Fassbinder's film is generally known as such, the full title is *Ali: Fear Eats the Soul*.

Chapter 6: Fragments of Darkness

1. Luo Feng also argues that *Yang ± Yin* is "the watershed in Stanley Kwan's filmmaking career and the start of a transition from his earlier 'women's films' to 'tongzhi cinema'" (2002, 44).

2. As Jane Shattuc argues in relation to Fassbinder's cinema, "although the sensationalism of an autobiographical reading is often discouraged by academic readings, which value more abstract and thematic understandings, it conditioned the social reception of Fassbinder's films" (1995, 127). I would argue that the public nature of Kwan's coming out—still a rarity, hence even more striking in the Chinese context— justifies if not demands an autobiographical reading of Kwan's films.

3. All quotation from the documentary's voice-over (narrated by Tony Rayns) is verbatim in the original English. Where conversations in the documentary are conducted in Cantonese, I have translated them in a more literal manner than the subtitles do.

4. Li's interview of Kwan was first published in Hong Kong in the original Chinese with an English translation. A slightly different Chinese version was subsequently reprinted in Taiwan, and I am drawing my own English translation from this.

5. For more on Yam Kin-fai, see Luo 2002, chapter 1.

6. Despite taking up only the final moments of the last chapter of the documentary, the significance of this sequence is out of proportion to its length. As Kwan reveals, many friends half jokingly said to him after watching the documentary that

the first part was just an appetizer, whereas the main course was his conversation with his mother (Li Xiaoxian 1997, 57).

7. In an interview on the documentary, the interviewer commented to Kwan that "I feel that [your mother] is supporting you with the best intentions. But like all mothers, no matter how much she disagrees with her children, she would comprehend and accept with an understanding attitude. I feel that's how she is." To which Kwan replied, "Of course that's how she is. But I feel that for a woman like my mother who is over sixty years old, didn't receive much education, toiled her whole life [and] didn't have many opportunities to come into contact with the outside world, what she has done is already a lot" (Li Xiaoxian 1997, 57–58).

8. The original Cantonese (here rendered in Mandarin Chinese) is *"yige ren ruguo you shenme..."* (if one has some...); the missing words could easily have been the familiar phrase *"sanchang liangduan"* (mishap or death).

9. Though Fassbinder had always been explicit about his sexuality in his real and reel lives, including his playing a homosexual in *Fox and His Friends* (1974), it was as late as 1979–1980, when, adapting Alfred Döblin's novel *Berlin Alexanderplatz* into a television series, that he acknowledged that the novel "enabled me to admit the agonizing fears which almost paralyzed me, to admit my homosexual desires" (*Die Zeit*, March 14, 1980; quoted in Silverman 1992, 215).

10. See, for example, the interviews quoted in Elsaesser (1980, 24) and Thomsen (1997, 180).

11. It must be noted, however, that Kwan had begun to include in his women's films references to homosexuality. For example, *Full Moon in New York* (*Ren zai Niuyue*, also known as *Sange nüren de gushi*, 1989) features a lesbian character, a conversation about homosexuality, and John Lahr's biography of the late British playwright Joe Orton (1933–1967).

12. However, Fassbinder's mother, unlike Kwan's, had had much more experience in front of her son's camera, as she appeared in eleven Fassbinder films (Shattuc 1995, 126).

13. When asked if he psychologically prepared his mother for the interview, Kwan answers: "No. I'm not sure if it is only today that my mother knows her son is gay. But the Chinese find it very difficult to talk about these things openly" (Li Xiaoxian 1997, 59).

14. The Chinese subtitle uses the male-gendered pronoun *ta* (which can also be gender-free) to refer to the friend and the person whom the friend loves the most. I am taking the linguistic hint as well as deducing from the context that both are male.

15. The terms *kuaile* and *duoluo* in Kwan's Chinese title rhyme in Cantonese as *failok* and *dolok*. The English title is the translation of the original screenplay's title, *Baojin ni, baojin ni*, written by Jimmy Ngai (Wei Shao'en). For the Chinese screenplay, see Ngai 1998. To add to the decadent/*duoluo* reference, one might also wish to note that Wong Kar-wai's film before *Happy Together* is *Duoluo tianshi* (*Fallen angels*, 1995).

16. According to Luo Feng, the line has now become a promotional slogan for

tongzhi theater in Hong Kong and even a statement encouraging *tongzhi* to come out (2002, 27).

17. I agree with the second half of Leung's statement but would qualify the first half by saying that the film is not *entirely* about gay identity.

18. Jie is the character's name as it appears in the subtitles, but he is more commonly called Xiaozhe in the film.

19. This scene recalls a similar arrangement in Kieślowski's Three Colors Trilogy. In three films corresponding to the colors of the French national flag—*Three Colors: Blue* (1993), *Three Colors: White* (1993), and *Three Colors: Red* (1994)—each features a female protagonist embodying the ideals of the French Revolution—namely liberty, equality, and fraternity—played respectively by Juliette Binoche, Julie Delpy, and Irène Jacob. Each film features a scene in which the three actresses appear together without acknowledging each other's presence.

20. This again is similar to Kieślowski's *The Double Life of Véronique,* in which the woman in Poland dies before the narrative concerning the French woman (both women played by Irène Jacob) begins.

21. In line with the intertwining of the personal with the political, Wai's relatives have all emigrated, and he is now alone in Hong Kong following Moon's death, thus opening up possibilities for a relationship (platonic or otherwise) with Tong later in the film.

22. Even though the camera pans very slowly across the poster and some words are visible on its bottom right corner, it is impossible to make them out. The published screenplay reveals the words as (in original English) "To my one and only beloved Tong: Happy Birthday, with lots of love and kisses, Eric, 1989" (Ngai 1998, 14). These words appear in the subtitles in the film's VCD (VCD1092) but not the DVD (DVD-178), both produced by Mei Ah Laser Disc.

23. Though the song would certainly be classified as Taiwanese rather than Cantonese pop, to be precise, its "national" identity is hard to define, as the singer-composer, Eric Moo (Wu Qixian), is a Malaysian who studied and launched his early music career in Singapore before making it big in Taiwan.

24. Prominent on the bookshelves next to the poster of *A City of Sadness* is the back cover of *A Brighter Summer Day (Gulingjie shaonian sharen shijian,* 1991), the screenplay of a film by another Taiwanese director, Edward Yang.

25. Kwan's 1989 film, *Full Moon in New York,* caused quite a furor in Taiwan's film circles when it swept eight awards, including best film, at Taiwan's Golden Horse Awards, while Hou's *A City of Sadness* was given only the best director award as consolation. More recently, Kwan's *Lan Yu* won five awards at the 2001 Golden Horse Awards, including best director for Kwan and best actor for Liu Ye, who plays the title role. Kwan's affinity to Taiwan's film circles can also be seen from his interview with many Taiwanese directors and critics in his documentary *Yang ± Yin.*

26. Not only does Tong wine and dine Wai with chilled crab, abalone, and Chardonnay, but he also removes his glasses for the first time before the meal in a move to appear more attractive.

27. The film does not portray any coming out scene, but it seems implausible that Wai does not know that Tong is gay. Their usual meeting place is a gay bar where Tong is a regular. On one occasion, Tong apologizes for being late, explaining that he had been held up at the (gay) sauna.

28. The initial relationship between Tong and Jie is more ambiguous. With Wai asleep in the back seat, both Tong and Jie seem to be testing each other by initiating physical contact (nudging each other on the shoulder) with the swerve of the car. After Jie announces that he alone will help Wai to the apartment, the tension between Jie and Tong becomes palpable.

29. It should be noted that a gender-free pronoun is used in the original Cantonese that cannot be rendered in the English translation. This lends a particular ambiguity to Tong's speech, as the sexual orientations of the two characters are presumably different. Even though Tong is addressing Wai here, I have chosen to use "him" in the translation as this speech may be read more accurately as Tong's internal monologue to himself. On the use of ungendered pronouns and its politics, see Glover and Kaplan 2000.

30. Both women have a large collection of perfumes. The trope of the sense of smell is also underscored in the MTV video of a Mandarin love ballad, *Smell (Weidao)*, rendered by the Taiwanese singer Hsin Hsiao-chi (Xin Xiaoqi). Appearing on the television set in Rosa's room in Taipei, the song carries the following line: "Thinking of your smile, thinking of your coat, thinking of your white socks and the smell of your body." Another connection between the two women concerns the reference to hotpot. Moon, on the morning of her flight to Taipei, promises to reward Wai with the food when she returns, and later Jie treats Rosa to a meal of hotpot in Taipei.

31. Andrew Grossman thinks that the object of Jie's fantasy is "unclear" (2000c, 175), primarily because he has mistaken Jie's sexual relationship with Moon as happening before, rather than after, this scene. Moreover, along with the sequence showing Jie's gaze on Wai, an earlier scene with Jie swimming alone with the reflection of the water surface (reminiscent of David Hockney's paintings) and another scene in which some gay teenagers flirt with Jie together provide enough gay subtexts to substantiate Jie's masturbatory fantasy as Wai.

32. Grossman also makes a similar observation as he wonders if Moon is just Wai's "intermediary" in Jie's sexual economy (2000c, 175).

33. The choice of Teng's song, while befitting the genre of romantic films alluded to here, may also have a geopolitical implication. Teng's songs became immensely popular in mainland China in the 1980s, a period that coincided with Deng Xiaoping's open door economic policy. However, because they share the same surname, Teng's songs—previously dismissed as bourgeois spiritual poison—can also be read as a covert oppositional discourse in China, as captured by the popular phrase, "Listen to old Deng [referring to the Chinese leader] by day and the little Deng [referring to the singer] by night" *(Baitian ting Lao Deng, wanshang ting Xiao Deng)*. Thus the use of Teng's song evokes both Taiwanese popular cinema and the geopolitical context of 1997.

34. Though Freud's theory of displacement refers to an activity in dreams, it is relevant to my discussion here as the displacement of Jie's homosexual desire also takes place in the unconscious.

35. Though some may choose to read Jie as a bisexual, I maintain that displacing homosexual desire as a heterosexual relationship is different from simultaneously desiring people of both sexes. That is, I do not see Jie's sexual relationship with Moon as driven by heterosexual desire but as a displacement of homosexuality as heterosexuality.

36. In addition to this psychoanalytic reading within the film's diegesis, the romantic sequence can also be accounted for in the more pragmatic terms of filmmaking. The Golden Harvest Studio approached Kwan to make a film starring the actress Chingmy Yau, who is otherwise better known for her soft-porn films. *Hold You Tight* plays an in-joke on Yau by having the video rental shop owner tell a caller on the phone that the shop does not carry Category III (that is, soft-porn) films just as Yau steps into the shop. While *Hold You Tight* is fairly explicit about homosexuality (for example, in the sex scene between Tong and another man in the sauna), the romantic sequence can be read as at once appealing to a heterosexual or mainstream audience while trafficking homosexual desire through displacement.

37. The film makes another reference to 1997 here as Rosa says, "They are doing the 1997 promotion for the cologne."

38. It remains unclear why Rosa and Jie visit the gay disco, though Rosa seems familiar with the scene as she meets a gay friend there (a cameo role by Tony Rayns). Her claim about having girlfriends whom she likes is perhaps not a suggestion of her possible bisexuality but her way of reassuring Jie that it is all right to be gay.

39. Kwan reveals in an interview that the portrayal of Wai and Moon's relationship is based on his own with his partner of several years and claims that many gay couples regard "straight" familial relationships such as Wai and Moon's as typically gay (Shan 1998, 71).

40. The film does not show Tong being given the phone number by a man. Instead, it shows Tong, having emerged from the sauna into the bustling street, wearing a smile as he takes out a piece of paper from his jacket pocket before tossing it away.

41. The film has also been read as hostile to heterosexuals and women at the expense of valorizing homosexuality. See Huang Shuxian 2000.

42. It can be deduced from the tempo of Wai's humming that it is the version by Faye Wong.

43. Wong, for example, has appeared on Hong Kong's gay radio station. See http://www.gaystation.com.hk/events.html (accessed December 7, 2002). For a similar queer reading of Wong's rendition of *Dark Surges,* see http://edu.sina.com.cn/literature/celebrity/vogue/4/2135.html (accessed December 7, 2002).

44. While I agree with Leung that the sauna scene is shot without pathos, I would suggest that pathos permeates more generally in the characterization of Tong, whose frequent double entendres in his speech belie a longing for companionship and love.

45. This statement is taken from the official Web site of *Lan Yu* and is dated 2001 (http://lanyu.gstage.com/english/director.html; accessed August 16, 2004). Kwan made a similar statement earlier in an interview on *Yang ± Yin* (Li Xiaoxian 1997, 57).

Conclusion

1. As Michael Warner notes, "Queer activists are also lesbians and gays in other contexts—as for example where leverage can be gained through bourgeois propriety, or through minority-rights discourse, or through more gender-marked language (it probably won't replace lesbian feminism)" (1993, xxviii).

2. On New Queer Cinema, see Aaron 2004.

3. *Chung Wai Literary Monthly (Zhongwai wenxue),* an academic journal published by the foreign language department at the National Taiwan University, featured four special issues on queer sexuality between 1996 and 2003, with the titles of the special issues rendered in both Chinese and English. While all the English titles used the term "queer," the Chinese titles ranged from *tongzhi* (June 1996; August 2003) to *ku'er* (August 1997) and *guaitai* (May 1998).

4. Smith makes a similar observation about the study of sexuality in Spanish and Spanish American literature: "content analysis goes hand in hand with the search for 'positive images': the literary text is to be judged against a set of pre-existing standards against which it is invariably found wanting" (1992, 3).

5. Since the 1990s, queer theory and politics have grown into a cottage industry in Taiwanese academic and intellectual circles, which are heavily influenced by Anglo-American discourses, owing to the large number of Taiwanese who have been trained in American universities or have experiences of living in the United States. In mainland China, Li Yinhe has translated key texts in queer theory into a book (2000). On the advent of queer theory in Taiwan, see Lim forthcoming-c.

6. See Lim forthcoming-a. On the contestation of the term "queer" in Anglo-American discourse, see Jagose (1996, chapter 8).

7. See, for example, Sinfield 1994a and Chang (2000, chapter 1).

8. For example, Grossman notes that "a great many of the most commercial/visible queer films are made by heterosexual directors whose intentions are often at odds with their queer audiences" (2000a, xv). Grossman's statement not only falls into the trap of the intentional fallacy, but also assumes a monolithic response to films from queer audiences.

Filmography

Citation style: English title (original title), director, company credits, year.

15, Royston Tan, Zhao Wei Films, 2003.

The 400 Blows (Les 400 coups), François Truffaut, Les Films du Carrosse/Sédif Productions, 1959.

2046, Wong Kar-wai, Block 2 Pictures/Paradis Films/Orly Films/Jet Tone, 2004.

Actress/Center Stage (Ruan Lingyu), Stanley Kwan, Golden Way Films, 1991.

Ali: Fear Eats the Soul (Angst essen Seele auf), Rainer Werner Fassbinder, Tango-Film, 1973.

As Tears Go By (Wangjiao Kamen/Rexue nan'er), Wong Kar-wai, In-Gear, 1988.

Ashes of Time (Dongxie Xidu), Wong Kar-wai, Jet Tone/Scholar Films/Beijing Film Studios/Tsui Siu-ming Productions/Pony Canyon, 1994.

Barton Fink, Joel Coen, Circle Films/Working Title Films, 1991.

Beauty for Boys (Meili shaonian), Mickey Chen Chun-chih, Taiwan Queer Pride Image House, 1999.

Beijing Bastards (Beijing zazhong), Zhang Yuan, Beijing Bastards Group, 1993.

Bend It like Beckham, Gurinder Chadha, Kintop Films, 2002.

Betty Blue: 37°2 le matin, Jean-Jacques Beineix, Constellation Productions/Cargo Films, 1986.

Bishōnen . . . (Meishaonian zhi lian), Yonfan, Far Sun Film, 1998.

Blue Gate Crossing (Lanse damen), Yee Chih-yen, Arc Light Films/Pyramide Productions, 2002.

The Boys in the Band, William Friedkin, Cinema Center 100 Productions/Leo Films/National General Pictures, 1970.

A Brighter Summer Day (Gulingjie shaonian sharen shijian), Edward Yang, ICA/Jane Balfour Films/Yang and His Gang Filmmakers, 1991.

Brokeback Mountain, Ang Lee, Alberta Filmworks/Focus Features/Good Machine/Paramount Pictures/This Is That Productions, scheduled for release in 2005.

Buenos Aires Zero Degree: The Making of Happy Together (Sheshi lingdu, chunguang zaixian), Kwan Pun-leung and Amos Lee, Block 2 Pictures, 1999.

Bugis Street (Yaojie huanghou), Yonfan, Jaytex Productions, 1995.

Café Lumière (Kōhī jikō/Kafei shiguang), Hou Hsiao-hsien, Shochiku/Asahi Shimbunsha/Sumitomo Corporation/Eisei Gekijo/Imagica, 2003.

Caravaggio, Derek Jarman, British Film Institute, 1986.

Un Chant d'amour, Jean Genet, Nico Papatakis, 1950.

Chungking Express (Chongqing senlin), Wong Kar-wai, Jet Tone, 1994.

A City of Sadness (Beiqing chengshi), Hou Hsiao-hsien, ERA International, 1989.

Crouching Tiger, Hidden Dragon (Wohu canglong), Ang Lee, Asia Union Film and Entertainment/China Film Co-Production Corporation/Columbia Pictures Film Production Asia/EDKO Film/Good Machine/Sony Pictures Classics/United China Vision/Zoom Hunt International Productions, 2000.

Days of Being Wild (A Fei zhengzhuan), Wong Kar-wai, In-Gear, 1990.

Do the Right Thing, Spike Lee, 40 Acres and a Mule Filmworks, 1989.

Doña Herlinda and Her Son (Doña Herlinda y su hijo), Jaime Humberto Hermosilio, Clasa Films Mundiales, 1985.

The Double Life of Véronique, Krzysztof Kieślowski, Sideral Productions/Tor Productions/Le Studio Canal, 1991.

East Palace, West Palace (Donggong xigong), Zhang Yuan, Amazon Entertainment/Ocean Films/Quelqu'un d'Autre Productions, 1996.

Eat Drink Man Woman (Yinshi nannü), Ang Lee, Central Motion Picture Corporation/Good Machine, 1994.

Edward II, Derek Jarman, BBC/British Screen Productions/Edward II/Working Title Films, 1991.

Enter the Clowns (Choujue dengchang), Cui Zi'en, Cuizi Film Studio, 2001.

Fallen Angels (Duoluo tianshi), Wong Kar-wai, Jet Tone, 1995.

Farewell My Concubine (Bawang bie ji), Chen Kaige, Tomson (HK) Films/China Film Co-Production Corporation/Beijing Film Studio, 1993.

Farewell My Concubine (Bawang bie ji), Alex Law, Radio Television Hong Kong TV, 1981.

Feeding Boys, Ayaya (Aiyaya, qu buru), Cui Zi'en, Cuizi Film Studio, 2003.

First Love and Other Pains (Xinhui), Simon Chung, First Run Features, 1999.

Fish and Elephant (Jinnian xiatian), Li Yu, Cheng Yong Productions, 2001.

Fleeing by Night (Yeben), Hsu Li-kong, Beijing Film Studios/Beijing Rosart Film/Broadband Films/Central Motion Pictures Corporation/China Film Co-Production Corporation/Zoom Hunt International Productions, 2000.

Formula 17 (Shiqisui de tiankong), Chen Ying-jung, Three Dots Entertainment, 2004.

Fox and His Friends (Faustrecht der Freiheit), Rainer Werner Fassbinder, Tango Films/City Film GmbH, 1974.

Full Moon in New York (Ren zai Niuyue/Sange nüren de gushi), Stanley Kwan, Shiobu, 1989.

Germany in Autumn (Deutschland im Herbst), Rainer Werner Fassbinder, Project Filmproduktion im Filmverlag der Autoren/Hallelujah Film/Kairos Film, 1978.

Golden Paddy Field (Huangjin daotian), Chou Teng, First Line Films Video Production, 1992.

Goodbye, Dragon Inn (Busan), Tsai Ming-liang, Homegreen Films, 2003.

Happy Together (Chunguang zhaxie), Wong Kar-wai, Block 2 Pictures/Prémon H./Seowoo Films/Jet Tone, 1997.

Hold You Tight (Yu kuaile yu duoluo), Stanley Kwan, Golden Harvest/Kwan's Creation Workshop, 1998.

The Hole (*Dong*), Tsai Ming-liang, Arc Light Films/Central Motion Pictures Corporation/China Television/Haut et Court/La Sept-Arte, 1998.

House of Flying Daggers (*Shimian maifu*), Zhang Yimou, Beijing New Picture Films/China Film Co-Production Corporation/EDKO Films/Elite Group Enterprises/Zhang Yimou Studio, 2004.

Hu-Du-Men (*Hudumen*), Shu Kei, Ko Chi-sum Productions, 1996.

Hulk, Ang Lee, Universal Pictures/Marvel Enterprises/Valhalla Motion Pictures/Good Machine, 2003.

I Only Want You to Love Me (*Ich will doch nur, dass Ihr mich liebt*), Rainer Werner Fassbinder, Bavaria Atelier/Westdeutscher Rundfunk, 1976.

The Ice Storm, Ang Lee, Good Machine, 1997.

In a Year with 13 Moons (*In einem Jahr mit 13 Monden*), Rainer Werner Fassbinder, Tango Films/Project Filmproduktion im Filmverlag der Autoren, 1978.

In the Mood for Love (*Huayang nianhua*), Wong Kar-wai, Block 2 Pictures/Paradis Films/Jet Tone, 2000.

Keep Cool (*You hua haohao shuo*), Zhang Yimou, Guangxi Film Studio, 1996.

Kill Bill series, Quentin Tarantino, Miramax Films/A Band Apart/Super Cool Man-Chu, 2003 and 2004.

Killing Me Softly, Chen Kaige, Metro-Goldwyn-Mayer/Noelle Entertainment/Montecito Pictures, 2002.

King of the Children (*Haiziwang*), Chen Kaige, Xi'an Film Studio, 1987.

Kiss of the Spider Woman, Hector Babenco, HB Filmes/Sugarloaf Films, 1985.

Lan Yu, Stanley Kwan, Kwan's Creation Workshop/Yongning Creation Workshop, 2001.

Life on a String (*Bianzou bianchang*), Chen Kaige, Beijing Film Studios/China Film Co-Production Corporation/Pandora Filmproduktion GmbH/Serene Productions, 1991.

The Living End, Gregg Araki, Desperate Pictures, 1991.

Lonely Hearts Club (*Jimo fangxin julebu*), Yee Chih-yen, Central Motion Pictures Corporation, 1995.

Looking for Langston, Isaac Julien, British Film Institute/Sankofa Film and Video, 1988.

The Love of Three Oranges (*San ju zhi lian*), Hung Hung, Kuaihuo yang dianying gongzuoshi, 1998.

Love Is Colder than Death (*Liebe ist kälter als der Tod*), Rainer Werner Fassbinder, Antiteater-X-film, 1969.

Love unto Waste (*Dixia qing*), Stanley Kwan, D and B Films, 1986.

M. Butterfly, David Cronenberg, Geffen Pictures/Miranda Productions, 1993.

Malcolm X, Spike Lee, 40 Acres and a Mule Filmworks/JVC Entertainment/Largo International, 1992.

Mama (*Mama*), Zhang Yuan, China, 1992.

The Map of Sex and Love (*Qingse ditu*), Evans Chan, Riverdrive Productions, 2001.

The Matrix trilogy, Andy Wachowski and Larry Wachowski, Groucho II Film Partnership/Silver Pictures/Village Roadshow Pictures, 1999 and 2003.

Men and Women (*Nannan Nünü*), Liu Bingjian, Apsaras Film and TV Productions, 1999.

Murmur of Youth (Meili zai changge), Lin Cheng-sheng, Central Motion Picture Corporation, 1997.

My New Friends (Wo xin renshi de pengyou), Tsai Ming-liang, Hong sidai gongzuo xiaozu/Dahao gongzuoshi, 1995.

Not Simply a Wedding Banquet . . . (Buzhishi xiyan), Mickey Chen Chun-chih and Mia Chen Ming-hsiu, Taiwan, 1997.

Oedipus Rex, Pier Paolo Pasolini, Arco Film S.r.L./Somafis, 1967.

Old Testament (Jiuyue), Cui Zi'en, Cuizi DV Studio, 2002.

One and Eight (Yige he bage), Zhang Junzhao, Guangxi Film Studio, 1984.

The Outsiders (Niezi), Yu Kan-ping, Taiwan, 1986.

Peony Pavilion (Youyuan jingmeng), Yonfan, Far Sun Films, 2001.

The Piano, Jane Campion, Australian Film Commission/CiBy 2000/New South Wales Film and Television Office, 1993.

Poison, Todd Haynes, Bronze Eye Production/Poison L.P., 1991.

Postman in the Mountains (Nashan naren nagou), Huo Jianqi, A Xiaoxiang Film Studio/Beijing Film Studios/Hunan Post Office Bureau, 1999.

Public Toilet (Hwajangshil eodieyo?/Renmin gongce), Fruit Chan, Digital Nega/Nicetop Independent, 2002.

Pulp Fiction, Quentin Tarantino, A Band Apart/Jersey Films/Miramax Films, 1994.

Pushing Hands (Tuishou), Ang Lee, Central Motion Picture Corporation, 1991.

A Queer Story (Jilao sishi), Shu Kei, Golden Harvest, 1996.

Querelle, Rainer Werner Fassbinder, Planet-Film/Albatros-Produktion/Gaumont in association with Sam Waynberg, 1982.

Rebels of the Neon God (Qingshaonian Nezha), Tsai Ming-liang, Central Motion Picture Corporation, 1992.

Red Rose, White Rose (Hong meigui, bai meigui), Stanley Kwan, Golden Flare Films, 1994.

Red Sorghum (Hong gaoliang), Zhang Yimou, Xi'an Film Studio, 1987.

Ride with the Devil, Ang Lee, Good Machine/Hollywood International Multimedia Group/Maplewood Productions/Universal Pictures, 1999.

The River (Heliu), Tsai Ming-liang, Central Motion Picture Corporation, 1997.

Rouge (Yanzhi kou), Stanley Kwan, Golden Harvest/Golden Way Films, 1988.

Sense and Sensibility, Ang Lee, Columbia Pictures Corporation/Mirage, 1995.

sex, lies and videotape, Steven Soderberg, Outlaw Productions/Virgin, 1989.

Sons (Erzi), Zhang Yuan, Beijing Expression Culture Communication Center, 1996.

Still Love You after All These (Nian ni ru xi), Stanley Kwan, China Television, 1997.

Strawberry and Chocolate (Fresa y chocolate), Tomás Gutiérrez Alea and Juan Carlos Tabio, Instituto Cubano del Arte e Industrias Cinematográficos/Instituto Mexicano de Cinematografia/Miramax Films/SGAE/Tabasco Films/TeleMadrid, 1993.

Three Colors: Blue (Trois Couleurs: Bleu), Krzysztof Kieślowski, CAB Productions/CED Productions/Eurimages/France 3 Cinéma/MK2 Productions/'Tor' Productions, 1993.

Three Colors: Red (Trois Couleurs: Rouge), Krzysztof Kieślowski, MK2 Productions/France 3 Cinema/CAB Productions, 1994.

Three Colors: White (Trois Couleurs: Blanc), Krzysztof Kieślowski, France 3 Cinéma/ CAB Productions/Le Studio Canal+/MK2 Productions/'Tor' Productions, 1993.

Too Young (Yemaque), Huang Ming-cheng, Taiwan, 1997.

Totally F***ed Up, Gregg Araki, Blurco/Desperate Pictures/Muscle + Hate Studios, 1993.

Vive l'amour (Aiqing wansui), Tsai Ming-liang, Central Motion Picture Corporation, 1994.

The Voyager, Volker Schlöndorff, Action Films/Bioskop Film/Stefi 2 Hellas, 1991.

The Wayward Cloud (Tianbian yiduo yun), Tsai Ming-liang, Arena Films/Homegreen Films, 2005.

The Wedding Banquet (Xiyan), Ang Lee, Central Motion Picture Corporation/Good Machine, 1993.

What Time Is It There? (Ni nabian jidian?), Tsai Ming-liang, Arena Films/Homegreen Films, 2001.

When Beckham Met Owen, Adam Wong, Anytime Pictures, 2004.

Wild at Heart, David Lynch, PolyGram Filmed Entertainment/Propaganda Films, 1990.

Women from the Lake of Scented Souls (Xianghunnü), Xie Fei, Changchun Film Studio/ China Film/Tianjin Film Studio, 1993.

Yang ± Yin: Gender in Chinese Cinema (Nansheng nüxiang), Stanley Kwan, British Film Institute, 1996.

Yellow Earth (Huang tudi), Chen Kaige, Guangxi Film Studio, 1984.

Young Soul Rebels, Isaac Julien, British Film Institute/Channel Four Films/Iberoamericana Films Producción S.A./Kinowelt Filmproduktion/La Sept/Sankofa Film and Video, 1991.

Glossary of Chinese Characters

A Fei zhengzhuan 阿飛正傳
Ah Bin 阿彬
Ah Gui 阿桂
Ah Lan 阿蘭
Ah Rong 阿榮
Ah Ze 阿澤
Aiqing wansui 愛情萬歲
Aiyaya, qu buru 哎呀呀，去哺乳
Anyong 暗湧
Baak Suet-sin (Bai Xuexian) 白雪仙
*Baitian ting Lao Deng, wanshang ting Xiao
    Deng* 白天聽老鄧，晚上聽小鄧
Baojin ni, baojin ni 抱緊你，抱緊你
Barazoku (Qiangweizu) 薔薇族
Bawang bie ji 霸王別姬
Beijing gushi 北京故事
Beijing Tongzhi 北京同志
Beijing zazhong 北京雜種
Beiqing chengshi 悲情城市
biantai 變態
Bianzou bianchang 邊走邊唱
boqi 勃起
bozi 脖子
buren buren huan xu ren 不認不認還須認
Busan 不散
Buzhishi xiyan 不只是喜宴
Chan, Evans (Chen Yaocheng) 陳耀成
Chan Kam-hung, Sunny (Chen
    Jinhong) 陳錦鴻
Chang (Zhang) 張
Chang Chen (Zhang Zhen) 張震
Chang Hsi-kuo (Zhang Xiguo) 張系國
Chang Hsiao-hung (Zhang
    Xiaohong) 張小虹
Changde (Street) 常德（街）
Chao, Winston (Zhao Wenxuan) 趙文
    瑄

Chen Chao-jung (Chen Zhaorong) 陳昭
    榮
Chen Chun-chih, Mickey (Chen Junzhi)
    陳俊志
Chen Kaige 陳凱歌
Chen Ming-hsiu, Mia (Chen Mingxiu)
    陳明秀
Chen Ying-jung (Chen Yingrong) 陳映
    蓉
Chen Yu-hsun (Chen Yuxun) 陳玉勳
Cheng Dieyi 程蝶衣
chenqie zhi dao 臣妾之道
Cheung Kwok-wing, Leslie (Zhang
    Guorong) 張國榮
Chiang Kai-shek (Jiang Jieshi) 蔣介石
Chin, May (Jin Sumei) 金素梅
Chongqing senlin 重慶森林
Chou Teng (Zhou Teng) 周騰
Choujue dengchang 丑角登場
Chu 楚
Chu T'ien-wen (Zhu Tianwen) 朱天文
Chung, Simon (Zhong Desheng) 鍾德
    勝
Chunguang zhaxie 春光乍洩
Cui Zi'en 崔子恩
dan 旦
danwei 單位
Deng Xiaoping 鄧小平
Dinühua 帝女花
diwudai 第五代
Dixia qing 地下情
dizhu 地主
Dong 洞
Donggong xigong 東宮西宮
Dongxie Xidu 東邪西毒
Duan Xiaolou 段小樓
duoluo (dolok) 墮落

217

Duoluo tianshi 墮落天使
Erzi 兒子
fangdong 房東
Fangjian li de yigui 房間裡的衣櫃
Fenbudao nide ai 分不到你的愛
Fengshen yanyi 封神演義
Fong, Allen (Fang Yuping) 方育平
gaizu 蓋族
Gao 高
Gao Wai-Tung (Gao Weitong) 高偉同
Ge You 葛優
gei (ji) 基
gei-lo (jilao) 基佬
Geming shang wei chenggong, tongzhi reng xu nuli 革命尚未成功，同志仍須努力
Gin Gin (Jin Jin) 晶晶
Gong Li 鞏俐
Gua Ah-Leh (Gui Yalei) 歸亞蕾
guaitai 怪胎
Gulingjie shaonian sharen shijian 牯嶺街少年殺人事件
guofu 國父
Haiziwang 孩子王
Han 漢
Hansen 韓森
Hei'an li dabukai de yishan men 黑暗裡打不開的一扇門
Heliu 河流
Ho Po-wing (He Baorong) 何寶榮
Hong gaoliang 紅高粱
Hong meigui, bai meigui 紅玫瑰，白玫瑰
Hong sidai de gushi 紅絲帶的故事
hongbao 紅包
Hou Hsiao-hsien (Hou Xiaoxian) 侯孝賢
Hsin Hsiao-chi (Xin Xiaoqi) 辛曉琪
Hsu Feng (Xu Feng) 徐楓
Hsu Li-kong (Xu Ligong) 徐立功
Hsu You-sheng (Xu Yousheng) 許佑生
Hu Jun 胡軍
Huang Ming-cheng (Huang Mingzheng) 黃銘正

Huang Shu-chun (Huang Shujun) 黃舒駿
Huang tudi 黃土地
Huangjin daotian 黃金稻田
Huangren shouji 荒人手記
Huayang nianhua 花樣年華
huayu dianying 華語電影
Hudumen 虎度門
Hui, Ann (Xu Anhua) 許鞍華
huigui zuguo 回歸祖國
Hung Hung (Hong Hong) 鴻鴻
Huo Jianqi 霍建起
jia 家
Jiang Zemin 江澤民
jianye 賤業
Jie (Xiaozhe) 小哲
jiefang 解放
Jilao sishi 基佬四十
Jimo fangxin julebu 寂寞芳心俱樂部
jingjie 境界
Jinnian xiatian 今年夏天
Jiuyue 舊約
Juxian 菊仙
Kafei shiguang (Kōhī jikō) 咖啡時光
Ko Yu-lun (Ke Yulun) 柯宇綸
koa-a-hi (gezaixi) 歌仔戲
kuaile (failok) 快樂
ku'er 酷兒
kunqu 崑曲
Kuomintang (Guomindang) 國民黨
Kwan, Stanley (Guan Jinpeng) 關錦鵬
Lai Yiu-fai (Li Yaohui) 黎耀輝
Lam, Edward (Lin Yihua) 林奕華
Lan Yu 藍宇
Lanse damen 藍色大門
Law, Alex (Luo Qirui) 羅啓銳
Lee, Ang (Li An) 李安
Lee Kang-sheng (Li Kangsheng) 李康生
Lee, Lilian (Li Bihua) 李碧華
Leung Chiu-wai, Tony (Liang Chaowei) 梁朝偉
Li Jing 李靖
Li sao 離騷
Li Yu 李玉
Liaoning (Street) 遼寧 (街)

lienü 烈女

Lienü zhuan 烈女傳

Lin Cheng-sheng (Lin Zhengsheng) 林
正盛

Lin Meimei 林美美

Ling Yan 凌煙

Linghui 靈慧

Liu Bingjian 劉冰鑒

Liu Xiang 劉向

Liu Ye 劉燁

Lu Hsiao-lin / Lu Yee-ching (Lu Xiaolin /
Lu Yijing) 陸筱琳 / 陸弈靜

luanlun 亂倫

Lung Hsiung (Lang Xiong) 郎雄

luoye guigen 落葉歸根

Ma Ying-jeou (Ma Yingjiu) 馬英九

Mai Ke 邁克

Mama 媽媽

Maomei / Wu Ren-ren 毛妹 / 吳仁仁

Mei Lanfang 梅蘭芳

Meili shaonian 美麗少年

Meili zai changge 美麗在唱歌

meiren 美人

Meishaonian zhi lian 美少年之戀

mianzi 面子

Miao Tian 苗天

Ming 明

Min-hsin (Minxin) 民心

Minsheng Bao 民生報

Moo, Eric (Wu Qixian) 巫啓賢

Moon (Wen) 紋

nan lai dian, nü lai dian 男來店，女來電

Nannan nünü 男男女女

Nansheng nüxiang 男生女相

naren 那人

Nashan naren nagou 那山那人那狗

Nezha zai ci 哪吒在此

Ngai, Jimmy (Wei Shao'en) 魏紹恩

Ni nabian jidian 你那邊幾點

Nian ni ru xi 念你如昔

Niezi 孽子

Ninü 逆女

Nishi wode weiyi 你是我的唯一

Pai Hsien-yung (Bai Xianyong) 白先勇

Peng, Neil (Feng Guangyuan) 馮光遠

Qing 清

qing 情

qingchun pian 青春片

Qinglang 晴朗

Qingse ditu 情色地圖

Qingshaonian Nezha 青少年哪吒

Qiu 囚

Qu Yuan 屈原

Ren zai Niuyue / Sange nüren de gushi 人
在紐約 / 三個女人的故事

Renmin gongce 人民公廁

rensheng ruji 人生如寄

Ruan Lingyu 阮玲玉

Ruhua 如花

San ju zhi lian 三橘之戀

sanchang liangduan 三長兩短

Shenzhen 深圳

Sheshi lingdu, chunguang zaixian 攝氏零
度，春光再現

Shimian maifu 十面埋伏

Shiqisui de tiankong 十七歲的天空

shise, xingye 食色，性也

Shisheng huamei 失聲畫眉

Shitou 石頭

Shu Kei (Shu Qi) 舒琪

shui 水

si 私

Si Han 司汗

Sifan 思凡

Sishui rouqing 似水柔情

sixiaoshuo (shishōsetsu) 私小說

Sun Yat-sen (Sun Yixian / Sun Zhongshan)
孫逸仙 / 孫中山

Sushi zhajiangmian 速食醡醬麵

ta (male gendered) 他

Taichung (Taizhong) 台中

taijiao 胎教

Taiwan Xindianying 台灣新電影

Tan, Royston (Chen Ziqian) 陳子謙

Tang Xianzu 湯顯祖

Tat Ming Pair (Daming Yipai) 達明
一派

Teng, Teresa (Deng Lijun) 鄧麗君

Tian Zhuangzhuang 田壯壯

Tiananmen 天安門

Tianbian yiduo yun 天邊一朵雲
tianren heyi 天人合一
Tong (Tang) 唐
tong zhong qiu yi 同中求異
tongxing lian'ai 同性戀愛
tongxing'ai (doseiai) 同性愛
tongxinglian 同性戀
tongzhi (doshi) 同志
Tsai Ming-liang (Cai Mingliang) 蔡明亮
Tsang, Eric (Zeng Zhiwei) 曾志偉
Tsing Ma Bridge (Qingma Daqiao) 青馬大橋
Tu Hsiu-lan (Du Xiulan) 杜修蘭
tuifei 頹廢
Tuishou 推手
Wai (Wei) 偉
waidu 歪讀
Wangjiao Kamen / Rexue nan'er 旺角卡門 / 熱血男兒
Wei-Wei (Weiwei) 威威
Weidao 味道
wenhua re 文化熱
Wo xin renshi de pengyou 我新認識的朋友
Wohu canglong 臥虎藏龍
Wong, Anthony (Huang Yaoming) 黃耀明
Wong, Faye (Wang Fei) 王菲
Wong Kan Seng (Huang Gencheng) 黃根成
Wong Kar-wai (Wang Jiawei) 王家衛
woshi nüde 我是女的
Wu Yi Julebu 五一俱樂部
xiahai 下海
xiangcao 香草
Xianghunnü 香魂女
Xiao Douzi 小豆子
Xiaokang 小康
Xiaoshi 小史
Xiaosi 小四
Xie Fei 謝飛
Xinhui 心灰
xinlangchao 新浪潮

xinrenlei 新人類
Xiyan 喜宴
xungen pai 尋根派
Yam Kin-fai (Ren Jianhui) 任劍輝
yang 陽
Yang, Edward (Yang Dechang) 楊德昌
Yang Kuei-mei (Yang Guimei) 楊貴媚
Yanzhi kou 胭脂扣
Yaojie huanghou 妖街皇后
Yau, Chingmy (Qiu Shuzhen) 邱淑貞
Yeben 夜奔
Yee Chih-yen (Yi Zhiyan) 易智言
Yemaque 野麻雀
yi si wu jun 以死悟君
yi zhong qiu tong 異中求同
Yige he bage 一個和八個
yige ren ruguo you shenme 一個人如果有什麼
yigui 衣櫃
yin 陰
Yinshi nannü 飲食男女
Yonfan (Yang Fan) 楊凡
You hua haohao shuo 有話好好說
Youyuan jingmeng 遊園驚夢
Yu Ji 虞姬
Yu Kan-ping 虞戡平
Yu kuaile yu duoluo 愈快樂愈墮落
Yuan Shiqing 袁世卿
yuanyi 願意
Yuen Wo-ping (Yuan Heping) 袁和平
Zhang Beichuan 張北川
Zhang Fengyi 張豐毅
Zhang Junzhao 張軍釗
Zhang Yimou 張藝謀
Zhang Yongning 張永寧
Zhang Yuan 張元
zhitongzhi 直同志
zhixiang 志向
Zhongguo lücheng 中國旅程
Zhongguo Wenhua Daxue 中國文化大學
zhongwen dianying 中文電影
zu (zoku) 族

Works Cited

Aaron, Michele, ed. 2004. *New Queer Cinema: A Critical Reader*. Edinburgh: Edinburgh University Press.

Abbas, Ackbar. 1997. *Hong Kong: Culture and the Politics of Disappearance*. Minneapolis and London: University of Minnesota Press.

Adorno, Theodor. 1978. *Minima Moralia*. London and New York: Verso.

Ahmed, Sara. 2000. *Strange Encounters: Embodied Others in Post-Coloniality*. London and New York: Routledge.

Allan, Sarah. 1997. *The Way of Water and Sprouts of Virtue*. Albany: State University of New York Press.

An Keqiang 安克強. 1995. *Hong taiyang xia de hei linghun: Dalu tongxinglian xianchang baodao* 紅太陽下的黑靈魂：大陸同性戀現場報導 (Black souls under the red sun: Live report on homosexuality in mainland China). Taipei: Shibao.

Anderson, Benedict. 1991. *Imagined Communities: Reflections on the Origin and Spread of Nationalism*, rev. ed. London and New York: Verso.

Andrew, Dudley. 1986. "Film and Society: Public Rituals and Private Space." *East-West Film Journal* 1 (1): 7–22.

Ang, Ien. 2001. *On Not Speaking Chinese: Living between Asia and the West*. London and New York: Routledge.

Aoki, Darren. 2004. "The Rose Tribes: Sexual Solidarity and the Ethico-Aesthetics of Manliness in Japan in the Early 1970s." PhD diss., University of Cambridge.

Appadurai, Arjun. 1990. "Disjuncture and Difference in the Global Cultural Economy." *Theory, Culture and Society* 7 (2/3): 295–310.

Appiah, K. Anthony. 1994. "Identity, Authenticity, Survival: Multicultural Societies and Social Reproduction." In Gutmann 1994, 149–163.

Arnold, Matthew. 1998. *Matthew Arnold*. Selected and edited by Nicholas Shrimpton. London: Everyman.

Arroyo, José. 1997. "Film Studies." In Medhurst and Munt 1997, 67–83.

Ashcroft, Bill, Gareth Griffiths, and Helen Tiffin. 1989. *The Empire Writes Back: Theory and Practice in Post-Colonial Literatures*. London and New York: Routledge.

Barmé, Geremie R. 1999. *In the Red: On Contemporary Chinese Culture*. New York: Columbia University Press.

Barthes, Roland. 1975. *The Pleasure of the Text*. Trans. Richard Miller. New York: Hill and Wang.

———. 1983. *Empire of Signs*. Trans. Richard Howard. London: Jonathan Cape.

———. 1990. *A Lover's Discourse: Fragments*. Trans. Richard Howard. Harmondsworth, England: Penguin Books.

Bawer, Bruce, ed. 1996. *Beyond Queer: Challenging Gay Left Orthodoxy*. New York: Free Press.

Beijing Tongzhi 北京同志. 2002. *Lan Yu* 藍宇 (Lan Yu). Taipei: Dongfan.

Berlant, Lauren, and Elizabeth Freeman. 1992. "Queer Nationality." *boundary 2* 19 (1): 149–180.

Berlant, Lauren, and Michael Warner. 1998. "Sex in Public." *Critical Inquiry* 24 (2): 547–566.

Berry, Chris. 1992. "Race: Chinese Film and the Politics of Nationalism." *Cinema Journal* 31 (2): 45–58.

———. 1993a. "*Farewell My Concubine*: At What Price Success?" *Cinemaya* 20: 20–22.

———. 1993b. "Taiwanese Melodrama Returns with a Twist in *The Wedding Banquet*." *Cinemaya* 21: 52–54.

———. 1996a. "Sexual DisOrientations: Homosexual Rights, East Asian Films, and Postmodern Postnationalism." In X. Tang and Snyder 1996, 157–182.

———. 1996b. "Zhang Yuan: Thriving in the Face of Adversity." *Cinemaya* 32: 40–43.

———. 1997. "Globalisation and Localisation: Queer Films from Asia." In *The Bent Lens: A World Guide to Gay and Lesbian Film*. Ed. Claire Jackson and Peter Tapp, 14–17. St. Kilda, Victoria: Australian Catalogue Company.

———. 1998. "*East Palace, West Palace*: Staging Gay Life in China." *Jump Cut* 42: 84–99.

———. 2000a. "If China Can Say No, Can China Make Movies? Or, Do Movies Make China? Rethinking National Cinema and National Agency." In Chow 2000b, 159–180.

———. 2000b. "Happy Alone? Sad Young Men in East Asian Gay Cinema." In Grossman 2000b, 187–200.

———, ed. 2003a. *Chinese Films in Focus: 25 New Takes*. London: BFI.

———. 2003b. "Introduction: One Film at a Time." In Berry 2003a, 1–7.

———. 2003c. "*Wedding Banquet*: A Family (Melodrama) Affair." In Berry 2003a, 183–190.

———. 2004. "The Sacred, the Profane, and the Domestic in Cui Zi'en's Cinema." *positions* 12 (1): 195–201.

Berry, Chris, and Mary Farquhar. 2001. "From National Cinemas to Cinema and the National: Rethinking the National in Transnational Chinese Cinemas." *Journal of Modern Literature in Chinese* 4 (2): 109–122.

Berry, Chris, and Feii Lu, eds. 2005. *Island on the Edge: Taiwan New Cinema and After*. Hong Kong: Hong Kong University Press.

Betsky, Aaron. 1997. *Queer Space: Architecture and Same-Sex Desire*. New York: William Morrow.

Bloch, Ernst. 1988. "Something's Missing: A Discussion between Ernst Bloch and Theodor W. Adorno on the Contradictions of Utopian Longing." In *The Utopian Function of Art and Literature: Selected Essays*. Trans. Jack Zipes and Frank Mecklenburg. Cambridge, Mass.: MIT Press. Quoted in Silverman 1992, 247.

Bono, Chastity, with Billie Fitzpatrick. 1998. *Family Outing: A Guide to the Coming-Out Process for Gays, Lesbians and Their Families*. New York: Little, Brown.

Bordwell, David. 2000. *Planet Hong Kong: Popular Cinema and the Art of Entertainment*. Cambridge, Mass., and London: Harvard University Press.

Borhek, Mary V. 1993. *Coming Out to Parents: A Two-Way Survival Guide for Lesbians and Gay Men and Their Parents*. Cleveland: Pilgrim Press.

Braziel, Jana Evans, and Anita Mannur. 2003. "Nation, Migration, Globalization: Points of Contention in Diaspora Studies." In *Theorizing Diaspora: A Reader*. Ed. Jana Evans Braziel and Anita Mannur. Malden, Mass.: Blackwell.

Brown, Melissa J. 2004. *Is Taiwan Chinese? The Impact of Culture, Power, and Migration on Changing Identities*. Berkeley and London: University of California Press.

Browne, Nick. 1994. "Introduction." In Browne et al. 1994, 1–11.

Browne, Nick, Paul G. Pickowicz, Vivian Sobchack, and Esther Yau, eds. 1994. *New Chinese Cinemas: Forms, Identities, Politics*. Cambridge: Cambridge University Press.

Bullock, Alan, and Stephen Trombley, eds. 1999. *The New Fontana Dictionary of Modern Thought*, 3rd ed. London: HarperCollins.

Bulmer, Martin, and John Solomos, eds. 1999. *Ethnic and Racial Studies Today*. London and New York: Routledge.

Butler, Judith. 1990. *Gender Trouble: Feminism and the Subversion of Identity*. New York and London: Routledge.

———. 1991. "Imitation and Gender Insubordination." In Fuss 1991, 13–31.

———. 1995. "Desire." In Lentricchia and McLaughlin 1995, 369–386.

Calinescu, Matei. 1987. *Five Faces of Modernity: Modernism, Avant-Garde, Decadence, Kitsch, Postmodernism*. Durham, N.C., and London: Duke University Press.

Carlitz, Katherine. 1991. "The Social Uses of Female Virtue in Late Ming Editions of *Lienü Zhuan*." *Late Imperial China* 12 (2): 117–148.

Chambers, Iain. 1994. *Migrancy, Culture, Identity*. London and New York: Routledge.

Chanan, Michael. 1997. "The Changing Geography of Third Cinema." *Screen* 38 (4): 372–388.

Chang Hsiao-hung 張小虹 (Zhang Xiaohong). 1996. *Yuwang xin ditu: Xingbie, tongzhixue* 慾望新地圖: 性別、同志學 (Queer desire: Gender and sexuality). Taipei: Lianhe wenxue.

———. 2000. *Guaitai jiating luomanshi* 怪胎家庭羅曼史 (A queer family romance). Taipei: Shibao.

Chauncey, George. 1996. "'Privacy Could Only Be Had in Public': Gay Uses of the Streets." In *Stud: Architectures of Masculinity*. Ed. Joel Sanders. New York: Princeton Architectural Press.

Chen Baoxu 陳寶旭. 1997. "Yuwang, yapo, bengjie de shengming: Fang Cai Mingliang" 慾望、壓迫、崩解的生命: 訪蔡明亮 (Desire, oppression, disintegrating lives: Interview with Tsai Ming-liang). In Chiao 1997b, 52–70.

Chen, Kuan-hsing. 1998. "Taiwanese New Cinema." In Hill and Gibson 1998, 557–561.

Chen Yongcheng 陳永成. 2001. "Cong *Beijing Gushi* dao *Lan Yu*" 從北京故事到藍宇 (From *Beijing Stories* to *Lan Yu*). *Dianying shuangzhoukan* 電影雙週刊 (City entertainment) 590: 52.

Chiang, Mark. 2002. "Coming Out into the Global System: Postmodern Patriarchies and Transnational Sexualities in *The Wedding Banquet*." In *Screening Asian Americans*. Ed. Peter X. Feng. New Brunswick, N.J.: Rutgers University Press.

Chiao Hsiung-ping Peggy 焦雄屏 (Jiao Xiongping). 1997a. *"Happy Together:* Hong Kong's Absence." *Cinemaya* 38: 17–21.

———, ed. 1997b. *Heliu* 河流 (The river). Taipei: Huangguan.

———. 1998. *Fengyun jihui: Yu dangdai Zhongguo dianying duihua* - 風雲際會：與當代中國電影對話 (Rendezvous of wind and cloud: Dialogues with contemporary Chinese cinema). Taipei: Yuanliu.

Chiao Hsiung-ping 焦雄屏 (Jiao Xiongping) and Tsai Ming-liang 蔡明亮 (Cai Mingliang). 1998. *Dong: Dianying juben yu pinglun* 洞：電影劇本與評論 (*The Hole:* Screenplay and reviews). Taipei: Wanxiang.

Chou Wah-shan 周華山 (Zhou Huashan). 1996a. *Beijing tongzhi gushi* 北京同志故事 (Beijing comrade stories). Hong Kong: Xianggang tongzhi yanjiushe.

———. 1996b. *Xianggang tongzhi gushi* 香港同志故事 (Hong Kong comrade stories). Hong Kong: Xianggang tongzhi yanjiushe.

———. 1997. *Houzhimin tongzhi* 後殖民同志 (Postcolonial comrades). Hong Kong: Xianggang tongzhi yanjiushe.

———. 2000. *Tongzhi: Politics of Same-Sex Eroticism in Chinese Societies.* New York: Haworth Press.

Chou Wah-shan and Andy Chiu 趙文宗 (Zhao Wenzong). 1995. *"Yigui" xingshi: Xianggang ji Yingmei tongzhi yundong* "衣櫃"性史：香港及英美同志運動 (Sexual history of the "closet": Gay movements in Hong Kong, Britain, and America). Hong Kong: Xianggang tongzhi yanjiushe.

Chow, Rey. 1991. *Woman and Chinese Modernity: The Politics of Reading between West and East.* Minnesota and London: University of Minnesota Press.

———. 1993. *Writing Diaspora: Tactics of Intervention in Contemporary Cultural Studies.* Bloomington and Indianapolis: Indiana University Press.

———. 1998. *Ethics after Idealism: Theory-Culture-Ethnicity-Reading.* Bloomington and Indianapolis: Indiana University Press.

———. 1999. "Nostalgia of the New Wave: Structure in Wong Kar-wai's *Happy Together."* *Camera Obscura* 42: 30–49.

———. 2000a. "Introduction: On Chineseness as a Theoretical Problem." In Chow 2000b, 1–25.

———, ed. 2000b. *Modern Chinese Literary and Cultural Studies in the Age of Theory: Reimagining a Field.* Durham, N.C., and London: Duke University Press.

———. 2002. *The Protestant Ethnic and the Spirit of Capitalism.* New York: Columbia University Press.

———. 2004. "A Pain in the Neck, a Scene of 'Incest,' and Other Enigmas of an Allegorical Cinema: Tsai Ming-liang's *The River." New Centennial Review* 4 (1): 123–142.

Chu T'ien-wen 朱天文 (Zhu Tianwen). 1994. "Xin de beizhi" 新的碑誌 (New milestone). In Tsai Ming-liang et al. 1994, 165–168.

———. 1999. *Notes of a Desolate Man.* Trans. Howard Goldblatt and Sylvia Li-chun Lin. New York: Columbia University Press.

Chu Wei-cheng Raymond 朱偉誠 (Zhu Weicheng). 1994. "Shi diren haishi 'tongzhi'? Ye tan *Bawang bie ji*" 是敵人還是同志？也談霸王別姬 (Enemy or "comrade"? Also on *Farewell My Concubine*). *Dangdai* 當代 (Contemporary) 100 (August): 142–149.

———. 1997. "Some Ethnic Gays Are Coming Home: Or, the Trouble with Interraciality." *Textual Practice* 11 (2): 219–235.

Chua, Ling-yen. 1999. "The Cinematic Representation of Asian Homosexuality in *The Wedding Banquet*." *Journal of Homosexuality* 36 (3/4): 99–112.

Chun, Allen. 1996. "Fuck Chineseness: On the Ambiguities of Ethnicity as Culture as Identity." *boundary 2* 23 (2): 111–138.

Chung Wai Literary Monthly 中外文學 *(Zhongwai wenxue)*. 1996. Special issue on *Tongzhi lunshu* 同志論述 (Queer studies) (June).

———. 1997. Special issue on *Yanyi xing yu xingbie: Ku'er xiaoshuo yu yanjiu* 衍異性與性別：酷兒小說與研究 (Proliferating sexual and gender differences: Queer study and queer fiction) (August).

———. 1998. Special issue on *Guaitai qingyuxue* 怪胎情慾學 (Queer sexuality) (May).

———. 2003. Special issue on *Tongzhi zaixian* 同志再現 (Queer Re[-]presentation) (August).

Clifford, James. 1989. "Notes on Travel and Theory." *Inscriptions* 5: 177–186.

———. 1997. "Diasporas." In Guibernau and Rex 1997, 283–290.

Crimp, Douglas, ed. 1988. *AIDS: Cultural Analysis, Cultural Activism*. Cambridge, Mass., and London: MIT Press.

Cristini, Remy. 2005. "The Rise of Comrade Literature: Development and Significance of a New Chinese Genre." MA thesis, Leiden University.

Cui, Shuqin. 2005. "Working from the Margins: Urban Cinema and Independent Directors in Contemporary China." In Lu and Yeh 2005a, 96–119.

Cui, Zi'en. 2002. "Filtered Voices: Representing Gay People in Today's China." Trans. Chi Ta-wei. *IIAS Newsletter* 29: 13.

Culler, Jonathan. 1975. *Structuralist Poetics: Structualism, Linguistics and the Study of Literature*. Ithaca, N.Y.: Cornell University Press.

———. 1983. *Roland Barthes*. New York: Oxford University Press.

———. 1997. *Literary Theory: A Very Short Introduction*. Oxford and New York: Oxford University Press.

Dai Jinhua 戴錦華. 1991. "Xin Zhongguo dianying: Disanshijie piping de biji" 新中國電影：第三世界批評的筆記 (The new Chinese cinema: Notes on third world criticism). *Dianying yishu* 電影藝術 (January): 46–54.

Dariotis, Wei Ming, and Eileen Fung. 1997. "Breaking the Soy Sauce Jar: Diaspora and Displacement in the Films of Ang Lee." In Lu 1997c, 187–220.

de Kloet, Jeroen. 2005. "Saved by Betrayal? Ang Lee's Translations of 'Chinese' Family Ideology." In *Shooting the Family: Transnational Media and Intercultural Values*. Ed. Patricia Pister and Wim Staat, 117–132. Amsterdam: Amsterdam University Press.

Deleuze, Gilles, and Leopold von Sacher-Masoch. 1991. *Masochism: Coldness and Cruelty by Gilles Deleuze/Venus in Furs by Leopold von Sacher-Masoch*. New York: Zone Books.

Dikötter, Frank, ed. 1997. *The Construction of Racial Identities in China and Japan: Historical and Contemporary Perspectives*. London: Hurst.

Dissanayake, Wimal, ed. 1993. *Melodrama and Asian Cinema*. Cambridge: Cambridge University Press.

———. 1996. "Cinema and the Public Sphere: The Films of Ōshima Nagisa." In X. Tang and Snyder 1996, 137–156.

Dolby, William. 1976. *A History of Chinese Drama*. London: Paul Elek.

Dollimore, Jonathan. 1991. *Sexual Dissidence: Augustine to Wilde, Freud to Foucault*. Oxford: Clarendon Press.

Dollimore, Jonathan, and Alan Sinfield. 1985. "Foreword: Cultural Materialism." In *Political Shakespeare: New Essays in Cultural Materialism*. Ed. Jonathan Dollimore and Alan Sinfield, vii-viii. Manchester: Manchester University Press.

Doyle, Christopher. 1997. *Christopher Doyle's Photographic Journal of* Happy Together, *a Wong Kar-wai Film*. Hong Kong: City Entertainment.

———. 1998. "Don't Try for Me, Argentina." In *Projections 8: Film-Makers on Filmmaking*. Ed. John Boorman and Walter Donohue, 154-182. London and Boston: Faber and Faber.

Duyvendak, Jan Willem. 1996. "The Depoliticization of the Dutch Gay Identity, or Why Dutch Gays Aren't Queer." In *Queer Theory/Sociology*. Ed. Steven Seidman, 421-438. Cambridge, Mass., and Oxford: Blackwell.

Dyer, Richard. 1990. *Now You See It: Studies on Lesbian and Gay Film*. London and New York: Routledge.

———. 1991. "Believing in Fairies: The Author and the Homosexual." In Fuss 1991, 185-201.

———. 1993. *The Matter of Images: Essays on Representation*. London and New York: Routledge.

Elsaessser, Thomas. 1980. "A Cinema of Vicious Circles." In *Fassbinder*. Ed. Tony Rayns, rev. and exp. ed., 24-36. London: BFI.

Eng, David L. 1997. "Out Here and Over There: Queerness and Diaspora in Asian American Studies." *Social Text* 52/53: 31-52.

Evans, Harriet. 1997. *Women and Sexuality in China: Female Sexuality and Gender since 1949*. New York: Continuum.

Fang Gang 方剛. 1995. *Tongxinglian zai Zhongguo* 同性戀在中國 (Homosexuality in China). Changchun: Jilin renmin chubanshe.

Fassbinder, Rainer Werner. 1975. Interview by Finn Holten Hansen. Danmarks Radio/TV. Quoted in Thomsen 1997, 180.

Fenton, Steve. 2003. *Ethnicity*. Cambridge: Polity.

Foucault, Michel. 1990. *The History of Sexuality*, vol. 1: *An Introduction*. Trans. Robert Hurley. Harmondsworth, England: Penguin Books.

———. 1998. "A Preface to *Transgression*." In *Aesthetics, Method, and Epistemology: Essential Works of Foucault, 1954-1984*, vol. 2. Ed. James D. Faubion. Trans. Robert Hurley et al., 69-87. London: Allen Lane, Penguin Press.

Fowler, Edward. 1988. *The Rhetoric of Confession: Shishōsetsu in Early Twentieth-Century Japanese Fiction*. Berkeley, Los Angeles, and London: University of California Press.

Freud, Sigmund. 1991. *The Interpretation of Dreams*. Ed. Angela Richards. Trans. James Strachey. Harmondsworth, England: Penguin Books.

Frye, Northrop. 1965. *Anatomy of Criticism*. New York: Atheneum. Quoted in Culler 1975: 119.

Fung, Richard. 1995. "The Trouble with 'Asians.'" In *Negotiating Lesbian and Gay Subjects*. Ed. Monica Dorenkamp and Richard Henke, 123-130. New York and London: Routledge.

Fuss, Diana. 1989. *Essentially Speaking: Feminism, Nature and Difference*. New York and London: Routledge.

———, ed. 1991. *Inside/Out: Lesbian Theories, Gay Theories*. New York and London: Routledge.

Garber, Marjorie. 1993. *Vested Interests: Cross-Dressing and Cultural Anxiety*. Harmondsworth, England: Penguin Books.

Garnham, Nicholas. 1992. "The Media and the Public Sphere." In *Habermas and the Public Sphere*. Ed. Craig Calhoun, 357–376. Cambridge, Mass., and London: MIT Press.

Genet, Jean. 1967. *The Thief's Journal*. Trans. Bernard Frechtman. Harmondsworth, England: Penguin Books.

Giles, Jane. 2002. *Criminal Desires: Jean Genet and Cinema*. New York: Creation Books.

Gledhill, Christine, ed. 1987. *Home Is Where the Heart Is: Studies in Melodrama and the Woman's Film*. London: BFI.

Glover, David, and Cora Kaplan. 2000. *Genders*. London and New York: Routledge.

Goldstein, Joshua. 1999. "Mei Lanfang and the Nationalization of Peking Opera, 1912–1930." *positions* 7 (2): 377–420.

Goody, Jack. 1997. *Representations and Contradictions: Ambivalence towards Images, Theatre, Fiction, Relics and Sexuality*. Oxford: Blackwell.

Gottlieb, Andrew R., ed. 2004. *Side by Side: On Having a Lesbian or Gay Sibling*. New York: Haworth Press.

Gray, Martin. 1992. *A Dictionary of Literary Terms*, 2nd ed. Beirut: York Press, and Essex: Longman.

Grossman, Andrew. 2000a. "Preface." In Grossman 2000b, xv–xx.

———, ed. 2000b. *Queer Asian Cinema: Shadows in the Shade*. New York: Harrington Park Press.

———. 2000c. "The Rise of Homosexuality and the Dawn of Communism in Hong Kong Film: 1993–1998." In Grossman 2000b, 149–186.

Guibernau, Montserrat, and John Rex, eds. 1997. *The Ethnicity Reader: Nationalism, Multiculturalism and Migration*. Cambridge: Polity.

Gutmann, Amy, ed. 1994. *Multiculturalism: Examining the Politics of Recognition*. Princeton, N.J.: Princeton University Press.

Habermas, Jürgen. 1992. *The Structural Transformation of the Public Sphere*. Cambridge, Mass.: MIT Press.

Hall, Stuart. 1996. "New Ethnicities." In *Stuart Hall: Critical Dialogues in Cultural Studies*. Ed. David Morley and Kuan-Hsing Chen. London and New York: Routledge.

Halperin, David M. 1998. "Forgetting Foucault: Acts, Identities, and the History of Sexuality." *Representations* 6 (3): 93–120.

Hansen, Miriam. 1983. "Alexander Kluge, Cinema and the Public Sphere: The Construction Site of Counter-History." *Discourse* 6: 53–74.

———. 1993. "Early Cinema, Late Cinema: Permutations of the Public Sphere." *Screen* 34 (3): 197–210.

Harris, Paul. 2004. "Hollywood to Break Last Taboo with Gay Cowboys." *The Observer* (London), January 18. http://observer.guardian.co.uk/international/story/0,6903,1125637,00.html (accessed July 27, 2005).

Havis, Richard James. 1997. "Wong Kar-Wai: One Entrance, Many Exits." *Cinemaya* 38: 15–16.

Hawthorn, Jeremy. 1997. *A Concise Glossary of Contemporary Literary Theory,* 2nd ed. London and New York: Edward Arnold.

He, Xiaopei. 2002. "Birthday in Beijing: Women Tongzhi Organizing in 1990s China." Trans. Susie Jolly. *IIAS Newsletter* 29: 10.

Herdt, Gilbert, and Bruce Koff. 2000. *Something to Tell You: The Road Families Travel When a Child Is Gay.* New York: Columbia University Press.

Hijiya-Kirschnereit, Irmela. 1996. *Rituals of Self-Revelation: Shishōsetsu as Literary Genre and Socio-Cultural Phenomenon.* Cambridge, Mass.: Council on East Asian Studies, Harvard University.

Hill, John, and Pamela Church Gibson, eds. 1998. *The Oxford Guide to Film Studies.* Oxford: Oxford University Press.

Hinsch, Bret. 1990. *Passions of the Cut Sleeve: The Male Homosexual Tradition in China.* Berkeley and Los Angeles: University of California Press.

Hjort, Mette, and Scott MacKenzie, eds. 2000. *Cinema and Nation.* London and New York: Routledge.

Ho, S. Y. Petula. 1997. "Politicising Identity: Decriminalisation of Homosexuality and the Emergence of Gay Identity in Hong Kong." PhD diss., University of Essex.

Howard, Richard. 1975. "A Note on the Text." In Barthes 1975, v–viii.

Hsia, C. T. 1971. *A History of Modern Chinese Fiction,* 2nd ed. New Haven and London: Yale University Press.

Hu, Hsing-chi. 1998. "*The Stories of Red Ribbons:* Red Ribbons in Asia." *Jump Cut* 42: 116–120.

Hu Youfeng 胡幼鳳. 1997. "Zhongguo de Jieke Pailiansi: Miao Tian" 中國的傑克派連斯: 苗天 (The Chinese Jack Palance: Miao Tian). In Chiao 1997b, 106–111.

Huang Jianhong 黃建宏. 1998. "Chenmo de yingxiang" 沉默的影像 (Silent images). *Dianying xinshang* 電影欣賞 (Film appreciation journal) 93 (May/June): 52–55.

Huang, Nicole. 2003. "Eileen Chang and Alternative Wartime Narrative." In *Columbia Companion to Modern East Asian Literatures.* Ed. Joshua Mostow, 458–462. New York: Columbia University Press.

Huang Shuxian 黃淑嫻. 2000. "Xingxiang de jueli: Lun jiuba nian sanchu Xianggang dianying de changshi [jielu]" 性向的角力: 論九八年三齣香港電影的嘗試 [節錄] (Wrestling with sexuality: On the attempt of three Hong Kong films from 1998 [Excerpt]). In *1998 Xianggang dianying huigu* 1998 香港電影回顧 (Review of 1998 Hong Kong films). Ed. Lie Fu, 251–254. Hong Kong: Xianggang dianying pinglun xuehui.

Huang Wulan 黃寤蘭, ed. 1999. *Dangdai Zhongguo dianying: 1998* 當代中國電影: 一九九八 (Contemporary Chinese cinemas: 1998). Taipei: Shibao.

Iser, Wolfgang. 1987. "Representation: A Performative Act." In *The Aims of Representation: Subject/Text/History.* Ed. Murray Kreiger, 217–232. New York: Columbia University Press.

Jagose, Annamarie. 1996. *Queer Theory: An Introduction.* New York: New York University Press.

Jameson, Fredric. 1971. "Metacommentary." *PMLA* 86: 9–18. Quoted in Culler 1975, 151.

———. 1998. "Notes on Globalization as a Philosophical Issue." In *The Cultures of Globalization*. Ed. Fredric Jameson and Masao Miyoshi. Durham, N.C., and London: Duke University Press.

Ji Yu 季余. 1994. "*Bawang bie ji gei guanzhong dailai le shenme?*" 霸王別姬給觀眾帶來了什麼 (What has *Farewell My Concubine* brought to the audience?) *Qiushi* 求是 134 (2): 45–47.

Jones, Kent. 1998. "*Cucao yu pinghua*" 粗糙與平滑 (Coarseness and smoothness). In Chiao and Tsai 1998, 145–168.

Jousse, Thierry. 1997. "*Happy Together* de Wong Kar-wai." *Cahiers du cinéma* 514 (June): 20. Quoted in Siegel 2001, 279.

Kang Zhengguo 康正果. 1996. *Chongshen fengyue jian: Xing yu Zhongguo gudian wenxue* 重審風月鑑：性與中國古典文學 (Aspects of sexuality and literature in ancient China). Taipei: Maitian.

Kaplan, Caren. 1996. *Questions of Travel: Postmodern Discourses of Displacement*. Durham, N.C., and London: Duke University Press.

Kaplan, E. Ann. 1997. "Reading Formations and Chen Kaige's *Farewell My Concubine*." In Lu 1997c, 265–275.

———, ed. 2000. *Feminism and Film*. Oxford: Oxford University Press.

Kellner, Douglas. 1998. "New Taiwan Cinema in the 80s." *Jump Cut* 42: 101–115.

King, Yeo-chi Ambrose. 1994. "Kuan-hsi and Network Building: A Sociological Interpretation." In Tu 1994b, 109–126.

Kluge, Alexander. 1981/1982. "On Film and the Public Sphere." *New German Critique* 24/25: 206–220.

Kong, S. K. Travis. 2002. "The Seduction of the Golden Boy: The Body Politics of Hong Kong Gay Men." *Body and Society* 8 (1): 29–48.

———. 2005. "Queering Masculinity in Hong Kong Movies." In Pang and Wong 2005, 57–80.

Kopelson, Kevin. 1994. *Love's Litany: The Writing of Modern Homoerotics*. Stanford, Calif.: Stanford University Press.

Kraicer, Shelly. 2000. "Interview with Tsai Ming-liang." *positions* 8 (2): 579–588.

Kuzniar, Alice A. 2000. *The Queer German Cinema*. Stanford, Calif.: Stanford University Press.

Kwan, Stanley. 1993. "Carrying the Past Lightly." *Cinemaya* 19: 10–13.

Lalanne, Jean-Marc. 1997. "Images from the Inside." Trans. Stephen Wright. In Lalanne et al. 1997, 9–27

Lalanne, Jean-Marc, David Martinez, Ackbar Abbas, Jimmy Ngai, and Wong Kar-wai. 1997. *Wong Kar-Wai*. Paris: Dis Voir.

Lam, Edward 林奕華 (Lin Yihua). 1993. "Yichang huanxi yichang kong: *Xiyan* hougan" 一場歡喜一場空：喜宴後感 (Happy for nothing: Afterthought on *The Wedding Banquet*). *Yingxiang* 影響 (Imagekeeper monthly) 36 (April): 69–72.

———. 1998. "*Chunguang* beihou, *Kuaile* jintou" 春光背後，快樂盡頭 (Behind *Happy Together*, at the end of *Hold You Tight*). *Dianying shuangzhoukan* 電影雙週刊 (City entertainment) 495: 80–81.

Landry, Donna, and Gerald MacLean, eds. 1996. *The Spivak Reader: Selected Works of Gayatri Chakravorty Spivak*. New York and London: Routledge.

Larson, Wendy. 1997. "The Concubine and the Figure of History: Chen Kaige's *Farewell My Concubine*." In Lu 1997c, 331–346.

Lau, Jenny Kwok Wah. 1995. *"Farewell My Concubine:* History, Melodrama, and Ideology in Contemporary Pan-Chinese Cinema." *Film Quarterly* 49 (1): 16–27.

Lee, Ang. 1994. *Eat Drink Man Woman/The Wedding Banquet: Two Films by Ang Lee.* Woodstock, N.Y.: Overlook Press.

Lee, Ang 李安 (Li An), and Neil Peng 馮光遠 (Feng Guangyuan). 1993. *Xiyan* 喜宴 *(The Wedding Banquet).* Taipei: Shibao.

Lee Ou-fan Leo 李歐梵 (Li Oufan). 1998. "Xiang yiwei xiandai yishujia zhijing" 向一位現代藝術家致敬 (A Tribute to a modern artist). In Chiao and Tsai 1998, 169–176.

Lentricchia, Frank, and Thomas McLaughlin, eds. 1995. *Critical Terms for Literary Study,* 2nd ed. Chicago and London: University of Chicago Press.

Leung, Helen Hok-sze. 2001. "Queerscapes in Contemporary Hong Kong Cinema." *positions* 9 (2): 423–447.

Leung Ping-kwan 梁秉鈞 (Liang Bingjun). 1995. "Minzu dianying yu Xianggang wenhua shenfen: Cong *Bawang bie ji, Qiwang, Ruan Lingyu* kan wenhua dingwei" 民族電影與香港文化身份：從霸王別姬、棋王、阮玲玉看文化定位 (National cinema and Hong Kong's cultural identity: Examining cultural positioning in *Farewell My Concubine, King of Chess, Center Stage*). In Zhang Jingyuan 1995, 355–373.

Li, Cheuk-to. 1994. "The Return of the Father: Hong Kong New Wave and Its Chinese Context in the 1980s." In Browne et al. 1994, 160–179.

Li, Siu Leung. 2003. *Cross-Dressing in Chinese Opera.* Hong Kong: Hong Kong University Press.

Li Tianduo 李天鐸, ed. 1996. *Dangdai huayu dianying lunshu* 當代華語電影論述 (Discourses on contemporary Chinese-language films). Taipei: Shibao.

Li, Wai-yee. 1993. *Enchantment and Disenchantment: Love and Illusion in Chinese Literature.* Princeton, N.J.: Princeton University Press.

Li Xiaoxian 黎肖嫻. 1997. "Guan Jinpeng zouchu yigui zhihou: Tan *Nansheng Nüxiang*" 關錦鵬走出衣櫃之後：談男生女相 (After Stanley Kwan walked out of the closet: On *Yang ± Yin: Gender in Chinese Cinema*). *Dianying xinshang* 電影欣賞 (Film appreciation journal) 88 (August): 55–60.

Li Yinhe 李銀河. 1998. *Tongxinglian yawenhua* 同性戀亞文化 (Subculture of homosexuality). Beijing: Jinri Zhongguo chubanshe.

———, trans. 2000. *Ku'er lilun: Xifang jiuling niandai xing sichao* 酷兒理論：西方 90 年代性思潮 (Queer theory: Western sexual thought in the 1990s). Beijing: Shishi chubanshe.

Li Yinhe 李銀河 and Wang Xiaobo 王小波. 1992. *Tamen de shijie: Zhongguo nantongxinglian qunluo toushi* 他們的世界：中國男同性戀群落透視 (Their world: A clear look into China's male homosexual community). Shanxi: Shanxi renmin chubanshe.

Li Zhaoxing 李照興. 2002. "*Lan Yu:* Guan Jinpeng de tongzhi shuxie" 藍宇：關錦鵬的同志書寫 (*Lan Yu:* Stanley Kwan's comrade writing). In *Xianggang dianying mianmian guan 2001–2002* 香港電影面面觀 2001–2002 (Hong Kong panorama 2001–2002), 62–63. Hong Kong: Hong Kong Arts Development Council.

Liao Ping-hui 廖炳惠 (Liao Binghui). 1994. *Huigu xiandai: Houxiandai yu houzhimin lun-wenji* 回顧現代：後現代與後殖民論文集 (Modernity in Re-vision: Reading postmodern/postcolonial theories). Taipei: Maitian.

———. 2000. "Postcolonial Studies and Multiculturalism in Taiwan: Issues in Critical Debates." Pullman: Washington State University, Department of Comparative American Cultures, 1–16. Working Paper Series.

Lilley, Rozanna. 1998. *Staging Hong Kong: Gender and Performance in Transition.* Surrey: Curzon Press.

Lim, Song Hwee 林松輝 (Lin Songhui). Forthcoming-a. "Fanyi ku'er: Jiuling niandai yilai Taiwan dui ku'er huayu de yinjie yu shijian" 翻譯酷兒：九０年代以來台灣對酷兒話語的引介與實踐 (Translating queer: Introduction and practice of a queer discourse in Taiwan since the 1990s). In *Guojia jiangjie yu wenhua tu-xiang: nüxing yu xingbie de lunshu* 國家疆界與文化圖像：女性與性別的論述 (National boundaries and cultural configurations: Issues of women and gender). Ed. Hsien-kuan Hsiung. Singapore: Global Publishing.

———. Forthcoming-b. "How to Be Queer in Taiwan: Translation, Appropriation and the Construction of a Queer Identity in Taiwan." In *AsiaPacifiQueer: Rethinking Gender and Sexuality in the Asia-Pacific.* Ed. Peter A. Jackson, Mark McLelland, Fran Martin, and Audrey Yue. Champaign: University of Illinois Press.

———. Forthcoming-c. "Queer Theory Goes to Taiwan." In *Critical InQueery: An Inter-disciplinary Queer Studies Reader.* Ed. Noreen Giffney and Michael O'Rourke. Perth, Western Australia: Black Swan Press.

———. Forthcoming-d. "Queering Chineseness: Searching for Roots and the Politics of Shame in (Post)Colonial Singapore." In *Cosmopatriots: Globalization, Patriot-ism, Cosmopolitanism in Contemporary Asian Culture/s.* Ed. Edwin Jurriens and Je-roen de Kloet. Amsterdam and New York: Rodopi.

Liu Jen-peng 劉人鵬 (Liu Renpeng) and Ding Naifei 丁乃非. 1998. "Wangliang wen jing: Hanxu meixue yu ku'er zhenglüe" 罔兩問景：含蓄美學與酷兒政略 (Reticent poetics, queer politics). *Xing/bie yanjiu* 性/別研究 (Working papers in gender/sexuality studies) 3/4: 109–155.

Liu, Cynthia W. 1995. "'To Love, Honor and Dismay': Subverting the Feminine in Ang Lee's Trilogy of Resuscitated Patriarchs." *Hitting Critical Mass: A Journal of Asian American Cultural Criticism* 3 (1): 37–40.

Liu, Lydia H. 1995. *Translingual Practice: Literature, National Culture and Translated Mo-dernity: China 1900–1937.* Stanford, Calif.: Stanford University Press.

Liu Zeyuan 劉澤源. 1997. "Happy Together with Leslie." *Dianying shuangzhoukan* 電影雙週刊 (City entertainment) 474: 32–33.

Louie, Kam. 2002. *Theorising Chinese Masculinity: Society and Gender in China.* Cam-bridge: Cambridge University Press.

Lu, Sheldon Hsiao-peng. 1997a. "Historical Introduction: Chinese Cinemas (1896–1996) and Transnational Film Studies." In Lu 1997c, 1–31.

———. 1997b. "National Cinema, Cultural Critique, Transnational Capital: The Films of Zhang Yimou." In Lu 1997c, 105–136.

———, ed. 1997c. *Transnational Chinese Cinemas: Identity, Nationhood, Gender.* Hono-lulu: University of Hawai'i Press.

Lu, Hsiao-peng Sheldon, and Emilie Yueh-yu Yeh, eds. 2005a. *Chinese-Language Film: Historiography, Poetics, Politics*. Honolulu: University of Hawai'i Press.

———. 2005b. "Introduction: Mapping the Field of Chinese-Language Cinema." In Lu and Yeh 2005a, 1–24.

Luo Feng 洛楓. 2002. *Shengshi bianyuan: Xianggang dianying de xingbie, teji yu jiuqi zhengzhi* 盛世邊緣：香港電影的性別、特技與九七政治 (City on the edge of time). Hong Kong: Oxford University Press.

Ma, Sheng-mei. 1996. "Ang Lee's Domestic Tragicomedy: Immigrant Nostalgia, Exotic/Ethnic Tour, Global Market." *Journal of Popular Culture* 30 (1): 191–201.

Ma Yingli 馬英力. 1997. "Rensheng jiu xiang yitiao he: Yu Cai Ming-liang tan *Heliu*" 人生就像一條河：與蔡明亮談河流 (Life Is just like a river: Conversations with Tsai Ming-liang on *The River*). *Dianying shuangzhoukan* 電影雙週刊 (City entertainment) 460: 40–42.

Macey, David. 1995. *The Lives of Michel Foucault*. New York: Vintage Books.

Mackerras, Colin P. 1975. *The Chinese Theatre in Modern Times: From 1840 to the Present Day*. London: Thames and Hudson.

Mai Ke 邁克. 2003. *Huchui buru danda* 互吹不如單打 (Single-minded, double entendre). Hong Kong: Oxford University Press.

Manalansan, Martin F., IV. 1995. "In the Shadows of Stonewall: Examining Gay Transnational Politics and the Diasporic Dilemma." *GLQ* 2 (4): 425–438.

Mann, Susan. 1997. *Precious Records: Women in China's Long Eighteenth Century*. Stanford, Calif.: Stanford University Press.

Mann, Thomas. 1971. *Death in Venice*. Trans. H. T. Lowe-Porter. Harmondsworth, England: Penguin Books.

Marchetti, Gina. 1998. "Plural and Transnational." *Jump Cut* 42: 68–72.

———. 2000. "*The Wedding Banquet*: Global Chinese Cinema and the Asian American Experience." In *Countervisions: Asian American Film Criticism*. Ed. Darrell Y. Hamamoto and Sandra Liu, 275–297. Philadelphia: Temple University Press.

Martel, Frédéric. 1999. *The Pink and the Black: Homosexuals in France since 1968*. Trans. Marie Todd. Stanford, Calif.: Stanford University Press.

Martin, Fran, trans. 2003a. *Angelwings: Contemporary Queer Fiction from Taiwan*. Honolulu: University of Hawai'i Press.

———. 2003b. "Introduction: Taiwan's Literature of Transgressive Sexuality." In Martin 2003a, 1–28.

———. 2003c. *Situating Sexualities: Queer Representation in Taiwanese Fiction, Film and Public Culture*. Hong Kong: Hong Kong University Press.

Martinez, David. 1997. "Chasing the Metaphysical Express." Trans. Andrew Rothwell. In Lalanne et al. 1997, 29–35.

McLelland, Mark. 2000. "Interview with Samshasha, Hong Kong's First Gay Rights Activist and Author." *Intersections* 4, http://wwwsshe.murdoch.edu.au/intersections/issue4/interview_mclelland.html (accessed March 8, 2004).

———. 2005. *Queer Japan from the Pacific War to the Internet Age*. Lanham, Md.: Rowman and Littlefield.

Medhurst, Andy. 1984. "Notes on Recent Gay Film Criticism." In *Gays and Film*. Ed. Richard Dyer. New York: New York Zoetrope.

Medhurst, Andy, and Sally R. Munt, eds. 1997. *Lesbian and Gay Studies: A Critical Introduction*. London and Washington, D.C.: Cassell.

Mencius. 1970. *Mencius,* vol. 1. Trans. D. C. Lau. Harmondsworth, England: Penguin Books.

Mercer, Kobena. 1990. "Black Art and the Burden of Representation." *Third Text* 10: 61–78.

Mitchell, W. J. T. 1995. "Representation." In Lentricchia and McLaughlin 1995, 11–22.

Moi, Toril. 1985. *Sexual/Textual Politics: Feminist Literary Theory*. London and New York: Methuen.

Mullaney, Thomas S., ed. 2004. "Ethnic Classification." Special issue, *China Information* 18 (2) (July).

Munt, Sally R. 1997. "The Personal, Experience, and the Self." In Medhurst and Munt 1997, 186–197.

Naficy, Hamid. 2001. *An Accented Cinema: Exilic and Diasporic Filmmaking*. Princeton, N.J.: Princeton University Press.

Ngai, Jimmy 魏紹恩 (Wei Shao'en). 1998. *Baojin ni, baojin ni* 抱緊你，抱緊你 (Hold you tight, hold you tight). Hong Kong: Hongye.

Ngai, Jimmy 魏紹恩 (Wei Shao'en), and Wong Kar-wai. 1997. "A Dialogue with Wong Kar-wai: Cutting between Time and Two Cities." In Lalanne et al. 1997, 83–117.

Nichols, Bill. 1994a. *Blurred Boundaries: Questions of Meaning in Contemporary Culture*. Bloomington and Indianapolis: Indiana University Press.

———. 1994b. "Global Image Consumption in the Age of Late Capitalism." *East-West Film Journal* 8 (1): 68–85.

Nowell-Smith, Geoffrey, ed. 1997. *The Oxford History of World Cinema*. Oxford: Oxford University Press.

OED (Oxford English Dictionary). Online ed. S.v. "Abjection," http://dictionary.oed.com/cgi/entry/50000420?single=1&query_type=word&queryword=abjection&first=1&max_to_show=10 (accessed August 30, 2005).

Ong, Aihwa, and Donald M. Nonini. 1997. "Toward a Cultural Politics of Diaspora and Transnationalism." In *Ungrounded Empires: The Cultural Politics of Modern Chinese Transnationalism*. Ed. Aihwa Ong and Donald M. Nonini, 323–332. New York and London: Routledge.

O'Sullivan, Charlotte. 1998. Review of *Happy Together*. *Sight and Sound,* May, 49.

Pai, Hsien-yung. 1995. *Crystal Boys*. Trans. Howard Goldblatt. San Francisco: Gay Sunshine Press.

Pang, Laikwan, and Day Wong, eds. 2005. *Masculinities and Hong Kong Cinema*. Hong Kong: Hong Kong University Press.

Peng Yiping 彭怡平. 1997. "*Chunguang zhaxie:* Jiuqi qian rang women kuaile zai yiqi" 春光乍洩：九七前讓我們快樂在一起 (*Happy Together:* Let Us Be Happy Together before 97). *Dianying shuangzhoukan* 電影雙週刊 (City entertainment) 473: 40–45.

Pines, Jim, and Paul Willemen, eds. 1989. *Questions of Third Cinema*. London: BFI.

Radhakrishnan, R. 1996. *Diasporic Mediations: Between Home and Location*. Minneapolis and London: University of Minnesota Press.

Rayns, Tony. 1994a. Review of *Farewell My Concubine*. *Sight and Sound*, January, 41–42.

———. 1994b. "The Narrow Path: Chen Kaige in Conversation with Tony Rayns." In *Projections 3: Film-Makers on Film-Making*. Ed. John Boorman and Walter Donohue, 46–58. London: Faber and Faber.

———. 1994c. Review of *The Wedding Banquet*. In *Sight and Sound Film Review Volume, January 1993–December 1993*, 208. London: British Film Institute.

———. 1996. "Provoking Desire." *Sight and Sound*, July, 26–29.

———. 1997. "The Chinese Syndrome." *Sight and Sound*, July, 25.

Reynaud, Bérénice. 1997. "Gay Overtures: Zhang Yuan's *Dong Gong, Xi Gong*." *Cinemaya* 36: 31–33.

Rich, B. Ruby. 1993. "Reflections on a Queer Screen." *GLQ* 1 (1): 83–91.

Rivière, Danièle, and Tsai Ming-liang. 1999. "Scouting." In *Tsai Ming-liang*, by Jean-Pierre Rehm, Olivier Joyard, and Danièle Rivière. Paris: Dis Voir.

Roberts, Martin. 1998. "*Baraka*: World Cinema and the Global Culture Industry." *Cinema Journal* 37 (3): 62–82.

Rofel, Lisa. 1999. "Qualities of Desire: Imagining Gay Identities in China." *GLQ* 5 (4): 451–474.

Rojas, Carlos. 2003. "'Nezha Was Here': Structures of Dis/placement in Tsai Ming-liang's *Rebels of the Neon God*." *Modern Chinese Literature and Culture* 15 (1): 63–89.

Ross, Michael W. 1983. *The Married Homosexual: A Psychological Study*. London, Boston, Melbourne, and Henley: Routledge and Kegan Paul.

Ruan, Fang-fu. 1991. *Sex in China: Studies in Sexology in Chinese Culture*. New York and London: Plenum Press.

Russo, Vito. 1987. *The Celluloid Closet: Homosexuality in the Movies*, rev. ed. New York: Harper and Row.

Ryan, Michael. 1988. "The Politics of Film: Discourse, Psychoanalysis, Ideology." In *Marxism and the Interpretation of Culture*. Ed. Cary Nelson and Lawrence Grossberg, 477–486. Hampshire and London: Macmillan Education.

Said, Edward W. 1994. *Representations of the Intellectual: 1993 Reith Lectures*. London: Vintage.

Sang Tze-lan Deborah 桑梓蘭 (Sang Zilan). 1993. "Cheng Dieyi: Yige quanshi de qidian" 程蝶衣： 一個詮釋的起點 (Cheng Dieyi: A starting point for interpretation). *Dangdai* 當代 (Contemporary) 96 (April): 54–73.

———. 1999. "Translating Homosexuality: The Discourse of Tongxing'ai in Republican China (1912–1949)." In *Tokens of Exchange: The Problem of Translation in Global Circulations*. Ed. Lydia H. Liu, 276–304. Durham, N.C., and London: Duke University Press.

———. 2003. *The Emerging Lesbian: Female Same-Sex Desire in Modern China*. Chicago and London: University of Chicago Press.

Sangren, P. Steven. 2000. *Chinese Sociologics: An Anthropological Account of the Role of Alienation in Social Reproduction*. London and New Brunswick, N.J.: Athlone Press.

Sartre, Jean-Paul. 1988. *Saint Genet: Actor and Martyr*. Trans. Bernard Frechtman. London: Heinemann.

Savin-Williams, Ritch C. 2000. *Mom, Dad, I'm Gay: How Families Negotiate Coming Out*. Washington, D.C.: American Psychological Association.

Schneider, Laurence A. 1980. *A Madman of Ch'u: The Chinese Myth of Loyalty and Dissent.* Berkeley and Los Angeles: University of California Press.

Scott, Joan W. 1992. "'Experience.'" In *Feminists Theorize the Political.* Ed. Judith Butler and Joan W. Scott, 22–40. New York and London: Routledge.

Sedgwick, Eve Kosofsky. 1990. *Epistemology of the Closet.* Berkeley and Los Angeles: University of California Press.

Shan Zhimin 單志民. 1998. "Cong relian dao pingwen guanxi dao waiyu: *Yu kuaile yu duoluo,* fangwen Guan Jinpeng" 從熱戀到平穩關係到外遇：愈快樂愈墮落，訪問關錦鵬 (From madly in love to stable relationship to extramarital affair: *Hold You Tight,* interview with Stanley Kwan). In *Xianggang dianying mianmian guan 1997-1998* 香港電影面面觀 1997-1998 *(Hong Kong Panorama 1997-1998),* 68–69. Hong Kong: Provisional Urban Council of Hong Kong.

Shattuc, Jane. 1995. *Televisions, Tabloids, and Tears: Fassbinder and Popular Culture.* Minneapolis and London: University of Minnesota Press.

Shaviro, Steven. 1993. *The Cinematic Body.* Minneapolis and London: University of Minnesota Press.

Shen, Shiao-ying. 1995. "Where Has All the Capital Gone? The State of Taiwan's Film Investment." *Cinemaya* 30: 4–12.

Shih, Shu-mei. 2000. "Globalisation and Minoritisation: Ang Lee and the Politics of Flexibility." *New Formations* 40: 86–101.

Shohat, Ella, and Robert Stam. 1994. *Unthinking Eurocentrism: Multiculturalism and the Media.* London and New York: Routledge.

Shu, Kei. 1993. "Letter to Chen Kaige." *Cinemaya* 20: 18–20.

Siegel, Marc. 2001. "The Intimate Spaces of Wong Kar-wai." In *At Full Speed: Hong Kong in a Borderless World.* Ed. Esther C. M. Yau, 277–294. Minneapolis and London: University of Minnesota Press.

Silbergeld, Jerome. 1999. *China into Film: Frames of Reference in Contemporary Chinese Cinema.* London: Reaktion Books.

Silverman, Kaja. 1992. *Male Subjectivity at the Margins.* New York and London: Routledge.

Silvio, Teri. 1999. "Reflexivity, Bodily Praxis and Identity in Taiwanese Opera." *GLQ* 5 (4): 585–604.

———. 2002. "Chinese Opera, Global Cinema, and the Ontology of the Person: Chen Kaige's *Farewell My Concubine.*" In *Between Opera and Cinema.* Ed. Jeongwon Joe and Rose Theresa, 177–197. New York and London: Routledge.

Simon, Scott. 2004. "From Hidden Kingdom to Rainbow Community: The Making of Gay and Lesbian Identity in Taiwan." In *The Minor Arts of Daily Life: Popular Culture in Taiwan.* Ed. David K. Jordan, Andrew D. Morris, and Marc L. Moskowitz, 67–88. Honolulu: University of Hawai'i Press.

Simpson, Mark, ed. 1996. *Anti-Gay.* London and New York: Freedom Editions.

Sinfield, Alan. 1994a. *Cultural Politics: Queer Reading.* London and New York: Routledge.

———. 1994b. *The Wilde Century: Effeminacy, Oscar Wilde and the Queer Moment.* London and New York: Cassell.

Sklair, Leslie. 1995. *Sociology of the Global System,* 2nd ed. Baltimore, Md.: Johns Hopkins University Press. Quoted in Chiang 2002, 275.

Sklar, Robert. 1996. "Beyond Hoopla: The Cannes Film Festival and Cultural Significance." *Cineaste* 22 (3): 18–20.

Smith, Paul Julian. 1992. *The Body Hispanic: Gender and Sexuality in Spanish and Spanish American Literature*. Oxford: Clarendon Press.

———. 1996. *Vision Machines: Cinema, Literature and Sexuality in Spain and Cuba, 1983–93*. London and New York: Verso.

Sontag, Susan. 1991. *Illness as Metaphor* and *AIDS and Its Metaphors*. Harmondsworth, England: Penguin Books.

Stein, Edward, ed. 1992. *Forms of Desire: Sexual Orientation and the Social Constructionist Controversy*. New York and London: Routledge.

Stewart, William. 1995. *Cassell's Queer Companion: A Dictionary of Lesbian and Gay Life and Culture*. London and New York: Cassell.

Stokes, Lisa Odham, and Michael Hoover. 1999. *City on Fire: Hong Kong Cinema*. London and New York: Verso.

Sullivan, Andrew. 1995. *Virtually Normal: An Argument about Homosexuality*. New York: Alfred A. Knopf.

Sun Cizhou 孫次舟. 1944. "Qu Yuan shi 'wenxue nongchen' de fayi: Jian da Qu Yuan chongbaizhe" 屈原是 '文學弄臣' 的發疑: 兼答屈原崇拜者 (Questioning Qu Yuan as "literary jester": Also answering Qu Yuan worshippers). *Zhongyang Ribao* 中央日報, September 6, 7, and 8, Chengdu edition.

Suner, Asuman. 1998. "Postmodern Double Cross: Reading David Cronenberg's *M. Butterfly* as a Horror Story." *Cinema Journal* 37: 49–64.

Sutcliffe, Lynn. 1996. *There Must Be 50 Ways to Tell Your Mother: Coming Out Stories*. New York and London: Continuum.

Suzuki, Tomi. 1996. *Narrating the Self: Fictions of Japanese Modernity*. Stanford, Calif.: Stanford University Press.

Tam, Kwok-kan, and Wimal Dissanayake. 1998. *New Chinese Cinema*. Hong Kong, Oxford, and New York: Oxford University Press.

Tambling, Jeremy. 1990. *Confession: Sexuality, Sin, the Subject*. Manchester and New York: Manchester University Press.

———. 2003. *Wong Kar-wai's Happy Together*. Hong Kong: Hong Kong University Press.

Tang Qiandai 唐千代 and Xu Ruilan 許瑞蘭. 1995. "Xu Ligong tan canzhan xinde yu yingzhan celüe" 徐立功談參展心得與影展策略 (Hsu Li-kong on lessons from and strategies in participating in film festivals). *Yingxiang* 影響 (Imagekeeper monthly) 61 (May): 51–57.

Tang, Xiaobing, and Stephen Snyder, eds. 1996. *In Pursuit of Contemporary East Asian Culture*. Boulder, Colo.: Westview Press.

Tay, William 鄭樹森 (Zheng Shusen), ed. 1995. *Wenhua piping yu huayu dianying* 文化批評與華語電影 (Cultural criticism and Chinese cinema). Taipei: Maitian.

Taylor, Charles. 1994. "The Politics of Recognition." In Gutmann 1994, 25–73.

Teng, Jinhua Emma. 2004. *Taiwan's Imagined Geography: Chinese Colonial Travel Writing and Pictures, 1683–1895*. Cambridge, Mass., and London: Harvard University Asia Center.

Teo, Stephen. 1998. "Hong Kong Cinema. (a) Discovery and Pre-discovery." In Hill and Gibson 1998, 550–553.

Thomsen, Christian Braad. 1997. *Fassbinder: The Life and Work of a Provocative Genius*. Trans. Martin Chalmers. London and Boston: Faber and Faber.

Tsai Kang-yung 蔡康永 (Cai Kangyong). 1994. "'Canren yu wenrou': Cai Mingliang de *Aiqing wansui*" "殘忍與溫柔": 蔡明亮的愛情萬歲 ("Cruelty and tenderness": Tsai Ming-liang's *Vive l'amour*). In Tsai et al. 1994, 160–164.

Tsai Ming-liang 蔡明亮 (Cai Mingliang). 1993. *Fangjian li de yigui* 房間裡的衣櫃 *(The Wardrobe in the Room)*. Taipei: Zhou Kai juchang jijinhui.

Tsai Ming-liang 蔡明亮 (Cai Mingliang) et al. 1994. *Aiqing wansui* 愛情萬歲 *(Vive l'amour)*. Taipei: Wanxiang.

Tu, Wei-ming. 1994a. "Cultural China: The Periphery as the Center." In Tu 1994b, 1–34.

———, ed. 1994b. *The Living Tree: The Changing Meaning of Being Chinese Today*. Stanford, Calif.: Stanford University Press.

Vitiello, Giovanni. 1992. "The Dragon's Whim: Ming and Qing Homoerotic Tales from *The Cut Sleeve*." *T'oung Pao* 78: 341–372.

Wachman, Alan M. 1994. *Taiwan: National Identity and Democratization*. Armonk, N.Y., and London: M. E. Sharpe.

Wan, Yanhai. 2001. "Becoming a Gay Activist in Contemporary China." Trans. Chris Berry. In *Gay and Lesbian Asia: Culture, Identity, Community*. Ed. Gerard Sullivan and Peter A. Jackson, 47–64. New York: Harrington Park Press.

Wang, Der-wei David. 1997. *Fin-de-siècle Splendor: Repressed Modernities of Late Qing Fiction, 1848–1911*. Stanford, Calif.: Stanford University Press.

Wang Hongzhi 王宏志, Li Xiaoliang 李小良, and Chen Qingqiao 陳清僑. 1997. *Fouxiang Xianggang: Lishi, wenhua, weilai* 否想香港：歷史、文化、未來 (Hong Kong unimagined: History, culture, and the future). Taipei: Maitian.

Wang, Ping, and Amie Parry. 2000. "Documenting a Beautiful Youth: *Boys for Beauty* and *2, 1*." *Inter-Asia Cultural Studies* 1 (1): 181–184.

Wang, Qi. 2004. "The Ruin Is Already a New Outcome: An Interview with Cui Zi'en." *positions* 12 (1): 181–194.

Wang Xiaobo 王小波. 1998. *Dijiu tianchang: Wang Xiaobo xiaoshuo juben ji* 地久天長：王小波小說劇本集 (Till the end of the world: Collected novels and plays of Wang Xiaobo). Changchun: Shidai wenyi chubanshe.

Wang Yage 王雅各. 1999. *Taiwan nantongzhi pingquan yundongshi* 台灣男同志平權運動史 (History of the male homosexual equal rights movement in Taiwan). Taipei: Kaixin yangguang.

Wang Zhicheng 王志成. 1999. "*Yu kuaile yu duoluo*: Baojin aiyu, shengpa luokong" 愈快樂愈墮落：抱緊愛慾，生怕落空 (*Hold You Tight*: Holding desire tight for fear of losing). In Huang Wulan 1999, 41–43.

Warner, Michael. 1993. "Introduction." In *Fear of a Queer Planet: Queer Politics and Social Theory*. Ed. Michael Warner, vii–xxxi. Minneapolis and London: University of Minnesota Press.

———. 1999. *The Trouble with Normal: Sex, Politics, and the Ethics of Queer Life*. New York: Free Press.

Wen T'ien-hsiang 聞天祥 (Wen Tianxiang). 2002. *Guangying dingge: Cai Mingliang de xinling changyu* 光影定格：蔡明亮的心靈場域 (Freeze-frame of light and image: The field of Tsai Ming-liang's heart and soul). Taipei: Hengxing.

Wen Yiduo 聞一多. 1948. "Qu Yuan wenti: Jing zhi Sun Cizhou xiansheng" 屈原問題：敬質孫次舟先生 (The question of Qu Yuan: Respectfully querying Mr. Sun Cizhou). In *Wen Yiduo quanji* 聞一多全集 (The complete works of Wen Yiduo), vol. 1. Ed. Zhu Ziqing, Guo Moruo, Wu Han, and Ye Shengtao, 245-258. Shanghai: Kaiming shuju.

West, Cornel. 1990. "The New Cultural Politics of Difference." In *Out There: Marginalization and Contemporary Cultures*. Ed. Russell Ferguson, Martha Gever, Trinh T. Minh-ha, and Cornel West, 19-36. New York: New Museum of Contemporary Art, and Cambridge, Mass., and London: MIT Press.

Weston, Kath. 1995. "Get Thee to a Big City: Sexual Imaginary and the Great Gay Migration." *GLQ* 2 (3): 253-277.

Wilson, Elizabeth. 1993. "Is Transgression Transgressive?" In *Activating Theory: Lesbian, Gay, Bisexual Politics*. Ed. Joseph Bristow and Angelia R. Wilson, 107-117. London: Lawrence and Wishart.

Wright, Elizabeth. 1999. *Speaking Desires Can Be Dangerous: The Poetics of the Unconscious*. Cambridge: Polity Press.

Wu, Cun Cun. 2004. *Homoerotic Sensibilities in Late Imperial China*. London and New York: Routledge Curzon.

Wu Jintao 吳金桃. 1998. "Shui, xing, yanghuan: Wosi wokan *Heliu zai Lundun*" 水、性、陽滉：我思我看河流在倫敦 (Water, sex, masculine plague: Thinking and watching *The River* in London). *Dianying xinshang* 電影欣賞 (Film appreciation journal) 95 (September/October): 101-104.

Wythe, Douglas, Andrew Merling, Roslyn Merling, and Sheldon Merling. 2000. *The Wedding: A Family's Coming Out Story*. New York: Avon Books.

Xiao Wenhui 蕭文慧. 1994. "Zhege ren feichang Lin Yihua" 這個人非常林奕華 (This guy is very Edward Lam). *Chengpin yuedu* 誠品閱讀 (eslitebookreview) 17 (August): 54-56.

Xu, Ben. 1997. "*Farewell My Concubine* and Its Nativist Critics." *Quarterly Review of Film and Video* 16 (2): 155-170.

Yau, C. M. Esther. 1993. "International Fantasy and the 'New Chinese Cinema.'" *Quarterly Review of Film and Video* 14 (3): 95-107.

Ye Yueyu 葉月瑜, Zhuo Botang 卓伯棠, and Wu Hao 吳昊, eds. 1999. *Sandi chuanqi: Huayu dianying ershi nian* 三地傳奇：華語電影二十年 (Romance of three cities: Studies in Chinese cinemas). Taipei: Guojia dianying ziliaoguan.

Yeh, Yueh-yu. 1998. "Defining 'Chinese.'" *Jump Cut* 42: 73-76.

———. 1999. "A Life of Its Own: Musical Discourses in Wong Kar-wai's Films." *PostScript* 19 (1): 120-136.

Yeh, Yueh-yu Emilie, and Darrell William Davis. 2005. *Taiwan Film Directors: A Treasure Island*. New York: Columbia University Press.

Yin Hong 尹鴻. 1996. "Guojihua yujing zhong de dangqian Zhongguo dianying" 國際化語境中的當前中國電影 (Current Chinese cinema in the context of internationalization). *Dangdai dianying* 當代電影, November, 21-29.

Yu Zhenfei 俞振飛, ed. 1982. *Zhenfei qupu* 振飛曲譜 (Zhenfei's scores). Shanghai: Shanghai wenyi chubanshe.

Yue, Audrey. 2000. "What's So Queer about *Happy Together*? A.k.a. Queer (N)Asian: Interface, Community, Belonging." *Inter-Asia Cultural Studies* 1 (2): 251–264.

Zeng Wobu 曾我部. 2001. "*Lan Yu*/Nanyu" 藍宇 / 男語 (*Lan Yu*/male talk). *Dianying shuangzhoukan* 電影雙週刊 (City entertainment) 590: 50–52.

Zha, Jianying. 1994. "Beijing Subnotebooks." *Public Culture* 6 (2): 397–406.

Zhang Ailing 張愛玲 (Eileen Chang). 1984. *Liuyan* 流言 (Rumor). Taipei: Huangguan.

———. 1996. "My Writing." Trans. Wendy Larson. In *Modern Chinese Literary Thought: Writings on Literature, 1893–1945*. Ed. Kirk A. Denton, 436–442. Stanford, Calif.: Stanford University Press.

Zhang Beichuan 張北川. 1994. *Tongxing'ai* 同性愛 (Homosexuality). Shandong: Shandong kexue jishu chubanshe.

Zhang, Benzi. 1999. "Figures of Violence and Tropes of Homophobia: Reading *Farewell My Concubine* between East and West." *Journal of Popular Culture* 33 (2): 101–109.

Zhang Jingbei 張靚蓓. 1994. "Shishi beijing qian huodong de renmen: Chen Kaige tan *Bawang bie ji*" 史詩背景前活動的人們：陳凱歌談霸王別姬 (People moving in front of epic background: Chen Kaige on *Farewell My Concubine*). *Dianying xinshang* 電影欣賞 (Film appreciation journal) 67 (January/February): 68–74.

———. 2002. *Shinian yijiao dianying meng* 十年一覺電影夢 (Ten years of dreaming about cinema). Taipei: Shibao.

Zhang Jingyuan 張京媛, ed. 1995. *Houzhimin lilun yu wenhua rentong* 後殖民理論與文化認同 (Postcolonial criticism and cultural identity). Taipei: Maitian.

Zhang Yingjin 張英進. 1996. "Chongsi kuawenhua yanjiu: Xifang Zhongguo dianying yanjiu zhong de quanwei, quanli ji chayi wenti" 重思跨文化研究：西方中國電影研究中的權威、權力及差異問題 (Rethinking transcultural studies: Authority, power, and difference in Western studies of Chinese films). *Dianying yishu* 電影藝術, March, 19–23.

———. 1997. "From 'Minority Film' to 'Minority Discourse': Questions of Nationhood and Ethnicity in Chinese Cinema." In Lu 1997c, 81–104.

———. 1998. "Chinese Cinema and Transnational Cultural Politics: Reflections on Film Festivals, Film Productions, and Film Studies." *Journal of Modern Literature in Chinese* 2 (1): 105–132.

———. 2002. *Screening China: Critical Interventions, Cinematic Reconfigurations, and the Transnational Imaginary in Contemporary Chinese Cinema*. Ann Arbor: Center for Chinese Studies, University of Michigan.

———. 2004. *Chinese National Cinema*. New York and London: Routledge.

Zhang, Yingjin, and Xiao Zhiwei, eds. 1998. *Encyclopedia of Chinese Film*. London and New York: Routledge.

Zhang Yiwu 張頤武. 1995. "Quanqiuxing houzhimin yujing zhong de Zhang Yimou" 全球性後殖民語境中的張藝謀 (Zhang Yimou in the context of global postcoloniality). In Zhang Jingyuan 1995, 401–420.

Zhong Xueping. 2000. *Masculinity Besieged? Issues of Modernity and Male Subjectivity in Chinese Literature of the Late Twentieth Century*. Durham, N.C., and London: Duke University Press.

Zhonghuaminguo bashiyi nian dianying nianjian 中華民國八十一年電影年鑑 (Cinema in the Republic of China, yearbook). 1992. Taipei: Guojia dianying ziliaoguan.

Index

femininity, in relation to homosexuality. See *Farewell My Concubine*

film festivals, 20, 30, 35–36; Berlin, 41, 127, 190n.3, 193n.1, 194n.10; Cannes, 22, 25, 30, 32, 41, 99, 190n.3, 191n.11; Hong Kong lesbian and gay, 11, 37, 189n.22; Venice, 127, 164, 190n.3

Foucault, Michel, 7, 194n.8; on confession, 50–51, 91, 93, 128, 130, 137; on sexuality, 8–9, 118, 153

Fowler, Edward, 128–129

Freud, Sigmund, 74, 81, 106, 146, 170

Frye, Northrop, 131

Fung, Eileen, 52, 55–56, 61, 195n.18, 196n.24

Fung, Richard, 48, 68, 78

Fuss, Diana, 15

Garnham, Nicholas, 27, 55, 58

gay liberation, 50–51, 53, 158, 181

gay liberationist discourse, 14, 16–17, 41, 50, 55

gender, 1, 9, 12–13, 17–18, 48, 50, 67–68, 115, 120, 126, 133, 138–142, 147, 149, 180, 184–185, 202n.16, 205n.14, 207n.29, 209n.1; performance and performativity, 21, 72–73, 82, 91. *See also* Butler, Judith; *Wedding Banquet, The*

Genet, Jean: *Un Chant d'amour*, 94, 199n.24, 201n.12; *Querelle*, 94, 142, 159; *The Thief's Journal*, 94

Giles, Jane, 94, 199n.24

globalization, 4, 17, 24–25, 59, 107, 191n.9

Goldstein, Joshua, 71, 197n.10

Gong, Li, 31, 73

Goody, Jack, 43, 46

Grossman, Andrew, 165, 170, 183, 207nn.31, 32, 209n.8

guaitai, 12, 181, 183, 209n.3

Habermas, Jürgen, 25–26, 118

Hall, Stuart, 77–78

Halperin, David, 9–10

Hansen, Miriam, 19, 25, 27, 191n.12

Happy Together (Wong Kar-wai), 17, 19, 38, 177, 182, 199n.2, 205n.15; and *Betty Blue: 37°2 le matin* (Jean-Jaques Beineix), 100, 104; and domesticity, 108, 113, 117, 120, 124; and Rainer Werner Fassbinder, 103–105, 200n.9; and *flânerie*, 109, 112–114, 117, 120; and Hong Kong's return to the PRC, 101–102, 121–125, 199n.5, 200n.7; and travel, 99–100, 102, 105, 106–108, 117. *See also* class; patriarchy

heteronormativity, 114, 118–121, 200n.14

Hinsch, Bret, 8, 10, 188n.19

HIV, 135–137, 181, 202n.21. *See also* AIDS

Hold You Tight (Stanley Kwan), 18, 27, 38, 208nn.36, 39; and abjection, 154, 157, 163, 167–169, 173; and *A City of Sadness*, 164–165, 177, 206nn.24, 25; and decadence, 160–163, 177–178; and displacement, 163, 166–167, 170, 172–174, 208nn.34, 35, 36; and duality, 163–167; and Hong Kong's return to the PRC, 160–166, 175; and Krzysztof Kieślowski, 164, 206nn.19, 20; use of music in, 166, 169, 170, 174–177, 206n.23, 207nn.30, 33, 208n.43

Hollywood, 19–20, 22, 25, 184, 191n.11

homophobia, 53, 55, 70, 81, 83, 120

homosexuality, 7–13; in China (PRC), 28–33, 89, 96–98, 101; in Hong Kong, 11, 18, 37–40, 103, 158, 189n.22, 193n.28; in Taiwan, 33–37

Hong Kong: film industry in, 20; New Wave, 26, 190n.2; return to the PRC, 37–40. See also *Happy Together*; *Hold You Tight*; homosexuality

Hoover, Michael, 113, 116, 200n.12

Hou, Hsiao-hsien, 5, 20, 127–128, 164; *A City of Sadness*, 26, 190n.3. See also *Hold You Tight*

Hsu, Li-kong, 35–36, 192n.25

identity politics, 1, 14, 16, 34, 41–42, 65, 67, 79, 119–120, 154, 178, 193nn.3, 5

Tambling, Jeremy: on confession, 91, 93, 198n.21; on *Happy Together*, 58, 102–103, 107, 116–117, 199nn.2, 4, 200nn.7, 10, 12, 16

Taiwan, 123, 188n.15, 191n.13, 192n.26; February 28 incident in, 26, 165–166, 191n.13; Golden Horse Award in, 11, 36, 40, 200n.2, 203n.34, 206n.25; in *Happy Together*, 102, 124; in *Hold You Tight*, 164–167; independence movement, 2, 102, 128; New Cinema, 20, 26; and the United States, 59–60. *See also* homosexuality

Taylor, Charles, 45

Teo, Stephen, 20

Third Cinema, 6, 24–25, 191n.10

Thomsen, Christian Brand, 104, 159–160, 205n.10

tongxinglian/tongxing'ai, 8, 10–11, 189n.23

tongzhi, 11–12, 34, 39, 180–181, 183, 189nn.21, 23, 193n.31, 204n.1, 205n.16, 209n.3

transvestism and transgenderism, 90, 95, 170, 181, 197n.5. *See also* Chinese opera; *East Palace, West Palace*; *Farewell My Concubine*

Tsai, Ming-liang, 17, 36, 192n.26, 200n.2, 202nn.20, 25, 203n.34; and confession, 127–130, 133–134, 136–137; *Goodbye Dragon Inn*, 203n.34; *The Hole*, 149, 200n.2, 202nn.21, 25, 203n.34; *My New Friends*, 135–137; as overseas Chinese, 127, 200n.4; poetics of desire in, 130–132; *Rebels of the Neon God*, 18, 36, 126, 137–142, 148–149, 202nn.24, 25, 203n.34; *The River*, 18, 19, 35–36, 127, 142–150, 201n.9, 202n.25, 203nn.27, 31, 32, 34; theater productions of, 132–135, 202nn.15, 17; *Vive l'amour*, 127–128, 137–138, 149, 151–152, 202n.25, 203n.34; *The Wayward Cloud*, 36, 203n.34; *What Time Is It There?*, 138, 201nn.11, 14. *See also* AIDS/HIV; patriarchy

Tu, Wei-ming, 2–3, 187n.7

United States, 20; gay community, activism and organizations in, 14, 63, 67, 136, 196n.20, 202n.19. *See also* Taiwan

Vitiello, Giovanni, 71–72, 193n.31

Wang, Der-wei David, 71

Wang, Xiaobo, 28, 89, 189n.23, 198n.20

Warner, Michael, 16, 118, 184, 200n.13, 209n.1

Wedding Banquet, The, 17, 19, 34, 35–36, 41–42, 107, 108, 190nn.3, 8, 193n.2, 194nn.10, 13, 195n.18; and *Bend It like Beckham* (Gurinder Chadha), 62–63; coming out in, 50–56; and *Doña Herlinda and Her Son* (Jamie Humberto Hermosillo), 63; gender in, 56–60; race and ethnicity in, 56–57, 62, 194n.14. *See also* class; patriarchy

Wen, T'ien-hsiang, 127–128, 132, 135, 151, 200nn.1, 3, 201n.11, 202nn.15, 17, 203n.27

West, Cornel, 78

Weston, Kath, 14–15

Wilde, Oscar, 80, 159

Willemen, Paul, 6, 191n.10

Wong, Kar-wai, 17, 27, 38, 58, 199nn.1, 5, 6; *2046*, 99, 199n.5; *As Tears Go By*, 99; *Ashes of Time*, 99; *Chungking Express*, 99; *Days of Being Wild*, 99, 122; *Fallen Angels*, 99, 205n.15; *In the Mood for Love*, 99, 199n.5; use of color, 102, 109–111; use of music, 110, 113, 122, 124, 175; use of voice-over, 100, 104, 111, 114, 116–117, 123–124, 199n.3. *See also* *Happy Together*

World Wide Web, 11, 24–25, 39, 193nn.6, 31

Wright, Elizabeth, 130

Xu, Ben, 22, 26, 197n.5

Yam, Kim-fai, 155–156, 162, 204n.5

Yang, Edward, 20, 127, 206n.24

About the Author

Song Hwee Lim is lecturer in film (world cinemas) at the Department of Film Studies, University of Exeter, UK. He is the co-editor of *Remapping World Cinema: Identity, Culture and Politics in Film* (Wallflower Press, 2006), and the editor of the *Journal of Chinese Cinemas*.